This is a Call

This is a Call: the life and times of DaveGrohl

By Paul Brannigan

HarperCollins*Publishers*

HarperCollins*Publishers*
77–85 Fulham Palace Road,
Hammersmith, London W6 8JB

www.harpercollins.co.uk

First published by HarperCollins*Publishers* 2011

1 3 5 7 9 10 8 6 4 2

© Paul Brannigan 2011

Paul Brannigan asserts the moral right to be
identified as the author of this work

A catalogue record of this book is
available from the British Library

ISBN 978-0-00-739122-6

Printed and bound in Australia
by Griffin Press

Contents

Acknowledgements

Although *This is a Call* is not an authorised biography, I would like at the outset to extend my sincere thanks to Dave Grohl for his generosity and kindness to me over the years, not least during the writing of this book. Thank you, Dave, for the music, the memories and for being living proof that sometimes good guys don't wear white.

Thank you too to everyone who graciously agreed to be interviewed for *This is a Call*. Without your insights, reminiscences, trust and inspiration this book would not have been possible. Thanks are also due to friends and colleagues who offered support throughout the process. Love and respect to: Steve Albini, Phil Alexander and everyone at *MOJO* magazine, Greg Anderson, Brian Baker, Vicky Ball, Frank Black, Scarlet Borg, Tracey Bradford, Kurt Brecht, Nichola Browne and everyone at *Kerrang!* magazine, Peter Buck, Michael Burkert, Donald Butcher, Nick Christy, Tim Clarkin, Jaz Coleman, E.L. Copeland, Scott Crawford, Cronos, Charles R. Cross, Lee Dorrian, Jack Endino, Colin Fennelly, Jennifer Finch, Jon Fitzgerald, Shaun Fulton, Richard Gibson, Mike Gitter, Stone Gossard, Sohrab Habibion, Kevin Fox Haley, Ross Halfin, Page Hamilton, Larry Hinkle, Josh

This is a Call

Homme, Sabira Hud, Barrett Jones, Darryl Jenifer, Lisa Johnson, Barrett Jones, Paul Jones at www.fooarchive.com (unquestionably the world's finest, most comprehensive, online Foo Fighters resource), Mark Kates, Nick Knowles, Bobbie Lane, Robert Lang, Jared Leto, Chet Lott, J. Mascis, Chris McCormack, Joel McIver, Ian MacKaye, Dave Markey, Ben Mitchell, Craig Montgomery, Slim Moon, Jason Narducy, Gil Norton, Chris Page, Charles Peterson, Karen Pinegar, Reuben Radding, Nick Raskulinecz, Paul Rees and everyone at *Q* magazine, J. Robbins, Brent Sigmeth, Slash, Franz Stahl, Pete Stahl, Bobby Sullivan, Jenny Toomey, Paul Travers, Butch Vig, Russell Warby, Mike Watt, Paul Wieser and Don Zientara.

I am also indebted to Anton Brookes at Bad Moon PR and to John Silva and Gaby Skolnek at Silva Artist Management for facilitating access to Foo Fighters across the past fifteen years. Respect and thanks also to Pat Smear, Chris Shiflett, Nate Mendel and Taylor Hawkins for their patience and kindness during my various incursions into the Foo family.

This is a Call wouldn't exist without the faith, guidance and endless patience shown by Natalie Jerome at HarperCollins and Ben Schafer at Da Capo Press, and by my fabulous, indefatigable agents Matthew Hamilton and Anna Stein at Aitken Alexander Associates. I would also like to extend my gratitude to Martin Noble for his eagle-eyed attention to detail and judicious text pruning.

Extra special thanks to Ian Winwood, proud citizen of the Socialist Republic of South Yorkshire and tireless advocate of London Town, for encouragement, advice, abuse and friendship above and beyond the call of duty.

Above all, words alone cannot express my debt to the Brannigan and Kato families, and in particular to my beautiful, brilliant wife Hiroko, my daughter Yuki and my son Tyler for their sacrifices, selflessness, patience and understanding and for making me smile each and every day.

Paul Brannigan
July 2011

Foreword

Dave Grohl has just slapped me across the face. It's the early hours of 20 December 2005, and he and I are in a central London rock bar. Neither of us is meant to be here. Grohl is supposed to be in Ireland, resting up before his band Foo Fighters headline Dublin's 8,000 capacity Point Depot; I had only dropped in to the Crobar for a swift pre-Christmas beer with colleagues. But sometimes, particularly for those of us with Irish blood, nights in bars take on a momentum all their own.

Surprised to see one another, Grohl and I caught up quickly: I had recently become a father and Dave's wife Jordyn was five months pregnant, so babies and fatherhood dominated the early conversation. Then Grohl brought two trays laden with Jägermeister shots to our table and the evening began to get a little unhinged. Soon enough, all sensible conversation was abandoned. As the Crobar's excellent jukebox spat the sounds of Metallica, Minor Threat, Venom, Black Flag, Slayer and the Sex Pistols into the night air Grohl and I started doing what men of a certain age do while listening to very loud rock music when very drunk – screaming out lyrics, thrusting clenched fists skywards and headbanging furiously. And it was in the midst of this unedifying frenzy that Dave Grohl asked me to give him a slap in the face, an ancient male bonding ritual that only those conversant in the hesher tradition will truly understand.

'I can't do that,' I protested.

'Why not?' he asked.

'Well, because … because … you're Dave Grohl,' I stammered.

'Okay, I'll go first then,' said Grohl.

And with that, Foo Fighters' grinning frontman unleashed a stinging right hander which almost lifted me off the sticky barroom floor. Out of politeness, then, it seemed only fair to hit him back …

I first met Dave Grohl in November 1997 in London. The afternoon was memorable for all the wrong reasons. I had been commissioned to interview Foo Fighters' 28-year-old frontman for an end-of-year cover story for *Kerrang!* magazine, but, travelling back home following the interview, I discovered to my horror that our entire conversation had been wiped from the cassette in my dictaphone. Mortified, I begged Grohl's long-standing PR man Anton Brookes to schedule another interview. Days later, I spoke with Grohl again backstage at London's Brixton Academy: he had the manners and good grace not to laugh at my misfortune.

Over the next decade, I would run into the singer fairly regularly – at gigs, in TV studios, on the set of video shoots and in dingy rock clubs across the world; sometimes we would have business to conduct, at other times our contact was limited to the briefest of greetings. Relationships within the music industry are often conducted at such a level.

'I would consider the two of us to be friends,' Grohl told me as we had lunch at the Sunset Marquis hotel in West Hollywood in 2009 while conducting a lengthy interview for *MOJO* magazine. 'This is the basis of our relationship, this working thing, but let's go have a fucking beer, you know what I mean? But it would take a long time for you to really know me.'

Foreword

In the eighteen months it has taken me to write this book, that sentence has entered my head one hundred times. In truth, *everyone* thinks they know Dave Grohl. In an age where social networking has made Marshall McLuhan's 1960s vision of a global village a reality, where Twitter and Facebook and Tumblr and Flickr conspire to log and classify every waking moment, Grohl's public profile has been distilled down to one simple epithet: he is, by common consent, 'The Nicest Man in Rock'. But in effect this rather meaningless, reductive phrase has allowed the 'real' Dave Grohl to remain hidden in plain sight, unknown to all but his closest friends.

Based upon insights drawn from first-hand interviews with Grohl's friends, peers and associates, and from my conversations with the man himself, this is my attempt to tell Dave Grohl's story. It is an epic tale, documenting a journey which has taken Grohl from Washington DC's scuzziest punk rock clubs to the White House and the world's most imposing stadia. It's a story which ties together strands from fifty years of rock 'n' roll history, from Bob Dylan, The Beatles and Led Zeppelin through to Sonic Youth, Queens of the Stone Age and The Prodigy in a singular career, one which speaks volumes about both the evolution of the recording industry and the manner in which music soundtracks our lives. On a more basic level, it's a story about family and a musical community which continues to inspire, empower and engage.

During the course of writing this book, I spoke to Dave Grohl both on and off-record, and he was kind enough to permit me to visit his family home in California during the making of Foo Fighters' current album *Wasting Light*. The last time I talked with Dave was on 3 July 2011, minutes after his band performed in front of 65,000 people for a second consecutive evening at the National Bowl in Milton Keynes, England. That was a special night, a night for celebration, but also one which felt like the beginning of a whole new chapter for this most resolute of musicians. That future is unwritten; this is the story so far.

Paul Brannigan
London, July 2011

Learn to fly

A big rock 'n' roll moment for me was going to see AC/DC's *Let There Be Rock* movie. That was the first time I heard music that made me want to break shit. That was maybe the first moment where I really felt like a fucking punk, like I just wanted to tear that movie theatre to shreds watching this rock 'n' roll band …

Dave Grohl

In 1980, in a song named after their Los Angeles hometown, the punk band X sang of a female acquaintance who had lost her way, lost her innocence and lost her patience with the City of Angels, a friend desperate to flee the squalid, druggy Hollywood scene and unforgiving streets where '*days change at night, change in an instant*'. But even as Farrah Fawcett Minor was dying to get out, get out, one young punk on the East Coast was dreaming of heading in the opposite direction.

As a child, Dave Grohl had a recurring dream, one that stole into his head in the hours of darkness 'a thousand fucking times'. In this dream, he was riding a tiny bike from his home in Springfield, Virginia to Los Angeles, cruising slowly along the side of the highway as cars whizzed past with horns blaring and tail pipes smoking. Generations of bored, restless suburban kids have harboured similar fantasies of escaping suffocating small-town life for the glister of Hollywood. Deep in the national psyche LA remains synonymous with freedom, opportunity and boundless glamour, and the city's entertainment industries, both legal and less legal, have grown fat feasting upon the wide-eyed *ingénues* who spill daily from incoming Greyhound coaches and Amtrak trains,

1

but young Grohl's imagination was fired less by the shimmering promises of the Golden State than by the excitement of whatever swerves and undulations might have to be negotiated on his westward odyssey.

In September 2009 I had lunch with Foo Fighters' frontman at West Hollywood's chic Sunset Marquis hotel. As he picked at a Caesar salad, Grohl, modern rock's most convincing renaissance man, described the early days of his life's journey as being informed by a 'sense of adventure', of 'not knowing what lay ahead'.

'In that dream I had so far to go,' he said, 'and I was going so slow, but I was moving.'

Los Angeles is a city which holds memories both good and bad for Grohl. A decade ago he would tell anyone who'd listen that he hated this town, hated the Hollywood lifestyle, and hated pretty much everyone he met here:

'It's kinda funny for a while,' he conceded, 'then annoying, then depressing, finally it gets terrifying because you start wondering if these people are rubbing off on you. It's like one giant frenzy of aspiration and lies.'

But now Los Angeles, or more specifically Encino, 15 miles northwest of Sunset Boulevard's celebrity haunts, and a neighbourhood Grohl once defined as a place where 'porn stars become grocery clerks and rock stars come to die', is his home. Here, overlooking the San Fernando Valley, Dave Grohl literally has Los Angeles at his feet.

Grohl bought his house, a tasteful four-bedroom 1950s villa set on almost 4,000 square feet of prime Californian real estate, for $2.2 million in April 2003; four months later, surrounded by friends and family, he married MTV producer Jordyn Blum on the tennis court at the rear of the property. And it was here that Grohl elected to record Foo Fighters' seventh studio album *Wasting Light* in autumn 2010, eschewing digital studio technology in favour of tracking to analogue tape, a process largely viewed as antiquated within the modern recording industry.

From the outset, it seemed like a curious move, verging on the perverse: Grohl has his very own state-of-the-art recording complex,

Learn to fly

Studio 606, in Northridge, California, not ten minutes' drive from his home, and though his house in Encino also contains a compact home studio built around a 24-track mixing desk, the set-up is very much that of a family home, not some rock star bolthole. In contrast to houses in Los Angeles' more fashionable zip codes, there are no high fences surrounding the Grohl residence, no signs warning of armed security guards patrolling the perimeters: a plaque on the left-hand side of the driveway simply reads The Grohls. When you step inside the front door there are no gold or platinum discs on the hallway walls, no framed magazine covers, no posed portraits with celebrity friends, nothing to signpost the road Dave Grohl has travelled to get here: instead there are family snapshots and brightly coloured crayon-drawn abstract artwork tacked to the walls, the work of artists-in-residence Violet Maye Grohl and Harper Willow Grohl, Dave and Jordyn's young daughters.

In November 2010 I was invited to the Grohl family home to interview Foo Fighters about their work-in-progress. I arrived to find the man of the house in his garage, holding up scuffed album sleeves and fingerprint-smudged CD cases from his personal record collection to a webcam delivering images for a 24/7 live stream on Foo Fighters' website. Among them were Bad Brains' *Rock for Light*, Metallica's *Master of Puppets*, AC/DC's *Back in Black*, Thin Lizzy's *Live and Dangerous*, Ted Nugent's *Cat Scratch Fever*, Pixies' *Trompe Le Monde* and Led Zeppelin's *Houses of the Holy*, each album a strand of Grohl's musical DNA, each one a part of the soundtrack of his life. Behind him, producer Butch Vig stood splicing two-inch analogue tape on a 24-track Studer A800 reel-to-reel tape machine. In the room next door, eighteen of Grohl's guitars stood erect in flight cases, tuned and ready for use. In the adjoining garage, usually reserved for Grohl's Harley Davidson motorcycles, Taylor Hawkins's drum kit sat encircled by mic stands.

'It gets fucking *loud* in there,' said Grohl, closing the door with a smile.

Upstairs in the studio control room, band members Pat Smear, Chris Shiftlet, Nate Mendel and Hawkins sat sharing cartons of takeaway food. Around them Grohl strode animated, enthusing about his belief that *Wasting Light* would be Foo Fighters' definitive work. And as he spoke, his decision to record here began to make sense, indeed began to look inspired.

'It only seemed like a good idea to do it here,' Grohl insisted. 'I wasn't nervous about it at all. What we're doing here is in some ways making sense of everything we've done for the last fifteen years.

'It all came together as one big idea. Let's work with Butch, but let's not use computers, let's only use tape. Let's not do it at 606, let's do it in my garage. And let's make a movie that tells the history of the band as we're making the new album, so that somehow it all makes sense together in the grand scheme of things. I feel like you can actually hear the whole process in the album.'

For Grohl, the notion of time, its passing, its deathless march and the value and importance of seizing precious moments, is central to *Wasting Light*. But later that night, as I played back the cassette recording of the day's conversations, it struck me that the process unfolding in Encino was perhaps more personal than Dave Grohl would care to acknowledge explicitly: as he spoke of garage demos and life-changing albums, of collaborations with heroes and friends, of teenage desires and adult responsibilities, it seemed that in making Foo Fighters' seventh album Dave Grohl was seeking not merely to define his band's career, but also to make sense of his own life to date. And who could blame him? For his has been a journey more dramatic than that adolescent dreamer back in Virginia could ever have imagined.

◡

Between 1880 and 1920 almost 24 million immigrants arrived in the United States, the majority of them from Southern and Eastern European nations. Pursuing his own dreams, Dave Grohl's great-grandfather was among their number.

Born in Slovakia, then a part of the powerful Austro-Hungarian Empire, John Grohol was admitted to America in 1886, the same year in which the Statue of Liberty was erected on Bedloe's Island in New York Harbor. Like the vast majority of Slovaks who boarded dangerously overcrowded, unsanitary steamer ships for the twelve-day voyage to America's eastern seaboard, Grohol was an economic migrant:

without a trade to his name when he arrived in the USA, he was drawn to the state of Pennsylvania by the promise of unskilled labour in the region's coalfields and steel mills. The state was a popular destination for Slovak immigrants: when Grohol made his home in the small town of Houtzdale in Clearfield County, he was just one of approximately 250,000 Slovaks to put down roots within the borders of the Keystone State between 1880 and 1920. This influx of new labour engendered a certain amount of tension in the region.

Racist attitudes towards the settling Eastern European community were laid out in the bluntest terms by a report commissioned by the US Immigration Commission, published in 1911. Presented to Congress by the Republican Senator for Vermont, William P. Dillingham, Volume 16 of the *Reports of the Immigration Commission: Immigrants in Industries* dealt with studies into communities built around 'Copper Mining and Smelting; Iron Ore Mining; Anthracite Coal Mining; [and] Oil Refining' in Michigan, Minnesota and Pennsylvania, and concluded that white, American-born workers were being displaced by 'the more recent settlers of the community', referred to elsewhere in the report as 'the ignorant foreigner'.

One excerpt of Dillingham's report stated:

The social and moral deterioration of the community through the infusion of a large element of foreign blood may be described under the heads of the two principal sources of its evil effects: (a) The conditions due directly to the peculiarities of the foreign body itself; and (b) those which arise from the reactions upon each other of two non-homogeneous social elements – the native and the alien classes – when brought into close association. Among the effects under the first-named class may be enumerated the following:

A lowering of the average intelligence, restraint, sensitivity, orderliness, and efficiency of the community through the greater deficiency of the immigrants in all of these respects.

An increase of intemperance and the crime resulting from inebriety due to the drink habits of the immigrants.

This is a Call

> An increase of sexual immorality due to the excess of males over females …

Baldly put, the 'new immigrants' were regarded as a dangerous breed of subhumans.

The Dillingham Commission concluded that immigration from Southern and Eastern Europe posed a significant threat to American society and should in the future be greatly reduced. These findings were used to justify a series of new laws in the 1920s which served to place restrictions on immigration, and which also served to place a veneer of legitimacy on increasingly hostile, often blatantly discriminatory employment practices towards foreign-born workers.

Faced with such widespread attitudes and beliefs, it's understandable that when John Grohol and his wife Anna, herself a Slovakian immigrant, started their own family, their four sons – Joseph, John, Alois and Andrew – were encouraged to adopt the less obviously Slovakian, more Americanised surname Grohl in order to better assimilate into the prevailing culture.

Ethnic conflict was not, however, confined to the United States. Tensions were also running high in Europe, with questions of sovereignty, race and national self-determination causing division and toxic discord. The 1914 assassination of Archduke Franz Ferdinand, heir presumptive to the Austro-Hungarian throne, by Yugoslav nationalist Gavrilo Princip acted as the catalyst for a breakdown in international diplomacy in the Balkans, a situation which ultimately led to the outbreak of the First World War.

By the time America entered the Great War in April 1917, the Grohol family themselves had crossed state lines and moved to Canton, Ohio, setting up home at 116 Rowland Avenue, in the north-east of the city.

Canton was a hard, working-class town, built around its steel mills, which had embarked upon massive recruitment drives required to accommodate the increased productivity needed for the war effort. As his second eldest boy, John Stephen, enlisted in the United States army, John Grohol senior took up a position as a hammerman in one such factory. During this period Canton's population swelled significantly

– the 1920 census recorded the town as being home to 90,000 residents, a leap of almost 40,000 from figures collated just a decade previously – but among this new influx of citizens were less savoury elements, attracted by the town's increased prosperity.

By the mid 1920s Canton had acquired the unwanted nickname 'Little Chicago' in recognition of the growth of underworld gangs busying themselves with organised prostitution, bootlegging and gambling operations in the town's newly established red-light districts. Suspicious of the local police force's apparent unwillingness to crack down on such illicit activities, newspaper editor Donald Ring Mellet conducted his own investigations, exposing the collusion between gangsters and police in a series of searing articles published in the *Canton Daily News*. Mellet paid a high price for his crusading efforts: on 16 July 1926 the journalist was shot dead at his home in a cold-blooded execution which sent shockwaves through the local community. This was not the American Dream as John Grohol had envisaged it. It was time for his family to move on once more. They headed north-east, this time for Ohio's industrial heartland.

Residents of Warren, Ohio refer to their hometown as 'The Festival City' in recognition of the various celebrations of heritage, culture and art held throughout the year for the local community. In the summer of 2009, one such event – the inaugural Music Is Art festival – attracted thousands of music fans to the city's downtown Courthouse Square. On display from 26 July to the first day of August were no less than 48 acts, a rich variety of musicians and artists. But on the afternoon of 1 August there was little debate as to the festival's headline attraction.

'Is this the most beautiful day of your life?' Dave Grohl asked the crowd gathered on the lawn of the Trumbull County Courthouse as he was presented with the key to the city on the Music Is Art stage. 'Because it is mine.'

'I was born here, at the hospital just down the street, over at Trumbull Memorial,' Grohl continued. 'Most of my family is from the Niles and the Youngstown and the Warren area: my mother went to Boardman High School, my father went to the Academy ...'

Standing alongside Grohl's father James and mother Virginia, Warren Police Sergeant Joe O'Grady felt a surge of pride as he watched the city's most famous son address his audience. Dave Grohl had perfected the art of speaking to a large group as if he were having an intimate one-to-one conversation with a close friend, and the crowd listened rapt as he spoke in his easy-going, everyman manner of his family's history in Ohio: about his paternal grandfather Alois Grohl's work at Republic Steel in Youngstown, his maternal grandfather John Hanlon's employment as a civil engineer on the Mosquito Dam building project in the 1940s, and his own pride in hailing from the town.

The Music Is Art festival was Sgt Joe O'Grady's brainchild, and it was his idea too to lobby the city council to rename a downtown street in Dave Grohl's honour. This tribute, he argued, would bolster civic pride, and in saluting Grohl's musical achievements the city elders would send an inspirational message to the youth of Warren about fulfilling their own potential. In September 2008 Warren City Council passed O'Grady's resolution, and Market Street Alley was officially renamed David Grohl Alley.

On the morning of the dedication ceremony, Joe O'Grady walked Dave Grohl through downtown Warren to meet with one young man whose story had become entwined with the police officer's own vision and passion for the project.

Throughout the summer of 2009, Jacob Robinson, an eighteen-year-old skater and aspiring rapper, had worked long days in David Grohl Alley, sweeping the asphalt street and removing weeds and leaves from every crack in the bordering walls, so that artists from the Trumbull Art Gallery could paint murals along its length. Initially these chores were undertaken as part of a community service programme, after a fracas with a local police officer who'd apprehended him for skateboarding on a public street (a misdemeanour under the city's penal code).

But as O'Grady explained to Grohl, as Robinson's involvement in the project deepened so too did the teenager's sense of self-esteem. In

Learn to fly

Robinson's story Grohl heard an echo of his own formative years: himself a self-confessed 'little vandal' during adolescence, he saw in Robinson another creative, frustrated, headstrong young man in need of direction. In a log cabin adjacent to Monument Park he spoke with the young skater as he signed his skate deck, telling him, 'You and I are a lot alike.'

'When I was your age, I was into skateboarding and I was into music,' said Grohl. 'I did my best to be myself and stay out of trouble ...'

The sentence was left hanging, but its subtext was clear enough to both Robinson and the listening Joe O'Grady. This was precisely the kind of non-judgemental pep talk to which Robinson could connect, the kind of positive message the progressive policeman would himself repeat in the months and years ahead to other kids who felt both disillusioned and disenfranchised growing up in Warren.

'A kid who's fifteen years old doesn't feel there's hope,' O'Grady told a local entertainment website. 'But just because you're born here doesn't mean you're a nobody.'

❧

David Eric Grohl was born on 14 January 1969 at Trumbull Memorial Hospital in Warren, just one mile from the street that now bears his name. He was James and Virginia Grohl's second child, and a brother for their daughter Lisa, then still a month shy of her third birthday. Speaking with Nirvana biographer Michael Azerrad in 1993, Grohl described his parents as being positioned 'pretty much at other ends of the spectrum': in his eyes, his father was 'a real conservative, neat, Washington DC kind of man', his mother 'a liberal, free-thinking, creative' type, but in the early years of the couple's relationship their shared passions evidently eclipsed such ideological divisions.

Virginia Jean Hanlon met James Harper Grohl while working in community theatre in Trumbull County. She was a striking, smart and sassy trainee teacher, he a quick-witted, charming and confident young journalist. Grohl was a classically trained flautist – nothing less than a 'child prodigy', according to his son – and a keen jazz buff; Hanlon sang with high school friends in an a cappella vocal group named the

Three Belles. The pair also shared a love of poetry and literature, particularly the provocative counter-culture writings of Beat Generation authors Jack Kerouac, William Burroughs and Allen Ginsberg. In later years, in the company of his son's more artistic, liberal-minded friends, James Grohl was fond of wheeling out an anecdote about Ginsberg (unsuccessfully) hitting on him when the pair moved in the same bohemian circles, a pointed reminder to his son that he wasn't always such a strait-laced square.

At the time of his son's birth, James Grohl was a journalist for the Scripps Howard news agency, a division of the multi-platform communications empire built up by the tough-talking Illinois-born media mogul Edward Willis Scripps. With a culture encouraging independent thinking, instincts for social reform and a healthy disrespect for authority, it was a fecund environment for any ambitious young journalist. For James Grohl, this avowed policy of fearless, scrupulous news-gathering was never more important than when he was called upon to cover the student protests at Kent State University in nearby Kent, Ohio in May 1970.

Founded in 1910 as a teacher training college, Kent State was officially accorded university status in 1935; then, as now, the college prided itself upon a commitment to 'excellence in action'. By 1970 the student body, which included future Pretenders singer Chrissie Hynde, then an eighteen-year-old art student, numbered 21,000 across all programmes. That student body had become enraged when US President Richard Nixon, a man elected two years earlier on a pledge to end the war in Vietnam, announced on 30 April 1970 that US combat forces had invaded neighbouring Cambodia, an act widely interpreted as an escalation of the conflict.

When sporadic rioting broke out in the city in the wake of an antiwar demonstration on the university campus on 1 May, Mayor Leroy Satrom declared a state of emergency, and Ohio Governor James Allen Rhodes sent the National Guard to Kent to quell the disturbances and restore order.

On 4 May, when 2,000 protestors gathered on the university commons for another scheduled protest, they were ordered to disperse.

Learn to fly

When it became clear that the protestors were not prepared to comply with this injunction, the Guardsmen fired first tear gas, then live ammunition, into their midst. Four students were killed, and nine more injured.

Dubbed 'the Kent State Massacre' by the media, the killings galvanised the American anti-war movement. In the wake of the shootings, angry demonstrations were held on college campuses nationwide, and on 9 May an estimated 100,000 people converged upon Washington DC to protest against the Vietnam War and the horrifying events in Ohio. In response, the Nixon administration called upon the military to defend government offices, as the President was secreted from the District of Columbia to Camp David in Maryland for his own safety. White House staffers viewed the tense stand-off with mounting panic: upon seeing armed soldiers in the basement of the executive offices, one Nixon aide later commented, 'You're thinking "This can't be the United States of America. This is not the greatest free democracy in the world. This is a nation at war with itself."'

James Grohl's dispatches from Ohio marked him out as a rising star within the Scripps Howard news service. In 1972, while working in Columbus, Ohio, he was asked to consider a move to Washington DC, the nation's capital and political nerve centre, to develop his career further. For Grohl, the timing was perfect. This was the age of the crusading journalist, with *Washington Post* reporters Carl Bernstein and Bob Woodward being hailed as American heroes for their incisive and explosive investigations into a seemingly trivial burglary at the Watergate Hotel on 17 June 1972, which exposed a botched attempt to bug the offices of the Democratic National Committee offices and uncovered a paper trail all the way to the White House, leading to the resignation of 'Tricky Dickie' Nixon on 8 August 1974. What upwardly mobile young reporter wouldn't wish to join the pair on the frontline in their tenacious pursuit of the truth? It was an opportunity Grohl accepted without reservation.

Like so many other transplants to the DC metropolitan area, he chose to relocate his family not in the District of Columbia itself, but in the outlying suburbs. Springfield, Virginia lay six miles down the I-95, just inside the Capital Beltway, and like the neighbouring towns of Arlington, Annandale and Alexandria it was a popular destination for commuters working in the city or at the nearby Pentagon offices. As with other Northern Virginian towns, it had a transient population, with the shifting dynamics of working on Capitol Hill leading many families to relocate after four or five years in the area. Despite this, residents worked hard to foster and maintain a strong community spirit.

At the dawn of the 1970s the Grohls' new hometown was a location suited to the patronising sobriquet 'white-bread'. But, befitting a town '15 minutes from chicken farmers, and 15 minutes from the White House', as Dave Grohl would later describe it, Springfield, VA also had a more schizophrenic character. Here, urbane, moneyed politicos – those 'fortunate sons' eviscerated in song by Creedence Clearwater Revival – shared street space with blue-collar Southerners with gun racks on their pickup trucks and Skynyrd and Zeppelin blasting from their Camaros and Ford Mustangs.

The family lived on Kathleen Place, a quiet cul-de-sac, in a house Dave Grohl remembers as 'a tiny shoebox'. The children settled quickly into their new home. Lisa Grohl enrolled at North Springfield Elementary School, while Dave, fondly remembered by his mother as 'a pretty rambunctious kid' with a taste for mischief that cherubic looks and a beatific smile couldn't always mask, was left to explore his new surroundings on his go-kart, with his faithful companion, a somewhat bedraggled Winnie the Pooh bear, glued to his side.

'Springfield was a great neighbourhood to grow up in,' recalls Nick Christy, the frontman of Grohl's first real band Nameless, whose own family moved to Springfield from Massachusetts in the early 1970s. 'A kid could have a lot of fun there. The houses weren't fancy or spectacular, but it was a nice friendly neighbourhood. It was all middle-income white families, and people looked out for one another. I only later found out that all my friends' parents were in the FBI or CIA or were senators from Washington.'

Seduced by the electric, politically charged atmosphere of his new environs, James Grohl switched careers soon after settling in Springfield, quitting journalism to take up a new position as a speech writer/

campaign manager for Robert Taft Jr, the Republican Senator for Ohio and grandson of former US President William Howard Taft. His wife also secured new employment, teaching English and drama at Thomas Jefferson High School in nearby Alexandria, where she was a popular addition to the staff.

'Virginia Grohl was a great teacher,' recalls Chet Lott, a student at Thomas Jefferson High from 1981 to 1984. 'She was the type of teacher that took an interest in you personally, and got to know everyone, and she was definitely one of the stand-out teachers in my whole schooling. She was very cool, a very nice lady.'

In private, though, things were not going quite so well for the Grohls. Behind closed doors, and out of earshot of their children, James and Virginia Grohl's marriage was slowly falling apart. In 1975 James Grohl walked out on his wife and young family. Virginia Grohl faced what would have undoubtedly been a difficult, stress-filled time with dignity and admirable stoicism, shielding her two children from both the harsh realities of separation and her own fears and concerns for the future.

'Of course it caused a lot of pain and it caused a lot of struggle, but I don't think I really understood what was going on,' Dave would later recall. 'By the time I got a hold of the situation, it was too late for me to have a freak-out. It just seemed abnormal for all my friends to have a father. I thought growing up with my mother and sister was just the way it was supposed to be.'

On a practical level, Virginia Grohl quickly realised that her $18,000 salary as a high school teacher in the Fairfax County public school system was never going to cover the cost of raising two children single-handedly. To supplement her income she took on part-time work: week-day evenings were spent working in a department store, while weekends were occupied by administration duties for a local carpet cleaning company.

In order to keep her children occupied and entertained while she was working weekends, Virginia Grohl would allow Lisa and Dave to listen to her record collection on a stereo borrowed from Thomas Jefferson

High School. One day while the family were out shopping in a local drugstore Dave nagged his mother into buying him an album of his own, a K-Tel compilation which had been heavily advertised on television. Released in 1976, *Block Buster* promised '20 original hits by original stars', and featured some of the biggest anthems of the era, from KC and The Sunshine Band's 'That's the Way (I Like It)' to Alice Cooper's 'Only Women Bleed'. Back home at Kathleen Place, Dave commandeered the stereo for the next few weekends, bugging the shit out of his big sister by lifting the stylus every three and a half minutes to play one particular track over and over and over again.

The Edgar Winter Group's 'Frankenstein' was one of the 1970s' more unlikely Number 1 singles. Originally a sprawling live jam, allowing the Texas-born Winter to demonstrate his virtuosity on a variety of instruments on his 1972 album *They Only Come Out at Night*, 'Frankenstein' was a spacey, synthesiser-led, progressive rock instrumental, featuring a spiralling saxophone solo and mid-song drum duel. The following year the track was used as the B-side of the band's 'Hangin' Around' single, but as disc jockeys nationwide began playing the track in response to listener requests, Winter's label Epic flipped the seven inch and began plugging 'Frankenstein' as the single. In May 1973 the song reached Number 1 on the *Billboard* Hot 100, eventually selling more than one million copies. As track nine on the *Block Buster* compilation, it would change one little boy's life forever.

'To me that was just the best sound I had ever heard in my life,' Grohl later enthused. 'To this day [it's] still one of the most amazing songs you've ever heard in your life. Every time I hear "Frankenstein" it reminds me of being that young, just rocking out in my bedroom.'

On the wall of that bedroom, Grohl had tacked a poster of the cockpit of a 747 aeroplane. At the time the young man dreamt of becoming a pilot, of leaving Springfield behind and escaping to new places, experiencing new things. But if his next musical discovery taught him anything, it was that he didn't actually need to leave his small bedroom in order to escape the realities of day-to-day life.

For American teenagers from Long Island to Long Beach, and all points in between, obsessing over Kiss was a rite of passage. On 31

Learn to fly

October 1976 the quartet from New York stomped onto ABC's *The Paul Lynde Halloween Special* in Kabuki make-up and stackheels, and proceeded to pout and prance through lip-synched versions of 'Detroit Rock City', 'Beth' and 'King of the Night Time World' for a national TV audience that numbered millions. For a generation of wide-eyed, awestruck young viewers this was their 'The Beatles on *The Ed Sullivan Show*' moment, only with added flashbombs.

Kiss were four cartoon superheroes – Starchild, The Demon, Space Ace and Catman – both larger and louder than life; figures who breathed fire, spat blood, fired rockets from their guitars and made rock 'n' roll seem like the most impossibly exciting vocation. A self-confessed 'show-off', fond of dressing up in clothes 'as outlandish and ridiculous as possible', the seven-year-old Dave Grohl thought they were just about the coolest thing he'd ever seen. Soon enough, Virginia Grohl was pestered into buying *Rock and Roll Over* (and later *Kiss Alive II*), but in truth Dave spent more time looking at the album sleeves than actually listening to the vinyl within. The true magic lay elsewhere. Kiss breathed fire! They spat blood! They played guitars that fired rockets! A poster of the band posing atop the Empire State Building soon occupied pride of place on Grohl's bedroom wall. It was surely no coincidence that his interest in playing guitar started soon afterwards.

'My mother bought my father a nylon string flamenco-type guitar when I was three or four years old,' he recalls. 'He never learned to play so it just sat around the house, and by the time I was nine I'd broken four of the six strings on it. But with the two left I'd learned how to make a chord and learned [Deep Purple standard] "Smoke on the Water" … very *Beavis and Butthead*. And that was how I started playing guitar.'

While Grohl was getting to grips with his first powerchords, his mother's new boyfriend, Chip Donaldson, a fellow English teacher and Vietnam War veteran, moved into the family home. Far from resenting this new alpha male presence, Grohl was in awe of the new arrival, and Donaldson's arrival started the fledgling guitarist's musical education in earnest.

'Chip was a fucking brilliant man, who I totally looked up to,' he told me in 2009. 'He was a real wild, "outdoors man" guy, who was just as book smart as he was at home in nature: we would go on these crazy nature walks, and he taught me to hunt when I was ten. He moved in with us for a few years and brought his record collection with him. Our living room went from being a conservative suburban Virginia home living room to crates of albums on the walls, and maybe deer antlers, and a gun rack … it basically turned into a hunting lodge, with really good music.

'I learned a lot from his record collection. It was everything from Jethro Tull to the Grateful Dead to the Rolling Stones to Phoebe Snow to Zeppelin to Jefferson Airplane to Dylan, all late sixties and seventies shit. Lynyrd Skynyrd was another big one. I remember listening to "Freebird" when I was ten years old and thinking, "God, if some day I could just play a solo like that …" and Chip saying, "Well, if you practise, maybe some day …" But I knew with all my heart he was wrong, that even if I practised for years I'd never be able to play that guitar part. And I still can't play that guitar part!'

Pleased that Dave had a hobby that was keeping him out of trouble, Virginia Grohl paid for guitar lessons for her son, until after a year the student pronounced them 'boring', and quit. In place of these lessons, Dave Grohl calmly revealed that he had formed a band.

❧

The HG Hancock Band was a duo, a partnership between Grohl and North Springfield Elementary School classmate, and near neighbour, Larry Hinkle. Grohl viewed the group as nothing less than North Springfield Elementary's answer to Southern rock heroes Lynyrd Skynyrd. Having discovered that the Jacksonville, Florida band had taken their name in mocking tribute to their former PE teacher Leonard Skinner, he and Hinkle borrowed the name of their own PE teacher Ms Hancock for their new outfit: the HG prefix stood for Hinkle/Grohl.

The pair shared classes together in fifth grade, and were now inseparable, always in and out of one another's houses, forever hatching schemes and making mischief. Now a self-employed woodworker living in Fredericksburg, Virginia, Hinkle has fond memories of his time as Grohl's partner-in-crime.

Learn to fly

'Dave was pretty funny, and fun to be around,' he recalls. 'We sat close to each other in class, he didn't live too far away from where I lived, and he was just a good guy to hang out with.

'We did do some things that weren't too cool,' Hinkle admits. 'I used to spend the night at Dave's house and we'd sneak out and go to this one road late at night and throw crab apples at cars and try to get them to chase us. That could have got us into a lot of trouble. Another time I remember we were teasing some girl on the school bus and we grabbed her purse and threw it out of the bus window. We forgot all about it until we were called into the principal's office the next day. We weren't bad kids, just kinda goofy.

'But Dave was always *really* into music. He always had his guitar with him, a beat-up old acoustic with broken strings. Hanging out with him it was hard not to get into music.'

When they weren't terrorising the local community, Grohl and Hinkle spent their free time listening to local classic rock station DC 101 with classmate Jimmy Swanson, sniggering at 'shock jock' Howard Stern's gleefully puerile banter and playing air guitar to a soundtrack of AC/DC, Led Zeppelin, Cheap Trick, Black Sabbath, Ted Nugent, Alice Cooper, Van Halen and, naturally, Lynyrd Skynyrd.

'Dave played his guitar with the broken strings,' says Hinkle, 'and I played drums, which was made up of his mom's knitting needles and laundry basket and pots and pans. His mom was always very welcoming, always really nice to us. But God only knows what she thought of the noises we were making.'

In truth, Virginia Grohl had long since learned to tune out the noises emanating from her son's bedroom. Since a cousin had given him a copy of Canadian prog-rockers Rush's 1976 album *2112*, Grohl had been teaching himself how to play drums, using the furniture in his room as a crude approximation of a kit. Now the thump-*thwack*-thump-*thwack* coming from her boy's bedroom was as natural to Virginia Grohl as birdsong, and scarcely more intrusive.

'I had a chair that was next to my bed, and I would kneel down on the floor and put a pillow between my legs to use as my snare,' said Grohl, explaining his rudimentary set-up to *Modern Drummer* magazine in 2004. 'I would use the chair to my left as the hi-hat and use the bed as toms and cymbals. And I would play to these records until there was condensation dripping from the windows.'

Encouraged by the promise displayed in the first HG Hancock Band rehearsals, Grohl decided it was time to start committing some of his own original material to tape. The HG Hancock Band's first song, 'Bitch', was a tribute to the Grohl family dog BeeGee. The second song presented to Hinkle by his musical partner was titled 'Three Steps'.

'In class this one day he gave me a piece of paper and said, "Here's this new song I've wrote, let's do it!"' Hinkle recalls. 'He played it for me and I said, "Wow, this is great!" And then later that afternoon he was feeling kinda weird about it and he admitted that he didn't write the song, that it was a Lynyrd Skynyrd song, "Gimme Three Steps". We wondered if we could get into trouble for playing it. We were kinda nervous for the rest of the day.'

'I certainly didn't consider myself a songwriter, they were just little experiments, little challenges,' says Grohl of his earliest, non-plagiarised songs. 'I honestly wasn't aiming for anything. But I figured out for myself that I could record multitrack at home with two cassette players. I could hit Record on one cassette player, play the guitar, stop, rewind, take that cassette and put it into the other cassette player, hit Play, get another cassette to record on in the first one and sing over the top. And then you have a two-track recording. I would listen back to it and I didn't necessarily like the sound of my voice but the reward was simple: proof that I could.'

In 2009, as part of the liner notes to Foo Fighters' *Greatest Hits* album, Grohl laid out this primitive recording process in marginally more detail in a four-step mini essay entitled 'How to Multitrack at Home'. The final step read simply 'Start band'.

⁓

As the 1970s drew to a close, Dave Grohl's life had settled into a familiar groove: school, soccer matches, small-scale vandalism, stereo-hogging. He was a popular kid in the neighbourhood, and a diligent student at school, even if his hyperactivity was a concern to his teachers: 'They always said the same thing: "David could be a great student if he could just stay in his fucking seat,"' he later recalled.

On school holidays the family returned to Ohio to see James Grohl and his parents Alois and Ruth, and Virginia Grohl's mother Violet. The whole family would rendezvous in Breeze Manor in Breezewood, 'get a couple of rooms, eat fried chicken and swim in the pool for the weekend'. These were happy, uncomplicated times: 'I had it made,' Grohl later reflected.

But as a new decade dawned, young David was given a glimpse into an alternate reality. On the evening of 26 January 1980 he snuck out of his home to hang out with his big sister, who was babysitting for a neighbourhood family. With her charges tucked up in bed, Lisa Grohl was watching *Saturday Night Live*, the nation's most popular comedy and variety television show. Dave joined his sister on the sofa. As *SNL* host Terri Garr introduced the night's musical guests, however, he almost tumbled from his seat in astonishment.

The band on TV were *weird*, seriously weird. The skinny singer in the oversized jacket was talking gibberish, the big-haired girls – one blonde, one a redhead – were shrieking and wriggling as if, quite literally, they had ants in their pants, the guitarist was playing with what sounded like just two out-of-tune strings, just as Dave himself had done before he mastered basic chord shapes. The noise they were making was all wrong, twitching and jerking like an anaphylactic shock. To add to the tumult, after two minutes on-screen the singer and the blonde girl simply fell over and lay twitching on the studio floor like they'd been shot. The Grohl children were witnessing Athens, Georgia's New Wave heroes The B-52s in full flight.

'I remember that moment like some people remember the Kennedy assassination,' says Grohl. 'When the B-52s played "Rock Lobster", honestly, that moment changed my life. The importance and impact of that on me was huge. That people that were so strange could play this music that sounded so foreign to me and for it to be so moving ... growing up in suburban Virginia, I had never even imagined something so bizarre was possible. It made me want to be weird. It just immediately made me want to give everyone the middle finger and be like, "Fuck you, I wanna be like *that*!"

'A big rock 'n' roll moment for me was going to see AC/DC's *Let There Be Rock* movie, because that was the first time I heard music that made me want to break shit. Like after the first number. Larry Hinkle and I went to see it at some theatre downtown in Washington DC and they had a club PA in the movie theatre, and it was the two of us and two people smoking weed in the back, and that was it. And that fucking movie was so loud … honestly, that was maybe the first moment where I really felt like a fucking punk, you know, like I just wanted to tear that movie theatre to shreds watching this rock 'n' roll band. It was fucking awesome.

'But the B-52s thing really had an impact on me, because it made me realise that there was something powerful about music that was different. It made everything else seem so vanilla. I didn't shave a mohawk in my head, and I still loved the melodies and lyrics in my rock 'n' roll records, but that sent me on this mission to find things that were unusual, music that wasn't considered normal.

'Those guitars! Two strings! How cool! Those drums! Slap slap slap! Dead easy! The women looked like they were from outer space and everything was linked in – the sleeves, the sound, the clothes, the iconography, the logo, everything. I think when you're a kid that's what you're after, a real unified feel to a band, and that's what the B-52s offered. Their songs were so easy to learn, they got me into playing really easily. This was definitely the first thing after Kiss or Rush that totally absorbed me like that.'

Virginia Grohl rewarded Dave's continued interest in music by buying him his first 'real' guitar, a 1963 Sears Silvertone with an amplifier built into the guitar case, as a Christmas present in 1981. Grohl received another gift in the form of two Beatles albums – *The Beatles 1962–1966* (aka 'The Red Album') and *The Beatles 1967–1970* (aka 'The Blue Album'). Opening with the giddy euphoria of 'Love Me Do' and 'Please Please Me' and winding down with the stately, elegiac 'Across the Universe' and 'The Long and Winding Road', these two extraordinary compilations served not only to document the Fab Four's astonishing creative evolution, but also provided an inspirational blue-print for artists seeking to redefine the rock 'n' roll landscape on their own terms. A young musician could have no finer template upon which to build.

'Around that time too my mother bought me this songbook, *The Complete Beatles*, that was all their songs transcribed with chord charts,' recalls Grohl. 'I can't read music, but I could read chord charts, so I'd put on those records and start to play along. And at that age everything was a puzzle, like any child now with a video game you just want to conquer that level and get to the next. So for me it was really about figuring out a song so I could move on to the next: maybe I could do "Day Tripper" but I hadn't figured out "A Day in the Life". So from then on if I wasn't outside walking around the creeks and the back yard looking for crawfish, I was inside with a guitar. That was my entertainment.'

Following the dissolution of the HG Hancock Band (which fell apart when Larry Hinkle moved away from Springfield to live in Maryland with his father, following his parents' divorce), Grohl was on the look-out for a new musical foil, a Lennon to his McCartney. Fortunately, he would not have far to look or long to wait. Living just a few blocks from Kathleen Place, at the age of thirteen Nick Christy was already a competent guitar player and a fine singer, blessed with a sense of self-confidence and self-possession rare in young men of his age. A fan of The Who, The Beatles and Rolling Stones, Christy was looking to put together his own band, and invited Grohl over to his parents' basement to jam. The two clicked immediately.

'After that we were *always* in that basement, always looking for an audience and more people to join us,' recalls Christy, now president of an award-winning landscaping company and a part-time musician back in his native Massachusetts. 'We played in a lot of little projects together, and just started bands with whoever we could find. We would throw our own parties in my basement, or in his house, and invite all our classmates just to have a party so we could play in front of people.

'We'd also do little duets, just the two of us. Dave's mom was amaz-ingly supportive, just the best, and she would take us out to a local restaurant called Treebeards, where there were open mic nights on a Wednesday night and we would perform in front of people. There'd be people in their twenties or thirties performing and then these two eighth grade kids popping up to play their stuff.'

'It's hard to book gigs when you're twelve years old!' Grohl says with a laugh. 'Usually we'd just play in our own back yards, and like six or seven people would watch. But I'd find out that the kid two blocks away played the bass and I'd be like, "*That* kid plays the bass? Really? Because Alex has a drum set: tell Alex to bring the drum set over to Nicky's house on Sunday at two." It was twelve- and thirteen-year-old kids in a basement, man, it was great, totally fun. It was better than stealing cars!'

'When we would rehearse, Dave was just a wildcard,' remembers Christy. 'He was the funniest guy you'd ever meet. He had so much energy and drive. But I was always that A-type personality, I wanted to lead the show and I'd be saying, "Okay, this is what we're doing next" – but he'd be going a mile a minute, wanting to do this and that. He was the lead guitar player and I was rhythm, but he'd be jumping on the drums any chance he could get, like in between songs. He'd just start whaling on those frigging drums, and it was annoying as hell, because I wanted to practise. I'd be saying, "Cut the shit, dude, we've gotta practise and you're not a fucking drummer." If he'd listened to me he'd never have been a drummer. If he'd listened to me, he might not have got anywhere …'

But the journey had already begun.

22

This is a call

The whole night was like a scene from *Lord of the Rings* where there's twelve people that have to fight their way through an army of orcs, and there's just no way they can possibly win – that's how it felt to be a punk rocker in the middle of five million rednecks in Washington DC on the 4th of July. I had just discovered punk rock, and it was so unbelievably moving. It was like our own personal Altamont, our Woodstock. And that's when I said, 'Fuck the world, I'm doing this …'

Dave Grohl

It was 3 July 1983, Independence Day weekend, and America was in the mood to party. The sun was shining in Washington DC and Irene Cara's hit single *Flashdance … What a Feeling*, sitting pretty at the summit of the *Billboard* Hot 100 for a fifth consecutive week, blasted from every shopfront, souvenir stall and boombox in the nation's capital. The stately tree-lined avenues around the National Mall were a bustle of colour, movement and noise, as tens of thousands of tourists and DC metropolitan area residents jockeyed for the best vantage points for that evening's celebratory fireworks display.

Chatting and laughing, Dave Grohl and Larry Hinkle weaved their way through the crowds, heading towards the Lincoln Memorial, in whose shadow a free concert was being held. Timed to coincide with DC's annual pro-marijuana legalisation Smoke-In event, the Rock Against Reagan concert had been organised by the Youth International Party, a leftist counter-cultural collective, and boasted a line-up featuring some of the finest American hardcore bands of the day, among them Reagan Youth, Crucifucks, Toxic Reasons, M.D.C. (aka Millions of Dead Cops) and headliners Dead Kennedys.

23

As they neared the concert site, Grohl and Hinkle sensed a change in the atmosphere. There were DC police *everywhere*, some patting down concertgoers against squad cars, others patrolling the site on horseback, dozens more sitting in buses in full riot gear. In a field adjacent to the Lincoln Memorial 800 punk rockers watched Houston's D.R.I. hammer through their hate songs in E minor, with vocalist Kurt Brecht railing against American consumerism, the military-industrial complex and the evil deathmonger in residence at 1600 Pennsylvania Avenue, over guitarist Spike Cassidy's filthy, gnarled, slamdance-on-a-dime riffs. When the band finally stopped to draw breath, an impressed Dave Grohl immediately walked over to their tour van and bought a copy of their self-titled 22-song seven-inch EP from the sweating, panting Brecht.

As the sky darkened, so too did the mood on the Mall. The punks grew mouthier, the tourists more bellicose. There were catcalls, confrontations and scuffles, raised voices and raised fists. Drunken college students pushed beer kegs around in shopping trolleys and stoned, naked hippies frolicked in the Reflecting Pool. The police got edgier and the bands played on, harder, faster, louder. As the sun dipped below the skyline, the Dead Kennedys walked on stage to face pandemonium.

'I get chills just thinking about it,' says Grohl. 'There were police helicopters going around with their lights on the audience and cops on horseback just fucking billy-clubbing punk rockers. Dead Kennedys are playing "Holiday in Cambodia" and Jello Biafra is pointing at the Washington Monument with its two blinking red lights and he's saying, "With the great Klansman in the sky with his two blinking red eyes …", it was unbelievable, it was like *Apocalypse Now*. The whole night was like a scene from *Lord of the Rings* where there's twelve people that have to fight their way through an army of orcs, and there's just no way they can possibly win – that's how it felt to be a punk rocker in the middle of five million rednecks in Washington DC on the 4th of July. I had just discovered punk rock, and it was so unbelievably moving. It was like our own personal Altamont, our Woodstock. And that's when I said, "Fuck the world, I'm doing *this* …"'

This is a call

Music historians will argue forever about the origins of punk rock.
Some lay the blame at the feet of Ann Arbor, Michigan's The Stooges,
blank-eyed degenerates who channelled desperation and isolation and
boredom and violence and sex and confusion into brutish, nihilistic
numbskull anthems. On '1969', the opening track of their self-titled
début album, released in the year of Dave Grohl's birth, vocalist Iggy
Pop looked outside his window to see 'war across the USA', before
turning his disgust inwards, mocking his own sullen self-pity (*'last year
I was 21 | I didn't have a lot of fun'*) with a deceptively throwaway,
infantile bubblegum-pop lyric – *'I say Oh-my and a boo-hoo'* – positively
dripping with sarcasm and self-loathing. Every bit as combative and
confrontational as the cold, hard stares of the four lank-haired thugs
glaring out from the cover artwork, *The Stooges* was also music to beat
yourself up to, a recurring theme in punk rock to the present day.

Other music critics see the form as pre-dating The Stooges, with its
roots in the primitive, animalistic poundings of The Sonics, The Seeds,
The Wailers and a thousand more unsung hooligan-blues heroes of the
early 1960s who never meant jack-shit outside the bare brick walls of
their own suburban garages. These bands took the thrust-and-drag
dynamics of The Kingsmen's 1963 version of Richard Berry's deathless rock 'n' roll standard 'Louie Louie' and The Kinks' 1964 hit 'You
Really Got Me' and amplified them with brute force and ignorance,
getting high on volume and fuzz and speaker-hiss and adrenaline.
Drawn together on *Rolling Stone* writer Lenny Kaye's seminal 1972
compilation album *Nuggets*, bands such as The Barbarians and The
Mojo Men and The Amboy Dukes made a forceful case for being the
true defenders of the spirit of rock 'n' roll.

In the early seventies, though, rock critics seemed keen to label just
about anyone punk. To *New York Times* writer Grace Lichtenstein, Alice
Cooper was a punk. To England's *New Musical Express* Gene Vincent
was a punk, as was Eddie Cochran. To *Zigzag* magazine Bruce
Springsteen was 'a rock 'n' roll punk'. To Greg Shaw of *Rolling Stone*
magazine, fifties teen idol Dion was 'the original punk'. As English rock
writer Mick Houghton cannily observed in 1975, 'the term "punk" is
bandied about an awful lot these days. It seems to describe almost any

rock performer who camps it up to any degree, on or off-stage, or who displays an arrogance and contempt for his audience.'

By consensus, however, New York and London are generally acclaimed as the parent cities of the modern punk sound. The New York punk scene revolved around the CBGB club on Bowery on Manhattan's Lower East Side, a scuzzy, graffiti-covered fleapit which, from 1974, played host to nonconformist, experimental artists such as Ramones, The New York Dolls, The Heartbreakers, Suicide, Blondie, Television, Talking Heads and Richard Hell and the Voidoids. London's vibrant scene, centred around the Sex Pistols, The Clash, The Damned, X-Ray Spex, The Slits and The Adverts, kicked in two years later, in 1976. But it was the latter scene which first received mainstream press coverage in the US, when *Rolling Stone* writer Charles M. Young was dispatched to London in August 1977 to write a cover story on the Sex Pistols, then still unsigned in America.

The Sex Pistols were England's most notorious rock band, even before their first single, the electrifying *Anarchy in the UK*, débuted in the UK charts. In their very first press interview guitarist Steve Jones commented, 'We're not into music. We're into chaos,' words that would prove astonishingly prescient. Following a fractious appearance on primetime television show *Today* on 1 December 1976 – where the Pistols responded to host Bill Grundy's goading putdowns by calling him a 'dirty fucker' and a 'fucking rotter' – the band graduated from the covers of Britain's four weekly music papers – *New Musical Express*, *Melody Maker*, *Sounds* and *Record Mirror* – to the nation's sensational-ist, scandal-thirsty tabloid newspapers, who gleefully set about portray-ing the young Londoners as dangerous revolutionaries hellbent on destroying the very fabric of British society. The band's inflammatory decision to release their caustic second single, *God Save the Queen*, in the run-up to Queen Elizabeth II's Silver Jubilee only heightened their infamy.

Charles Young was not met with open arms in London. Initially, in fact, he was not met at all, for Malcolm McClaren, the Sex Pistols' mischievous, maverick manager, simply ignored the writer's phone calls during his first two days in the city. Though *Rolling Stone* took pride in its roots as a counter-cultural magazine, by the mid-seventies it was firmly part of the establishment, in thrall to Laurel Canyon songwriters and MOR superstars: cover stars in 1976 included Neil Diamond, Jackson Browne, Paul Simon, Peter Frampton, teen pinup Donny Osmond and Christian crooner Pat Boone. When McClaren finally deigned to receive Young at his central London flat, he regarded the journalist as one might regard a ball of phlegm hacked up in a porcelain sink.

'This band hates you,' he loftily informed Young. 'It hates your culture. Why can't you lethargic, complacent hippies understand that? You need to be smashed.'

When he finally met McClaren's charges, Young was horrified and fascinated in equal measure by the 'four proletarian kids' who'd provoked such outrage and revulsion in the UK. In a beautifully written article, titled 'Rock Is Sick and Living in London', the writer sketched out pen portraits of the men behind the myths: in his eyes, guitarist Steve Jones was a brash, lairy Jack The Lad who revelled in his band's 'bad boy' status, drummer Paul Cook was thoughtful and unassuming, while cartoon-like bassist Sid Vicious was a somewhat pitiful, childlike, self-abusing simpleton.

Young found the band's witheringly sarcastic frontman Johnny Rotten a more complex character to categorise. Despite Rotten doing his level best to be as obnoxious as possible to the visiting scribe, Young was impressed by the singer's passion and obvious intelligence, and found the 21-year-old a not entirely dislikeable character.

On 19 August Young travelled to Wolverhampton to see the Pistols in concert. When the band took to the stage of Club Lafayette at the stroke of midnight, the writer was transfixed by the chaotic, violent spectacle in front of him and by Rotten in particular, whom he later hailed as 'perhaps the most captivating performer I've ever seen'. He was convinced that the Pistols could be just the wake-up call that the moribund US music scene was crying out for.

'Kids destroyed schools to the tune of $600 million in the U.S. last year,' he noted towards the end of his article. 'That's a lot of anger that the Southern-California-Cocaine-and-Unrequited-Love Axis isn't capable of tapping.'

This is a Call

By the time the Sex Pistols finally hit America's West Coast in January 1978, however, they were a very different band. Vicious was by now a full-blown heroin addict, Rotten was at loggerheads with McClaren over his manipulative managerial style and Jones and Cook were tiring of the self-destructive circus that had long since enveloped their band. With perverse, puckish logic, McClaren had shied away from booking the Pistols into America's most Anglophile, punk-cognisant cities – New York, Los Angeles, Boston, Detroit – opting instead to schedule dates in Pittsburgh, Atlanta, Memphis, San Antonio, Baton Rouge, Dallas, Tulsa and San Francisco, gambling that America's media would lap up the opportunity to see how the more conservative Bible Belt states would react to these delinquent scumbags pitching up in their towns. Hysterical television reports sensationalising the violence at the band's English gigs duly followed: Atlanta's Channel 2 news team upped the ante by claiming that the band routinely vomited and committed 'sex acts' upon one another as part of their stage show.

Those hoping to witness Caligulan frenzy on the Pistols' début US tour would have been horribly disappointed: the shows were remarkable only for the sense of anti-climax which accompanied them. The biggest problem the Pistols faced lay in the yawning chasm between their terrifying reputation and the rather more prosaic reality: audiences expecting to see the Four Horsemen of the Apocalypse were confronted instead with little more than a workmanlike rock 'n' roll band.

By the time the Pistols pitched up at San Francisco's Winterland Ballroom on 14 January it was all over bar the shouting. The Winterland show saw the quartet play to a crowd of over 5,000 people – more than they'd drawn in the previous six shows combined – but by now Rotten was sick to his cavities of the whole sorry pantomime. At the end of a perfunctory set the band returned for one encore, a ramshackle, seemingly interminable trawl through The Stooges' 'No Fun'. As the song limped to its climax, Rotten knelt at the lip of the stage, his arms folded across his chest, fixing his audience with a sullen glare.

'Ah-ha-ha,' he laughed joylessly. 'Ever get the feeling you've been cheated? Good night.' His microphone clunked to the floor, and the Pistols' great rock 'n' roll swindle was over.

This is a call

Among the audience at Winterland that night were 19-year-old Eric Boucher, a freshman at the University of California, Santa Cruz, and two friends from Hermosa Beach, California, 22-year-old Keith Morris and 23-year-old Greg Ginn, who played together in a Stooges/MC5-influenced garage rock band called Panic. Far from feeling cheated, and unaware that the Pistols had just played their last show – Johnny Rotten would announce his exit from the group just four days later – all three young men walked out of Winterland feeling elated, energised and inspired by what they had seen. Six months later Boucher formed his own punk band, Dead Kennedys, and adopted the stage name Jello Biafra. Six months after that, Ginn and Morris changed the name of their band to the more militant, threatening-sounding Black Flag.

∽

It would be a gross over-simplification to suggest that the American hardcore movement was born, like a phoenix from the ashes, out of the death of the Sex Pistols' punk rock dream. By the summer of 1977, while the Pistols were finishing up the recording of their début album *Never Mind the Bollocks* at Wessex Sound Studios in London, there was already a fertile, diverse punk rock scene in Los Angeles, centred around the Masque, a dingy basement club just off Hollywood Boulevard. Here bands such as the Weirdos, The Zeros, X, The Bags and The Germs – the latter fronted by charismatic, nihilistic Iggy/Bowie acolyte Darby Crash and his guitar-playing best friend Pat Smear – played short, riotous sets for messed-up Hollywood club kids.

Keith Morris and Greg Ginn were occasional visitors to the Masque but found themselves out of step with the self-absorbed, narcissistic, peacocking club regulars, who took one withering look at the suburban beach kids with their long hair, faded jeans and T-shirts, and slammed doors in their faces.

'We weren't in it for the fashion,' Morris told Black Flag biographer Stevie Chick, 'we were in it for the music, its intensity, and the volume.' The cliquish snobbery they encountered in Hollywood only enhanced the alienation felt by Morris and his friends, and strengthened their desire to create a new noise, without waiting for anyone's permission or acceptance.

Black Flag's début EP then was a startling declaration of independence, in both content and form. Released on guitarist Greg Ginn's own newly created SST label in January 1979, the *Nervous Breakdown* EP featured four taut, wired tales of caucasian psychosis, delivered at breakneck speed, with extreme aggression. From Keith Morris's agitated delivery of Ginn's tension-filled lyrics – '*I'm about to have a nervous breakdown | My head really hurts | If I don't find a way outta here | I'm gonna go berserk …*' – through to the pen-drawn cover art (contributed by Ginn's brother Raymond Pettibon) which depicted a terrified-looking man holding up a chair to fend off another visibly distressed, aggravated individual with clenched fists raised, it was a record every bit as viciously confrontational as The Stooges' 1969 début.

By the time filmmaker Penelope Spheeris began documenting the LA punk scene for her 1981 movie *The Decline of Western Civilization*, Morris and Ginn were no longer playing together (the singer having bailed out to form his own band, the more frantic but less threatening Circle Jerks) but the *Nervous Breakdown* EP had become one of the cornerstones of a new punk rock community.

Born in South Bay towns such as Hermosa Beach, San Pedro, Santa Ana and Huntingdon Beach, American hardcore was, in its earliest incarnation, the sound of California screaming. Growing from childhood to adolescence while former Hollywood actor Ronald Reagan reigned as Governor of California, teenagers in these towns were raised to believe that theirs was the golden generation, that they were the heirs apparent to the fabled American Dream: for many, such promises were a joke without a punchline. Living in the suburbs, and still dependent on their parents, these kids felt like flies caught in a jam-jar jail: they understood that a bigger world lay somewhere out there, but they themselves stood trapped in their everyday world, frustrated and constrained by the invisible walls they believed surrounded them.

To those with such a mindset, punk rock offered both succour and a sense of escape. It did not matter that by 1979 the mainstream was already pronouncing punk 'dead' – indeed this was the year that trail-blazing fanzine *PUNK* ceased publication – it didn't matter that the Sex Pistols were defunct and that The Clash had broken their chains with the expansive *London Calling*: for the kids who had just discovered the genre, this was a new form of music from which they weren't about to walk away. Instead they stripped away the elements they didn't like – the posturing, the obsession with fashion, the elitism – and rebooted the genre, amplifying its volume, simplifying its structure, accelerating the velocity, ratcheting up the aggression. What emerged was hardcore: music made by, made for and made about America's angry, alienated youth, a true riot of their own.

In the 2006 documentary *American Hardcore*, based upon writer Steve Blush's 2001 book of the same name, Keith Morris gave an eloquent summation of hardcore's appeal for suburban teens.

'I'm working Monday through Friday, here comes Friday night and I'm just gonna go *off*,' said Morris. 'I hate my boss, I hate the people that I work with, I hate my parents, I hate all these authoritative figures, I hate politicians, I hate people in government, I hate the police: everybody is kinda pointing the finger at me, everybody is picking at me, everybody is poking at me and now I have a chance to be with a bunch of my own type of people, and I have a chance to go off. And that's basically what it was … BOOM!'

Dave Grohl's first punk rock epiphany came not in one of the community centres, church halls or housing co-op basements that provided the setting for the incubation of Washington DC's nationally regarded hardcore scene, but in Evanston, Illinois, a prosperous suburb of Chicago. Located on the shores of Lake Michigan, Evanston was largely populated by wealthy old money families, aspirational middle-class professionals and a transient student population taking classes at the nearby Northwestern University. It was also home to Virginia Grohl's best friend, her former Boardman High School classmate and Three Belles bandmate Sherry Pelz, by then the married Sherry Bradford, and her teenage daughter Tracey, a sassy, feisty punk rock girl who within the space of ten days in the summer of 1982 turned Dave Grohl's world upside down.

This is a Call

Tracey Bradford became a punk after seeing Dead Kennedys and Chicago's own Naked Raygun and Articles of Faith destroy her hometown's Club COD one 'fun, crazy' night in September 1981. An instant convert to the cause, within weeks she had shorn her long brown hair and swapped pretty, preppy dresses for bondage pants and ripped T-shirts. None of this, however, had been relayed to Dave Grohl before he knocked on the Bradfords' front door that summer.

'So we showed up that year,' he recalls, 'and Tracey came down to the door in engineer boots, bondage pants and an Anti-Pasti T-shirt, with a crew cut and a fucking motorcycle chain around her neck and spikes. And I was like, "You are my hero!"'

'We ran up the stairs of their mansion to her bedroom and she had, honestly, a collection of punk rock singles that would be worth like $100,000 today, singles that are considered impossible to find, like first-pressing Dischord singles, legendary shit you just don't see. And I went through every single one of those records. And that definitely set my life in the direction it's been in for thirty fucking years.'

Now a care home nurse living in Florida, Tracey Bradford has fond memories of her 'cousin' Dave's visit.

'It's funny, I don't ever remember thinking, "Wow, Dave thinks I'm cool!",' she laughs. 'I don't really recall him being really impressed. I just remember that Dave was always a really nice guy. He was pretty young the first time he came to visit – I remember him visiting with his little Winnie the Pooh bear – and he was a good kid, always super, super nice.'

As Grohl rifled through her record collection, Bradford dropped another bombshell: she wasn't just a punk rock fan, she was also the singer in her own punk rock band, Verboten.

'Verboten were a pretty cool little band,' remembers Steve Albini, now frontman of noise rock provocateurs Shellac and a world-renowned recording engineer, then a journalism and fine art student at Northwestern University, taking his first faltering steps towards punk rock godhead with his misanthropic dorm room solo project Big Black. 'Chicago had such a small punk rock scene and everybody knew everybody. That was a really inspirational period: it seemed like everything was permissible, like all the misfits and losers and people who couldn't function in regular society could get along quite comfortably with each other and that sort of created a punk rock scene. There was nothing fashionable or chic about it like it was in Los Angeles or New York where you'd have hip socialites dropping in on the punk scene, or where wealthy patrons took bands under their wings. That didn't happen in Chicago, it was very much a street-level scene and by the mid-eighties it had extended to misfits of all ages. The kids in Verboten would prob-ably have been the youngest kids involved.'

Verboten, in which 14-year-old Bradford was joined by 10-year-old guitarist Jason Narducy, 12-year-old bassist Chris Kean and 11-year-old drummer Zack Kantor, played their first show at Chicago's Cubby Bear, a dank, dark rock club opposite Wrigley Field, home of the Chicago Cubs baseball team, in January 1982, opening up for Naked Raygun and Rights of the Accused. Video footage of the gig shows Verboten to be a tight little unit, with their young guitarist emerging as the star of the show, ripping out a blistering Angus Young-style solo during a chaotic cover of 'Louie Louie' as stage invaders swamp his singer and front row punks take the piss with good-humoured 'We're not worthy!' bows.

'It was all a big laugh,' remembers Bradford, 'all about having a good time.'

As Naked Raygun and Rights of the Accused were back at the Cubby Bear while the Grohls were staying in Evanston, Bradford asked Grohl and Hinkle if they would be interested in coming along to see a punk rock show with her.

'I had to sit them down and give them the Punk Rock 101 speech before we left,' laughs Bradford. 'And they had to look the part so we wouldn't stand out. I'd dated the drummer of Rights of the Accused and then the guitarist, they were both boys that I knew, so it was impor-tant that I wasn't bringing two little geeks to the show.'

Yet to release a single, in 1982 Naked Raygun were still one of the Chicago punk scene's best-kept secrets. Influenced by second-wave British punk acts Wire, Gang of Four and Stiff Little Fingers, the band dealt in abrasive, scratchy, teeth-on-edge post-punk, with Santiago

Durango's metallic, drilling guitar lines tempered by vocalist Jeff Pezzati's keen melodic instincts: the notoriously hard-to-please Steve Albini considered them the finest band in his adopted hometown.

Grohl was also blown away by the band, but more than that, he loved the tumultuous atmosphere in the Cubby Bear and the sense of community within its walls. Tracey Bradford introduced him to Pezzati and her friends in Rights of the Accused, and the Chicago punks adopted him for the evening, filling his head with stories of legendary gigs and must-have records, and scooping him off the venue's sticky floor when the propulsive ebb and flow of the pit threatened to pull him under. It was an eye-opening, life-changing night for the youngsters from Virginia: 'When we walked out I remember Dave saying, "That was fucking crazy!"' says Bradford.

'I stood there and thought, "I could do this, I can play drums, and you don't even have to sing – you can just scream your balls off,"' Grohl recalled two decades later. 'I talked to the singer and I jumped on someone's head and I felt completely at ease with the band and the audience. It was just a bunch of people having a good time.

'Most people who were kids back then, when they talk about their first concert it's like, "Yeah, I saw Dio opening for Ozzy," or "I saw Fastway opening for Van Halen," but mine was Rights of the Accused opening for Naked Raygun. That was my point of reference, and still to this day it remains some sort of reference as to how music should be experienced live.'

Before he left Evanston, Grohl had one more revelatory experience, one which would shape the rest of his adolescence, and provide a moral framework that continues to inform his life. It came with the discovery that, back on the East Coast, one of punk rock's most vibrant, vital communities was virtually on his doorstep.

'I remember looking at Tracey's singles,' he told me in 2009, 'and picking up an S.O.A. single or a Minor Threat single – a Dischord single anyway – and looking at the address and going, "Woah, this one is from Washington DC!" And then Tracey said, "Dude, listen to this!" and she played me a Bad Brains record. And it was like, "Holy shit! They're from DC too?" And then we listened to Faith and Void and all the real cool shit from Dischord's early days. And a lot of these bands were still going at that time, so now I had a mission for when I got back home, to check out that scene. It took me about a year before I finally found it. And then I couldn't get out of it.'

✎

If liberal, leafy Evanston, Illinois was an unlikely breeding ground for punk rock revolution, the same could be said of Washington DC's affluent, elegant Georgetown district, home to politicians, foreign diplomats and some of the city's most influential, wealthy and well-connected families. Before he was elected as the 35th President of the United States in 1961, Senator John F. Kennedy owned a house in the district; former US President Bill Clinton also lived in the area while studying at Georgetown University, America's oldest and most prestigious Catholic university. The hub of Washington's glamorous social scene, Georgetown is best known for its refined architecture, upscale boutiques and high-end restaurants, but it was in this genteel, gentrified district that the punk rock scene which changed Dave Grohl's life was spawned.

Ian MacKaye is the godfather of that community. A most reluctant punk rock icon, MacKaye's name has nonetheless become a by-word for uncompromised integrity, independent thought and unyielding, principled self-determination. The Clash's Joe Strummer once commented: 'Ian's the only one who ever did the punk thing right from Day One and followed through on it all the way.' Dischord, the record label MacKaye co-founded in 1980 to document his hometown's nascent scene, stands as an inspirational example of the potential of the punk rock underground. Preferring handshake deals over legal contracts, selling its releases at affordable prices and splitting all profits evenly between artists and the label, Dischord is a collective that values community above commerce, and offers an alternative, ethical framework to standard record industry practices. The trailblazing bands Ian MacKaye fronted – among them Minor Threat, Embrace and Fugazi – operated defiantly out of step with the music business; his current group The Evens continue happily to do so.

This is a Call

Like Dave Grohl, MacKaye is the son of a journalist father and a schoolteacher mother: unlike Grohl, one can easily imagine him excelling in either profession. Often portrayed as an austere, intimidating character, in person MacKaye is thoughtful, eloquent and disarmingly direct, blessed with a dry wit and an encyclopaedic knowledge of, and boundless enthusiasm for, music.

MacKaye's introduction to punk rock came on the night of 3 February 1979, when he attended an all-ages concert featuring New York's trashy punkabilly ghouls The Cramps and Washington DC New Wave outfit Urban Verbs at Georgetown University's Hall of Nations. He remembers that night as 'one of the greatest nights of my life'.

'At that show I entered into a whole new universe,' he told me in 1992, as we conducted an interview in a Georgetown café three blocks from 36th and Prospect Street, the former location of the Hall of Nations. 'I met a lot of really interesting people who challenged me artistically and emotionally and politically and sexually, people who threw up all these different ideas and alternative ways of living. And when the music you listen to challenges established notions of how music should sound, it gives you the message that rules can be broken. It was the most unbelievable, mind-blowing night.'

The Cramps' show was a benefit gig to raise money to save WGTB, Georgetown University's radio station, which had recently been shut down after having its broadcast licence and FM frequency sold to the University of the District of Columbia for just $1. With its provocative left-wing political bias and vocal support for gay rights, abortion rights and the anti-war movement, WGTB had long been a thorn in the side of the university's Jesuit administration.

The majority of those in attendance at the Hall of Nations, however, were less concerned about the suppression of the station's subversive news bulletins than by the loss of WGTB's eclectic, playlist-free programming, which had brought punk rock to the DC airwaves for the first time. Then a 17-year-old senior at Woodrow Wilson High School, MacKaye went along to the show with friends to add his voice to the protests. Also present was his future Fugazi bandmate Guy

Picciotto, then a 13-year-old student at DC's private Georgetown Day School.

As The Cramps kicked into their ramalama rock 'n' roll rumble, vocalist Lux Interior went into a frenzy, scaling amps, hurling microphone stands around, diving into the crowd and vomiting on the stage. Urged on by this demented master of ceremonies, the Hall of Nations' audience responded in kind, its largely teenage occupants pinballing around the room, overturning tables and hurling chairs through windows. For Ian MacKaye, whose previous concertgoing experience was limited to arena shows by hard rock behemoths Led Zeppelin, Ted Nugent and Queen, it was an impossibly thrilling, unforgettable experience, one which instantly transformed him, in his own words, into 'a punk rock motherfucker'.

Two weeks later, on 15 February 1979, MacKaye and his friends Jeff Nelson and Henry Garfield (now better known to the world as ex-Black Flag vocalist-turned-punk rock renaissance man Henry Rollins) went to see The Clash play DC's Ontario Theatre on their Pearl Harbor Tour, their first US trek. London's finest opened up with the provocative 'I'm So Bored with the USA' – with Joe Strummer spitting *Never mind the Stars and Stripes, let's print the Watergate tapes*' – and closed with the incendiary 'White Riot', during which a frustrated Mick Jones repeatedly smashed his Les Paul guitar against an amplifier stack until its headstock snapped off. MacKaye, Rollins and Nelson were transfixed by the band's fire, ferocity and fury.

'They were detonating every song, like "use once and destroy",' recalled Rollins in Clash associate Don Letts's punk rock documentary *Punk: Attitude*. 'They were burning through the music like napalm. They weren't even playing it, they were just chewing it up and eviscerating it as they went through it, like after the show there'd be no more Clash. And we walked out of there stunned. The Ramones were great, but it was like The Beach Boys compared to that … The Clash came through and just went, "Wake up, let's go!"'

Asked in 2004 to describe Washington's music scene at the tail end of the seventies, Ian MacKaye responded, 'There was no music scene in Washington really, that's my answer.' As an erudite scholar of his hometown's cultural history, in the late seventies MacKaye would have been keenly aware of popular local bands such The Razz, Urban Verbs and the Slickee Boys and indeed Washington's vibrant funk-driven Go-Go scene, but those bands said little to MacKaye about his own life. The Cramps and The Clash gave him the impetus to change that.

Within weeks of attending his first punk shows, the teenager had picked up a bass guitar and formed his own punk band, The Slinkees, with Nelson on drums. The band managed to play one show in a friend's garage before singer Mark Sullivan quit in order to attend university in New York. Undeterred, MacKaye promptly recruited a new singer, Nathan Strejcek, and changed the quartet's name to the Teen Idles.

Another young DC band who'd fallen under The Clash's spell were Bad Brains, four young Rastafarians from the south-east of the city. Formerly a jazz-fusion collective named Mind Power, influenced by Stevie Wonder, Sly and the Family Stone, Chick Corea's Return to Forever and John McLaughlin's Mahavishnu Orchestra, Paul Hudson (aka H.R.), Earl Hudson, Gary Miller (aka Dr Know) and Darryl Jenifer had been introduced to punk rock by their friend Sid McCray, a fan of The Damned, the Dead Boys and the Sex Pistols. By 1979 Bad Brains were determined to outpunk *everyone*, mixing fat dub reggae bass lines with blur-speed rhythms, jarring tempo changes and frenetic, feral energy. At that point no band played faster, or swung harder. But Bad Brains had another mission too, to spread a doctrine of Positive Mental Attitude via vocalist H.R.'s empowering, motivational lyrics, themselves inspired by *Think and Grow Rich*, a self-help, personal development manual written and published by author Napoleon Hill during the Great Depression. To say that DC rock clubs, then more used to hosting coolly detached New Wave acts and rootsy rock 'n' roll bands, were unprepared for this whirlwind of energy blowing their way is something of an understatement.

'Bad Brains were some black youths who wanted to play punk rock and hard rock and a couple of club owners were confused and a little frightened,' Darryl Jenifer told me in 1996. 'Punk rock was a *vulgar* thing, and maybe some people wanted to look at the black situation too as a vulgar thing: one time this guy said, "We ain't having no punk stuff in here, and damn sure we ain't having no black punk stuff." But we had the PMA with us at that time, Positive Metal Attitude, and the "quitters never win" concept, so these little obstacles didn't mean that much to us.'

Inspired by stories they had heard of The Clash playing free shows in community centres in England, the quartet began setting up gigs in housing co-ops and friends' basements, as a 'fuck you' gesture to the club owners who'd banned them from their premises. In doing so, the quartet helped create an alternative gig circuit in their hometown, and a template for self-sufficiency other DC bands would soon seek to emulate.

After they'd blown his band off-stage at a June 1979 show at Georgetown rock venue the Bayou, The Damned's drummer Rat Scabies offered to help Bad Brains put together an English tour, convinced that their righteous energy would revive the UK's flagging punk scene. That autumn, after honing their chops with a succession of shows on New York's Lower East Side, the band decided to make the trip. They would soon discover that their PMA was no match for over-officious English bureaucracy. Arriving at London's Gatwick airport without work visas, the quartet were detained, questioned and summarily dumped onto the next outbound flight to New York. To rub salt in the wound, all their gear was stolen.

Back in New York, the city's punk community rallied around the band, lending them instruments and squeezing them onto bills where they could: Jimi Quidd and Leigh Sioris from The Dots even paid for a studio session for the band, during which Bad Brains recorded two songs, 'Stay Close to Me' and 'Pay to Cum'. The latter, a one minute 33 seconds rush of breathless, bawling positivity, flamethrower guitar and blur-speed rhythms, would eventually become the A-side of the band's début single, and a musical benchmark for every hardcore band that followed in their wake. But for all the support they received in NYC, just three months after departing Washington Bad Brains were back in the city, penniless and homeless. MacKaye's Teen Idles stepped in to help, inviting their brethren to use their equipment and practice space in the basement of Nathan Strejcek's parents' house. Watching the older punks rehearse was an education for the kids from Wilson High.

'Bad Brains influenced us incredibly with their speed and frenzied delivery,' Jeff Nelson admitted in the excellent DC punk scene memoir *Dance of Days*. 'We went from sounding like the Sex Pistols to playing every song as fast and as hard as we could.'

'H.R. was the energizer,' MacKaye stated in 2001. 'He was really passionate about what he did. He was a visionary. He really got a lot of us kids thinking we could do anything. He was really full of great ideas and was always the one who said "Go". They were a complete inspiration as a band.'

'Dr Know always used to say, "Each one teach one,"' Darryl Jenifer told me when I asked about his band's influence on the DC scene and beyond. 'It's a musical tapestry we got going here. It don't start with us. Respect is due to the magic of music, not Bad Brains.'

As the new decade dawned, stories of other bands playing urgent, raging punk rock across America were reaching DC. In the racks of Yesterday and Today records in Rockville, Maryland, an independent record store owned by former DJ Skip Groff and largely frequented by teenage punks eager to hear the latest import singles arriving from England, new releases from West Coast labels Dangerhouse, Slash, Frontier and Alternative Tentacles records were arriving weekly, bringing to the attention of Ian MacKaye and his friends bands such as The Germs, The Weirdos, Deadbeats, The Flyboys and Dead Kennedys. After graduating from Woodrow Wilson High in June 1980, MacKaye and Nelson hatched a plan to check out the nascent West Coast scene, booking shows for the Teen Idles in LA and San Francisco.

As with the Bad Brains' proposed UK trip, things didn't go according to plan for the adventurous young punks. In LA the quartet found themselves sharing a bill at the Hong Kong Café with obnoxious Seattle shock rockers The Mentors, Masque club regulars Vox Pop and brutal 'biker punks' Puke, Spit and Guts, who sang of murder and rape and looked like they would happily slit the Teen Idles' throats for the price of a cup of coffee. More disappointingly, in San Francisco the quartet were bumped at the last minute from their promised slot on a Dead Kennedys/Circle Jerks/Flipper show at the Mabuhay Gardens by promoter Dirk Dirksen, who only reluctantly agreed to rebook them on a bill with New Wave outfits The Wrong Brothers and Lost Angeles at the venue the following evening following lobbying efforts on the band's behalf from the Circle Jerks.

California nonetheless left indelible impressions on the young band. They took note of how punks from the Golden State – most notably the feared Huntingdon Beach crew who followed the Circle Jerks and Black Flag from show to show – conducted themselves, taking shit from no one: this was a revelation for the DC youths, who were routinely hassled and abused on the streets of Georgetown. They also noticed that the Mabuhay Gardens had instituted an 'all-ages' policy for gigs, marking a large black 'X' on the hands of audience members too young to drink alcohol to distinguish them from patrons legally allowed to purchase intoxicating liquor. On their three-day bus trip back to the East Coast the young punks talked excitedly about introducing these practices to their hometown. Washington DC was about to get a noisy wake-up call.

Back on home turf, though, cracks began to appear in the group dynamic. The experiences of the past year had left the articulate MacKaye with plenty to say, but he no longer felt comfortable putting his words into Strejcek's mouth. The band agreed to split, but before doing so the decision was made to document their time together by releasing a seven-inch single on their own label, funded by the $600 they had amassed from their 35 live shows. The quartet had already recorded an eight-song tape with local sound engineer Don Zientara at Inner Ear Studios – a four-track tape recorder set up in Zientara's suburban home in Arlington, Virginia – and sought advice from Skip Groff, who had his own small record label Limp Records, on the mechanics of putting out a record.

In December 1980, a month after the band played their final show at DC's 9:30 club, the Teen Idles' seven-inch *Minor Disturbance* EP emerged as the first release on the newly created Dischord record label. The cover featured a photograph of Alec MacKaye, Ian's younger brother, with an inked 'X' on each of his clenched fists, an image which neatly captured the defiant mood of the emerging youth community. MacKaye and Nelson pledged that if they managed to sell enough copies of the EP to recoup some of their investment, they would use the money to put out records by their friends' bands. It was a proud moment for the teenage punks but, never one for nostalgia, MacKaye had already moved on. By the time Skip Groff put the *Minor Disturbance* EP on sale at Yesterday and Today, MacKaye's new band Minor Threat had already played their first show.

~

'Revolution is not the uprising against pre-existing order, but the setting up of a new order contradictory to the traditional one.' Printed on the inner sleeve of Fugazi's 1990 album *Repeater*, this quote from Spanish liberal philosopher José Ortega y Gasset's 1929 text *La rebelión de las masas (The Revolt of the Masses)* offers an insight into Ian MacKaye's *modus operandi* since the night he first discovered punk rock. Raised by liberal, free-thinking, intellectual parents, for MacKaye the notion of an independent counterculture was not some intangible pipe dream, but rather a viable and attainable reality. It is this conviction that has driven his life's work.

In October 1981 MacKaye's first step towards independence saw him move out of his parents' Beecher Street home in North-West Washington and take up residence in a rented four-bedroom house in Arlington with Jeff Nelson and three punk rock friends. Dischord House, as the property was known, soon became the creative and spiritual epicentre of the emerging DC hardcore community. An office for MacKaye and Nelson's label was set up in a small room next to the kitchen, while the basement of the house was utilised as a rehearsal space for bands, among them Henry Garfield's State of Alert (S.O.A.), Alec MacKaye's The Untouchables, Iron Cross and MacKaye and Nelson's new outfit Minor Threat.

When their bands weren't practising, the young musicians spent their time at Dischord House hand-cutting and pasting record sleeves for Dischord releases (the second of which was S.O.A.'s bruising *No*

Policy EP), designing flyers for upcoming shows, dubbing demo cassettes to trade with penpals, scribbling columns for fanzines and writing letters to record store owners, promoters and college radio DJs nationwide, anything to spread the DC punk gospel. The first Dischord releases were mailed out bearing the slogan 'Putting D.C. on the Map', but there was genuine pride and conviction behind the tongue-in-cheek sentiment: MacKaye regarded each release as another stepping stone towards the creation of a truly independent artistic community in his hometown. To MacKaye, Dischord was about nothing if not its sense of engagement, involvement and connection.

'From the very beginning of the label we were told time and again that the way we were approaching the business was unrealistic, idealistic and ultimately unworkable,' he recalled in 2004. 'They said that it couldn't work, and that it wouldn't. Obviously it fucking worked.'

Dischord's most popular, passionate and influential band was Minor Threat, arguably *the* defining act of the American hardcore movement. Featuring MacKaye on vocals, Jeff Nelson on drums and Georgetown Day School students Lyle Preslar and Brian Baker on guitar and bass respectively, Minor Threat played super-fast, super-tight, morally righteous punk rock that blazed with an incandescent fury which left all who saw them indelibly marked. Though Minor Threat would record just two EPs and one full-length album, their influence on the nascent hardcore movement was incalculable, their commitment to breaking down the barrier between 'artist' and 'audience' unequalled.

The band's début release, the *Minor Threat* seven-inch EP was a revelation. Rather than pointing a finger at the Republican administration in the White House (as was *de rigueur* in hardcore circles at the time), MacKaye's scathing, indignant lyrics targeted both his own community and everything it stood in opposition to, sparing no one, friend or foe. The EP's most infamous song was 'Straight Edge', the clean-living MacKaye's apoplectic response to substance-abusing punk rock fuck-ups who took Sid Vicious's self-destructive cartoon nihilism as a template for their own lives.

Elsewhere he tackled themes of peer apathy, masculinity, violence and failing friendships, with equally unambiguous, thrillingly direct anger. If Black Flag's *Nervous Breakdown* EP was a declaration of independence, the *Minor Threat* EP was a declaration of war, a war MacKaye was determined to wage all across the nation. To do so meant tapping into what author Michael Azerrad called hardcore's 'cultural underground railroad', an interlinked community of promoters, fanzine writers, college radio stations, independent record stores and alternative venues.

Prior to the arrival of Black Flag there was no national grassroots touring circuit for America's punk bands. That group's pioneering attempts to establish a network, using phone numbers bassist Chuck Dukowski copied from the sleeves of the earliest hardcore seven-inch singles, was partly born out of necessity – by 1981 Black Flag's hometown shows were notorious for pitched battles between punk kids and the brutal LAPD, making it increasingly difficult for the band to secure bookings *anywhere* – and partly derived from Greg Ginn's desire to replicate the violent, untrammelled energy of his group's LA shows in every town and city in the union. For Ginn and Dukowski, the idea of stepping into the unknown to confront and challenge was integral to the punk rock experience.

'We like to play out of town,' Ginn told *Flipside* in December 1980. 'You've gotta threaten people sometimes.'

'We think everybody should be subjected to us, if they like it or not,' the guitarist added in another interview.

'There's more impact in playing for people who aren't just soaking up the punk thing,' Dukowski explained to *Outcry* fanzine in 1980. 'It's actually more stimulating to play for an audience that has not heard it and probably has a prejudice against it. You almost don't know what to do when you're in front of people who love it. It's much easier when you're in front of people who are sort of neutral or anti what you're doing. You get all these people out there who've never seen it, don't know what to expect and you get out there and blow 'em away.'

'Greg Ginn had a ham radio thing as a teenager and through that he knew all about fucking up people from other towns – he just extended that to the idea of playing gigs,' explains Mike Watt, now playing with The Stooges, then the bassist with Black Flag's SST labelmates/touring partners, San Pedro agit-funk punks The Minutemen. 'Before Black Flag there was no template. We literally had to invent this thing for ourselves. The rock 'n' rollers really hated punk, so it was hard to play their clubs, so we'd play ethnic halls, gay discos, VFW halls, anywhere that would have us, because we also learned from Black Flag that when you ain't playing you're paying.'

Black Flag seemed to invite confrontation – whether this be with cops, promoters or indeed their own fans – with their every move, and each day on the road brought both fresh challenges and familiar entanglements. Henry Rollins's Black Flag tour diaries, published in 1994 as *Get in the Van*, offer the most searing account of the experience of touring the USA in a hardcore band in the early 1980s, mapping out the scene's lawless, anarchic landscape with unflinching detail. Rollins's diary entry for 7 July 1984 was not untypical:

> In the middle of the show, I took a knife off a guy and started swinging it at people in the front row. I put my other hand in front of my eyes so that they could see that I couldn't see. I hope it bummed them out. Next, a guy handed me a syringe that looked full. He said that there was coke in it. I took it and threw it into Greg's cabinet screen. It stuck like a dart. After the show, some fucked-up guy was trying to crawl into the van with us. I pulled out Dukowski's .45 and put the barrel on the man's forehead and told him to get the fuck away.

On the road Minor Threat themselves faced trouble at every turn. The didactic tone of their EP infuriated just as many punks as it inspired, with many of the group's detractors interpreting MacKaye's militant lyrics as a personal assault upon their lifestyle. Each night on tour MacKaye faced drunken hecklers and macho lunkheads hellbent on imparting a little attitude adjustment of their own. With tedious regularity, violence ensued.

Such hostility only added to the escalating stresses of life on the DIY circuit. Money was tight, drives were long and mind-numbing, comforts were scarce. Soon enough, the band was at war not just with the outside world, but also within: internecine arguments raged around divergent views on questions of materialism, ethics, aspirations and intentions. Yet, for all the bullshit they encountered, Minor Threat in full flight were truly transcendent, providing a visceral experience few bands of their generation could hope to match. 'Ian MacKaye sings with more meaning and honesty than anyone I have seen,' noted a reviewer for *Flipside* when the band played The Barn in Torrance, California in July 1982. 'The crowd went nuts singing along with every song. If you miss these guys live I feel sorry for you.'

‹∼

While Ian MacKaye and his friends travelled America's highways and byways inspiring and empowering a new nationwide punk rock community, back in Washington DC Dave Grohl was embarking upon his own personal revolution.

To mark his allegiance to the punk tribe, in 1983 he gave himself his first tattoo using a needle and pen ink, a primitive technique he picked up from watching *Christiane F. – Wir Kinder vom Bahnhof Zoo (We Children from Bahnhof Zoo)*, a 1981 film about the drugs scene in seventies Berlin. His intention was to ink Black Flag's iconic four bars logo on his left forearm: he managed to etch three of the four bars into his flesh before the pain proved too much to handle.

Guided by Tracey Bradford's recommendations, and the reviews of records he read in *Flipside* and its more politically conscious San Franciscan counterpart *maximumrocknroll*, he began seeking out punk rock wherever he could find it, the noisier and nastier the better.

'Dave and I played lacrosse in junior high school and we went to a lacrosse camp at the University of Maryland the summer we were turned on to punk rock,' remembers Larry Hinkle. 'We both had a little spending money that week, and during a break we checked out the university's student union book store and record store. I bought some stupid souvenir like a baseball cap or shorts or something, but Dave bought an Angry Samoans record, *Back from Samoa*, from the record store. It was one of his first punk records and he couldn't wait to get home and listen to it at the end of the week. I remember asking him why he would buy a record at a lacrosse camp when he could spend his money on some cool crap like I had. I don't remember exactly what he said, but he definitely couldn't care less about all that stupid souvenir shit. From then on, it was all about the music.'

'The first hardcore record I fell in love with was a *maximumrocknroll* compilation called *Not So Quiet on the Western Front*,' Grohl recalls. 'It was a double LP with over 40 bands from the Bay Area, so it had everyone from Flipper to Fang to M.D.C. to Pariah, and that and the Dead Kennedys' *In God We Trust* and Bad Brains' *Rock for Light*, those were the first three records I absolutely fell in love with. And to be honest, that's all you need, that's enough.

'I was so excited by this new discovery that it became all I would listen to. I didn't have time to listen to my old Rush and AC/DC records. I didn't dislike them and I didn't disown them, I was just too busy trying to find something new. It was exciting to buy albums that were a total mystery until the needle dropped. I remember buying an XTC single because I thought it would sound like GBH – I love XTC now, but goddammit at the time I was really pissed off that I'd spent those $5 on that single! But punk rock and industrial noise is a slippery slope: you start with something like The Ramones and go, Wow, now I want something faster! And then you get to D.R.I. and you go, Wow, I want something noisier! And then you get to Voivod and it's, I want something crazier! And then you get to Psychic TV and go, I want something more insane! Pretty soon you wind up just listening to white noise and thinking it's the greatest thing ever. But while I was listening to hardcore punk my sister Lisa was listening to Siouxsie and the Banshees and R.E.M., and we'd sometimes meet in the middle, say on Hüsker Dü. So through her I discovered Bowie and Talking Heads and stuff like that. To this day I credit her with a lot of musical influence, because had I not had an older sister like Lisa I would not have heard [Buzzcocks'] *Singles Going Steady* or [R.E.M.'s] *Murmur* or [Talking Heads'] *Stop Making Sense*. There was a lot of cool music in my house.'

While journeying into the dark heart of punk rock, Grohl remained preoccupied by the idea of playing guitar in a band. The circumstances which finally enabled him to do so were unorthodox. In autumn 1983

This is a Call

Tony Morosini, a student at Thomas Jefferson High School, spotted Grohl and Christy entertaining the elderly residents of an Alexandra nursing home, playing cover versions of Rolling Stones and Who songs on their guitars. The gig had been organised by their school's Key Club, a civic-minded student organisation whose stated aim was to provide members with 'opportunities to provide service, build character, and develop leadership' by undertaking tasks to help the local community. 'Dave and I just joined for the keg parties,' Christy admits today.

'So we played for a room full of people whose average age was maybe, I don't know … 10,000?' recalls Grohl. 'And we played "Time Is on My Side". *Time Is on My Side?* Did they enjoy it? I don't even know if they could hear it!'

Morosini, a talented drummer, had been jamming with two fellow Thomas Jefferson High upperclassmen in the basement of his Alexandria home, and he saw the confident, charismatic Christy as the missing piece in his rock 'n' roll jigsaw. That same week Morosini approached Christy in the school corridor and enquired as to whether the freshman student would be interested in fronting his band. Christy offered to give it a shot, but on one condition. He told Morosini, 'It's a package deal, though: I got Dave, and where I go Dave goes.' Morosini shrugged his shoulders. Sure, he said, whatever, bring Dave too, we'll be a five-piece.

The band practised regularly in the basement of Morosini's parents' house, hammering out covers of classic rock anthems: Bowie's 'Suffragette City', The Who's 'My Generation', some Stones, Chuck Berry's 'Johnny B. Goode' and, perhaps inevitably, that evergreen punk staple 'Louie Louie'. With a few appearances at backyard parties already under their belts, by the end of the '83–'84 school year the band felt confident enough to put their name forward for Thomas Jefferson High School's annual variety show competition – or rather they would have put their name forward had their band actually been in possession of a name.

'When we registered for the show we were asked for the band name and we said "We're nameless,"' says Nick Christy. 'So that's how we got billed on this variety show, Nameless.'

This is a call

The competition saw Nameless pitted against the school's reigning variety show champions, Three for the Road, a three-piece garage band from the school's senior year, fronted by Mississippi Senator Trent Lott's son, Chet Lott. A degree of rivalry existed between the two bands – 'Three for the Road always seemed like they were better than us,' remembers Nick Christy – and the entire student body was aware that this year's competition carried with it a new edge.

'We had won this contest every year so we just assumed we were going to win it forever,' recalls Chet Lott, now a 44-year-old political lobbyist working alongside his father and former Louisiana Senator John Breaux at the Breaux Lott Leadership Group in Washington DC. 'Maybe we were a little naïve. When they showed up it was like, "Oh, hell, now we got some real competition here!"'

On the day of the competition Nameless played well, blasting through raucous covers of The Who's 'Squeezebox', Chuck Berry's 'Johnny B. Goode' and their trump card, Kenny Loggins's recent *Billboard* chart-topper 'Footloose'. Three for the Road followed with a strong set of their own, turning in powerful versions of the Rolling Stones' 'Honky Tonk Women', The Who's 'Can't Explain' and Creedence Clearwater Revival's 'Have You Ever Seen the Rain?' The fate of both bands lay in the hands of their audience, quite literally, as the contest was to be decided by the volume of applause garnered by each act. Ultimately, to Grohl's intense disappointment, Three for the Road triumphed once more. 'All the chicks loved them,' a rueful Grohl admitted 25 years on.

'Those guys had some real chemistry in their band, and obviously some great musicians,' recalls Chet Lott, an accomplished musician himself, with two albums of soulful, country rock to his name. 'In Three for the Road we were not great musicians individually, but as a unit we were pretty good. And because we'd been around since freshman year that helped us a little bit in the talent show as we already had a bit of a following. I don't think Dave Grohl has lost out too often since that day …'

The June 1984 Thomas Jefferson High School variety concert was to be one of the Nameless's final appearances. Just a few months later, following his parents' divorce, Nick Christy's mother moved her family back to Massachusetts; without their frontman the band soon petered out. Amusingly, in 2009, when I asked Grohl about the band's demise, he put his own tongue-in-cheek, mythologising spin on the breakup: 'We lost a couple of members to drugs, women and fast cars,' he said with a shrug. 'Hey, it was North Virginia, it was crazy …'

∽

By 1984 the American hardcore scene itself was slowly disintegrating. Many of the musicians who had helped build the community no longer recognised or respected it. Violence and drug abuse prevailed, younger acts seemed content to ape their heroes rather than search for their own voice, and arguments about politics, sexism, racism and ethics played out in the letters pages of fanzines. The civil war tearing the scene apart was one of the topics under debate when *maximumrocknroll* brought together Ian MacKaye, Articles of Faith's Vic Bondi and M.D.C.'s Dave Dictor for a round-table discussion in the summer of 1983. MacKaye's exasperation was all too evident when at one point he asserted, 'Punk rock has more assholes, in a ratio sense, than any other kind of music. They don't have respect for anything, it drives me crazy.' Something had to give. And in September 1983, as the issue went on sale, his band Minor Threat played their final show.

In truth, the members of this volatile and relatively short-lived group were never the best of best friends, and would argue constantly – about songwriting, about MacKaye's lyrics, about their relationship with Dischord and their future plans. 'I have some really great practice tapes with about seven minutes of music and about eighty-three minutes of arguing,' MacKaye would wryly note years later.

By the time the quartet recorded their début album *Out of Step* with Don Zientara in January 1983, MacKaye was already directing much of the anger in songs such as 'Betray', 'Look Back and Laugh' and 'Cashing In' squarely at Preslar, Baker and Nelson. Minor Threat may have been out of step with the world, but they were also increasingly out of step with one another, and their status as kingpins of the national hardcore scene only exacerbated divisions within a band that bassist

Baker once scathingly dismissed as 'an after-school hobby for some over-privileged kids'.

'Part of the split was that Lyle and I – what a surprise, the private school kids – wanted to continue to build and to see where this could go,' Baker told me in 2010. 'I mean Minor Threat never left the United States and we wanted to see the rest of the world: we thought that there was potential to keep moving forward. And that really wasn't in the cards and so basically that's what split us up. Aspirations tend to ruin the best of intentions.'

On 23 September 1983 Minor Threat played their final show, opening up for DC Go-Go legends Trouble Funk at the Landsburgh Center. They aired a new song for the first, and last, time.

'Salad Days' was MacKaye's unflinching dismissal of a scene he felt had become stagnant and compromised, driven by sounds of fury which came increasingly to signify nothing. The song's bitter lyrics were all the more powerful coming from a man whose belief in the power of music and art to empower, engage and inspire had been so well documented.

The mood of the song struck a resounding chord with many in the punk community. In spring 1984 *maximumrocknroll* placed the bald question 'DOES PUNK SUCK???' on its front cover. That same spring, 12-year-old Scott Crawford interviewed Ian MacKaye for the first issue of a new DC scene fanzine called *Metrozine*. Though more than six months had passed since Minor Threat's final show, the young writer found MacKaye unwilling or unable to drag himself out of his slough of despond.

'He was so down, so totally over the whole scene,' says Crawford, now the editor of *Blurt* magazine. 'There was no suggestion of him forming another band, he was so disillusioned and disenchanted. It was actually pretty painful to see.'

Interviewed by *Flipside* around the same time, Black Market Baby frontman Boyd Farrell offered another doomy insider's prognosis of the DC scene.

'It's sad, all those little kids that were on skateboards a year or two ago are on heroin now,' Farrell commented. 'It's like DC lost its innocence. It's been deteriorating since the end of Minor Threat, though obviously it isn't their fault. It's like a fashion thing now. It's like it lost the sincerity, the anger, and became more cynical. You used to be able to go to the clubs and get a buzz from the bands' energy.'

One year on, in April 1985, Skip Groff filed Minor Threat's final single alongside the Teen Idles' *Minor Disturbance* EP, State of Alert's *No Policy* EP, Government Issue's *Legless Bull* EP and Youth Brigade's *Possible* EP in the Dischord rack at Yesterday and Today. Recorded on 14 December 1983, almost two months after the band had played their final show, *Salad Days* felt like the requiem for a shared dream. Yet, typical of the DC punk scene's capacity for death and renewal, in the same month that the single went on sale another young area band were entering a recording studio to record their début EP. This would be the first seven-inch single to bear Dave Grohl's name.

Chaotic hardcore underage delinquents

For bands in Washington DC a career in music was never the intention. The motivation was, 'Let's get together and fucking blow this place up ...'

Dave Grohl

On the afternoon of 21 January 1985 Ronald Reagan stood in the magnificent Capitol Rotunda for the swearing-in ceremony that would begin his second term as President of the United States of America. Re-elected following a landslide victory over Democratic Party candidate Walter Mondale, Reagan promised a new dawn for a nation emerging from the deepest recession since the Great Depression.

'My fellow citizens, our nation is poised for greatness,' he told the American people in his second inaugural address. 'We must do what we know is right and do it with all our might. Let history say of us, "These were golden years ..."'

In the same month that President Reagan was filling a cold January day with hot air, across the Potomac River, in Arlington, Virginia, a new band was formed. For vocalist Chris Page, guitarist Bryant 'Ralph' Mason, bassist Dave Smith and 16-year-old drummer Dave Grohl, Mission Impossible represented their own new beginning, as all four band members had previously played together in Freak Baby, one of the new acts who had emerged on the DC scene in mid '84, around the time *maxiumumrocknroll* published its contentious 'Does Punk Suck?'

issue. Freak Baby were by no means the best of DC punk's second-wave bands – indeed Dave Grohl fondly remembers them as being 'awful'. But the quartet were possessed of a boundless energy and a knack for short sharp shock pit anthems, the best of which ('Love in the Back of My Mind', '20–20 Hindsight' and 'No Words') rang out like Stiff Little Fingers played at 78 rpm. In 17-year-old skatekid vocalist Page, Mission Impossible also had a frontman with genuine charisma and presence.

Now a married father of two working on environmental education projects in his native Seattle, Chris Page discovered punk rock in 1983, when he heard his Yorktown High School classmate Brian Samuels blasting Bad Brains' self-titled ROIR cassette on a boombox in the school playground: 'As with Dave, my dad left the family, and I was angry and confused at the time,' he recalls. 'And this was like nothing I'd ever heard before. I thought it was amazing, just incredible. That and the first Minor Threat record were my introduction to this world.'

Samuels helped Page navigate his way into Washington DC's underground punk network: on weekends the pair would ride the DC Metro's Orange and Blue lines from Rosslyn into the city to check out the scene. Page recalls his initial journeys into the heart of DC being 'an adventure' – 'There's all kinds of dark stuff in the city that you don't see in the suburbs,' he notes – and the shows being characterised by 'pure, explosive, sweaty energy'.

'There was definitely something special happening in DC at that time,' agrees Hollywood film star and 30 Seconds to Mars frontman Jared Leto, who lived in the city from 1983 to 1984. 'That scene was really vibrant, and the characters in it were such individuals. I worked in a nightclub right across the street from the 9:30 so I could walk in there every night and we saw some crazy shit. The shows were just free-for-all madness, with the singers jumping off the stage into the audience and passing the mic around. It was definitely a fun time.'

For Dave Grohl, the 1983 Rock Against Reagan show helped shine a light on this underground community. That July day was the first time he saw flyers advertising all-ages punk shows, hosted in off-the-beaten-track venues never listed in the *Washington Post*'s Arts section or DC's newly established free listings paper the *City Paper* – hole-in-the-wall city centre clubs like dc space and Space II Arcade, suburban community centres such as the Wilson Center and hardcore gig-friendly restaurants such as Food for Thought in Dupont Circle. Emboldened by memories of his night at the Cubby Bear, he stage-dived headlong into the scene.

'No one was sniping my neighbourhood with Black Flag flyers on the weekend,' he remembers, 'so initially that scene stayed pretty underground. But as soon as I found out about these shows I was like, "Man, if I could just get a ride …" All day long I'd mow lawns to make enough money to go into the city at the weekend: I'd have my Walkman on, blasting out Dead Kennedys *In God We Trust* and Bad Brains *Rock for Light* and Minor Threat's *Out of Step* and the *Faith/Void* album and I'd be wondering what the weekend would have in store.

'I'd get dropped off or take the Metro down to the shows in inner city DC on my own, and initially I didn't know *anyone*. At that time in Washington DC there were three or four people getting killed every night over drugs: there was crack cocaine and a new drug called Love Boat – nobody knew what the fuck it was, it could have been embalming fluid, but you smoked it and it would burn white hot like an electrical fire and make you feel like you were sitting in your own blood for about four hours. It would make people kill each other. It was fucking crazy. So here I was, a 14-year-old kid on my own, on a Friday night in the murder capital of the world …

'But then you'd go into these shows, and they'd be amazing. There was always the sense that anything could happen. There were people selling fanzines and people giving out stickers, and there'd be broken glass and fights and every once in a while someone would get stabbed. The venues were shitty, the PAs never worked and there were always technical difficulties, but you didn't judge a band on performance as much as you judged them on audience participation. And your new favourite band could sound completely different than they did on the single you'd bought last week.

'Trading tapes and buying singles and ordering fanzines by mail, all of those things became so special to you. You'd get a single by a band from Sweden in your mailbox and then a year later they were playing the shithole down the street? You can imagine the feeling: you'd walk in and see them in person and then they'd plug in and play the songs that you loved from that single that you ordered for two dollars a year ago and it meant the world to you, it was fucking huge. So that spirit, I consider it now to be just the spirit of rock 'n' roll, that spirit of music meant more to me than anything else.'

On his trips into the city, two local bands in particular stole Grohl's heart: Bad Brains and Virginian hardcore heroes Scream.

'The first time I saw Scream was at one of those Rock Against Reagan shows,' he recalls. 'Scream was legendary in DC. They were from my neighbourhood, from Bailey's Crossroads in suburban Virginia, which was maybe ten miles away from North Springfield, and if ever the DC scene seemed elitist or insular or hard to crack it didn't matter, because Scream were from my fucking neighbourhood! We were so proud of that because not only were they one of the best American hardcore bands, but they were the best in DC: Bad Brains had moved to New York, Minor Threat were gone and Rites of Spring were amazing, but they weren't playing hardcore. And Scream played *everything*. You would go to see them and they would play the first three songs off [their 1983 début album] *Still Screaming*, which are unbelievably bad-ass hardcore songs, and then bust into [Steppenwolf's] "Magic Carpet Ride" and then do some weird space-dub shit for a couple of minutes and then pile back into something that sounded like Motörhead. They were so fucking good. They didn't give a fuck what anyone thought of them, they didn't give a shit. They were the underdogs because they were from Virginia. And we looked up to them so much.

'But nobody else blew me away as much as Bad Brains,' Grohl admitted in 2010. 'I'll say it now, I have never ever, ever, ever, ever seen a band do anything even close to what Bad Brains used to do live. Seeing them live was, without a doubt, always one of the most intense, powerful experiences you could ever have. They were just … Oh God, words fail me … incredible. They were connected in a way I'd never seen before. They made me absolutely determined to become a musician, they basically changed my life, and changed the lives of everyone who saw them.

'It was a time when hardcore bands were these skinny white guys, with shaved heads, who didn't drink and didn't smoke and made fast, stiff and rigid breakbeat noise. But the Bad Brains when they came out, it was like if James Brown was to play hardcore or punk rock! It was so smooth and so fucking powerful – they were gods, man, they were way more than human. To see that kind of energy and hear that kind of power just from a guitar, bass, some drums and a singer was unbelievable. It was something more than music and those four people onstage. It was just fucking unreal.

'The DC scene wasn't a huge scene,' Grohl remembers. 'If a local band like Scream or Black Market Baby or Void played you'd probably have maybe 200 people show up, the same 200 people every time: if you had a band like Black Flag play, then there'd maybe be 500 or 600 people there. We called those extra people the "Quincy Punks", people who had seen one punk rock episode of [popular NBC crime drama] *Quincy* and then heard that Black Flag was coming to town. Those were usually the shows that had the most trouble. But the other gigs would have just a few people so you just started seeing the same people around. I'd be starstruck and intimidated when I would see, like, Mike Hampton from Faith or Guy [Picciotto], because these people were my musical heroes and I knew every word to every one of their songs, but you'd be singing along with a band and ten minutes later they'd be diving on top of your head when the next band was on. There was no separation between "bands" and "fans", and that was my idea of some sort of community.

'For me, punk rock was an escape, and it was rebellion. It was this fantasy land that you could visit every Friday evening at eight o'clock and beat each other to bits in front of the stage and then go home.'

It was at a Wilson Center show by Void, a chaotic, impossibly intense punk-metal quartet from Columbia, Maryland, that Grohl first met Brian Samuels in autumn 1984. At the time Samuels's band Freak Baby were seeking to add a second guitar player to their line-up, just as scene elders Minor Threat, Faith and Scream had done the previous year, and

Samuels invited the young guitarist to an audition at the group's practice spot in drummer Dave Smith's basement. Grohl wasn't the best guitar player the band had ever seen – Chris Page remembers him as being merely 'competent' – but what he lacked in technical dexterity he made up for in terms of the energy, enthusiasm and infectious humour he brought to the band. In addition, Grohl's simple but effective rhythm playing neatly complemented Bryant Mason's more proficient lead guitar work. Freak Baby's newest member made his début with the band that winter, playing as support to Trouble Funk at Arlington's liberal-minded, 'alternative' high school H-B Woodlawn. It would prove to be the band's one and only show as a quintet.

Freak Baby's demise was sudden and brutal. One afternoon in late 1984 Grohl was behind Dave Smith's kit at practice, trying out some of the rolls, fills, ruffs and flams he had been practising for years in his bedroom of his family home in Springfield. He had his head down, and eyes closed: his arms and legs became a blur as he hammered out beats to the Minor Threat and Bad Brains riffs running through his head. Lost in music, Grohl was oblivious to his bandmates urging him to get back to his guitar. Standing six foot five inches tall, and weighing in at around 270 pounds, skinhead Samuels was not a figure used to being ignored. Grohl didn't notice his hulking bandmate rise from the sofa, so when Samuels yanked him off the drum stool by his hair and dragged him to the ground, he was more shocked than hurt. The rest of his band, however, were mortified. They had felt that Samuels had been increasingly trying to assert his authority and control over the band, but this was too much. As Grohl stumbled back to his feet, Chris Page called time on the day's session. Within the week he would call time on Freak Baby too, reshuffling the line-up to move Grohl to drums, Smith to bass, and Samuels out the door. With the new line-up came a new name: Mission Impossible.

With the domineering Samuels out of the picture, initial Mission Impossible rehearsal sessions were playful, productive and wildly energetic: all four band members skated, and at times Smith's basement resembled a skate park more than a rehearsal room, with the teenagers bouncing off the walls and spinning and tumbling over amps and furniture as they played. But there was also an intensity and focus to their rehearsals. Songs flowed freely as they bounced around ideas, fed off the energy in the room and experimented with structure, tone, pacing and dynamics. Just two months after forming, the band felt confident enough to record a demo tape with local sound engineer and musician Barrett Jones, who had helmed a previous session for Freak Baby. Jones fronted a college rock band called 11th Hour, North Virginia's home-grown answer to R.E.M., and operated a tiny recording studio called Laundry Room, so called because his Tascam four-track tape deck and twelve-channel Peavey mixing board were located in the laundry room of his parents' Arlington home. Now running a rather more sophisticated and expansive version of Laundry Room Studios out of South Park, Seattle, Jones has fond memories of the session.

'I'd recorded a tape for Freak Baby with Dave on guitar, but when he switched to drums their band was just so much better,' he recalls. 'They went from doing one-minute hardcore songs to doing … two-minute hardcore songs! But those songs were more ambitious and involved and dynamic.

'Back then Dave was probably the most hyper person I'd ever met,' he adds. 'When we did that first Freak Baby demo he was literally bouncing off the walls. They were a hardcore band, so they all had that energy, but he was something else. But musically his decision to switch to drums was definitely the right one.'

'Once Dave got behind the drums he was very obviously something special,' says Chris Page. 'He was doing stuff that nobody else was doing, incorporating little riffs and ideas that he'd pinched from some of the great rock drummers he listened to. He took great pride in us being the fastest band in the DC area, but there was so much more to his playing than just speed and power. And that started to affect our songwriting, because even though our songs were maybe only one minute or a minute and a half long we wanted to showcase his talent and build in space for those parts.'

The first Mission Impossible demo neatly captured the quartet's combustible energy. It provides a snapshot of a band in transition, mixing up vestigial Freak Baby tracks and goofy cover versions (most notably a take on Lalo Scifirin's theme for the *Mission Impossible* TV series, with which the band opened every gig) with more nuanced shards of hardcore rage. Across twenty tracks the shifts in tone occasionally grate – the decision to include a screeching romp through a BandAids advertising jingle alongside a thoughtful, articulate song such as 'Neglect', in which Page delivers a spoken-word lyric juxtaposing the privileged consumer lifestyles of the suburbs with the poverty and pain he encountered on visits to inner-city DC, rather betrays the quartet's youthful over-exuberance – but at their best Mission Impossible were a genuinely thrilling prospect.

Among the more light-hearted selections on the tape, two tracks stand out: 'Butch Thrasher' is Grohl's mocking paean to the macho knuckledraggers who considered punk rock moshpits their private battlefields, while 'Chud', inspired by the kitschy 1984 horror movie *C.H.U.D.*, sees Page screaming '*Chaotic Hardcore Underage Delinquents! Cannibalistic Humanoid Underground Dwellers!*' while trying to keep a straight face. Of the more sober tracks, 'Different' deals with the hassles devotees of punk rock faced from parents and peers unsympathetic to the lifestyle, while 'Life Already Drawn' echoes the sentiments Ian MacKaye expressed in the song 'Minor Threat' with Page screaming '*Slow down!*' at teen peers who seemed in an unseemly haste to join the adult rat-race.

Two Dave Grohl-penned originals also warrant mention: 'New Ideas' stands as the fastest song in MI's repertoire, packing whammy bar divebombs, squealing harmonics, two verses, three choruses and a jittery, atonal Bryant Mason solo into just 74 seconds. Elsewhere 'To Err Is Human' was arguably the demo's most sophisticated track, its driving rhythms and sudden dynamic shifts in tempo and key bearing the influence of Grohl's favourite new band, SST's Hüsker Dü, the brilliant Minneapolis trio whose stunning 1984 double album *Zen Arcade* had rendered hardcore's perceived boundaries obsolete, and drawn favourable comparisons to The Clash's *London Calling* album in mainstream music publications. 'To Err ...' was significant not only for highlighting the increased maturity of Grohl's songwriting, but also for flagging up to his new friends issues in his personal life, specifically in regard to his relationship with his father.

Over the years Dave Grohl has stubbornly resisted journalists' attempts to play amateur psychologist over the impact his parents' divorce had upon his life. It would make for a convenient narrative if his drive, energy, work ethic and subsequent success could be linked back to a teenage desire, conscious or subconscious, to scream 'Look at me now!' at the man who walked out on his family; if his entire artistic *raison d'être* could be traced back to the rejection, resentment, anger and pain he felt as the child of a broken home. But time and again Grohl has rejected this analysis. 'There was some Nirvana book that glorified my parents' divorce as if it were my inspiration to play music,' he protested in 2005. 'Completely untrue. The fucking Beatles were the inspiration for me to play music.'

Nevertheless, Dave had James Grohl in mind when in spring 1985 he scribbled the lyrics to 'To Err Is Human' in his notebook: '*To err is human,*' he wrote, '*so what the fuck are you? Working so hard to make me perfect too …*'

At the time, Grohl's visits to see his estranged father in Ohio were regularly punctuated by finger-pointing lectures, explosive arguments and sullen, protracted silences. As a speechwriter for the Republican Party, James Grohl was a master of the dark art of transforming trenchant opinions on morality, ethics and law and order into screeds of fiery rhetoric, and he was never shy of sharing his views with his teenage son, regardless of whether Dave wanted to hear them or not: 'Imagine the lectures I'd get if I fucked up,' Grohl commented in 2002. 'I'd get the State of the Union address!'

With his grounding in classical music, James had firm views too on the self-discipline required of performing musicians – 'He thought that unless you practised for six hours a day you couldn't call yourself a musician,' his son once noted – and Dave's basement thrashings didn't exactly match up to his lofty ideals. Even after Nirvana's *Nevermind* album became a worldwide phenomenon, Dave Grohl was still mindful of his father's occasionally dismissive attitude to his career. 'Dave and I were at his house one night,' his friend Jenny Toomey told me during the research for this book, 'and I remember him talking about his father being critical of him for not being a "real" musician and I thought that was really sad,' so one can only imagine the snarky, offhand comments that would have been directed towards him during his formative years in the DC punk underground.

During these difficult times music provided Dave with both a pressure valve and an escape hatch. His spirits were buoyed as Mission Impossible's demo quickly built up a word-of-mouth buzz on the tape-trading underground, attracting plaudits both nationally and overseas. The band were name checked by *maximumrocknroll* editor Tim Yohannon in a review of *Metrozine*'s DC area cassette compilation *Can It Be?* (which featured MI's 'New Ideas'), and secured their first international release around the same time when French punk rock label 77KK included 'Life Already Drawn' alongside tracks by D.O.A., California's Youth Brigade, Red Tide and the best up-and-coming French punk acts on their début release, a compilation album also titled *77KK*.

In April 1985 Mission Impossible returned to Laundry Room Studios to cut a second demo. The quartet were now writing collaboratively, pushing one another to create more complex, challenging material, and a new-found self-assurance shone through in each of the six new tracks demoed with Barrett Jones. Hardcore's 'loud fast rules!' ethic still provided a foundation for the new material, but MI had learnt that silence and space could be harnessed to accentuate volume and weight as readily as thrashing powerchords. Chris Page was growing in confidence as a lyric-writer too, and the conviction with which he delivered each word rendered his tales of teenage travails wholly believable.

Of the songs on this second demo 'I Can Only Try' is a classic slice of teen angst (*'I can't promise perfection, I can only try'*), 'Into Your Shell' is a rallying call for noisy self-expression (*'If you're really upset and you don't know what to do, then shout it out or talk it out, don't crawl into your shell'*) while 'Paradoxic Sense', 'Wonderful World' and 'Helpless' tackle issues of growing up without giving in. The demo's final track, 'Now I'm Alone', finds the singer picking over his father's decision to leave the family home – 'You could say that disappointment with fathers was a minor theme with MI,' Page now wryly reflects – and celebrating the freedoms that came with his immersion in the DC punk community.

Delivering fully on the promise of their first demo, the tape showcases a committed, articulate, progressive young band gearing up for adult life with defiant self-belief: *'Now I'm off to face a new horizon,'* Chris Page sings, *'but I don't think I'll be alone.'* These words would carry an added emotional resonance in the months ahead.

⁓

In spring 1985 unmarked envelopes were pushed through the letterboxes of a number of homes in Washington DC and suburban Virginia. Each envelope contained a photocopied leaflet, styled to resemble a kidnap ransom note, bearing messages such as 'Wake up! This is … REVOLUTION SUMMER!' and 'Be on your toes. This is … REVOLUTION SUMMER'. Recipients of the letters were initially bemused, then intrigued, curious not only to discover the identity of the anonymous letter-writer and the meaning of the note, but also as to who else might have received one. A common thread quickly emerged: everyone sent a 'Revolution Summer' missive had been active on the DC hardcore scene at the beginning of the decade.

The letters were traced back to the office of the Neighbourhood Planning Council, a small administrative body set up by the DC Mayor's office to host community meetings and schedule an annual free summer concert series in nearby Fort Reno Park. Located next to Woodrow Wilson High School, the office had become a *de facto* drop-in centre for local punks to hang out and drink sodas. While they were there they had access to Xerox machines in order to run off flyers, posters and fanzines. It subsequently emerged that the letters had been sent out by Dischord staffer Amy Pickering as a playful way to get old friends talking together once again.

The plan proved extremely effective. Pickering's missives opened up new dialogues among the hardcore class of '81, who began mulling over their own involvement in the punk community, debating whether it was the scene, or they themselves, that had changed with the passing years. They wondered if, and how, the idealism and integrity that had fuelled that nascent community could be rekindled. As these conversations continued, many within the group made a conscious decision to try to redefine their world. Some started new bands, others formulated new ideas and made renewed commitments to re-engaging with the social and political issues affecting their community. As Ian MacKaye explained to *Suburban Voice* fanzine in 1990, the phrase 'Revolution Summer' itself meant 'everything and nothing', but it was the 'kick in the ass' he and his friends needed.

'We all decided that this is it, Revolution Summer,' MacKaye told the fanzine. 'Get a band, get active, write poetry, write books, paint, take photos, just do *something*.'

For Beefeater frontman Thomas Squip, another resident of Dischord House, Revolution Summer was more than just a time of musical rebirth. As he explained to *Flipside* in a July 1985 interview, he considered Revolution Summer to be about 'putting the protest back in punk'. The Swiss-born singer was soon backing up his words with action. That same month he helped organise the Punk Percussion Protest, a noisy anti-apartheid rally which saw scores of young punks gather on Massachusetts Avenue to bang on drums, buckets and bins outside the South African Embassy. Soon, in close co-operation with newly formed activist group Positive Force, DC punks – including the members of Mission Impossible – were lending their voices to a wide range of causes, from protests against America's clandestine war in Nicaragua to benefit concerns for civil liberties organisations, community clinics and homeless shelters. Chris Page remembers the time as 'eye-opening, empowering and transformative'. With delicious irony, DC punks were taking Reagan's 'we must do what we know is right and do it with all our might' words to heart, and using them in opposition to some of his most reactionary policies.

In June the new wave of DC punk was showcased by a seven-inch compilation, put together by *Metrozine* editor Scott Crawford in collaboration with Gray Matter man Geoff Turner's label WGNS. Its title, *Alive & Kicking*, was intended as a defiant rebuttal to those hardcore zealots who considered the DC scene as dead as the American Dream.

Chaotic hardcore underage delinquents

Crawford selected for inclusion Mission Impossible's 'I Can Only Try', alongside tracks by Beefeater, Marginal Man, United Mutations, Gray Matter and Cereal Killer: once again, over in Berkeley, *maximumrockn-roll* gave positive feedback.

That same month also saw the release of the first record on Dischord for two years, the first, in fact, since Minor Threat's *Salad Days* single. The self-titled début album by Guy Picciotto's Rites of Spring could hardly have been more symbolic of the scene's regeneration.

By common consent, Rites of Spring were Revolution Summer's most inspirational band. They sang of love, loss, wasted potential and spiritual rebirth while attacking their instruments with a commitment, intensity and kinetic fury that saw guitars and amps reduced to match-wood. Their wiry, sinewy, high-tensile compositions eschewed hardcore formulas, choosing instead to strip away the genre's machismo in order to expose its raw, sensitive, bleeding heart. RoS shows were genuine events that saw audiences moved to tears by the group's passionate and cathartic outpourings. They would play just fifteen shows in their short history, and Dave Grohl says that he was present at every one of them.

'A lot of people don't realise the importance of that band, but for us they were the most important band in the world,' he remembers. 'They really changed a lot in DC. They played every show like it was their last night on earth. They didn't last long, but then for bands in Washington DC a career in music was never the intention. The motivation was "Let's get together and fucking blow this place up, until we can't blow it up any more." Once the inspiration or electricity felt like it was fading, or once a band started to feel like a responsibility, they'd just break up. It was all about that moment. But those moments were so special to us.'

July 1985 also saw the return to the stage of DC hardcore's spiritual leader. Ian MacKaye's new band Embrace may not have been as musically adventurous as Rites of Spring, but they were a powerful, emotive unit in their own right. As with his previous band Minor Threat, Embrace asked a lot of questions, but this time MacKaye's rage was for the most part directed inwards, as he dissected his own foibles and flaws in unflinching, forensic detail. In part, this soul-searching was sparked by MacKaye's admiration for DC's younger punk set. When he looked at bands such as Mission Impossible and their peers Kid$ for Ca$h and Lünchmeat, MacKaye saw a new breed of idealistic, gung-ho teen punks operating in blissful, stubborn denial of hardcore's demise, a poignant echo of his own reaction to premature reports of the death of punk rock: it made him wonder at what point he stopped believing. 'Those kids were super enthusiastic and it reminded us of our younger selves,' he recalls. 'It was inspiring to see high school kids playing again.'

'The American hardcore movement may have been all over by 1984, but none of us wanted to believe it,' admits Lünchmeat vocalist Bobby Sullivan. 'It was hard for us to measure up to what had already happened, but we were all fans of Minor Threat and Bad Brains and we wanted to carry on the tradition, in the right way.'

Dave Grohl and Bobby Sullivan were regular visitors to Dischord House in the summer of '85. Ian MacKaye had known Sullivan for years, as he was the younger brother of his former Slinkees bandmate Mark Sullivan, and he remembers Grohl as a nice kid to have around, always positive, friendly and full of enthusiasm. He first saw the pair's bands play together at a tiny community centre in Burke, Virginia that July. For all the positive energy surrounding Revolution Summer, a number of prominent venues, including the 9:30 Club and Grohl's beloved Wilson Center, had that summer stopped booking hardcore bills due to the attendant violence and vandalism. Lake Braddock Community Center in the new-build community of Burke had emerged as a new venue after Kid$ for Ca$h guitarist Sohrab Habibion persuaded his mother to sign up as a sponsor to allow him to use the hall for all-ages shows. In keeping with the inclusive vibe of these gigs, the new venue lacked even a stage, the division between the audience and performers having been distilled down to nothing more prohibitive than a line of duct tape marked on the ground. Mission Impossible and Lünchmeat shared this 'stage' for the first time on 25 July 1985; Ian MacKaye was in the audience to see them.

'Everyone said, "You gotta see this drummer, this kid, he's 16, he's been playing for two months and he's out of control,"' MacKaye recalls. 'And then I saw them, and Dave was just *maniacal*. He didn't have all the chops down, but he was dialling it in from the gods, his drumming was so out of control, and he wanted to play so hard and so fast, it was kinda phenomenal. Everybody was like, "Woah, that guy is incredible!"'

'One night Ian came up and told me that he thought I played just like [D.O.A./Black Flag/Circle Jerks drummer] Chuck Biscuits,' recalls Grohl. 'To me that was like saying, "You are just like Keith Moon," because Chuck Biscuits was a *huge* inspiration to me. So from then I became that kid in town who played like that, I had this reputation as being this super-fast, fucking out-of-control hardcore drummer.'

'Honestly, from the moment you saw Dave play, you were just in shock, because he seemed superhuman,' laughs Sohrab Habibion, now playing guitar in the excellent Sub Pop post-hardcore band Obits. 'I liked Mission Impossible, Chris was a really cool singer and they had great songs, but you'd see them play and there'd be this *monster* on the drums. Dave sat in with my band Kid$ for Ca$h for a couple of shows and it was hilarious, because the whole band was instantly transformed to a higher calibre. We played one show out at Lake Braddock with 7 Seconds and they were all just staring at him, like, "Who is this guy?"'

'People definitely talked about him,' agrees Kevin Fox Haley, a Woodrow Wilson High School student at the time. 'Everyone would say, "You gotta see this kid on drums, he's *insane*." To me it seemed like it stemmed from hyperactivity, because he was kinda a spazz, and I don't mean that in a bad way, but he was so goofy and full of energy. I'm from Washington DC and I'm sorry to say that myself, and some people from Dischord, were pretty snobby about looking down on the kids from the suburbs, so maybe at the time I was still stuck in that snobbiness where I was like, "Yeah, he's good, but he's from *out there* ..." But he definitely stood out.'

For all the momentum and buzz accumulated by Mission Impossible, their days were numbered. As with so many DC bands before them, the lure of higher education was to prove irresistible. Around the time the quartet recorded their second demo tape Chris Page had been accepted to study at Williams College in Massachusetts, while Bryant Mason had been offered a place at the University of Virginia in Charlottesville, meaning the break-up of the band was inevitable. Mission Impossible played its final show at Fort Reno park on 24 August alongside local art-punks Age of Consent, preceded by one last emotional show with Lünchmeat at Lake Braddock, at which the two bands decided to cement their friendship by releasing a posthumous split single. A co-release between Dischord and Sammich, a label set up by Ian MacKaye's younger sister Amanda and her Wilson High School friends Kevin Fox Haley and Eli Janney, the EP featured three tracks taken from Mission Impossible's April '85 demo – 'Helpless', 'Into Your Shell' and 'Now I'm Alone' – alongside three Lünchmeat originals – 'Looking Around', 'No Need' and 'Under the Glare'. As the summer drew to a close, both bands and the Sammich kids commandeered the Neighbourhood Planning Council office to cut out, fold, paste and hand-decorate sleeves for the EP. For Grohl and his friends it was a bittersweet experience. Everyone involved in the project understood that both Mission Impossible and Lünchmeat had more to offer, but the young musicians remained positive and optimistic to the end, writing slogans such as 'Revolution Summer is for always!' on every sleeve. As a final gesture towards the community which had nurtured, supported and empowered them both as individuals and as bands, they decided to title the EP *Thanks*.

'The Do-It-Yourself element made everything more special,' Grohl recalled in 2007. 'When your band put the money together to go into a studio, record some songs, take the tape, send it to the plant, get a test pressing, print the labels and stuff the sleeves yourselves, the final product in your hand is just amazing. Because you know you built that shit from scratch from the ground up.'

The sun had set on Revolution Summer long before the *Thanks* EP received its first review. Writing in the March 1986 issue of *maximumrocknroll*, reviewer Martin Sprouse commented, 'Both outfits create and exhibit three high energy melodic thrashers backed by interesting lyrics. Neither outfit falls into the DC stereotype of musical direction but really do break the ice for a lot of the underground bands from that area. Worth looking into.' By then of course both bands were already defunct.

Chaotic hardcore underage delinquents

When all 500 copies of the *Thanks* EP sold out, it was re-pressed and re-released under the rather more punk rock title *Getting Shit for Growing Up Different.* The new title was all too apt for Dave Grohl. His relationship with his own father James hit its lowest point around the same time, when Virginia Grohl informed her ex-husband that she had found a bong belonging to their son under the driver's seat of her Ford Fiesta prior to a morning school run. Grohl and Jimmy Swanson had discovered marijuana around the same time they fell in love with punk rock and thrash metal: they embraced the herb with equal vigour. Unbeknown to his father, by 1985 Dave was also partial to huffing lighter fluid and necking hallucinogenic drugs. During one memorable Christmas party at Kathleen Place he was tripping on mushrooms to such an obvious degree that one of Virginia Grohl's friends steered him away from the other revellers and politely enquired if he was doing cocaine. But pot remained his drug of choice: 'I was smoking all day long,' he admitted in 1996. 'I was such a burn-out. My best friend was the bong. Me and Jimmy were bonded in pot; bonded by herb.

'The first time I took acid was in Ocean City, Maryland in 1985,' he recalls. 'I was forced to take it. All of my other friends had taken it. They were like, "Come on! Take it! Take it!" I said, "I don't want to take it," and they said, "If you don't take it we're just going to put it in your drink," so I said, "Okay, I'd rather know I've taken it." I liked it so much I took another about six hours in …

'When we were teenagers, me and Jimmy were outcasts,' he laughs. 'We weren't jocks, we weren't nerds, we had created our own little world: we were all about mischief and just being petty criminals. I'm sure most people thought that we were freaks, or just uncool: we were incredibly weird and geeky but we never gave a fuck. Being "cool" in suburban Virginia was like how big of a bong hit you could take. It didn't matter what haircut you had, or what car you had, or what pants you had on, if you could burn a whole bowl in one bong hit, you were fucking cool.'

When James Grohl looked at his son in 1985, though, he did not see Virginia's coolest teenager. Instead he saw a smart kid whose future seemed literally to be going up in smoke. He was concerned that Dave's teenage rebellion was rooted in deeper psychiatric problems, perhaps linked to the break-up of the family unit a decade earlier, but two sessions with a guidance counsellor failed to divine any underlying issues. In a last resort attempt to impose some much-needed discipline on the boy, it was decided that Dave should transfer from Thomas Jefferson High to Alexandria's Bishop Ireton High School, a Catholic private school, run by priests from the Religious Congregation of the Oblates of St Francis de Sales and nuns from the Sisters of the Holy Cross, known for its strict disciplinary regime. This was not a decision likely to build any bridges between father and son.

'I'd never cracked a Bible in my life and all of a sudden I've started studying the Old Testament,' Dave complained in 2007. 'It's like, "Dude, all I did was take acid and spray-paint shit! Why am I here?"'

Bishop Ireton's ecclesiastical stormtroopers faced a losing battle in trying to convert the school's newest recruit to the gospel of Christ: by late 1985 Dave Grohl was already in thrall to new gods – British rock legends Led Zeppelin. Dave first heard hard rock's most powerful band when 'Stairway to Heaven' poured out of his mother's AM radio when he was six or seven years old – 'Growing up in the seventies,' Steve Albini once told me, 'Led Zeppelin were *everywhere*, so saying you were a fan of Zeppelin was like saying you were a fan of air' – but it wasn't until the mid-eighties that the band's majestic *Sturm und Drang* became an obsession for him. Every weekend Grohl and Jimmy Swanson would call around to Barrett Jones's house in Arlington armed with a bag of weed. Together with Jones and his roommate, Age of Consent bassist Reuben Radding, the pair would get high while listening to Zeppelin's fifth album *Houses of the Holy* on Jones's new CD player. In later years, Grohl would claim to have listened so intently to the album that he could hear every squeak of drummer John Bonham's bass drum pedal.

'To me, Zeppelin were spiritually inspirational,' Grohl wrote in a 2004 essay for *Rolling Stone*. 'I was going to Catholic school and questioning God, but I believed in Led Zeppelin. I wasn't really buying into this Christianity thing, but I had faith in Led Zeppelin as a spiritual entity. They showed me that human beings could channel this music somehow and that it was coming from somewhere. It wasn't coming from a songbook. It wasn't coming from a producer. It wasn't coming from an instructor. It was coming from somewhere else.'

To Grohl, Zeppelin were the ultimate rock band, experimental, ambitious, mysterious, dangerous, sexual and dazzlingly adroit, capable of shifting from thunderous blues-rock riffing to gossamer-fine acoustic lullabies at a flick of Jimmy Page's plectrum. That US music critics largely *despised* Zeppelin (for all their subsequent sycophantic backtracking, *Rolling Stone*'s review of the quartet's self-titled début album, released on 12 January 1969, just two days before Grohl's birth, dismissed the band's songs as 'weak' and 'unimaginative') only enhanced their standing in Grohl's eyes. To Grohl, guitarist Page, the conductor of Zeppelin's light and magic, was a 'genius possessed' while bassist John Paul Jones was 'a musical giant'. But it was John Bonham's masterful drumming which truly blew his mind.

'Led Zeppelin, and John Bonham's drumming especially, opened up my ears,' he told *MOJO* magazine in 2005. 'I was into hardcore punk rock; reckless, powerful drumming, a beat that sounded like a shotgun firing in a cement cellar. *Houses of the Holy* changed everything.

'As a 17-year-old kid raised playing punk-rock drums, I just fell in love with John Bonham's playing – his recklessness, his precision. There were times when he sounded to me like a punk-rock drummer. [Led Zeppelin] were so out of control. They were more out of control than a Dead Kennedys record.

'Bonham played directly from the heart. His drumming was by no means perfect, but when he hit a groove it was so deep it was like a heartbeat. He had this manic sense of cacophony, but he also had the ultimate feel. He could swing, he could get on top, or he could pull back … I learned to play by ear. I wasn't trained and I can't read music. What I play comes straight from the soul – and that's what I hear in John Bonham's drumming.'

Given his new-found obsession with Zeppelin, it was natural that Jimmy Page's band would provide a foundation for Grohl's next musical project. Former Minor Threat man Brian Baker had offered Grohl the chance to play with his new band Dag Nasty, but the drummer was now looking to play something more challenging than four-to-the-floor punk rock: ('He turned me down,' recalls Baker, 'but you have to remember that we were children then, so it wasn't like he turned me down flat, it was more like, "Oh, that sounds like fun, but I have to practise with these guys and … oh, hold on, Mom, I'm coming …"') He also wanted to continue playing with bassist Dave Smith, with whom he had developed an almost telepathic understanding. The biggest problem for the pair initially was finding a guitarist who operated on the same wavelength, and could boast the musicianship to match. Both Larry Hinkle and Sohrab Habibion jammed with the pair – by now known to friends by the nicknames Grave (Grohl) and Smave (Smith) – but both guitarists readily concede now that their chops weren't up to scratch at the time. It was Dave Smith who suggested that the duo might try hooking up with his friend Reuben Radding, as Age of Consent had just recently broken up.

The Georgetown-born son of two classical musicians – his father was a violinist in the National Symphony Orchestra, his mother an opera singer – at 18 Radding had already been a touring musician for three years. Now a well-respected jazz musician based in Brooklyn, New York, Radding – like Grohl – was a childhood Beatles fan and originally a guitarist but had switched to bass when an opportunity arose to join the Gang of Four/PiL/The Jam-influenced Age of Consent. On a personal level, Radding didn't know Grohl particularly well – 'To me he was this very goofy but charismatic guy who was at once both shy and extroverted,' he recalls – but he was well aware of the teenager's prowess as a drummer.

'Dave's reputation as a drummer began spreading from the first time he got behind the drums at a Mission Impossible rehearsal, well before any live gigs,' he recalls. 'Dave Smith had been one of my best friends for years, he lived with his parents right up the hill from me on the same tree-lined street, and one day I got a phone call, saying, "Dude, you have got to come up here and check out Dave Grohl playing drums. You won't believe it. He's better than Jeff Nelson!" Jeff Nelson was pretty much considered by everybody to be the best hardcore drummer around, so if Dave said that Grohl was better it was something I had to check out … it had to at least be worth a walk up the hill.

Chaotic hardcore underage delinquents

'What I saw was exactly what had been described, and more. Grohl was flat out ridiculous. It was like watching a young Keith Moon, but he was sort of simultaneously being it and being outside it with a surprised look on his face, almost like he was watching it too and didn't know what was making his hands and feet do these energetic and musical things. He was fun to watch right from the start. Whatever he lacked in metronomic solidity he made up for in raw excitement.

'Mission Impossible and my band were scene friends. We loved supporting them and they were frequent followers of our shows and tapes. Stylistically we were worlds apart – I loved hardcore but I looked like a flower child or New Waver, more likely to wear paisley shirts and hand-painted sneakers than torn T-shirts and Doc Martens or Vans – but good musicians are into good music, and we shared that nonconformist, open-minded mindset of early punk rock.

'When Mission Impossible dissolved I didn't think that Dave and Dave's next move would possibly involve me,' Radding admits. 'Even more than my lack of hardcore cred, I'd become a bass player and whatever reputation I had – not much beyond our Arlington circle, believe me – was as a bass player, an innovative one: switching back to guitar was not something I foresaw myself doing. I still owned one, though, and when Dave Smith asked if I would come do a jam session on guitar I jumped at the chance, not because I thought it was going to be a band, but because those guys were so great I wanted to experience playing with them. I dusted off my long-ignored electric guitar and got in Smave's van for the ride down to Springfield.'

When I spoke to Radding in 2010, his memories of his first jam session with Grohl some 25 years previously were still remarkably vivid.

'The Grohl residence was small,' he recalled. 'I remember Dave setting the drums up in the living room, and with Smave and I and our amps in front of them the front door to the house was only a couple feet away from my ass. They showed me the first of their "songs" – it was just a riff, really, a little guitar figure, and then the drums and bass came in in a call-and-response pattern: I don't think I'll ever forget what it felt like. It was not like playing music with anyone else. Listening to Dave

Grohl play the drums had always been a gas, but playing with him was instantly addictive and a total rush. It was like having your ass lifted in the air as if by magic.'

Grohl's own memories of the session were rather more prosaic: 'We smoked a whole bunch of pot,' he recalled, 'wrote four songs and Dain Bramage was born.'

Led Zeppelin may have provided the common link in Radding, Smith and Grohl's musical tastes, but their new band incorporated myriad diverse influences: Hüsker Dü, Moving Targets, Television, Mission of Burma, Black Sabbath, Neil Young and Metallica were just a handful of the bands who shaped the Dain Bramage sound. In Foo Fighters' first press biography, released to the world's media in 1995, Dave Grohl remembered Dain Bramage as being 'extremely experimental, usually experimenting with classic rock clichés in a noisy, punk kind of way'. When I interviewed him for a career retrospective cover story for UK music magazine *MOJO* in 2009, he summed up his experiences in the band in just one sentence, stating, 'Nobody fucking liked us, because we sounded like Foo Fighters.'

Here Grohl was being somewhat disingenuous. Ian MacKaye remembers Dain Bramage being 'a little less euphoric than Mission Impossible, and not quite so out of control, but cool', while some of Grohl's closest friends, Larry Hinkle and Jimmy Swanson among them, actually rated the three piece as superior to his previous band. The band's biggest problem was simply that they were in the wrong place at the wrong time: Dain Bramage's Led Zeppelin-referencing, hard rock-meets-art punk sound would have made perfect sense in Washington *state* circa 1985 or 1986, but in the capitol of punk, the group stood out like a drum solo at a Ramones concert. Which, to a large extent, was exactly what Radding, Smith and Grohl had intended.

'We felt like there wasn't really a model for what we were doing,' says Radding, 'and it was both frustrating and a source of pride. I mean, for us it was the fulfilment of a dream to be able to present something we felt was truly our own but it could be pretty lonely at times.'

Mindful of the distance they had placed between their new band and Mission Impossible's propulsive posi-punk, the trio approached their début gig at the Lake Braddock Community Center on 20 December 1985 with some trepidation.

'I remember feeling really excited to share what we were working on and I knew our group was special and something different for the hardcore scene,' says Radding, 'but I was worried about being accepted since I'd never really been part of that scene. Everyone else seemed to know who everyone was and I had kids coming up to me asking, "Who are you?" I had long hair and was wearing a sweater over a button-down shirt and in that environment I was somewhat of an enigma.'

Dain Bramage opened up their début gig with a song called 'In the Dark', a reflective, mid-tempo minor key number. As he sang into a battered SM-58 mic just inches from a sea of curious faces, Radding was convinced that Burke's young punks hated his band, but as the final notes rang out the assembled crowd broke into cheers and loud applause: 'I was never so happy or relieved to hear a reaction like that in my life,' he laughs.

Twenty-five years on, Radding has one other indelible memory of that first Dain Bramage performance.

'It was the first time as a front man that I ever experienced seeing an entire audience looking over my left shoulder through the whole gig,' he laughs. 'I had to get used to that pretty quickly, playing with Dave. I could play all the good guitar I wanted, and sing like a motherfucker, but all eyes were gonna be on Dave all the time. At first I resented it. Then I embraced it. We should have set up like a jazz band with him on the side facing in, then at least I could have watched too. Dave's charisma was ever-present, both in performance and off stage.

'He was always kind of hyperactive and he bears the distinction of being the only guy I ever knew who would smoke pot and become *more* hyper,' he continues. 'When he would get stoned he would act truly deranged and go into these episodes of extroverted performance, doing skits and voices, hilarious stuff. I can still remember us laughing till we were in serious pain at some of the stuff he would do when he got stoned. It was kind of like watching Robin Williams at his best – that energy and creative spontaneity – but better than a performance because it was real.

'At one point he earned a new nickname from Dave Smith. We were at some house partying and Grave had been totally going off. Next thing you know he's passed out under a pile of clothes in the corner and someone said something like, "Well, he's finally had it." And Smave just shook his head. "No," he cautioned, "he's just *energizing*." Sure enough, Dave was back up at full energy in about twenty minutes and just totally going nuts. So for a little while Dave was known as The Energizer.'

ᔕ

Shortly after their baptism of fire at Lake Braddock, Dain Bramage cut two demos with Barrett Jones. The first featured five tracks – 'In the Dark', 'Cheyenne', 'Watching It Bake', 'Space Car' and 'Bend' – while the second included a cover of Grand Funk Railroad's 1973 *Billboard* chart-topping blue-collar anthem 'We're an American Band', alongside originals such as 'Home Sweet Nowhere' and 'Flannery'. Given Mission Impossible's previous connection with Dischord it might have made sense for Grohl to approach Ian MacKaye about putting out a record, but the trio were (understandably) concerned that their artful post-hardcore might sound out of step with much of the didactic, righteous rage showcased on the nation's premier punk rock imprint.

'Looking back, we had a bunch of incorrect ideas in our heads by that time,' Radding admits. 'We were in a period of being down on Ian back then. We made fun of him behind his back. It's one of the bigger sources of guilt in my recollections of that time, because the main reason we were snotty about him was just that so many people admired him so we felt like we had to tear him down. How fucking childish. I have the utmost respect for Ian and Dischord even though I like relatively little of their music. What he has built over the years is nothing short of extraordinary, and if we'd been a little less young and stupid we might have done more to join forces with Dischord or somebody else who would have carried more weight. What were we thinking?'

Unusually for a DC area band, Dain Bramage ended up signing with a Californian record label, the inelegantly named Fartblossom Records, a new venture for punk rock promoter Bob Durkee (later 'immortalised' in scathing, scabrous verse in the song 'Bob Turkee' on NOFX's 1986 EP *So What If We're on Mystic!*). Asked what Fartblossom offered that other labels could not, Radding is disarmingly honest: 'Frankly the appeal was that he asked us,' he concedes.

In June 1986 the band booked a four-day recording session at RK-1 Recording Studios in Crofton, Maryland with engineers E.L. Copeland and Dan Kozak (formerly the guitarist in Radding's band Age of Consent) to record their début album. The trio had suffered a falling out with Barrett Jones – 'They were rehearsing in our house using my PA, and there was some tension about them taking over the house and my equipment without ever really asking,' Jones recalls – and Radding convinced his bandmates that they needed to use a 'real' studio in order to get a bigger and better sound for their début album. Visiting RK-1 for a reconnaissance mission, Radding was somewhat alarmed to discover that this 'real' studio was little more than a soundproofed suburban garage, but he swallowed his instincts and said nothing. It was a decision he would come to regret.

The recording did not go smoothly. Within minutes of the band setting up their gear on 21 June, the local police interrupted the session, having been summoned by a noise complaint from Copeland's elderly college professor neighbour. No sooner had the cops departed than a thunderstorm knocked out all the power in the studio.

'The power went out in the whole neighbourhood,' Radding recalls. 'We took a "break" that went on for hours, all of us sitting on the screened back porch watching and listening to the storm and then finally giving up and packing up a lot of our gear by flashlight. The next day's dubbing/mixing session turned into an all-nighter. Little things seemed to take forever to accomplish.'

'It was probably the worst first weekend of recording I've ever had in my life,' Copeland, now the owner of Rock This House Audio and Mastering in Ohio, admitted to me in 2010. 'But the band were extremely organised and we quickly caught up. There wasn't a lot of fiddling around or double-takes, it was just *boom!* We blazed through the songs and it was over. All the guys in that band were really energetic, but Grohl was something special. I thought it was really weird to see somebody beat the living piss out of a drumkit, I'd never seen that kind of playing before. We had a blast, it was a good time.'

Copeland mixed the ten-track album in a day, at which point Radding sent the tape off to his label boss in Pomona. Some months later the group received in the post the test pressings of their first album, a number of songs from which the trio proudly previewed on a Sunday evening show on local 'alternative' radio station WHFS. Radding told the show's presenter that the album, to be titled *I Scream Not Coming Down*, would be released in a matter of weeks. Back at Kathleen Place later that evening, Grohl listened back proudly to his mother's cassette recording of the radio interview.

'I remember thinking that it was so fucking cool that there was a DJ introducing one of our band's songs, going out to maybe a couple of thousand people,' he told me in 2002.

'And that,' he added with a laugh and a theatrically raised eyebrow, 'was when I knew that eventually, one day, I'd become the world's greatest rock star.'

In the weeks that followed the WHFS interview, Grohl was repeatedly stopped by friends enquiring where they could buy his album. On each occasion he promised that the album would be out in a week or two. But when weeks turned into months, with a release date seemingly as distant as the line of the horizon, such questions faded into silence. Morale in the Dain Bramage camp dipped: it was a dispiriting, frustrating time.

Late in the autumn of 1986 Dave Grohl found himself buying new drumsticks in Rolls Music in Falls Church. It was here that he spotted a note pinned among the flyers on the shop's bulletin board. It read 'Scream looking for drummer. Call Franz'. At first disbelieving, Grohl re-read the note several times, before tearing it from the board and stuffing it into his pocket. With Dain Bramage in limbo, he figured that he might as well take the opportunity to jam with a band he considered heroes. When he got home, he picked up the phone and dialled the number.

Gods
look down

The feeling of driving across the country in a van with five other guys, stopping in every city to play, sleeping on people's floors, watching the sun come up over the desert as I drove, it was all too much. This was definitely where I belonged.

Dave Grohl

In late 1987, as they toured America's West Coast in support of their third album *Banging the Drum*, DC hardcore veterans Scream were interviewed for their first *maximumrocknroll* cover story. With its title inspired by Revolution Summer's Punk Percussion Protests, *Banging the Drum* was Scream's most socially conscious, politicised release to date, and writer Elizabeth Greene was keen to tease out the messages behind powerful new songs such as 'Walking by Myself' and 'When I Rise'. 'Are there any political issues that are especially important to you?' she asked the band.

'Apartheid,' said singer Pete Stahl.

'Censorship,' said his brother Franz, Scream's guitarist.

'We're kind of worried about nuclear war,' added Pete.

Scream's 18-year-old drummer, touring nationally with the band for the first time, chipped in with an answer of his own: 'The drinking age,' he replied.

Dave Grohl was just 17 years old when he joined America's last great hardcore band. Bruce Springsteen once sang of learning 'more *from a three-minute record than we ever learned in school*': similarly, three years in Scream's Dodge Ram van would provide Grohl with the finest education he could ever wish for. In a wonderfully evocative phrase which neatly illustrated the feral, lawless nature of the mid-eighties underground touring circuit, an ex-girlfriend once memorably claimed that Grohl was 'raised in a van by wolves': 25 years after joining Scream, Grohl still regards Pete and Franz Stahl as family.

Scream hailed from Bailey's Crossroads, VA, a rural no-horse town built around the intersection of Columbia Pike and Virginia's Route 7. The area owes its name to the fact that P.T. Barnum and James Anthony Bailey, proprietors of a circus they grandly billed as The Greatest Show on Earth, parked up their menagerie in the area in the off-season. Pete Stahl remembers his hometown as 'very Southern, very rural and somewhat segregated ... Norman Rockwellish in a way': many of Stahl's contemporaries on the DC punk scene simply use the epithet 'redneck' to describe the area and its residents.

Like Dave Grohl, the Stahl brothers had music in their bloodline: Arnold Stahl, their lawyer father, managed a popular rock 'n' roll group called The Hangmen who were the toast of Georgetown society parties in the mid-sixties. In February 1966 the band's 'What a Girl Can't Do' single knocked The Beatles' 'We Can Work It Out' from the top of the Virginia/Maryland/DC pop charts: that same month the Stahl kids got their first glimpse of rock 'n' roll's capacity to incite mayhem when local police were summoned to shut down The Hangmen's in-store performance at the Giant Record Shop in Falls Church after 2,000 screaming teenagers laid siege to the store. Franz Stahl bought his first guitar from the same shop ten years later.

Scream formed in 1979, though their story truly begins in 1977, when 15-year-old Franz first started jamming on Hendrix, Skynyrd, Kiss and Funkadelic covers in local garages with two J.E.B. Stuart High School classmates, drummer Kent Stax and bassist Skeeter Thompson. Soon enough, the teenagers were turned on to garage rock and punk via two cult radio programmes, WAMU's *Rock 'n' Roll Jukebox* and Steve Lorber's WHFS show *Mystic Eyes*; stomping standards by The Seeds, The Sonics and The Kingsmen were then added to their repertoire. The group were still searching for a sound and direction of their own when they first stumbled upon Washington DC's nascent hardcore scene. Upon seeing Bad Brains lay waste to the capital's basement dives, the scales fell from their eyes: in the rasta-punks' searing electrical storms Scream saw rock 'n' roll's future. To Pete Stahl, H.R.'s crew were nothing less than 'the greatest fucking band in the world'.

'The first time I saw them [Bad Brains] was at a Madam's Organ show and it scared the hell out of me!' he told *maximumrocknroll* in May 1983. 'I'd never seen a band like that. I just walked in and Doc, Darryl and Earl were just kind of back against the wall, and it was real crowded and dark, and all of a sudden H.R. just busted through the back of the crowd. It was just an intense feeling, just the tension and excitement, and as H.R. exploded through the crowd they exploded into their song! It just blew me away.'

Skeeter Thompson was equally mesmerised. Previously, the bassist had considered that he was the only black kid in the nation in thrall to punk rock: witnessing Bad Brains' righteous ferocity at close quarters was revelatory.

'One day Pete came over and said you've *got* to see this band,' recalled Thompson. 'When I first saw them it was just like, "Man, I want to do that!" So much power!'

Scream's earliest performances took place at keg parties – or 'beer blasts' – in the basement of the house the Stahl brothers shared in Falls Church. Shows at Scream House, as the property was soon known locally, were spectacularly messy affairs. Starved of entertainment options in rural Virginia, every hesher, jock, pot-head and freak within a ten-mile radius would turn up on their porch on party nights. The Stahls' basement floor would be awash with blood, sweat and beers long before the night's 'official' entertainment was scheduled to begin. Inspired by Pete Stahl's memories of his first Bad Brains show, Scream gigs always started with a violent explosion of energy: Stahl would crash through the tightly packed crowd like a raging bull, shunting beers and bodies to the four walls, and the band would kick in with concussive levels of volume. The room would duly erupt in a flurry of fists, elbows, swear words and screams. It was not uncommon for these shows to end amid squealing sirens and baton charges, as the Fairfax County police department piled in mob-handed to break up brawls.

'It was *insanity*,' laughs Franz Stahl. 'Kids didn't know what the hell to make of us. They were used to listening to Zeppelin or Foghat or the Allman Brothers, and what we were playing just freaked them out, it would put everybody on edge. It would get completely out of hand.'

'Our music *really* pissed off a lot of the jocks and rednecks,' agrees his elder brother. 'It was pretty wild. At the start people either laughed at us or wanted to kill us. But soon they started to get into it, attracted by the energy of what we were doing.'

Hardcore's bush telegraph soon carried reports of Scream's chaotic basement parties to Dischord House. Before long, Ian MacKaye and his friends stopped by Falls Church to scope out the scene. Their presence incensed territorial local jocks, and a confrontation ensued. Recognising the DC crew as kindred spirits, the Scream team backed up their punk brethren. Predictably, fists were soon flying. When order was restored, the bloodied but unbowed Dischord and Scream House crews forged an immediate alliance, and MacKaye pledged to find his new friends slots on hardcore shows in the city. The curtain dropped on Scream House's infamous parties soon afterwards: 'We couldn't afford the cleaning bills any more!' Franz Stahl laughs.

Despite MacKaye's endorsement, usually taken as gospel within the Dischord family, the DC punk community didn't immediately embrace Scream. In a scene notionally populated by the marginalised and disenfranchised, they were genuine outcasts, a racially mixed, blue-collar rock band wholly uninterested in kowtowing to codified musical, philosophical or sartorial scene norms. This nonconformist mindset caused confusion and hostility: to *Capitol Punishment* fanzine Scream were simply 'a bunch of jocks trying to be punk'.

The quartet's début show in DC could hardly have been more disastrous. Booked alongside Bad Brains and Minor Threat on a fifteen-band bill at the Wilson Center on 4 April 1981, the Stahl brothers, Thompson and Stax found themselves playing to an empty room when their potential audience walked out of the room en masse as the opening chords of their set rang out. Further humiliation was to follow at a

Gods look down

9 May show with Minor Threat, S.O.A., Youth Brigade and D.O.A. Again, the band had barely set foot on the stage of H-B Woodlawn High School when the audience melted away. To lose one crowd may have been regarded as misfortune, to lose both was a genuine kick in the teeth for the young Virginians. But for encouraging words from scene elders Ian MacKaye and Jello Biafra (in town with D.O.A.) Scream may have abandoned punk rock at that very moment.

'We were feeling pretty down,' remembers Pete Stahl, 'because we wanted to be in that scene: we identified with it and dug those bands and felt this was our natural home. So to have everyone diss us like that was pretty harsh. But Jello came up to me after we finished playing and said, "You guys are great, don't worry about what happened." He gave me his address and told me to send him a demo. That was a really sweet thing to do and it meant a lot.'

'Having people turn their backs and walk out was fairly typical of the DC scene early on,' admits Franz Stahl. 'But them snubbing their noses at us initially just gave us that much more of a drive to smoke these guys every time we played.'

'The first time Scream played nobody cared because they were better than all of us!' says Brian Baker, then playing in Minor Threat. 'They were a fantastic band, with fantastic musicians and great songs. There wasn't really a backlash against them, but trepidation was raised from the minute they started to play. Initially people thought they weren't cool because they had moustaches and they didn't wear the "approved" regalia and they lived twenty miles away ... and twenty miles in teenage terms is *hours* away. But then the moustaches disappeared, and someone bleached their hair and someone else bought a leather jacket and suddenly it was, "Hey! Now they're one of us! Come on in!" After that they were *revered* by all of the Dischord people.'

In January 1983 Scream's *Still Screaming* album became the first full-length release on Dischord. Produced by the band, Ian MacKaye, Eddie Janney and Don Zientara at Inner Ear, three decades on it stands up as a thrillingly urgent, impassioned and powerful collection, mixing up scratchy, Gang of Four-influenced punk-funk ('Hygiene'), loping, spacey dub-reggae ('Amerarockers'), Clash-style rock 'n' roll ('Piece of

Her Time') and thought-provoking, razor-sharp hardcore (everything else) to stunning effect. Pete Stahl lays out his band's manifesto on the fierce 'We're Fed Up', referencing his band's past while keeping both eyes firmly fixed on the future: '*We're from the basement / We're from underground / We want to break all barriers with our sound / We're sick and tired of fucking rejection / But we're not down 'cause we got a direction.*' It's a ferocious statement of intent.

Given the mix of apathy and outright hostility they faced at their earliest DC shows, it was unsurprising that Scream began booking shows nationally even before the release of *Still Screaming*. In *Putting DC on the Map* (a booklet included with the *20 Years of Dischord* box set) Ian MacKaye notes that Scream were the first act on his label to be paid 'royalties', when Dischord stepped in to help them pay for a van repair and a tour-related phone bill: this little detail speaks to the band's proud reputation as inveterate road dogs. No DC band was more committed to taking their music to the people.

'We didn't really have time to think about whether anybody accepted us or not,' says Franz Stahl, 'we wanted to play the world and we couldn't believe that there was this network that was already out there. DC wasn't that big and you could only play the 9:30 Club so many times. We got out of there pretty quickly.'

The responsibility for booking Scream shows fell to Pete Stahl. He remembers his band's earliest national tours coming together on a somewhat *ad hoc* basis – 'You'd phone someone who was a friend of a friend in another town and they'd say, "Okay, this guy is going to be at this record store between twelve and two and he'll help you put on a show"' – but over time he built up 'The Book', a comprehensive database of phone numbers and addresses for record stores, promoters, venues, fanzine writers, DJs, record labels and bands in every state. For all Stahl's meticulous planning, however, touring the nation was rarely predictable: on the road a certain 'Wild West' mentality prevailed. On more than one occasion the band found themselves literally staring down the barrel of a gun.

'We had a couple of shows where we had guns pulled on us,' recalls Franz Stahl. 'Once in Pennsylvania we didn't get paid and the guy pulled a gun because basically Skeeter was trying to kill him. Another time we played in New Orleans and this crazed redneck came storming into the club with a shotgun, saying, "Any y'all feel like being punk rock here?" This huge biker named Ace just stuck his hand out, whipped the shotgun out of the guy's hand and said, "We're not having any of that here." That could have ended badly.'

'You'd play a lot of crazy shows in those days,' agrees Pete Stahl. 'You'd have cops trying to shut down shows, there'd be tensions with skinheads – we had a black guy in the band, remember – and fights were pretty common. But we always got by.'

'Most of the confrontations we had were with drunks, people who just happened to come to the club for a drink and got stuck with us,' says Franz. 'But Skeeter was a big, cut dude and my brother was afraid of no one, so they'd shut down situations pretty quick. Pete was never scared to jump in the middle of potential fights. People would just back away saying, "These motherfuckers are crazy."'

Following the example set by Minor Threat and Faith, in spring 1983 Scream decided to flesh out their sound with the addition of a second guitar player. Their new recruit could hardly have been more at odds with the DC punk aesthetic. Robert Lee Davidson – better known by his nickname 'Harley' – played in a Judas Priest-influenced metal band called Tyrant, and first met the Stahl brothers while dating their sister Sabrina. Every bit as stubbornly independent as his new band-mates, the candy-floss-haired, studs-and-leather-wearing metal-head made absolutely no attempt to tone down his look to assimilate into the DC scene, horrifying elitist punk purists. This secretly gave Pete and Franz Stahl no small amount of pleasure.

Whatever his perceived sartorial shortcomings, Davidson was an undeniably gifted guitarist, and his fluid, technical hard-rock style helped Scream tap deeper into primal rock 'n' roll sources on their superb second album, 1985's *This Side Up*. The new guitarist's metallic influences are most evident on 'Iron Curtain', a not-entirely-convincing Aerosmith-meets-Judas Priest headbanger replete with squealing guitar leads, but elsewhere *This Side Up* swaggers and slams with a confidence and agility of which Bad Brains themselves would have been proud.

This is a Call

The rollicking 'Bet You Never Thought' could have fitted seamlessly onto The Clash's *London Calling*; the title track is an exhilarating tangle of Buzzcocks guitar and air-punching PMA (*'Yesterday it rained so hard I thought the roof was gonna give / But now today's so bright, just wanna let it all in'*) while the soulful 'Still Screaming' matches shimmering minor key reggae with skronking jazz saxophone. Elsewhere, 'I Look When You Walk' has a sexy garage rock groove, and album-closer 'Walking Song Dub' mixes arty, experimental found-sound collages with booming dub basslines, cut-and-paste vocal loops and a whistled melody line. Within a scene hovering dangerously close to self-parody in the mid-eighties, *This Side Up* was a genuine revelation. In 1997 Dave Grohl nominated it as one of the most significant albums of his adolescence.

'This is the album where Scream went from being a hardcore band into being a rock band,' he told England's now defunct *Melody Maker* magazine. 'They sounded like Aerosmith and I loved that. I liked the fact that they had long hair, that they weren't straight edge and that they played this kinda hard-rock/hardcore thing. It made me realise there was a place for me making music.'

With a superb new album to draw upon, and with their sound bolstered by Davidson's muscular fretwork, Scream quickly acquired a reputation as one of the punk scene's unmissable live draws. When the quintet came through Boston in April 1985, *Suburban Voice* editor Al Quint declared their set at the Paradise 'the best set of the year, so far'.

'The perfect combination of speed, power and melody,' Quint wrote. 'The new songs combine those attributes and more. Pete Stahl has charismatic stage presence, able to draw people together, while the band's versatile, uptempo sound, spearheaded by a two-guitar blitz, keeps on coming. The band's newer material has been lumped into the metal classification, but it's coming more from a late sixties hard-rock style – bands like Ten Years After, Steppenwolf (especially their 10-minute jam of "Magic Carpet Ride") or Blue Cheer have influenced their newer material. Scream are definitely in the top echelon of American bands.'

Gods look down

In autumn 1986 Kent Stax reluctantly came to the conclusion that he would have to leave Scream. Having recently become a father for the first time, the drummer felt that he could no longer commit to the band's arduous, loss-making touring schedule. He promised, however, to stick around until the band found a suitable replacement. To this day Dave Grohl maintains that he never imagined that this opportunity would fall to him. When he first made contact with Franz Stahl Grohl's ambitions were modest: he simply hoped to score a jam session with his favourite local band so he could brag about it to his friends. In conversation with Stahl, he mentioned his stints in Freak Baby, Mission Impossible and Dain Bramage and explained that he was a huge Scream fan. When Stahl asked Grohl his age, the 17-year-old drummer claimed to be 20, making the assumption that a nationally touring rock band wouldn't be interested in auditioning a rookie teenager. Stahl promised to be in touch.

As an emerging talent on the DC scene, Grohl wasn't a complete unknown to the members of Scream. Franz Stahl had seen Mission Impossible play at Lake Braddock, while both Stahl brothers and Skeeter Thompson had witnessed an early Dain Bramage show at dc space. Pete Stahl's memory of that particular night tallies with Reuben Radding's account of playing with Grohl: 'All I remember is everybody staring at Dave and not really watching the band,' Stahl says. 'Everyone was like, "Wow, this kid is really good."'

Given the instant impression that the young drummer had made that night, Franz Stahl's decision not to schedule an immediate audition for Grohl was mystifying, though the guitarist now admits that he has scant memory of the pair's first phone conversation. In fact, Grohl only secured an audition for Scream after calling Stahl a second time. The delay proved to be to Grohl's advantage, however. In the interim period he obtained Scream's demo recordings for what would become the *Banging the Drum* album and he had taught himself the drum parts to every song. When the drummer arrived for his audition at Scream's rehearsal space, situated beneath an Arlington 'head' shop, he felt confident and ready. Grohl would later describe the next two hours of his life as 'heaven'.

'Franz was the only member at that first audition,' he recalls. 'He was one of my heroes, and he just looked at me and said, "Alright kid, let's see what you got …"'

'I said, "What do you know?"' recalls Stahl, 'and he said, "Well, I know the first record." And then he blew through twenty songs with a fervour I'd never seen before. As soon as we were done I immediately got on the phone with Harley and Skeeter and said, "You guys have to fucking come down here, you have to check this kid out." To be honest, he had the gig after the first song.'

Grohl was asked to sit in on two or three full rehearsals with Scream before he was formally offered a position in the band. He now faced a difficult decision. He could join Scream, and ditch Radding and Smith, his two best friends; or he could pass up the opportunity to join one of his favourite bands in the world and remain in limbo with Dain Bramage. He drove around Alexandra in his VW Bug for a week listening to *Led Zeppelin III* while pondering his choices: finally he phoned Franz Stahl and apologetically declined his offer. With a guilty conscience, he then confessed to Reuben Radding and Dave Smith that he had been tempted to stray.

'I remember him saying how he was massively flattered but that it was more important to him to see things through with Dain Bramage,' recalls Radding. 'He said that he thought we were more original, and that he wasn't so psyched about being just a drummer after being in a band like ours that was such a collaboration. I was dark, but relieved.'

Scream were not the only band interested in securing Grohl's services in 1986. That same year the drummer received an offer to join 'Scumdogs of the Universe' Gwar, a Richmond, Virginia-based heavy metal collective whose outlandish sci-fi monster costumes and gory, over-the-top theatrics made Kiss look like The Osmonds. A local hard rock band called Wizard enquired about his availability too. And following the dissolution of Embrace, Ian MacKaye also called, inviting Grohl to Dischord House to jam with bassist Joe Lally in a new project that would become the brilliant, iconoclastic Fugazi. By then, however, Grohl had spoken to Franz Stahl again, to tell him that he had reconsidered his decision to join.

Gods look down

Reuben Radding learned of Grohl's change of heart only after over-hearing mutual friends discussing his defection to Scream. Later that same day, Grohl called to confirm his decision. By his own admission, Reuben Radding was 'devastated'.

'I both could and couldn't understand his decision,' he admits. 'I was pissed off and I stayed pissed off for a very long time. We had done a lot for Dave already, especially Smave. He used to drive Dave around, fix his drums … he sacrificed a hell of a lot. We loved Dave tremen-dously, but I didn't think I could trust him after that happened. Trying to talk him out of it wasn't in my head.'

'Dave was definitely torn as to what to do,' recalls Larry Hinkle. 'I remember thinking that he should have stayed with Dain Bramage, and I told him that. Scream was definitely cool, but Dain Bramage were up and coming, and they had a different sound than what was going on at the time. But he had already made up his mind.'

With cruel inevitability, finished copies of Dain Bramage's *I Scream Not Coming Down* album arrived at Reuben Radding's house just weeks after Grohl's decision to quit the band. Listening to the album did nothing to elevate Radding's spirits; indeed it added to the sense of disappointment he was already feeling. Compared with the demos his band had recorded with Barrett Jones, Radding considers *I Scream Not Coming Down* 'flat' and 'lifeless': 'The performances are not as comfortable and confident as the stuff we did before,' he says. 'The number of ways that the record doesn't sound like us are numerous.'

Nonetheless, *I Scream Not Coming Down* is not without its merits. The influence of Led Zeppelin is evident in the album's most powerful tracks 'Drag Queen', 'Stubble' and 'Flicker' (not least in the subtly tweaked 'Misty Mountain Hop' bass line in 'Flicker') but Radding's imaginative, non-linear guitar work and the rhythm section's varied, versatile dynamic shifts keep the songs from straying into monolithic hard rock territory. Elsewhere, 'Eyes Open' combines acoustic and electric guitars in a post-punk adrenalin rush reminiscent of latter-day Hüsker Dü and 'The Log' is a superbly adroit slice of progressive punk that recalls Boston's Moving Targets. The title track, co-written by

Radding and his former Age of Consent bandmate Dan Koazk, is another high point, though Radding's lyric '*The sky's my limit*' now serves as a rather poignant reminder of the band's dashed optimism and unfulfilled potential. Despite his understandable disappointment at how things panned out for Dain Bramage, when Reuben Radding reflects now upon his time creating and playing music alongside Dave Grohl he has few regrets.

'I was a kid, and my mistakes or questionable decisions are pretty easy for me to shrug off in that light,' he told me in 2010. 'Ever since Nirvana got big I've been surrounded by people who want or expect me to be bitter. Sorry, there's no grounds for that kind of bullshit. It was a hell of a lot of fun.'

I Scream Not Coming Down finally reached record stores nationwide on 28 February 1987. Lauded as 'a real rock 'n' roll record' of 'incredible depth and power' by Fartblossom, the album was largely met with positive reviews. Tim Yohannon of *maximumrocknroll* categorised it as 'quirky, jangly hard pop meets the DC sound', and hailed the band's 'complex' arrangements: the album, he noted, was 'a challenge'. *Suburban Voice* praised the album's 'heart, energy and guts' and 'knockout hooks', describing it as 'tuneful enough to stick in your head, with enough stylistic variation to make it come across as original'. Dave Grohl himself would later hail the album as 'a fine demonstration of our blend of rock, art punk and hardcore'. By the time of its release, however, he was working on a new Scream album.

In summer 1985, some six years on from the release of Black Flag's *Nervous Breakdown* EP, *Rolling Stone* finally acknowledged the existence of the American hardcore scene. Writer Michael Goldberg was tasked with bringing the magazine's readership up to speed with the music, mindset and mores of the punk rock underground, in what was *Rolling Stone*'s most significant report on the genre since Charles M. Young's October 1977 cover feature on the Sex Pistols. Goldberg's excellent article was titled 'Punk Lives'. 'They don't sound like the Ramones, and they don't look like the Sex Pistols,' stated the feature subhead, 'but bands like Black Flag, Hüsker Dü, the Minutemen and the Meat Puppets are keeping the spirit of '77 alive.'

Goldberg's article offered a neat précis of what he dubbed the 'neopunk' community. Focusing largely upon acts signed to Greg Ginn's SST label and Minneapolis' indie imprint Twin/Tone, the writer highlighted the scene's stubbornly independent Do-It-Yourself ethos and the tireless work ethic powering it, contrasting 'old school' punk's cartoon nihilism with the 'responsible', proactive, self-reliant mentality underpinning the hardcore movement.

In the closing paragraphs of his feature, Goldberg detailed a conversation he held with Hüsker Dü frontman Bob Mould in regard to the advantages and disadvantages of bands operating within an independent label framework. 'I think being outside the mainstream music business is good,' Mould told Goldberg. 'When you tie yourself down to a major label, you give up all your individual control over things. You become part of the machine. It wouldn't seem right for Hüsker Dü …' Yet, just nine months after the publication of Goldberg's article, Hüsker Dü's sixth studio album *Candy Apple Grey* was released on Warner Bros.

Though Hüsker Dü were not the first eighties 'neopunk' collective to sign to a major label – fellow Minneapolis act The Replacements had inked a deal with Sire shortly after the release of their brilliant 1984 album *Let It Be* – the trio's decision to sign with Warners was significant, and hotly debated at the time. While The Stooges, MC5, Ramones, the New York Dolls, Television and most other key players in the first wave of American punk rock all recorded within the major label system, the American hardcore movement had never actively sought its endorsement or patronage.

In 1981 Black Flag had signed a distribution deal with MCA Records affiliate Unicorn for their début album *Damaged* only to have MCA President Al Bergamo declare the album 'anti-parent' and refuse to authorise its release. The resulting lawsuit tied the band up in legal red tape for two years: when Ginn attempted to sneak the album out on SST both he and Dukowski were jailed for contempt of court. That Hüsker Dü, a fellow SST band, was now prepared to sleep with the enemy was viewed by many in the punk community as a traitorous betrayal of the scene in which they had honed their craft.

All too aware of the imminent backlash, in February 1986 – one month before the release of *Candy Apple Grey* – Bob Mould penned a column for *maximumrocknroll* (a fanzine with an editorial policy which dictated that no act signed to a major would feature in its Xeroxed pages) to face down such criticisms. Mould was at pains to point out that Hüsker Dü's Warners contract guaranteed his band 'complete artistic freedom' in terms of their music, artwork and image, and stressed that the trio were still self-managed, still committed to all-ages shows and still punk rockers at heart. 'I don't think Hüsker Dü signing to a major label will have an effect on the underground scene at all,' he wrote. 'If anything, it might be a sign that something is happening, that some people are finally listening to the underground, and they might even respect what's going on.'

Mould's comment was both perceptive and prescient. Michael Goldberg's *Rolling Stone* article was just one indicator that the mainstream no longer saw the underground as appealing solely to a demographic R.E.M.'s Michael Stipe pithily characterised as 'the freaks, the fags, the fat girls, the art students and the indie music fanatics'. In March 1986 MTV launched its own 'alternative' music show *120 Minutes*, giving national exposure to left-of-the-dial acts such as Gene Loves Jezebel, Killing Joke, The Smiths, The Cure and Hüsker Dü themselves.

In truth, Bob Mould's band were not the only punk act looking to break through a glass ceiling perceived to exist just inches above the moshpit floor. The burgeoning success of R.E.M. and U2, two bands who had started out on the post-punk circuit, offered hope and encouragement to other aspirant underground acts. R.E.M., who had previously taken bands such as The Replacements and The Minutemen on tour, secured their first US Gold record classification in 1986 when *Life's Rich Pageant* passed the 500,000 sales mark. While this level of mainstream acceptance remained a pipe dream for even the most ambitious young punks, such achievements did not go unnoticed in the underground community, as Greg Ginn told writer

Gods look down

Michael Azerrad in his highly regarded text *Our Band Could Be Your Life*.

'[Bands] started out with the ambition "If we could just be a touring band and go around and do this, that would be cool,"' Ginn noted. 'Then R.E.M. came into it and it was like, "Wow, we can make a career out of this." There was a sharp turn.'

Suspicious that this mindset was infecting his own band, in August 1986 Ginn broke up Black Flag. Four months later, following the release of his band's *Bedtime for Democracy* album, Jello Biafra called time on Dead Kennedys too. The American hardcore era was over: the age of 'Alternative Rock' was dawning.

'When we got really successful it kinda ruined the scene for everybody,' R.E.M. guitarist Peter Buck maintains. 'Everyone got big major label deals and I'm not sure it was a good thing.

'We got lucky and were relatively successful in the mid-eighties, but all my favourite groups – Hüsker Dü and The Replacements and hundreds of others – would come through towns and play to maybe 80 people. In 1984 I booked The Replacements to play a club in Athens [Georgia] and I personally dragged every single person to the club that night: there was 22 people there. It was completely under the radar. And that was fun. It was the Reagan years and you had us weird guys with dyed hair playing music that was never on the radio. It felt like us against the world.

'But then there was a period for about a year where I had to apologise every time the radio came on, because college radio was just bands that sounded like R.E.M. without the good stuff. And then the year after us everyone sounded like The Replacements. And then everyone sounded like Hüsker Dü. And then everyone sounded like Sonic Youth … Maybe ideally it'd have been better for us to have been less successful.'

Mark Lanegan, then the frontman of SST-signed psych-rockers Screaming Trees, later Dave Grohl's bandmate in Queens of the Stone Age, was equally cognisant of R.E.M. and U2's increasing influence upon the mid-eighties underground music scene.

'I remember we would go on SST tours which were notoriously long and you hit everywhere relentlessly,' he recalled in 2002. 'And everywhere we would hit we would try and guess if the [other] band [on the bill] today was gonna sound like R.E.M. or U2 – inevitably it would be one or the other.'

'When we discovered U2 it was pre-*Boy*,' says Brian Baker, 'and this was a band that was lyrically very powerful and sounded pretty tough to us relative to the time. To us it was just like Stiff Little Fingers or The Undertones, but just a bit slicker. They were a good example of what I thought was a punk ethic moving into a mainstream place.

'My band Dag Nasty existed from '85 through to '88 and at that point a lot of things had changed. The climate was definitely different. Punk rock was not as threatening as it used to be, it had become much more universally understood and less feared, which meant that there were many more places to play and people were willing to play your music on college radio. In that period, bands were definitely trying to connect on a broader scale.'

It was against this background that Scream left Dischord in 1987 to sign to DC reggae label RAS (Real Authentic Sound of Reggae). Founded in 1979 by WHFS disc jockey Doctor Dread (aka Gary Himelfarb), the label was looking to expand into the rock scene, and Himelfarb saw the powerful, passionate Scream as the ideal first non-reggae signing to his roster. In their interview with Elizabeth Greene from *maximumrocknroll*, the band could hardly have sounded more enthused about their new beginning.

'It'll be a clean, fresh start for Scream,' said Skeeter Thompson. 'Dischord is really limited in what they can do ... not really limited, they just don't have enough personnel I guess. They're not really interested in putting out more than 10,000 copies of an album. Now I think Scream is just ready to put out as much music as we can.'

'We've been sending out tapes for a long time, trying to get record companies interested in us,' admitted Pete Stahl. 'For one reason or another it never happened and RAS was really the first thing that ever came up. RAS really likes us and they like what we're saying and they'd like to help us fuckin' get our music out and make some money at the same time.'

Gods look down

'Ian [MacKaye] knew that we had aspirations to make a living as musicians and he was very gracious and supportive,' Stahl told me in 2010. 'He was like, "You might want to see where this can take you. You have a home here, but …" So we took a chance. It didn't really work out.'

⌒

In the autumn of 1987 Scream booked a lengthy US tour to preview material from their forthcoming RAS début *No More Censorship*. Before their new drummer could get in the van, he needed his mother's permission to drop out of high school. To his surprise, his mother acquiesced without hesitation.

'I said, "Hallelujah. Go,"' Virginia Grohl recalled in 2008. 'Because, of all the things he's done brilliantly in his life, school was never one of them.'

'Even then she knew me well enough to know I was better off following my heart,' Dave would later recall. 'All parents want their kids to do brilliantly at school. Still, why should I have stayed at school and learned things I wouldn't really need later, when I could do something I really loved and wanted to pursue with all my energy: music.'

As he readied himself to leave home for his first tour, Grohl received a phone call from his old friend and punk-rock mentor Tracey Bradford. Far from encouraging Grohl's pursuit of his musical dreams, however, Bradford desperately urged the teenager to reconsider his plans.

'I came home from college one day,' Bradford recalls, 'and my mom said, "Dave joined a band called Scream and he's dropping out of high school and he's going to go on tour." And so I called him and I was like, "God, David, don't drop out." I said, "David, look at all these bands I've seen who are still living in vans." It wasn't like Dave had a glamorous life, but with an education you can feed yourself and you can get an apartment. I said, "Your mom's a school teacher, so how does that look, dropping out of high school with no education? You're a smart kid, you're not dumb and you could be a great musician and still be a nothing." I was around some great musicians, really, really talented kids, and here was this guy saying, "I wanna be a rock star!" and I'm going, "Oh my God, please, just get something so you have a back-up." But he was like, "Nope, this is my big chance.'"

'Because I was still in high school I could never imagine getting out of suburban Virginia,' Grohl recalls. 'So I remember always being fascinated with the tour van. Any time I went to a gig I loved watching a band pack up their van, because I imagined it to be almost like a travelling tree-house. Tour vans represented freedom to me. So to get in a tour van for the first time felt like the start of a big adventure.'

Scream's autumn '87 tour itinerary took them across the Mid-West, into Canada and down the Pacific Coast. It took in venues such as Johns Hopkins University in Baltimore, the Community World Theatre in Tacoma, Washington (where Scream were supported by local punks Diddly Squat, featuring future Foo Fighter Nate Mendel) and the Speedway Café in Salt Lake City, where the quintet played as support to Keith Morris's Circle Jerks. Accompanied by his pal Jimmy Swanson, who had blagged a seat in the van as Scream's roadie, Grohl remembers the whole experience being an absolute blast. Every day brought new experiences. In Chicago Grohl scored his first-ever groupie ('some blonde heavy metal chick. It was lame, not good, not sexy at all'); in Denver he took so many magic mushrooms that he barely made it through the show. The feeling of freedom was intoxicating.

'I used to keep journals,' Grohl recalls, 'fucking good ones. Every single day I wrote an entry in my journal, with diagrams and line drawings and sketches of the venues. They were poorly written, for sure, but absolutely real. I'd revisit them every now and then when I was superhigh and look back and laugh.'

'I was 18 years old, doing exactly what I wanted to do. With $7 a day, I travelled to places I'd never dreamed of visiting. And all because of music. The feeling of driving across the country in a van with five other guys, stopping in every city to play, sleeping on people's floors, watching the sun come up over the desert as I drove, it was all too much. This was definitely where I belonged.'

'Dave was at home with the lifestyle from day one,' says Franz Stahl. 'And he had the personality to fit in. He was a hyperactive kid, on and off the drum stool: he always seemed like he'd just downed four Coca Colas. From the start I thought, "This kid's a star." I knew it from way back then, I felt it. Maybe that was why I wanted him to be in the band. I mean, it was his playing initially, but I could see through that and see that this kid was going to go someplace.'

Asked for his most vivid memory of his first-ever tour, Grohl likes to recall an incident which almost ended his career before it had barely begun. He and Swanson had been tasked with piloting Scream's Dodge Ram van on an overnight drive: unfortunately for his new bandmates, asleep in the back of the van, the irresponsible duo were rather more interested in roadtesting a new item of pot-smoking paraphernalia called the Easy Rider Aqua Pipe. As the van filled up with smoke, the two teenage potheads had an attack of the giggles, and lost control of the vehicle.

'The two of us were laughing so hysterically 'cos we could hardly see each other,' Grohl recalled. 'I remember looking at Jimmy's face 'cos he was looking at mine with two big bloodshot eyes, when all of a sudden the van starts rumbling 'cos we were way the fuck off the road, going about 70 miles per hour and the van's just quaking! Everybody wakes up from their sleeping bags in this cloud of smoke. We weren't allowed to drive again.'

Some two months after Scream set out upon their autumn '87 tour, Pete Stahl dropped Dave Grohl back at 5516 Kathleen Place. As Grohl clambered from the van, Stahl asked him if he held a valid passport. When Grohl looked confused, Stahl told him that Scream would be starting a European tour in February. As Scream's van pulled out of the cul-de-sac, their 18-year-old drummer was still standing on his mother's doorstep with his mouth hanging open.

✎

Scream toured Europe for the first time in 1985, becoming the first East Coast hardcore band to do so. European punk rockers didn't always take kindly to having American bands on their territory – when Black Flag débuted their *Damaged* album in the UK tour in December 1981 they were greeted with volleys of spit, anti-American abuse and skinhead violence at every show – but the Virginians' easy charm and raw magnetism won over crowds wherever they went.

'It was amazing,' says Pete Stahl. 'People seemed to have greater freedom in Europe to create little pockets of music and art and cinema and there was always people in those communities that would support us.'

Scream played squats and bombed-out youth centres, bonded with anarchist collectives over weed and industrial-strength cider and talked punk, politics and philosophy with fans who had driven across international borders just to attend their shows. When they returned to the continent in February 1988 (now a quartet once more, as 'Harley' Davidson had left the band at the end of their autumn '87 US tour) they had a fervent, passionate fan base in every city – and a drummer who couldn't quite believe that this alternate reality existed.

'The whole trip was a real eye-opening experience,' Grohl recalls. 'We'd fly standby from Washington DC on this Dutch airline called Martin Air – they had standby tickets that you could reserve, so you could get a flight from DC to Amsterdam for like $110 – so we'd have enough money to get there, but we'd never have enough money to get back. So we had to tour until we had enough money to get home. And we toured fucking hard. We'd go over for three months at a time and we were hanging on by a thread the whole time we were there.

'Going on the road in America in the early eighties bands really had no fucking idea what to expect, it was still like the Wild Wild West out there. But after that network was established in the mid-eighties it became a little easier: it was never *easy*, but maybe you had played that place last time around and maybe you'd have somewhere to crash so it wasn't a complete step into the dark every time. But Europe was so different. In Europe there were squats where we'd turn up and they'd still be building the stage, or someone would be out back tying wires together to pirate some electricity so that we could play. Or we'd show up to see them burning mattresses out front because there was scabies everywhere. Or there'd be riots where there'd be squatters chucking bottles and glass at the skinheads who were trying to evict them from the building … shit like that. It totally blew my mind.

Gods look down

'Coming over to Europe for the first time I had no idea what a squat was. We landed in Amsterdam – which was great for me because I was at the height of my pot-head career, my stoner phase – and everyone we worked with lived in squats. Our booking agent Hedi lived in a squat that was one of the most beautiful buildings I've ever been in in my life, so it was hard for me to wrap my head around this concept. I was like, really, if a building is not being used and you maintain it you can just live there? How the fuck is that possible? But just as the network that was the hardcore scene in America brought all these people together, you'd come over to Europe and see the same thing. I'd meet kids from all over the world in squats in Italy and Spain and Germany and they loved to come see American bands: Europe had great bands, amazing hardcore bands, but there were kids who wanted to see us because their dream was to go see America: they wanted to see the desert, or New York City or Los Angeles, California. That changed, at some point it became fuck your desert, and fuck New York and LA, but back then we were singing along with the rest of the world about how fucked up our country was. It was an amazing time.'

'Scream made a lot of friends out in Europe,' says Ian MacKaye, then touring the continent for the first time with Fugazi. 'They toured hard, and were well loved, well received and well respected. They'd hang out after shows and meet good people, and their reputation as nice guys and a great band spread. On Fugazi's first European tour we played something like 78 shows in three months and we didn't always stay for the party afterwards – we'd have an eight-hour drive so we wanted to get on the road quickly so we could destroy the next room the next night – but Scream always stayed for the party and won the affection of a lot of people.'

Lee Dorrian first met Scream at a party on the sixteenth floor of a Coventry council flat in 1985. Then a 17-year-old punk promoter, later the frontman of hugely influential grindcore band Napalm Death and now the vocalist of British doom rockers Cathedral and owner of the influential metal label Rise Above, Dorrian remembers the band being 'absolutely trashed', but good natured, likeable and friendly.

'Pete Stahl was a real cool guy,' he recalls. 'I went to see Scream a few times, and I remember one gig at the Hummingbird in Birmingham, which I think was the last gig on their tour, and he reeled off a list of about 50 people he'd met on the road, and he remembered everybody's name. That impressed me.'

'When they came back to England in '88 I put them on at a place called The Inn Hotel in Coventry. They had nowhere to stay and I had a council flat in Hillfields in Coventry, 52 Hillfields House, so they piled back to my flat. There were holes in the windows and doors made by some Dutch band who had stayed the week before, and I had to go around to a squat around the corner to nick some furniture. But they were just happy to have a roof over their heads. And they were good company. Dave was a particularly witty character. I remember my girl-friend at the time had a big Jimmy Page logo on the back of her jacket and Dave was in the back of the van going, "Does anyone like Led Zeppelin?", and she was all excited, saying, "Oh, I do, I do!" He was just teasing, of course, just pretending he hasn't noticed. He was really knowledgeable and excited about music too. Napalm had just recorded a session for [late, great, punk-championing DJ] John Peel and Dave really wanted to hear it, so I played it. It completely floored them, they thought it was nuts. I think Dave and I spent the rest of the night talking about Sabbath and Celtic Frost and Voivod.'

Back in Amsterdam after English dates with Concrete Sox and Subhumans, Scream's 28 March set at Van Hall was broadcast live on Dutch radio. Released later that same year on Konkurrel records as *Live! At Van Hall Amsterdam*, the recording stands as an excellent snapshot of a confident, dazzlingly capable band at the peak of their abilities. 'Don't ask me why they want an American band on the radio when there's so many good European bands,' says Pete Stahl after opener 'Who Knows? Who Cares?', but the incendiary 40-minute set that follows ably demonstrates just why Scream were generating such a strong word-of-mouth buzz on the continent: Grohl's frenetic drum solo on 'Feel Like That' alone justifies the price of admission.

Before leaving Amsterdam, Grohl decided to commemorate his first visit to Europe by getting John Bonham's three-circle logo from

Gods look down

Led Zeppelin IV tattooed on his right shoulder: he'd attempted to ink the symbol into his own skin at the age of 16, but was disappointed with the end result, later admitting, 'It looks like someone put a cigarette out on my fucking arm.' Ironically, though, it would be the discovery of another hard-hitting drummer, Melvins' Dale Crover, which would leave the biggest mark on Grohl in Amsterdam. And although he could not possibly have realised it at the time, this discovery would ultimately prove to be one of the most significant events of Dave Grohl's life.

'We were killing time between gigs, staying at a friend's house, smoking weed and doing nothing,' he recalled in 2004. 'I was literally playing through this guy's record collection, every single last one. When I got to Melvins' *Gluey Porch Treatments*, I thought, Here's another hardcore record. But when I put it on it really fucking blew my mind. This was the moment I fell in love with the dirge aesthetic. The songs were so slow you couldn't imagine how the band kept time. It was ten to fifteen seconds between each hit. I had never heard anything so heavy before, and the fact these were teenagers from Aberdeen, Washington, playing music heavier than Black Sabbath or any metal record I had heard was unbelievable.'

Hailed by the venerable Trouser Press Guide as 'inimitable steamrolling overlords of the slow-flowing magma', Melvins deal in oppressive downer anthems resembling the sound of the earth choking slowly on its own vomit. Fronted by Buzz 'King Buzzo' Osbourne, a maverick malcontent reared on a high-carb diet of Black Sabbath, Black Flag, Flipper, Kiss and Motörhead, the band were cult legends in the subterranean Pacific Northwest rock scene, and a huge influence upon their hometown Nirvana. To Dave Grohl, their viscous punk/metal gloop offered a whole new lexicon of aural abuse.

'I always thought I knew the definition of heavy,' Grohl admitted in 2001, 'but hearing *Gluey Porch Treatments* completely turned my musical perception on its side.'

This is a Call

Melvins were not the only band redefining the boundaries of underground rock in America in the late eighties. As the American hardcore dream turned sour, and the scene's early idealism gave way to bitterness, cynicism and in-fighting, a new breed of nihilistic, provocative noisemakers emerged: the finest of these were Steve Albini's Big Black, Texan audio terrorists Butthole Surfers and Scratch Acid, Washington DC's Pussy Galore, Wisconsin's Killdozer, Minneapolis' Cows and New York art-rockers Sonic Youth. Influenced by post-punk and No Wave acts such as The Birthday Party, Suicide, Killing Joke, Swans and John Lydon's Public Image Ltd, these disparate, dissolute artists were united in a quest to tear apart hardcore orthodoxy and challenge the punk mindset with excessive volume, confrontational ideas and extreme behaviour. A common overarching *raison d'être* for these bands was to prod, poke, irritate and inflame sensibilities to the point where even the most enlightened punk-cognisant audiences would wish to inflict physical harm upon them. In this mission they proved remarkably successful.

That this emerging scene was informed by, but not in thrall to, the hardcore movement is perhaps best illustrated by the earliest recordings made by Pussy Galore, the unsettling, hate-filled noise collective led by future Blues Explosion frontman Jon Spencer. Though the sleeve of Pussy Galore's début seven inch, the *Feel Good About Your Body* EP, bore the dedication 'Thanks to Ian and Jeff' (Dischord owners MacKaye and Nelson having helped guide the band in setting up their own label, Shove Records) the vinyl within mocked the hardcore scene's righteousness: 'HC Rebellion' featured bassist Julia Cafritz reading out letters printed in the September 1985 issue of *maximumrocknroll* as if they contained the answers to all of life's greatest mysteries. This determination to offend the punk community in their adopted hometown was even more evident on the band's second EP, *Groovy Hate Fuck*, released in June 1986. Amid atonal slabs of noise every bit as abrasive and unpleasant as their titles – 'Cunt Tease', 'Teen Pussy Power', 'Kill Yourself', 'Asshole' – *Groovy Hate Fuck* featured a brutally offensive song called 'You Look Like a Jew', which likened the DC punk uniform of shaved heads and thrift store clothing to concentration-camp 'chic' and celebrated *'smoke rising outta Dischord House'*. It's hard to imagine how Pussy Galore could have tried harder to burn bridges.

Both Pussy Galore EPs were recorded at Barrett Jones's Laundry Room studio. Jones knew that these sessions were going to be entirely unlike any he had previously helmed from the moment that Spencer and Cafritz produced a rusty chainsaw, hammers, a steel oil drum and several panes of glass as 'instruments'. The producer's abiding memories of the sessions are Spencer encouraging him to make the recordings as distorted and fucked-up as possible – 'He'd say, "That sounds too good – make it sound worse"' – and his roommates recoiling in horror as the leather-clad degenerates occupying their suburban home spent day after day assembling punishing walls of noise from screeching guitar feedback, brutish percussion and screamed lyrical obscenities. When Jones played the Pussy Galore tapes for Dave Grohl and Reuben Radding, his friends assumed the recordings were intended as a joke. Jon Spencer would doubtless have been delighted.

Music critics were at once repulsed and fascinated by this new punk aesthetic and their scabrous songs of loathe and hate, detecting a deep moral core buried beneath the layers of feedback, filth and fuzz. Reviewing Big Black's masterful début album *Atomizer*, Steve Albini's forensic dissection of the ugly urges churning beneath the surface of Ronald Reagan's whitewashed Pleasantville America, Robert Christgau noted, 'Though they don't want you to know it, these hateful little twerps are sensitive souls – they're moved to make this godawful racket by the godawful pain of the world.' Writing in the *Village Voice*, Christgau also coined the term 'pig-fuck' to describe the loosely affiliated noise-rock movement: perhaps unsurprisingly, this umbrella term failed to cross into mainstream music criticism, but it's a memorably unpleasant turn of phrase which goes some way to evoking the violent, perverse and knowingly obnoxious nature of the music in question. As an overview of the scene, Touch and Go's 1986 compilation *God's Favourite Dog*, featuring Big Black, Butthole Surfers, Killdozer, Scratch Acid, Happy Flowers (a Virginian duo featuring the incomparably named Mr Horribly Scarred Infant and Mr Anus) and Hose (featuring one Rick Rubin on guitar) is essential: one listen to Killdozer's drooling deconstruction of Lynyrd Skynyrd's 'Sweet Home Alabama' should quickly determine your tolerance for the 'pig-fuck' aesthetic.

In the summer of 1986, Steve Albini and Scratch Acid featured on another culturally significant compilation album. *Sub Pop 100* was the first vinyl release from a new Seattle imprint owned by local fanzine writer and DJ Bruce Pavitt. Showcasing a range of hard-edged underground sounds from punk to industrial dance, the compilation also featured Dave Grohl favourites Naked Raygun, Portland garage rockers Wipers, Sonic Youth and Seattle punks U-Men. Though Steve Albini's contribution was simply a short spoken-word intro, it set the tone superbly for the gloriously squally racket that followed. '*The spoken word is weak*,' he intoned solemnly over whining feedback. '*Scream, motherfuckers, scream!*'

Albini's bullish sentiments clearly struck a nerve with Chicago-born Pavitt: while a message on the album insert dedicated *Sub Pop 100* 'to K-Tel with love', the spine of the record carried the ludicrous statement 'SUB POP: the new thing: the big thing: the God thing: a mighty multinational entertainment conglomerate based in the Pacific Northwest'. If nothing else, it demonstrated that America's newest indie imprint had a certain sass and style.

Pavitt started *Subterranean Pop* fanzine in 1980 while studying for a degree at Evergreen State College in Olympia, Washington. He determined that his fanzine would focus upon the American indie scene and shine a spotlight on home-grown artists. The fifth issue of the fanzine, by then named *Sub Pop*, featured a 21-track cassette showcasing artists such as Portland's Neo Boys, Michigan's Jad Fair, Witchita's The Embarrassment and Seattle's Steve Fisk: when it was warmly received, Pavitt included a second 20-band compilation with issue number seven. He described these cassettes as 'audio maps to America's more remote locations'.

While promoting *Sub Pop 100* Pavitt was interviewed on the University of Washington's KCMU radio station by Jonathan Poneman, a Toledo, Ohio-born promoter and DJ. The two had a mutual friend in Kim Thayil, a philosophy student at UW by then playing guitar in a band called Soundgarden, and it was Thayil who suggested that the two music fanatics might want to consider working together. Excited by the challenge of starting a new label, the duo agreed. As Pavitt was already using the name Sub Pop for his own KCMU show and his weekly column in Seattle music paper *The Rocket*, it made sense to retain it for their new venture.

Pavitt and Poneman's gung-ho attitude was entirely in keeping with the mentality of the music scene they determined to document. From the early 1960s the Pacific Northwest musical community was motivated by one simple idea (later copyrighted as a slogan by one of the area's best-known corporations): Just Do It. From sixties pop/rock bands such as Paul Revere and the Raiders through to garage rockers The Kingsmen and proto-punks such as The Wailers and The Sonics, energy, attitude and soul took precedence over technical ability for local musicians: it was no coincidence that Seattle-born guitar hero Jimi Hendrix had to travel overseas to England for his virtuoso genius to be appreciated. But the area's ramshackle, adventurous spirit helped propagate one of the most fecund, experimental and visceral music scenes in the nation.

'In high school I had a guitar but I couldn't play very well,' says Seattle music scene veteran, and Pearl Jam guitarist, Stone Gossard. 'But one day I was talking to my friend Steve Turner and he said, "Don't learn to play your guitar, get a band! Don't figure it out, just do it!" Being in a garage rock band is the greatest!' I'd never in my life heard anyone talk about art that way, it was the most liberating thing. I was like, "I don't have to take lessons? Thank God!"'

In 1984 Gossard joined Green River, a punk/metal collective Turner had formed with his music-obsessed best friend Mark Arm. Named after the Green River Killer, a serial killer responsible for the murder of at least 50 women in Washington State in the early eighties, the band were influenced by Black Sabbath, Black Flag, The Stooges, The Sonics, Blue Cheer and Aerosmith: just like Dave Grohl's Dain Bramage on the other side of the nation, they aimed to subvert classic rock clichés in a noisy, ragged punk style. That same attitude fuelled other local bands. Malfunkshun, fronted by the charismatic Andrew 'L'Andrew the Love-Child' Wood, mixed the glam theatrics of Kiss and T-Rex with the street-level aggression of Discharge. Soundgarden, fronted by Wood's roommate Chris Cornell, formed to play 'Black Sabbath songs without the parts that suck', according to guitarist Thayil. Skin Yard occupied the middle ground between The Doors and Led Zeppelin. And Melvins showed everyone that playing slow and low was a really, really, *really* effective way to antagonise, irritate and aggravate causal rock 'n' roll fans who'd stumble into bars such as the Central Tavern and the Ditto Tavern expecting to have their night soundtracked by covers of 'Stairway to Heaven' and 'Freebird'.

Mark Arm once attributed the sound of the Pacific Northwest to isolation and inbreeding. To that he might have added intemperance, irascibility and irreverence. Like Liverpool, Belfast, Glasgow, New York and other tough, blue-collar port towns, Seattle bred men with bone-dry wits, quick fists and no-nonsense attitudes. The city's soundtrack was always going to be dense, raw and fearless.

'It's still essentially wilderness country up here,' Poneman once noted. 'It's attracted a lot of crazy people. But there's a lot of the rugged, do-it-yourself, survivalist, drifter types. Apply that to rock 'n' roll and that makes punk rock. Also, people who live out in the middle of nowhere like to party because there's nothing else to do, which is why the local music was unusually rowdy.'

In the summer of 1985, Skin Yard bassist Daniel House took the initiative to document Seattle's newest musical community, harvesting tracks from Green River, Malfunkshun, Soundgarden, Melvins, the U-Men and his own band for release on a compilation album entitled *Deep Six* on the C/Z Records label. Heard now, the resulting album is an uneven, rough-hewn collection of Sasquatch stomp-rock, but at the time it was compelling proof that something was stirring in the back-woods. It was also a massive inspiration to Poneman and Pavitt when they came to create Sub Pop.

To some extent, Sub Pop had advantages over other start-up busi-nesses. Pavitt and Poneman were already plugged into the underground community as a result of their work in press, radio and retail, and they had ready-made media platforms from which to hype their new enter-prise. But they were also shrewd enough to recognise something which

Gods look down

the owners of more earnest US hardcore imprints would never explicitly acknowledge – that the underground music industry was still, at heart, part of the entertainment business, and that in showbiz, packaging, promotion and perception are just as important as product. When Pavitt worked at Seattle's Bombshelter record store, he noticed that Anglophile music fans would pay exorbitant import prices for anything and everything released by 4AD, Postcard or Factory records, for those labels had developed an iconic identity which transcended the appeal of individual artists. He pondered as to how his fledgling label might create a similar aesthetic.

The answer came to him in spring 1987, while visiting friends at Room Nine House, a rented property shared by members of the psychedelic rock band Room Nine, local drummer Dan Peters, UW photography student Charles Peterson and an ever-changing cast of Seattle scenesters. A punk rock fan, Charles Peterson had been documenting live gigs in Seattle since the early eighties: his unfiltered, light-streaked and movement-blurred black and white images screamed with vitality and energy, slamming the viewer into the heart of the moshpit. Live shots of Green River, Malfunkshun and Soundgarden hung all over Room Nine House, reeking of sweat and alcohol, testosterone and adrenaline. Seeing them for the first time, Pavitt saw a visual identity for his fledgling label.

'I looked at those photos, and I immediately knew that he was catching the energy of the groups, and combining these images with the music would work,' he told Pitchfork.com in 2008. 'Every record label needs a visual motif to establish [itself], and those photos would help do it. Those photos inspired me to focus on trying to release records by Seattle groups.'

Sub Pop's first single-artist release was Green River's *Dry as a Bone* EP: music from Soundgarden, Blood Circus, Swallow, Fluid and Mudhoney (a post-Green River vehicle for Mark Arm, Steve Turner and friends Matt Lukin and Dan Peters) followed. The releases had a defined, uniform look: each had a black bar across the top with the band name written in capital letters, followed by the release name, all in a sans-serif font. Charles Peterson supplied the cover images. Text was kept to a minimum: more often than not only Peterson and producer Jack Endino were credited. The idea, as Pavitt explained in Sub Pop's official biog, was to 'pump up the visceral connection to the records' and add 'a sense of mystery'.

'Not only did we put an emphasis on design,' Pavitt told *NME* in 1992, 'but on consistency of design, *à la* Postcard or Blue Note. This was very key. If they liked the Mudhoney records and there was hype on Mudhoney and there was another record that came out that kinda looked similar, then people would automatically pick that up. It's the oldest scam in the book.'

The release of Mudhoney's début single *Touch Me, I'm Sick* created a genuine buzz around the label, nationally and internationally. Released in August 1988, 'Touch Me, I'm Sick' remains one of *the* great punk anthems, a glorious yowl of dissatisfaction and self-loathing powered by rusty Stooges-meets-The Sonics guitar slashes and a flat-out fucked drum pattern which threatens to collapse to the kerb at any given moment. Two decades on, it ranks alongside The Kingsmen's version of 'Louie Louie' as the timeless definition of Seattle rock.

For all the acclaim and attention *Touch Me, I'm Sick* generated in the underground, however, by the end of 1988 Sub Pop was fast running out of money. In a last-ditch gamble to build their industry profile, in February 1989 Pavitt and Poneman paid for *Melody Maker* journalist Everett True to visit Seattle to soak up the scene. The pair were aware that, in their constant, relentless search to uncover music's 'Next Big Thing', the weekly UK music magazines were given to hyperbole, their journalists rarely letting facts stand in the way of a great story. This suited Sub Pop's own marketing strategies just fine. And with Everett True they lucked out. His excitable, action-packed 18 March 1989 feature on 'Seattle: Rock City' made the Sub Pop scene look like the epicentre of a thrilling new rock revolution.

'Before Seattle I'd never been exposed to rock,' True admitted in 2006. 'Punk in 1977 had seen to that. It's unlikely I would have been half as enthusiastic about Seattle and its music if I, like my American counterparts, had grown up on a diet of Led Zeppelin and hardcore. But I hadn't, and neither had most of my British contemporaries.

Gods look down

Reared on a constantly changing musical culture where the press determined that bands grew old very quickly, we were always on the lookout for the thrill of the new. Consequently I was able to write about what was essentially traditional rock music with real enthusiasm. The Sub Pop rock bands, both in spirit and in sound, were new to this naïve English boy.

'Here were bands that achieved what I had thought hitherto impossible: they made metal sound cool. During the mid-eighties pop music was anti-guitar. Jon and Bruce's stroke of marketing genius was to push rock 'n' roll as rebellion – an ancient credo – while allowing people to listen to big dumb rock and retain their hipster credibility. Up until grunge, there had always been a line drawn between popular and underground music. Sub Pop confused that line once and for all.'

True's feature focused largely on Sub Pop's big hitters Mudhoney and Tad, a monstrously heavy, elephantine riff machine fronted by the super-sized Tad Doyle. While in Seattle, he was also taken to see one of Sub Pop's brightest new hopes, Aberdeen, Washington's Nirvana, a ragged 'power trio' featuring vocalist/guitarist Kurdt Kobain (as Kurt Cobain was spelling his name at the time), bassist Chris (Krist) Novoselic and drummer Chad Channing.

True had just made Nirvana's début single *Love Buzz/Big Cheese* one of his *Melody Maker* Singles of the Week. He had hailed the band as 'beauty incarnate' playing 'love songs for the psychotically disturbed'.

Now featuring a second guitarist, Jason Everman, in their line-up, Nirvana played their first show as a quartet at the University of Washington's HUB Ballroom on 25 February 1989. Seeing the band in the flesh for the first time, True was far from impressed. In his 2006 Nirvana biography *Nirvana: The True Story*, he described Nirvana as 'another formless compendium of noise for noise's sake'.

'I loved their single,' he wrote, 'but what was this mess of noise and hair and alcohol-fuelled banter?'

This, however, wasn't the story that he told the readers of *Melody Maker* in March 1988.

'Basically, this is the real thing,' he enthused. 'No rock star contrivance, no intellectual perspective, no master plan for world domination.

This is a Call

You're talking about four guys in their early twenties from rural Washington who wanna rock, who, if they weren't doing this, would be working in a supermarket or lumber yard, or fixing cars. Kurdt Kobain is a great tunesmith, although still a relatively young songwriter. He wields a riff with *passion.*'

The seeds of a new rock revolution had been sown.

~

'Jumping the shark' is what cultural commentators call the precise moment when an established brand or creative enterprise abandons its core premise and begins an irretrievable decline. For Scream, that moment comes with the penultimate track on 1988's *No More Censorship* album. 'Run to the Sun' is a painfully sincere sub-U2, arena rock tune which even Pete Stahl's heartfelt lyrics ('*I remember when we began / Getting together to make a band / Mixed-up teenagers, think you're strong-minded men / We started playing to take a stand*') cannot redeem. The track was barely recognisable as a Scream song; moreover it was symptomatic of a broader malaise within the band at the time: for the first time in their career, Scream sounded like followers, not leaders.

Neutered by a flat, featureless production job, *No More Censorship* isn't a bad album … but it's not within touching distance of greatness. While the title track and 'Fucked Without a Kiss', a graphic, unflinching tale of prison rape in a DC jail, are among the most compelling of Scream's career, too much of the album is mannered and mediocre, bearing little of the muscular flexibility showcased on *Live! At Van Hall.* Hyped up as a record to propel Scream out of the underground, in reality *No More Censorship* sounded suspiciously like the work of a band running desperately low on inspiration.

'Our idea of making this huge rock record didn't really pan out,' Grohl admitted, with some understatement.

In 1989, less than a year after the release of *No More Censorship*, Scream were dropped by RAS Records. The album had sold around 10,000 copies, a decent return for an underground band, but far less than both the band and Gary Himelfarb had anticipated: by way of comparison, Dag Nasty's 1988 album *Field Day* had shifted in excess of 30,000 copies while Hüsker Dü's *Candy Apple Grey* album was heading north of 120,000 sales. Scream were in danger of looking like yesterday's men.

This was not the only problem facing the band in 1989: Skeeter Thompson's drug use was also becoming an issue. As a collective, Scream had always been heavily into pot-smoking, but as their commitment to long tours intensified, so too did their drug use. More than one band member graduated from smoking pot to snorting powders. 'Drugs entered the picture towards the end of the band,' says Dave Grohl. 'There was cocaine and shit going around. Still to this day I've never done coke, one of the reasons being that I saw how it fucked everybody's lives up. I can't touch that shit, because if I did I would surely go down in a ball of flames. I got sent to hospital after drinking coffee, so imagine what fucking crack cocaine would do to me! I'd have no teeth and I'd be sucking dicks in like a month.'

During a 1989 tour of Europe, Skeeter Thompson disappeared, without a word to anyone. Efforts to track him down proved fruitless, so Pete Stahl promoted roadie Guy Pinhas to the vacant bass slot, and Scream completed their scheduled dates without him. When they returned to Virginia, they found Thompson waiting for them. The bassist blamed his absence upon 'girlfriend problems': his friends pried no further.

'It wasn't completely unusual for Skeeter to disappear in Europe,' says Franz Stahl. 'He was a handsome lad, and he had a special way with the ladies. In the States he'd be called a "nigger" and then he'd go to Europe and have all these white women just throwing themselves at him, and he took full advantage of that, like anybody would. It was like the Hendrix syndrome, and he dove headlong into it. He'd disappear for a bit and come back with a new suit of clothes, with some girl having bought him an all-new wardrobe. But this time his problems seemed to run deeper and he clearly needed space to get his life together.'

With Thompson temporarily incapacitated, Scream were desperate to regain some momentum. DC punk veteran Ben Pape was swiftly recruited for their next US road trip. Remarkably, he too bailed out without warning, walking out mid-tour to join The Four Horsemen, a new hard rock band assembled by Slayer/Beastie Boys producer Rick Rubin. The band immediately flew out ex-Government Issue bassist J. Robbins to complete the tour, but morale was sinking: 'I had a really good time with those guys, and it was super fun playing with Dave,' recalls Robbins. 'But even when I was in the band I was thinking, "Well, this is cool, but this isn't Scream."'

'Maybe we weren't perfectly content with the hand that had been dealt to us at that point, but we'd certainly accepted it as a reality,' says Grohl. 'Growing up the way we did in suburban Virginia I didn't feel like I had many opportunities. I had surrendered to, and resigned myself to, the idea that I would live the rest of my life there, doing the things that most people there do: like masonry, which I've done, or working in Furniture Warehouse, which I've done, or roofing. I just figured, Isn't the idea just to do what you love to do and be happy? Because how much do you need, really? I was playing music, and going on the road to Europe and not making any money but coming home and getting my job back, and then having enough money to buy weed and eat and then going on the road again. Then I'd sleep in the van and fucking jam with my buddies and come home and get another job. That was just how it worked. Skeeter sold weed, Pete worked at the *Washington Post* and Franz worked at a restaurant, so as much as we wanted to be a band that millions of people would appreciate, it just wasn't in the fucking cards. Hüsker Dü were playing places that held 1,200 people, and we considered them to be like U2. That was huge. If we had any aspirations it was that, and at that point even that was an impossibility.'

At a low ebb, the band returned to the basement of Scream House to demo some new material. Stung by the poor reception afforded to *No More Censorship*, and bitter about the ongoing problems shackling their progress, their anger and frustration manifested itself in songs darker, heavier and more aggressive than anything they had previously recorded. One track in particular, 'Gods Look Down', a seething, down-tuned dirge which sounded like the final anguished screams of a man drowning in quicksand, stood out. Originally demoed at Laundry Room Studios in 1988, this was Dave Grohl's first-ever solo track.

Gods look down

'Barrett Jones was in a band called Churn at the time and he'd some-times ask me to come over and play drums on his demos,' Grohl recalls. 'So then I thought, Maybe I'll ask if I can use the last bit of that reel and experiment, so I'd buy Barrett a little weed and he'd let me use the last bits of his tapes. I had a couple of riffs and I played them really quick, and then ran in and did the drum track and then the bass, and I listened to it and it sounded fucking great. And "Gods Look Down" was the first time I wrote a song, recorded it with vocals and had my own complete song.'

'I was totally blown away by how good it was,' says Barrett Jones. 'He had the exact arrangement in his head and he did the whole thing in twenty minutes, first take with everything, no mistakes. He made it look so easy. It was pretty incredible to see.'

Recorded in their darkest hour, Scream's new basement demos were a revelation, the sound of a band with their backs against a wall, lashing out ferociously with everything at their disposal. As tapes of the demo began circulating on the underground, word began building that Scream had created their masterpiece. Pete Stahl was contacted by Glenn E. Friedman, the North Carolina-born, LA-raised photographer whose images of the nascent skateboarding, hardcore and hiphop scenes had superbly captured the anarchic energy inherent in America's emergent youth culture: the photographer, who had previously helped broker LA skate-punks Suicidal Tendencies break into the mainstream, offered to help find Scream a new record deal. Through his work with the Beastie Boys, Run-DMC and Public Enemy, Friedman had become friends with Def Jam's owners, producer Rick Rubin and New York hiphop entrepreneur Russell Simmons, and the trio were in talks about launching Friedman's own imprint, to be called World Records. In the newly re-invigorated Scream, Friedman saw a credible marquee signing for his new enterprise.

The quartet returned to Europe in spring 1990 with a renewed fire in their bellies. They played 23 shows in 24 days, cutting a second live album at the Oberhaus in Alzey, Germany, on 4 May for the German independent label Your Choice. Attendances were strong and the band departed for the USA in good spirits. Back on home soil, their optimism was soon cruelly dashed. Friedman's label plans were on hold, and his A&R connections at major labels didn't share his enthusiasm for Scream's new demo. As an additional kick in the teeth, when Pete Stahl and Skeeter Thompson returned to DC they discovered that they had been evicted from their shared house. Scream's future suddenly looked bleaker than ever.

'Pete wound up staying in his van in front of my mother's house while we figured out what to do next,' says Grohl. 'And our plan was, let's just book a tour and get the fuck out of here. It was an escape, it was almost like we could survive on the road better than we could at home. But then we started that tour and shows were being cancelled all over the place. We were getting desperate.

'If you read through my journals, you'd see the gradual decline in morale as that tour went on. The struggle was getting more and more difficult. And as I was getting older, even though I was only 21 years old, I was starting to question this as a life decision. I was like, "Do I really want to be homeless for the rest of my life?" There was one entry from New Orleans where I was stranded on a fucking kerb in the middle of fucking nowhere for hours, waiting for the guys to pick me up. I had no money and no food and no smokes … nothing. I was completely stranded with no lifeline at all, just a backpack and my journal. And so I dug the pen a little deeper that day and I wrote about all the things I was tired of. I was tired of having absolutely nothing; I was tired of being hungry, tired of being lost, and tired of being tired. I just wanted to go home and work at the Furniture Warehouse, and have somewhere to take a shower, and go to bed every night and be with my friends and my family. Because it had been three or four years from 18 to 21 of just loving every moment of playing, but getting tired of that struggle … and there being no other option.

'When we got to LA, Skeeter disappeared. We woke up one morning and he wasn't there. We had a gig that night at a club called The Gaslight and we waited and waited and thought, Okay, so when do we cancel it? By 7 p.m., when he hadn't shown up, we cancelled. And then the next night we had a show booked in San Diego. So we waited and waited and we started calling everyone, like, "Have you seen Skeeter?" but no one had seen him. He had just disappeared. So that was it, we were stuck.'

It soon became apparent that Thompson wasn't coming back. Scream were now stranded, penniless and depressed on the West Coast, a broken band.

'We were in LA for a month, with nothing,' says Grohl. 'We were sleeping on the floor of this really nice house rented out by three girls who were mud wrestlers at the Hollywood Tropicana. One of them was Pete and Franz's sister Sabrina, a beautiful, sweet, good girl who happened to be making a lot of money mud-wrestling, to the dismay of her two older brothers, who just wanted her to change her life. But they were hardly in a position to start giving lectures. Every night these chicks would come home and dump out mountains of one dollar bills on the table and count them in front of us. They were nice girls, they took care of us and would take us out for Thai food, or let us ride their motorbikes, but still, we were living in poverty. And I thought, What, does it just end here? Now I'm gonna spend the rest of my life in Los Angeles? I had no way to get back home. I guess I could have called home and asked for the money for a Greyhound ticket, but I didn't even know if my mom could do that. We were just lost.'

While kicking his heels in Sabrina Stahl's house on Satsuma Avenue, Grohl read in the *LA Weekly* that Melvins were coming to town. Scream and Melvins had recently played together at San Francisco's I-Beam club, and the two bands were now firm friends, so Grohl placed a call to Buzz Osbourne to ask if he might be able to get a spot on their guest list for their upcoming LA show. Osbourne was surprised to hear that his friends were in Los Angeles, and asked Grohl what they were doing in the city. The drummer poured out the whole depressing tale.

'And then Buzz said, "Have you heard of Nirvana?"' Grohl recalls. 'He said, "They're looking for a drummer." And he gave me Chris's number.'

Grohl had heard of Nirvana, indeed he owned the Aberdeen trio's début album *Bleach*. But he knew nothing of the band beyond their music and their status as an underground buzz band: indeed, the previous month he had stood in the I-Beam's dressing room with Cobain and Novoselic without recognising either man.

'Someone told me who they were and I was thinking, What, *that's* Nirvana? Are you kidding? Because on the cover of *Bleach* they looked like psycho lumberjacks. I was like, "What, that little dude and that big motherfucker? You're kidding me." I laughed, like, "No way."

'But I loved *Bleach*, I thought it was great. It had everything that I really loved about music. It had The Beatles influence on "About a Girl" and then songs like "Paper Cuts" and "Sifting" were heavy as balls. And "Negative Creep" was *amazing*. And girls liked Nirvana. I had a girlfriend that liked Nirvana and I was like, "You like a band that I like? Wow!" So I knew that Nirvana were successful in the underground scene and surely that was some motivation for me to call.

'So then I talked to Chris and Kurt on the phone, but I didn't tell Pete and Franz I was talking to them. But when I first called, Chris said, "Oh man, Dan Peters from Mudhoney is our drummer now." And I said, "Oh, well, if you come down here, call me up and let's hang out … because I'm fucking stranded here!" And then he called back and said, "You know, actually let's talk about this …"

'Those guys liked Scream and they were bummed that we'd broken up, but they also loved Mudhoney, and they didn't want to be responsible for breaking Mudhoney up. So then I got on the phone with Kurt and in talking to the two of them we realised, Wow, we kinda come from the same place. I love Neil Young *and* Public Enemy, I love Celtic Frost *and* The Beatles, and they were the same in that way. We all came from divorced families. We all discovered punk rock and grew up listening to Black Flag but we also loved John Fogerty. We were all little dirtbags who loved to play rock music. So it seemed like we might have a connection.

'So then I was faced with this decision, maybe the hardest decision of my entire life. It was, do I leave Pete and Franz and move on and join another band, or do I stay in Los Angeles? Pete and Franz were my best friends. I looked up to Pete like he was my father, he taught me so much, and I respected him so much and we were so close. But to be honest I just didn't want to stay in Los Angeles and suffer any more. And for me to do that would mean leaving Pete and Franz …'

Gods look down

Agonising over his decision, Grohl picked up the phone and called Kathleen Place to ask his mother for her advice.

'She loved Pete and Franz as much as I did, we were family,' he says. 'And she basically said, of course you need to do what you need to do, but you have to look out for yourself in this situation.'

When he replaced the handset, Grohl made his decision.

'I remember saying to Franz, "I'm going to go up there to try out." And he said, "You ain't coming back." And I said, "Well, I don't know if I have the gig." And he shook his head and said, "You ain't coming back."

'And deep down I knew it too.'

Negative creep

Kurt was a human being. And maybe it's selective memory, but I don't want to think of him as some brooding, suicidal genius. He was a fucking nice guy. But I understand. That's how legends are made ...

Dave Grohl

There's a famous photograph of Kurt Cobain which Nirvana fans will instantly recognise. Shot by *NME* photographer Martyn Goodacre in London in October 1990 during Dave Grohl's first tour with the band, the image has featured on magazine covers worldwide and been reprinted on countless unofficial T-shirts, posters and live bootleg recordings. In the photo, Cobain stares down the camera from behind a tousled, mussed-up fringe, his eyes ringed with black 'guy-liner', his jaw set hard. It's a powerful piece of iconography, conveying vulnerability, defiance and soulful intensity: the singer's sullen expression evokes memories of classic movie anti-heroes, from Marlon Brando's outlaw biker Johnny Strabler in *The Wild One* to Matt Dillon's high school rebel Richie White in *Over the Edge*. It's an image that posits the idea of Cobain as a moody, brooding misfit, rock's last rebel without a cause.

On 4 March 1994, as news broke internationally that Nirvana's frontman was in a coma in Rome's Policlinico Umberto Primo hospital following a drug overdose in the city's Hotel Excelsior, one UK music magazine selected Goodacre's photo as a potential cover image to accompany its coverage of the story. The following day, after Cobain emerged from the coma and it became clear that he would survive the overdose, the image was placed back in the files. The time was not yet right for Cobain's beatification. Five weeks later, as reports reached London that a lifeless body had been found in a room above the garage of Cobain's home on Seattle's Washington Boulevard, the photo was pulled from the files once more. For even as Kurt Cobain's death was being reported, his immortality was being packaged and sold.

Former *NME* Editor Steve Sutherland, the man who originally commissioned Goodacre's session with Nirvana, once claimed that this image 'tells the story of grunge', that it 'tells Kurt Cobain's story'. But with all due respect to the photographer, it doesn't, it doesn't at all. It's too clean, too pretty, too stylised, too perfect. It's an image that would be better suited to advertising a Disney biopic of Cobain's life than the true dirt-under-the-fingernails story. It does, however, perfectly illustrate the *myth* of Cobain – the notion of Nirvana's frontman as a troubled poetic genius, an artist too sensitive and fragile for the cut-throat corporate entertainment industry into which he was propelled against his will by the phenomenal success of his band's 1991 album *Nevermind*. That romanticised narrative is neat, conventional and easily grasped, a powerful myth with enduring appeal.

Yet no one was more responsible for constructing myths around Kurt Cobain than the man himself. From the earliest entries in his journals through to his suicide note, Cobain obsessively and compulsively documented, distorted, revised and rewrote his own history, to the point where facts and fictions in his life story have blurred and coalesced into one. The singer used to tell a great story about how he pawned his stepfather's guns to buy his first guitar: it's a memorable anecdote, but not true. Then there was the moving tale of Cobain living under a bridge in Aberdeen as a homeless teenager: poignant, but again untrue. As another illustration of his unhappy, deprived childhood, Cobain would tell of receiving just a solitary lump of coal as a present from his parents one Christmas: this piece of heartrending Dickensian storytelling was pure fiction too. For the singer, truth was rarely allowed to stand in the way of a good story.

But if Cobain was, on occasion, an unreliable narrator, then he was following in an accepted tradition. The music business is a hall of smoke and mirrors, and rock 'n' roll had always provided opportunities for reinvention and rebranding: for all their undeniable integrity, the personas of 'Joe Strummer' and 'Iggy Pop' were calculated constructs for John Mellor and James Osterberg Jr just as surely as Ziggy Stardust and Alice Cooper were the inventions of David Jones and Vincent Furnier. And just as Robert Zimmerman's early yarns about being a hobo and a circus performer were pure fantasy, there's no doubt that padding out his own life experiences with exaggerations, obfuscations and lies damned lies appealed to the mischief-maker in Cobain. As a child, Cobain read about punk rock before he ever *heard* punk rock – courtesy of a *Creem* magazine report on the Sex Pistols' much-hyped 1978 US tour – and in reading of Malcolm McClaren's machinations and manipulations he instantly grasped how myths could serve to inspire and incite above and beyond base realities. Rewriting his own story, then, was Cobain's very own great rock 'n' roll swindle.

Writing about Nirvana's frontman in Ireland's *Hot Press* magazine in 1993, music critic Bill Graham noted, 'Small-town outsiders frequently believe more intensely in rock myths. Swallowing dreams whole, they can lack the worldliness, agnosticism and chameleon habits of big city scenemakers. Kurt Cobain's version of punk could be nothing but fundamentalist.' The intensity of this conviction would prove damning for the singer. On the afternoon of 5 April 1994, before placing the business end of a shotgun against his head, Cobain put pen to paper for the final time. 'All the warnings from the Punk Rock 101 courses over the years since my first introduction to the, shall we say, ethics involved with independence and the embracement of your community has proven to be very true,' he wrote. 'I haven't felt the excitement of listening to as well as creating music along with reading and writing for too many years now. I feel guilty beyond words about these things … The fact is, I can't fool you, any one of you. It simply isn't fair to you or me. The worst crime I can think of would be to rip people off by faking it and pretending as if I'm having 100% fun.'

'It's better to burn out than to fade away,' he concluded.

Negative creep

With these words, for better or worse, Cobain's status as a rock 'n' roll martyr was enshrined. But this reductive version of Nirvana's story sits uneasily with those, like Dave Grohl, who knew Kurt Cobain best.

'You have to understand, for me, Nirvana is more than it is for you,' Grohl told one inquisitive journalist in 2011. 'It was a really personal experience. I was a kid. Our lives were lifted and then turned upside down. And then our hearts were broken when Kurt died. The whole thing is much more personal than the logo or the T-shirt or the iconic image.'

'What do you think of when you think of Kurt?' Grohl asked me rhetorically in 2009. 'You think of a rock star that killed himself, because of this guilt of being a rock star, [because] he was unhappy with his success. But he was a complicated person, and it's hard for anyone still to this day to completely understand. He may have seemed like this punk rock iconoclastic misfit, but he still fucking loved Abba, we danced to Abba a hundred times. So, when *I* think of Kurt, I think of the way he giggled, or Abba, or him saying to me, "God man, I wish I could wear sweatpants," shit like that. He was a human being. And maybe it's selective memory, but I don't want to think of him as some brooding, suicidal genius. He was a fucking nice guy. But I understand. That's how legends are made.

'Reading John Lennon interviews you can see how he was so conflicted, how he was such a massive tangled ball of contradiction, how he was searching and confused and passionate and a genius. And in reading a lot of those interviews, personally, I see a lot of similarities [with Kurt]. Please don't quote me saying he was a songwriter like Lennon, but there are some similarities in those two personalities that made for some great contradictions and it's really complicated to figure them out. Did Kurt want to be considered the greatest songwriter in the world? I think he did. But was he cool about everything else that came along with that? No. Did it keep him from writing songs? No. At the end of the day, if you don't want to fucking do something, don't do it.

This is a Call

Kurt Donald Cobain was born on 20 February 1967 at Grays Harbor Community Hospital, on a hill overlooking Aberdeen, Washington. His mother, Wendy, was a homemaker, his father Donald a mechanic at a Chevron station in nearby Hoquiam, where the young newly-weds lived at 2830½ Aberdeen Avenue. Like Dave Grohl, Cobain had Northern European ancestry – his father's family had Irish roots, while Wendy Cobain's bloodline, the Fradenburgs, were of German descent. Like Grohl too, Cobain had music in his blood: his uncle Chuck Fradenburg played drums in Aberdeen garage rockers The Beachcombers (whose raucous take on garage standard 'Farmer John' can be heard alongside The Kingsmen's 'Louie Louie' and The Sonics' 'High Time' on the excellent compilation album *The History of Northwest Rock, Volume 2 – The Garage Years*) while Wendy's younger sister Mari played guitar and performed as a country 'n' western singer/songwriter in area nightclubs. By the age of two, Kurt was contributing enthusiastic takes on The Beatles' 'Hey Jude' and The Monkees' '(Theme From) The Monkees' to family singalongs: one of Mari Fradenburg's home audio recordings from 1969 finds her stubbornly independent nephew shouting 'I'll do it by myself!' when an adult offers to help out with lyrics.

'You could just say, "Hey Kurt, sing this!" and he would sing it,' Mari Fradenburg (then the married Mari Earl) told *Goldmine* magazine in 1997. 'He had a lot of charisma from a very young age.'

On 24 April 1970 the Cobain family was expanded with the arrival of Kurt's sister Kimberly. By then the family had moved to Aberdeen, Washington. Derived from the Pictish-Gaelic words *aber devan*, meaning 'at the meeting of two rivers', Aberdeen is located on the banks of the Wishkah and Chehalis Rivers, on the southern edge of the picturesque Olympic Peninsula. Developed around its logging and fishing industries, in the post-World War II years it was a thriving seaport and a gateway to the Pacific, with a reputation as a town in which hard, honest graft was handsomely rewarded. Those rewards were not always wholesome: local entrepreneurs recognised that the town's young, overwhelmingly male itinerant workforce had significant disposable income, and a slew of saloons, gambling dens and brothels grew up around

Negative creep

Hume Street to part them from their earnings. The area had a reputation for lawlessness: at a point, violence and villainy was so endemic that sailors kicking their heels in Aberdeen between voyages to Asia bestowed the unwanted nickname 'The Hellhole of the Pacific' upon the town. By the time the Cobain family set up home at 1210 East First Street, though, Aberdeen's streets had been cleaned up and its bordellos had long been shut down. So too, however, had most of its sawmills and fishing canneries. Unemployment, alcoholism and suicide rates were on the rise, homes and shops were being boarded up and abandoned, and Washington State politicians had chosen to avert their eyes from the town's problems. As the 1970s progressed, Aberdeen's prospects looked increasingly bleak: to many of its residents, this was a forgotten town drawing its last breaths.

Though he would come to despise his hometown, in the early years of his childhood at least Cobain was oblivious to its rapid deterioration. He was a hyperactive, bright, happy child, popular with his peers and teachers alike, with a flair for art and a gift for mimicry which made him the centre of attention at family parties. But in 1975 the youngster's self-confidence and self-esteem were dealt a crushing blow when his parents decided to divorce. This was also the year in which Virginia and James Grohl separated, but whereas the six-year-old Dave Grohl, too young to fully grasp the gravity of the situation, took his parents' divorce in his stride, Cobain, two years older than his future bandmate and shielded less from parental arguments, internalised the split and dwelt upon it constantly. In the summer of 1975 he wrote on his bedroom wall 'I hate Mom, I hate Dad. Dad hates Mom, Mom hates Dad. It simply makes you want to be so sad.'

'It just destroyed his life,' Wendy Cobain admitted to Michael Azerrad. 'He changed completely. I think he was ashamed. And he became very inward – he just held everything. He became real shy. He became real sullen, kind of mad and always frowning and ridiculing.'

Where Virginia and James Grohl's divorce was conducted with civility and mutual respect, and the split actually tightened the bonds between Dave and his mother and sister, the same was not true for Kurt Cobain. Wendy and Don Cobain's separation was acrimonious, and both Kurt's parents later admitted that their children were used as pawns in the bitter battle between them. Though Wendy Cobain was awarded custody of the couple's two children, soon after the divorce Kurt asked to live with his father in the nearby town of Montesano, as he despised his mother's new boyfriend. He found life with his father problematic too, however. Though Donald Cobain tried his best to develop a relationship with his boy, he was locked down emotionally, and not given to overt displays of affection. His attempts to bond with his artistic, sensitive son over baseball and wrestling were painfully ill-judged: a loathing of the 'jock' mentality stayed with Kurt throughout his life.

In truth, both Cobain males were lonely, unhappy and unfulfilled. While Don sought solace in a new relationship with a local divorcee, Kurt retreated to his bedroom, seeking escape in his father's record collection, through which he discovered bands such as Kiss, Led Zeppelin, Iron Maiden and Aerosmith. He took to drawing Iron Maiden's cadaverous mascot Eddie in notebooks and on his bedroom walls, bestowing the monster with violent, vengeful urges and a powerful presence he himself lacked.

Despite reassurances to his son that he would not remarry, in February 1978 Don Cobain did just that. His new wife and her two young children moved into his trailer park home soon afterwards. Feeling pushed out by the new arrivals, and increasingly starved of both attention and affection, Kurt's sense of rejection intensified: he decided it was time for him to move on once more. For the rest of his childhood the restless youngster bounced unhappily between both his parents, three different sets of aunts and uncles and his grandparents; in the coming years he would stay with no less than ten different families. But wherever he lay his head he felt like a burden, unwanted and unloved. Shunted between high schools in Aberdeen and Montesano, he found it hard to establish firm friendships and became increasingly withdrawn and isolated.

'I was a rodent-like, underdeveloped, hyperactive spaz … and I was frustrated,' he recalled in his journals in later years. 'I needed to let off some steam.'

Negative creep

In time-honoured fashion, Cobain soon fell in with a group of fellow misfits, older stoner kids who shared his love of classic rock and metal. But he felt ill-at-ease in the group, and was still unsure of his own identity. In the summer of 1983, however, the teenager finally found what he'd unconsciously began searching for, a world which gave him a sense of definition and belonging. This world was punk rock. Years after the event, he sketched out his personal punk rock epiphany in vivid detail in his journals.

He wrote: 'I remember hanging out at a Montesano, Washington Thriftway when this short-haired employee box boy who kinda looked like the guy in Air Supply handed me a flyer that read: "The Them Festival. Tomorrow night in the parking lot behind Thriftway. Free live rock music." Montesano, Washington was a place unaccustomed to having live rock acts in their little village, a population of a few thousand loggers and their subservient wives. I showed up with stoner friends in a van ... There stood the Air Supply box boy holding a Les Paul with a picture from a magazine of Kool cigarettes laminated on it, a mechanic red-headed biker boy and that tall Lukin guy ... They played faster than I had ever imagined music could be played and with more energy than my Iron Maiden records could provide. *This was what I was looking for.* Ah, punk rock. The other stoners were bored and kept shouting, "Play some Def Leppard." God, I hated those fucks more than ever. I came to the promised land of a grocery store and I found my special purpose.'

The 'Air Supply box boy' was Buzz Osbourne, his band Melvins. And this was the night that changed Kurt Cobain's life forever.

Or so one version of the story goes. Again, Cobain may have been taking some liberties with the truth here. In *Come As You Are*, Cobain told the author that he'd first seen Melvins play at a rehearsal session in the attic of a local house, before they'd gone punk, and were still playing Hendrix and Who covers.

Whatever the truth of Kurt's initial exposure to the band, there's no doubt that Melvins, and in particular Osbourne, their wild-haired frontman, had a massive impact upon his life. The teenager began hanging out at Melvins' practice sessions at drummer Dale Crover's house at

609 West Second Street in Aberdeen with a group of other nerdy metal-head stoners Osbourne dubbed 'The Cling-Ons', so-called because they clung on to every word of wisdom the older teenager dispensed. Among his peers at Montesano High School Osbourne was considered a freak: here on home turf, among the beaten-down, the ill-at-ease and the written-off, he was revered as a philosopher, a rock star, a mentor. And here, sheltering under Osbourne's wing with his fellow adolescent misfits, Cobain finally found the sense of community and familial security that he so craved in his domestic life.

It was Osbourne who introduced Cobain to punk rock, via a series of home-made compilation tapes featuring bands such as Flipper, Fang, MDC and Black Flag, the same bands Dave Grohl was obsessing over in his Springfield bedroom. According to legend, the first song on the first tape Osbourne handed to Cobain was Black Flag's 'Damaged II', one of the snarling, slamming highlights of the California band's 1981 début album. The track opens with vocalist Henry Rollins screaming '*Damaged by you / Damaged by me / I'm confused / Confused / Don't wanna be confused.*' This rage, this aggression, was music to young Cobain's ears.

On 25 September 1984 Cobain travelled to Seattle with Osbourne and Matt Lukin to see Greg Ginn's band play alongside Green River at the Mountaineers club on their My War tour. For Black Flag the show was unremarkable – Henry Rollins's diary entry for the night read simply, 'Show went good. Throat feeling better' – but for Cobain the night was a revelation. Though the Californian band were increasingly moving away from the relentless, clenched-fist hardcore of *Nervous Breakdown* towards a grinding, sludgy, Black Sabbath-influenced punk-metal crossover sound, their live shows remained every bit as confrontational and punishing as ever, and Cobain felt at home amid the chaos and violence. This was not Cobain's first concert – he had watched ex-Montrose (and future Van Halen) frontman Sammy Hagar rock the Seattle Center Coliseum in March 1983 and had checked out Judas Priest at the Tacoma Dome on their Defenders of the Faith tour in May 1984, almost a year on from his 'conversion' to punk rock – but the white heat of Black Flag's performance proved to be a transformative experience. On the drive back to Aberdeen Cobain spoke excitedly of his dream to start his own punk rock band.

Cobain originally fancied himself as a drummer, and had graduated from banging on Chuck Fradenburg's kit as an infant to playing drums in the Montesano Junior High School band by the time he reached seventh grade. But on his fourteenth birthday, in 1981, he had been gifted a guitar and a 10 watt amp by his uncle Chuck. The guitar was second-hand, Japanese and strung so high as to be barely playable, but Cobain carried it with him everywhere as a badge of pride. He began taking lessons from a local guitarist named Warren Mason, then playing in a band with his uncle, and soon learned the chords to AC/DC's 'Back in Black', The Cars' 'My Best Friend's Girl', Led Zeppelin's 'Stairway to Heaven' and, inevitably, Washington's unofficial state anthem The Kingsmen's 'Louie Louie'. With these cornerstones of rock 'n' roll in place, he began writing his first songs. The following year, over the Christmas holidays, he made his first recording, at his aunt Mari Earl's house in Seattle, utilising Earl's bass guitar, an empty suitcase and a pair of wooden spoons to provide rhythmic accompaniment. He labelled the cassette *Organized Confusion*.

'Most of what I remember about the songs was a lot of distortion on guitar, really heavy bass and the clucky sound of the wooden spoons,' Mari Earl told *Goldmine*'s Gillian G. Gaar in 1997. 'And his voice, sounding like he was mumbling under a big fluffy comforter, with some passionate screams once in a while. Musically, it was very repetitious. As far as really sharing his music with me, and saying, "What do you think of this?" or whatever, he really didn't do that. Kurt was very sensitive about the stuff that he wrote and he was very careful about who he let hear it.'

'I told him, "Kurt, you're totally welcome to use my computer drummer,"' Earl recalled to English documentary maker Nick Broomfield the following year. 'And he says, "Oh yeah, I don't want to use a computer, I want to keep my music pure."'

One person permitted to listen to Cobain's first recordings was Dale Crover. Though Kurt had flunked an audition to join Melvins as a second guitarist, their hard-hitting drummer was impressed by the teenager's rudimentary original material, and encouraged him in his songwriting. In 1985, when Cobain announced his intention to start a band called Fecal Matter with fellow 'Cling-On' Greg Hokanson on drums, Crover offered to help out on bass. But by the time Fecal Matter got around to recording their first demo tape back at Mari Earl's house in December, the Melvins man found himself playing drums too, as Hokanson was no longer part of the set-up.

While clearly indebted to Melvins, Scratch Acid, Black Sabbath and late period Black Flag, the most remarkable thing about Fecal Matter's *Illiteracy Will Prevail* demo is just how clearly it prefigures Nirvana's signature sound. Though the seven songs on the cassette are poorly recorded, and often overwhelmed by tape hiss, tinny distortion and peaking sound levels, Cobain's pit-of-the-stomach yowl, his acerbic, none-more-bleak lyrical obsessions, childlike melodic sensibilities and gift for crafting stubbornly hook-laden punk-metal riffs all shine through the grime.

The highlight of the tape is the feedback-drenched, spiky, 'jock'-baiting 'Class of '86', Cobain's acid commentary upon his high-school peer group. But the shape of Cobain's punk to come is perhaps best illustrated by the churning garage grind of 'Laminated Effect', with the 18-year-old lashing out at Aberdeen's small-town mores with provoca-tive, misanthropic lyrics calculated to offend. Track four, the seesawing cow-punk of 'Spank Thru', mocked wholesome teenage love, celebrated masturbation and would remain a fixture in Nirvana set-lists up through to 1992. The sessions at Mari Earl's house also yielded an early version of *Bleach*-era Nirvana track 'Downer': quite why Cobain held back this MDC-inspired politico-punk seether from inclusion on the demo while the noisy but unremarkable 'Sound of Dentage', 'Bambi Slaughter' and 'Blathers Log' made the cut is unclear, but in later years the singer admitted to a certain amount of embarrassment over its sophomoric, angry young man lyrics.

Packaged with the singer's hand-drawn scatological artwork depict-ing three flies buzzing around a freshly minted pile of shit, the *Illiteracy Will Prevail* demo created quite a buzz among Aberdeen's punk kids. With his tongue firmly in his cheek, Cobain informed friends that Fecal

Negative creep

Matter were going to be 'bigger than U2 or R.E.M.'. In reality, the band split without ever playing a gig, but their cassette did earn Cobain minor celebrity status within his peer group, and bestowed a genuine sense of self-worth upon him for the first time. In April 1986 Buzz Osbourne wrote a letter to another 'Cling-On' friend from Aberdeen who'd recently moved to Phoenix, Arizona in search of work, hailing his young protégé's burgeoning talent.

'Some of [Kurt's] songs are real killer!' Osbourne enthused. 'I think he could have some kind of a future in music if he keeps at it.'

The recipient of the letter was 20-year-old Chris Novoselic. The first-born son of Croatian immigrant parents, Krist Anthony Novoselic was born in Compton, California on 16 May 1965. In 1979, squeezed out of California by rising property prices, the Novoselic family moved to Aberdeen, setting up home at 1120 Fairfield Street on Think of Me Hill. Krist Novoselic senior took up a position as a machinist in one of the town's lumber mills while his wife Maria opened a hairdressing salon, unfussily titled Maria's Hair Design. Though Aberdeen had a sizeable Croatian community – 'There are a lot of Croatian people here, and that's why we are here,' Maria Novoselic told the *Seattle Times* in 1992 – the insular small town felt alien to the family. To teen-age brothers Krist and Robert, moving to Aberdeen felt like stepping back in time when stacked against the experience of growing up in California.

When the elder Novoselic boy enrolled at Aberdeen High School, he registered his name as 'Chris' rather than his birth name 'Krist' in a bid to better assimilate into his new surroundings. A name change alone, however, was never likely to be enough to help the teenager blur into the background: at six feet seven inches tall, young Novoselic stood out among his peers like a cow in a chicken coop.

Kurt Cobain first noticed Novoselic at an Aberdeen High School assembly. The pair shared no classes, and never actually spoke to one another during their school days, but Cobain remembered the older boy as 'hilarious … a really clever, funny loud-mouth', with a gift for subverting the most sombre educational rituals with manic outbursts of songs and poetry. For all his anarchic humour, however, Novoselic was utterly depressed by his new environs, to the extent that in the summer of 1980 his parents were so concerned about his mental well-being that he was sent to live with relatives in Croatia, then still part of Yugoslavia. It was during this summer that the teenager fell in love with punk rock.

A fan of Black Sabbath, Zeppelin and Aerosmith in his early teens, Novoselic had first discovered the Sex Pistols and Ramones while listening to a Sunday night radio show called Your Mother Won't Like It on Seattle's KZOK radio station. In Yugoslavia he was exposed both to the freshest punk sounds coming out of England and an impassioned, vibrant local scene. Empowered by a community which actively celebrated society's misshapes, he returned to Aberdeen on a mission to spread the punk gospel. It was inevitable that he'd run into the like-minded Buzz Osbourne sooner rather than later.

Through hanging out with Melvins at their practice pad, Novoselic was drawn into a number of Buzz Osbourne's short-lived side projects. It was while singing with one such band, the Stiff Woodies, that he first met Kurt Cobain, who would occasionally sit in with the group on guitar or drums. Though Novoselic was a wretched singer, the mere fact that he was aware of the existence of punk rock was enough for Cobain to view him as a potential collaborator.

'Kurt asked me if I wanted to be in a band with him and gave me that Fecal Matter tape,' Novoselic recalled in the sleevenotes accompanying Nirvana's *With the Lights Out* box set. 'I listened to it and thought, "Hey, this is really good." I thought it was cool. So I went, "Yeah, let's do it." Then we laboured to put the ensemble together, find a drummer … and a drum set.'

The duo recruited fellow 'Cling-On' Aaron Burckhard as their drummer: a metalhead stoner who lived down the street from Cobain, Burckhard didn't actually own a drum kit, but he was the only available drummer within spitting distance of Aberdeen. The trio began rehearsing in earnest in January 1987.

'We had the most intense jams,' Novoselic recalled in his 2004 autobiography, *Of Grunge and Government*. 'We'd simultaneously orbit inner *and* outer space. It was so serious, if we felt we sucked we were disappointed and we'd sit around bummed out after. It must have been about transcendence. If we didn't get that rush, that otherworldly sense of liberation, we were let down; it's hard to lose God after you've experienced it. These were not cover-song sessions or protracted blues jams. These were manifestations of a psychic dissonance.'

The trio had yet to decide upon a name when they played their first show in March '87, at a house party in nearby Raymond, a town even more isolated than Aberdeen. To the dismay of their hosts, the band played only two cover songs – a ragged take on Led Zeppelin's 'Heartbreaker' which crumbled into an even more shambolic, and quickly aborted, version of the same band's 'How Many More Times'. The bulk of their set featured brutish originals, among them the newly written 'Mexican Seafood', 'Hairspray Queen' and 'Aero Zeppelin', a gothic-sounding dismissal of mainstream rock 'n' roll featuring the withering lyric *'You could shit on the stage, they'll be fans.'*

'We were just snotty and jumped around,' Cobain later recalled. 'We rocked, though.'

It's a measure of Cobain's confidence in his new band that he booked the trio a live radio session at KAOS FM, the station at Olympia, Washington's progressive liberal arts college Evergreen State College, before he had even chosen a name for the group. Cobain loved Olympia, a college town with an artsy, bohemian, free-thinking aesthetic, its own independent record label (Calvin Johnson's K Records) and fanzine culture (Bruce Pavitt's *Sub Pop* and Richie Unterberger's *Option*) and a diverse cultural demographic embracing students, punk rockers, artists and oddball small-town eccentrics. Here, Cobain felt, was Nirvana's natural audience.

Released in 2004 on Nirvana's *With the Lights Out* box set, three tracks taken from the 17 April session (Cobain originals 'Anorexorcist' and 'Help Me, I'm Hungry' plus a cover of 'White Lace and Strange' by obscure Philadelphia psych-rockers Thunder and Roses) show the recently formed trio to be a powerful, locked-in unit, with Burckhard's John Bonhamesque pounding anchoring Cobain and Novoselic's lurching, lumbering 'Black Zeppelin' riffage. The following evening, when the trio débuted at the Community World Theater in nearby Tacoma, they finally had a name: Skid Row.

The name didn't stick. When the trio next played the Community World Theater on 27 June they were called Pen Cap Chew. On 9 August they performed at the same venue as Bliss. When they returned on 23 January 1988 they were billed as Ted, Ed, Fred. At other times they played house parties as Throat Oyster and Windowpane.

For all the confusing indecision over the band's moniker, though, their sound, and Cobain's ambition, remained focused and unwavering. Though he had now moved from Aberdeen to Olympia to live with his girlfriend Tracy Marander, Cobain was keen that the three-piece should come together to practise five times a week: when Aaron Burckhard expressed reservations about committing to this schedule, Cobain promptly fired him from the band. He took out an advert in the October '87 issue of Seattle music paper *The Rocket* seeking a replacement. His ad read: 'SERIOUS DRUMMER WANTED. Underground attitude. Black Flag, Melvins, Zeppelin, Scratch Acid, Ethel Merman. [No seriously]. Versatile as heck. Kurdt 352.0992.' While the search was on-going, Dale Crover stepped into the breach to help out his friends once more.

On the afternoon of 23 January 1988, before their scheduled gig in Tacoma, the trio cut a new demo at Seattle's Reciprocal Recording studio with producer Jack Endino, recording ten songs in just six hours. Only 'Spank Thru' and 'Downer' were retained from Fecal Matter's *Illiteracy Will Prevail* demo; newer tracks such as 'Floyd the Barber', 'Paper Cuts' and 'Beeswax' hinted that Cobain's songwriting was moving into darker, heavier and more melodic territory. Endino, who had previously helmed Sub Pop sessions for Soundgarden (the *Screaming Life* EP) and Mudhoney (the *Dry as a Bone* EP), was sufficiently impressed to make his own copy of the session. Some weeks later he passed a dubbed cassette of the demo to Jonathan Poneman, who was actively seeking to expand his new label's roster.

'I think initially he was intrigued by it, but he wasn't about to just release it,' said Endino in a video interview for the *Nirvana: Taking Punk to the Masses* exhibition at Seattle's Experience Music Project in

As Vice-President of his freshman class at Thomas Jefferson High, Grohl
would introduce morning classes by playing Black Flag and Bad Brains
over the school intercom.

Grohl (black shirt) and Larry Hinkle (yellow shirt) make a stand for
personal freedom in their lacrosse team photo. 'Dave told us he couldn't
come to every practice as he had a band,' recalls coach Donald Butcher.

Grohl (in Necros T-shirt) at Lake Braddock Community Center, shot for
the insert of the Mission Impossible/Lünchmeat *Thanks* EP.

With Reuben Radding and Dave Smith in Dain Bramage. 'Playing with Dave
Grohl was like having your ass lifted in the air as if by magic,' says Radding.

Post-gig beers for the Scream team in Holland, spring 1988.

Keeping a low profile behind Kurt Cobain at Krist Novoselic's house in
Tacoma, Washington, 23 September 1990.

Repping Led Zeppelin in London, October 1990.

Recording a VPRO radio session at NOB Audio in Hilversum, Holland, 25 November 1991.

Grohl and Krist Novoselic take a break from Nirvana's 'tornado of insanity.' in 1992.

Opposite: Nirvana in Belfast, 22 June 1992. The following day Cobain was rushed to the city's Royal Victoria Hospital with a 'weeping ulcer'.

Nirvana at Seattle's Edgewater Hotel, August 1993, during the promo tour for the *In Utero* album.

Foo Fighters' first ever headline club show, at the Satyricon in
Portland, Oregon, 3 March 1995.

At Robert Lang Studios in Shoreline, Seattle, 26 January 1996. (Left to
right) Nate Mendel, William Goldsmith, Dave Grohl, Barrett Jones, Robert
Lang, Pat Smear.

2011. 'He thought, "Hmmm, well, this is interesting; the singer's got character, let's see what happens with them." So his take was basically watchful waiting.'

In truth, Cobain had little interest in the new label on his doorstep: in 1989 he admitted, 'We had never heard of Sub Pop.' The singer was desperate to put out a record on Greg Ginn's SST label or Chicago's Touch and Go records, then home to his beloved Scratch Acid, Butthole Surfers and Steve Albini's typically provocative new band Rapeman. He sent about 20 copies of what became known as the *Dale Demo* to the Midwest label, each one accompanied by a small gift, if used condoms and snot-filled tissues can be defined as 'gifts'.

A reply was not forthcoming.

Cobain was also on the hunt for a new drummer. In spring 1988 he placed a second advert in *The Rocket*. This one read: 'DRUMMER WANTED: Play hard, sometimes light, underground, versatile, fast, medium, slow, versatile, serious, heavy, versatile, dorky, nirvana, hungry. Kurdt 352.0992.' This was the first public mention of what would be his band's new, and final, name: Nirvana.

Explaining the name in later years, Cobain declared: 'Punk is musical freedom. It's saying, doing and playing what you want. In Webster's terms, "nirvana" means freedom from pain, suffering and the external world, and that's pretty close to my definition of punk rock.'

On 24 April 1988 Jonathan Poneman booked Nirvana (now featuring new drummer Dave Foster) to support Blood Circus on a Sub Pop Sunday show at the tiny Vogue club in Seattle. Poneman cajoled his business partner Bruce Pavitt, Charles Peterson and members of Mudhoney and Soundgarden into coming down early to check out the band. Painfully aware that his songs were to be critiqued by peers he respected, Cobain was so nervous that he threw up in the venue's car park before taking the stage. By all accounts, the gig which followed was a disaster.

'I thought they sucked,' said Charles Peterson. 'I didn't understand why Jonathan wanted to sign this band. They just seemed like a bunch of mopey shoegazers. The music seemed off, it didn't do it for me. And stupidly, I didn't take any pictures of them that night. I just thought,

"This is probably the first and last time I'll ever see or hear from this band."'

'We were uptight,' Cobain later admitted to *Backlash* fanzine writer Dawn Anderson. 'It just didn't seem like a real show. We felt like we were being judged; it was like everyone should've had score cards.'

Anderson's article, which ran in her fanzine in August 1988 under the heading 'It May Be the Devil and It May Be the Lord ... But It Sure as Hell Ain't Human', was Nirvana's first published press feature. The writer referred to the band as 'the Melvins' fan club' and noted 'it's probably only fair to inform you that if you didn't like the Melvins, or if you did like the Melvins but think leadbelly music has run its course, you won't like Nirvana'.

'But it's also important to stress that this is not a clone band,' Anderson added. 'The group's already way ahead of most mortals in the songwriting department and, at the risk of sounding blasphemous, I honestly believe that with enough practice Nirvana could become ... *better than the Melvins!*'

By the time Anderson's article appeared in print, Nirvana had a new drummer – 21-year-old Chad Channing from Bainbridge Island, a small community located in Puget Sound – and the offer of a single release, plus a slot on the forthcoming *Sub Pop 200* compilation album, from the stubbornly supportive Poneman. Cobain was not altogether thrilled that for his band's first single Sub Pop wished to release 'Love Buzz', a tripped-out, hypnotic cover of an obscure cut by the Dutch pop band Shocking Blue, in preference to one of his own original songs, but he soon relented. In truth, no one was making Nirvana a better offer.

Love Buzz/Big Cheese was duly released as the first offering from the Sub Pop Singles Club, a service which delivered seven-inch vinyl releases on a monthly basis to the label's hardcore fans in return for an annual $35 subscription fee, in November 1988. In the customary Sub Pop tradition, promotional copies of the single came with a gloriously hyperbolic press release. This time, however, Cobain himself was the hype man. He wrote:

Negative creep

NIRVANA sounds like: Black Sabbath playing The Knack, Black Flag, Led ZEP, the Stooges and a pinch of Bay City Rollers.
Their personal musical influences include: H.R Puffnstuff, Marine Boy, divorces, drugs, sound effects records, the Beatles, Young Marble Giants, Slayer, Leadbelly and Iggy.

NIRVANA sees the underground music SEEN as becoming stagnant and more accessible towards commercialised major label interests.

Does NIRVANA feel a moral duty to change this cancerous evil?

No way! We want to cash in and suck butt of the big wigs in hopes that we too can GET HIGH and FUCK. GET HIGH and FUCK. GET HIGH and FUCK.

American rock bands who could deliver sarcasm and black humour as deftly as they harnessed volume and distortion were thin on the ground in 1988. American rock bands who could deliver sarcasm and black humour *and* land themselves a Single of the Week accolade in not one but *two* influential British music magazines in the same week were even more rare. Reviewing the *Love Buzz/Big Cheese* single in *Melody Maker* and *Sounds* respectively, writers Everett True and John Robb both hailed Nirvana as one of the finest new acts to emerge from the US underground scene in years. With the release of *Bleach* seven months later, the buzz around the band only intensified.

Sub Pop heralded the release of the album in its typically low-key manner. Hyping *Bleach* as 'hypnotic and righteous heaviness' and hailing the band as 'Olympia pop stars', they crowed, 'They're young, they own their own van and they're going to make us rich!'

'In our press releases we would announce that the Nirvana album was gonna go double platinum and stuff like that, never believing for a minute that would actually happen,' Bruce Pavitt admitted in 2008. 'By 1988 selling five to ten thousand copies a record was considered doing very good business. The idea of selling millions of records was almost inconceivable. A lot of what Jon and I were doing was living in this hyper-fantasy realm where we were pretending – it was almost like we were five years old – let's play record label!'

In the wake of the phenomenal success of *Nevermind*, it became fashionable to argue that *Bleach* was a much superior manifestation of Kurt Cobain's songwriting. This is nonsense. As the respected US rock critic Ira Robbins noted in his review for *Trouser Press*, *Bleach* is 'a punk album of its time, class and place', and nothing more. Kurt Cobain's own assessment of the album was equally blunt: for Cobain, *Bleach* was slow, grungey and 'one-dimensional', deliberately dumbed down to fit the Sub Pop aesthetic.

The album was recorded with Jack Endino over six studio sessions at Reciprocal between Christmas Eve 1988 and 24 January 1989. Its opening track 'Blew' is a testament to just how raw Nirvana were at the time: inspired by the doomy sounds of avant-garde Swiss metal collective Celtic Frost, on their first day in the studio Cobain and Novoselic tuned their guitars down two notes, forgetting that they had already tuned down two steps from a standard E setting to a 'drop D' tuning. As a result, 'Blew', a bleak rumination on entrapment, sounds even sludgier and more oppressive than originally intended.

The track sets the tone for much of what follows. 'Floyd the Barber', a tale of small-town fear and loathing, sounds choked and claustrophobic. 'Mr Moustache', in which Cobain lashes out at both the hyper-masculine culture of Aberdeen and the self-righteous political correctness he found in Olympia, eddies woozily around one circular six-note riff repeated *ad nauseam*. 'Big Cheese' lumbers and lurches to no great purpose, as Cobain vents his spleen against Jonathan Poneman's attempts to meddle with his art. And 'Sifting' is a sub-Melvins grind that should never have made it out of Nirvana's rehearsal room.

There were diamonds in the dirt, however. 'Love Buzz' remains a thrilling slab of grime-pop, with Cobain's reckless guitar slashes cutting across his bruised, ugly/beautiful vocals. 'Negative Creep' is a fabulously dead-eyed wail of self-loathing and self-pity (*'I'm a negative creep, I'm a negative creep, I'm a negative creep and I'm stoned'*). 'Swap Meet' is an atypically perky, if typically twisted, white trash love song, in which

Negative creep

Cobain cleverly masks concerns about his own faltering relationship with girlfriend Tracy Marander in a lyric ostensibly detailing the shared passions of a couple scrambling to make ends meet below the poverty line. And while on a musical level 'School' is clichéd sub-Stooges sludge, its biting lyric lashes out at the cliquey, incestuous Seattle music community, giving welcome early evidence of Cobain's stubborn nonconformist mindset.

'About a Girl' is the album's undoubted highlight, however, the one genuine indication that Nirvana had more to offer than standard-issue Sub Pop misanthropy and negativity. Cobain's most pure, open-hearted and unconditional love song, it was written for Tracy Marander following a heated domestic argument in which the singer was threatened with eviction from the couple's Pear Street home if he didn't find himself a job. Cobain would later claim that he listened to *Meet the Beatles* for three hours straight before writing the song's delicate melody for his girl. Wherever his inspiration came from, it had the desired effect: while he would never admit that the song was about Marander, his girlfriend saw through his sheepish, blushing denials and it bought him one more rent-free year.

Reviews of the album were largely positive. Writing in *The Rocket*, Gillian G. Gaar highlighted the album's potential to reach a broad church of rock fans, noting that *Bleach* drew its elemental power from 'garage grunge, alternative noise and hell-raising metal, without swearing allegiance to any of them'. *NME*'s Edwin Pouncey, another long-time supporter of the band, was even more effusive in his praise.

'This is the biggest, baddest sound that Sub Pop have so far managed to unearth,' he raved. 'So primitive that they manage to make label-mates Mudhoney sound like Genesis, Nirvana turn up the volume and spit and claw their way to the top of the musical garbage heap.'

The album cost $606.17 to record, a tiny amount compared to major label recording budgets, but more money than the members of Nirvana had access to at the time. Chad Channing's friend Jason Everman ended up covering the studio costs; in return he was credited with playing guitar on the album, though he didn't commit a single note to tape. On 22 June 1989, just one week after the album's release, the band piled into their Dodge van to begin their first ever national tour, scheduled to take in 26 shows. Everman was with them, on board as a second guitarist to beef up their live sound. The experiment didn't work out and the guitarist left the band after they returned home to Olympia.

Cobain's idea of adding a second guitarist into the mix was shelved as Sub Pop packed Nirvana off to Europe with labelmates Tad for a six-week co-headlining tour, billed as the Heavier Than Heaven tour. There was a genuine buzz surrounding the dates: Mudhoney had just blown through Europe with a series of incendiary shows that justified all the hype around Sub Pop, *Bleach* was in the Top Ten of the UK indie label charts and John Peel was airing cuts from both bands nightly on Radio 1. *Sounds* magazine previewed the UK leg of the tour with a Tad/Nirvana cover feature ... though it was Tad, then receiving rave reviews for their Jack Endino-produced *God's Balls* début, not Nirvana, who were chosen as the main cover image. When the tour hit London on 27 October 1989, 1,000 people packed into the 700-capacity School of Oriental and African Studies to see the show. On their own US tour one month previously, Nirvana were often incapable of drawing flies, so it's little wonder that the band were fired up for the gig. The following week *Melody Maker* hailed their performance as 'superb, cranked-up, desperate and loud'.

Transcendent nights such as this were not the norm, however. The Heavier Than Heaven tour schedule was brutal, encompassing 36 shows in 42 days across 9 countries, and Nirvana didn't even have their own van: rather they shared a rented 10-seat Fiat with the four members of Tad, tour manager Alex MacLeod, sound engineer Craig Montgomery and both bands' merchandise and equipment. The group had to contend with long overnight drives in sub-zero temperatures, their lodgings were spartan, showers were rare and food was a luxury. Almost everyone in the van fell ill during the tour. All three members of Nirvana vowed to quit the band at separate points.

The tour wound up back in London on 3 December 1989, where Nirvana and Tad were joined at the 2,000-capacity Astoria theatre by Mudhoney for a special Sub Pop showcase dubbed the Lame Fest. Nirvana were now homesick, road-weary and mentally fried: after missing their ferry from Belgium, they arrived at the venue just 30 minutes before the doors opened, with no time to soundcheck. Popular legend has it that Cobain and Tad Doyle flipped a coin to see who would open the show: Nirvana lost. This didn't bother their frontman, who by now just wanted the misery to end as quickly as possible.

Depending on who you talk to, Nirvana's ragged, nerve-shredding Lame Fest set was either an unmitigated disaster or one of the defining moments in their career. The trio tore through 15 songs, including a cover of The Stooges' 'I Wanna Be Your Dog' and two new Cobain originals titled 'Polly' and 'Breed', as their equipment threatened to flatline at any given second. At the climax of set closer 'Blew', Cobain took off his guitar and hurled it at Novoselic, who swung his bass at the incoming instrument and smashed it into pieces with one single swipe. Cobain was off the stage before his guitar hit the ground. It was a beautifully brutal conclusion to a messy, tension-filled night.

'The Lame Fest show was what really put Nirvana on the map in the UK,' says Anton Brookes, then a young publicist with his own company, Bad Moon, who represented Nirvana among other Sub Pop bands. 'The reviews the next week were like, "Forget Mudhoney, forget Tad, *this* is the band. This is the band, this is special." Everybody in the audience was stood there going "Wow". Everybody was just like, "This is amazing."'

Phil Alexander, then a contributor to heavy rock magazine *Raw*, now Editor-in-Chief of *MOJO* magazine, interviewed Cobain and Novoselic before they returned to the USA. He remembers the pair as articulate, thoughtful and affable young men, bearing scant resemblance to their Sub Pop-manufactured image as happy-go-lucky backwoods knuckle-draggers. Cobain had long since tired of Sub Pop's gamesmanship and hype – 'I feel like we've been tagged as illiterate, redneck, cousin-fucking kids that have no idea what's going on at all,' he complained to journalist Nils Bernstein from *The Rocket* that same month. 'That's completely untrue' – and as he spoke to Alexander over bottles of Newcastle Brown Ale in The Clachan bar on Kingly Street in Soho, Nirvana's singer made no secret of his ambition to transcend the scene which had spawned his band.

'I had just reviewed an album by an obscure band on SST called Slovenly, which seemed to pique Kurt's interest,' Alexander recalls. '"So you're the alternative rock guy?" he asked. I told him that I wasn't really sure that I was, but that also forced Krist into asking me what I thought of *Bleach*. I was fairly honest, and I told them that I was far more of a fan of *God's Balls*. "Everyone's got an opinion, everyone's got an asshole!" countered Krist, looking a little upset. But that set us off on a conversation about where the band were heading and what their ambitions were. It was at that point that Kurt told me unequivocally that he wanted to be in the biggest band in the world. It wasn't a boast, but neither did he mumble: he just said it as if this was the most normal thing in the world. In hindsight, you tend to think: be careful what you wish for ...'

As the new decade dawned, Sub Pop were keen to capitalise upon the growing buzz on Nirvana by getting the band back into the studio to make a second album. Jonathan Poneman targeted Butch Vig, an up-and-coming producer from Madison, Wisconsin, then making a name for himself in the underground thanks to his work on albums by Killdozer, Die Kreuzen and Urge Overkill, as the man to bottle Nirvana's magic.

'At the time I'd been doing a bunch of projects for Sub Pop,' says Vig, 'and so when Jonathan called and said, "Do you want to do a project with this band Nirvana?" I was like "Okay, cool." He said, "They could be the next Beatles." And I just sort of laughed and went, "Yeah, right."

'I'd heard *Bleach* before, and to be honest I was not that impressed. I liked a couple of songs on it, I thought "School" was pretty cool, but the one song that stood out to me, that I think everybody has recognised, was "About a Girl". Most of the record was very one-dimensional, but that song showed someone capable of writing a brilliant pop song; with the melodies and the lyrics and the chord progression, it was like a Beatles song. And looking back now, that was sort of the shape of what was to come, because Kurt's songwriting had started to grow a bit more sophisticated.'

Negative creep

Nirvana arrived at Vig's Smart Studios in Madison on the morning of 2 April 1990, after an overnight drive from Chicago, where they'd kicked off an eight-week national tour with a show at the city's Metro club the previous evening. The producer recalls three 'scraggly-looking, greasy, dirty kids' tumbling out of the Sub Pop van, unaccompanied by any road crew. As they lugged their gear into the studio, the producer remembers Novoselic and Channing being 'super-friendly, funny and out-going': their pal Kurt was rather harder to read.

'From day one, Kurt was somewhat of an enigma,' says Vig. 'He came in and said, "Hey, my name's Kurt," and he loaded in his amp and his guitar and then he just sat in the corner and didn't say anything for about half an hour. I thought something was wrong, either he didn't want to be there, or maybe he didn't like me from the second he saw me. I had no idea. But finally Chris pulled me aside and said, "It's okay, Kurt gets that way, he gets in these funks but he always snaps out of it." And I said, "Okay, well, I won't take anything personal, I'll just roll with it." And sure enough Kurt slowly came out of his shell.

'As it turned out it was great working with him. He was smart and funny and we developed a really good rapport. But it was just kinda strange that first day. I realised over the course of the week that he just had these incredible mood swings but that that was just a big part of his personality.'

The first song Nirvana played for Vig was a new track entitled 'In Bloom', a song Cobain had penned in tribute to his friend Dylan Carlson, which had received its live première the previous night. They then ran through a further six originals – 'Dive', 'Lithium', 'Immodium' (titled after the anti-diarrhoea medicine Tad Doyle had used on their European tour), 'Pay to Play', 'Sappy' and a stark acoustic track called 'Polly' (originally titled 'Hitchhiker') based upon the harrowing story of a 14-year-old girl who'd been abducted, raped and tortured at gunpoint following a punk rock show in Tacoma in 1987. Vig could scarcely believe that this was the same band who'd made *Bleach*.

'I realised, "God, there's some great, great, great songs here," and I was excited,' he recalls. 'Once they started playing they were a powerful-sounding band.'

Over the next four days the trio committed Cobain's new songs, plus a cover of the Velvet Underground's 'Here She Comes Now', to tape. Vig was impressed by their work ethic and professionalism.

'The only tension really that came from the session was that Kurt was arguing with Chad about the drumming a lot,' he recalls. 'Either it didn't sound intense enough or he didn't like the parts. Sometimes Kurt, who couldn't really play drums, would get behind the kit and go "Play it like this" or "Play this part" and he'd half be able to do it, but it was enough that Chad would get it.'

On 7 April, following a headline show at Madison's Club Underground, Nirvana climbed back into the Sub Pop van and headed for Milwaukee to resume their tour. Vig mixed the tracks the following week and sent the master tapes to Jonathan Poneman and cassette copies to the band. The plan was that Nirvana would return to Madison in June to finish the album, which was to be called *Sheep*, a title Cobain intended as a barbed joke on hipsters who would pick up the album based on Sub Pop's bullshit alone. But the Sub Pop van never reappeared in Madison, and as months passed without any communication from the label Vig feared he'd screwed up.

In reality, Sub Pop was facing its own problems. Always a hand-to-mouth operation – famously Poneman and Pavitt once had T-shirts printed up reading WHAT PART OF 'WE HAVE NO MONEY' DON'T YOU UNDERSTAND? – by the summer of 1990 the label was in serious danger of bankruptcy. Behind the scenes, Poneman and Pavitt were seeking to secure a licensing deal with a major label, using Nirvana's brilliant new demo as bait. Unbeknownst to the pair, initially at least, their brightest young stars were shopping the demo around too.

The notion that Kurt Cobain negotiated the music industry as a wide-eyed, guileless *naïf* is a lie. The publication of the singer's diaries as *Journals* in 2002 revealed that he plotted and planned his every musical and career move far in advance of their execution, and knew exactly how the industry worked. He was more than aware that Sub Pop viewed his band as a valuable commodity; his plan now was to cut out the middlemen and approach the labels directly. Nirvana's stint at

Negative creep

Smart Studios also convinced him of another cold hard fact – that his drummer was not good enough to take the step up to the next level with him.

One week after the end of the band's US tour, he and Novoselic drove out to Bainbridge Island and told Channing he was out of the band. That same week he also broke off his relationship with Tracy Marander. It was time for the singer to look after number one.

❧

On 11 July 1990 Cobain and Novoselic borrowed Mudhoney's drummer and Tad's gear to record a one-off song, 'Sliver', at Reciprocal for a Sub Pop single. A loosely autobiographical tale of an unhappy boy dropped off with his grandparents while his parents attended a rock show, it was Cobain's most immediate song to date, employing a quiet/ loud dynamic which saw stripped-back verses exploding into a distorted wall-of-sound chorus as Dan Peters's drums kicked in hard. A class apart from the rough-hewn sludge on *Bleach*, the *Sliver* single dropped into the underground rock scene like a grenade.

'Sub Pop has yet to find anything to top Nirvana's massive fusion of rock and perfect pop,' declared *NME*, hailing the single as 'The best record this label has put out since Mudhoney's *Touch Me I'm Sick*'.

'It wasn't until "Sliver" that anyone thought Nirvana could be a commercially successful band,' says Cobain biographer Charles R. Cross, then Editor of Seattle's *The Rocket*. 'Even as late as 1990 most people in Seattle thought Mudhoney would be the first band to break huge. Nirvana were the dark horse.'

In August 1990, at Thurston Moore's invitation, the band were invited to open a clutch of West Coast dates for Sonic Youth. Moore, his partner Kim Gordon and Dinosaur Jr's J. Mascis had caught a Nirvana show in New Jersey the previous summer, and had been blown away by the band's brutish power. Having acquired a dubbed copy of Nirvana's Smart Studios cassette, he was now talking the band up to everyone he knew. For Cobain, the opportunity to support the revered New York noiseniks was too good to pass up, irrespective of the fact that his band once again had no drummer. With Dan Peters committed to a European festival tour with Mudhoney, Cobain turned to his old friend Dale Crover for help once more.

Two days before the tour was due to start at Bogart's in Long Beach, California, Cobain, Novoselic and Craig Montgomery drove down to San Francisco to meet up with Crover at Buzz Osbourne's house. It was then that Osbourne suggested the party should head over to the I-Beam to watch his friends in Scream.

Cobain took some persuading. Together with his next-door neighbour Slim Moon, the owner of Olympia's Kill Rock Stars record label, the singer had gone to see the band from Bailey's Crossroads play Tacoma's Community World Theater back in October 1987, during Dave Grohl's first tour with the Stahl brothers. Expecting a set of righteous punk rock, Cobain was horrified to discover that Scream's live show was now largely built around the kind of strutting hard rock he himself was trying to disown.

'Kurt hated it,' remembers Slim Moon, still a respected figure in Olympia's tight-knit and fiercely independent musical community. 'He kept saying, "It sucks when good bands turn into Van Halen." For some reason he was particularly annoyed that they were playing guitar solos on Telecasters. He talked about how much he hated it for the whole drive home.'

Back in San Francisco, Cobain agreed to go to the I-Beam to keep the peace. This time he didn't notice what guitars Franz Stahl was playing, or that Pete Stahl dressed more like Sammy Hagar than Ian MacKaye. This time his focus was solely upon Scream's powerhouse drummer.

'I was standing with Kurt and Chris,' recalls former Nirvana soundman Craig Montgomery, 'and Kurt said, "That's the kind of drummer we need." Dave had an energy that was hard to miss and Kurt and Chris were pretty blown away by his playing. He seemed like a good fit for what they were doing.'

Six weeks later Dave Grohl packed his drums into a large cardboard box and boarded a flight bound for Seattle.

Negative creep

Grohl arrived in Seattle on the afternoon of Friday 21 September 1990. Cobain and Chris Novoselic were at the city's Sea-Tac airport to greet him. As Novoselic nudged his Volkswagen van out of the airport for the 29-kilometre drive to his home in Tacoma, where Grohl was due to crash for his first few weeks in Washington, the drummer offered Cobain an apple to break the ice.

'No thanks,' said Cobain. 'It'll make my teeth bleed.'

The rest of the journey was conducted in silence.

The following evening Nirvana were billed to play an all-ages show with local punks Derelict, Dwarves and Melvins at Seattle's 1,500-capacity Motor Sports International Garage. The gig was a huge deal for the band: it was by far their biggest hometown headline show to date, and Sub Pop had flown journalist Keith Cameron and photographer Ian Tilton from *Sounds* magazine across from London to write a cover story on the group ahead of their first full UK headline tour in October. With Mudhoney on hiatus while guitarist Steve Turner finished college, Cobain had asked Dan Peters to play drums for the evening. That afternoon Cobain informed Grohl that he wouldn't really be able to speak to him, or introduce him to friends, at the show, as the sudden appearance of an unknown drummer at the gig might set tongues wagging among local scenesters. A bemused Grohl duly watched the show from the crowd, soaking in the atmosphere. He was astonished to see that every other kid in the room seemed to be wearing one of Nirvana's new Fudge Packin' Crack Smokin' Satan Worshippin' Motherfuckers T-shirts.

While standing in the crowd, Grohl was recognised by 20-year-old Greg Anderson, a local metalhead who'd caught a Scream show in Olympia just a few weeks previously. The pair struck up a conversation about old school heavy metal while waiting for Melvins to take the stage. Anderson, who had played alongside future Foo Fighter Nate Mendel in local punk acts and now runs heavyweight US metal imprint Southern Lord in addition to playing guitar in a host of experimental/stoner/doom bands – including the Pete Stahl-fronted Goatsnake – recalls that Grohl was rather more enthused about seeing Buzz Osbourne's band than his prospective new employers.

This is a Call

The following day the Novoselics threw a barbecue at their house for the visiting British journalists, and the drummer sat quietly in the background chowing down on surf and turf as Cobain, Novoselic and Peters outlined their future plans to Keith Cameron. The next day he joined Cobain and Novoselic at the Dutchman, the grubby Seattle rehearsal room where the pair had written 'Sliver' with Peters just a few months earlier, and auditioned for a vacancy Peters understandably thought had already been filled. Before the trio had finished running through their opening number, Cobain and Novoselic knew that they'd got their man.

The following day Kurt Cobain dropped in unannounced to Calvin Johnson's KAOS radio show to play an impromptu four-song acoustic session. During the show he casually informed Johnson that Nirvana had a new drummer, nothing less than 'the drummer of our dreams'.

'His name is Dave and he's a baby Dale Crover,' he enthused. 'He plays almost as good as Dale. And within a few years' practice he may even give him a run for his money.'

'This new kid on the block can't dance as good as your MTV favorites but he beats the drums like he's beating the shit out of their heads!' Cobain wrote in an excitable Sub Pop press release. 'His name is Dave Grohl. Dave is formerly of the Washington D. band Scream. He passed thru the gruelling Nirvana initiation ritual with flying colors and is now an important cornerstone in the Nirvana institution.'

Dan Peters missed Cobain's surprise announcement on KAOS. So when Nirvana's frontman called him the following day, Peters assumed Cobain wanted to talk about the band's imminent UK tour. Instead, he was sheepishly informed that the band had recruited a new permanent drummer. Communication had never been one of Cobain's strong points, as Grohl himself had immediately discovered.

'I don't remember them saying, "You're in the band,"' he admitted years later. 'We just continued.'

Nirvana's new drummer played his first gig with the band at the North Shore Surf Club in Olympia on 11 October 1990. The

300-capacity club had sold out within a day of the tickets going on sale, a feat which so impressed Grohl that he felt compelled to phone home to share the news with his mother.

'The venue was down the street from where Kurt and I lived,' he recalled in 2005. 'We soundchecked and I went to get something to eat. When I got back there was a line around the block. I called my mother and said, "Mother, there's at least 200 people in line!" I was amazed. With Scream the band usually outnumbered the audience.'

The show was sweaty, frenzied and intense. Grohl had to start the set's opening number, a cover of the Vaselines' 'Son of a Gun', no less than three times, as the band kept blowing the power in the tiny venue. A few songs later the bare-chested drummer put his sticks right through his snare drum skin: Cobain held the broken drum aloft like a war trophy to the cheering crowd. Grohl had officially arrived.

'I felt I had something to prove,' he later recalled. 'I knew we sounded good as a band. And we were fucking good that night. Absolutely, I was nervous. I didn't know anyone – no one in the audience, no one in the band. I was completely on my own. That was the only thing that mattered, that hour on stage. That's what I was focused on.'

'Grohl was simply a monster,' says Charles R. Cross. 'Chad Channing is often underrated; he was a great drummer for the early van-touring Nirvana because he was an affable guy, a talented drummer and he played the punk-era songs of Nirvana as well as anyone. However, with Dave Grohl Nirvana became a very different beast. He powered Nirvana's shows and made them spectacular events. It was Grohl who turned Nirvana into the powerhouse it became.'

'His contribution transformed us into a force of nature,' said Novoselic. 'Nirvana was now a beast that walked the earth.'

Lounge act

I didn't really think that much of 'Teen Spirit' at first. I thought it was just another one of the jams that we were doing: we had so many jams like that, that we'd record onto a boombox tape and then lose the cassette and lose the song forever. But 'Teen Spirit' was one we kept coming back to …

Dave Grohl

In the darkness, no one could see the tears streaming down Dave Grohl's face. It was the evening of 20 October 1990, and Grohl and Kurt Cobain had sneaked into London's Brixton Academy to catch the final show of Boston alt. rock alchemists Pixies' sold-out UK tour. Having stepped off an 11-hour trans-Atlantic flight that same afternoon, Grohl was jetlagged and a little spaced out, but as he looked around the cavernous converted theatre and saw the sheer exhilaration etched on the faces of 4,500 sweat-drenched indie-rock fans screaming Black Francis's surrealist lyrics about 'slicing up eyeballs' back at the stage, the euphoria of the evening overcame him and he cried tears of pure joy. That a band this wired, this warped, this utterly uncompromising could connect on such a visceral, human level in a room this size so far from home seemed to Grohl truly transcendent. Just like the B-52s' appearance on *Saturday Night Live* a decade previously, it represented a small, but significant, victory for the outsiders, for the freaks. One day, Grohl thought as he blinked back the tears, I want to be up on that stage.

Nirvana had stages of their own to conquer in the week ahead, in Birmingham, Leeds, Edinburgh, Nottingham, Norwich and London, where the 2,000-capacity Astoria theatre had sold out one month in advance of their arrival. There was a tangible street-level buzz around the band, and Kurt Cobain sensed it. With Grohl behind him, though, he knew his band was ready. For the very first time, Nirvana had a swagger in their step.

A surprise awaited Grohl in Birmingham on the opening night of the tour. Nirvana's support band, all-girl rockers L7, were already inside Goldwyn's Suite when the headliner's van pulled up outside, and Grohl heard his name being called as soon as he stepped into the venue. L7 bassist Jennifer Finch had booked Scream on a Bad Religion bill in Los Angeles some months previously, and she recognised their former drummer immediately. Before the night was over the pair were making out like teenagers.

Though the past four years of his life had largely been spent cooped up in foul-smelling tour vans with punk rock lifers for company, finding girlfriends was rarely a problem for Grohl. Holding onto them was a little trickier. His first love, at age 13, was Sandy Moran, the most 'gorgeous, angelic' girl in the seventh grade at Oliver Wendell Holmes Middle School. The pair dated for two whole weeks – 'We'd meet at her locker after every period and give each other hickeys,' Grohl would later recall – before the feather-haired heartbreaker told her infatuated boyfriend that she didn't want to get tied down, and dumped him. The following year, aged 14, he lost his virginity to a high school female basketball player two years his senior at a house party; when he returned to school the next week he discovered that his partner had quit school and moved from the area. At 16 he fell 'hopelessly in love' with a girl named Wendy, only to see her move to Arizona with her family just weeks after the pair started dating. Looking back, Grohl admits he used to fall in love much too easily. But he had never met a girl like Jennifer Finch.

A street-smart, ballsy, tomboy-cute 24-year-old, Finch had started playing guitar at age 10 and saw the Ramones as her first punk rock show aged 11. By 14 she was living on the streets of Los Angeles, shooting up drugs during the day and shooting hardcore bands for fanzines at night. She was, in short, the most punk rock girl Dave

Grohl had ever met. The pair were inseparable for the remainder of the tour.

'We started dating from the second we met,' recalls Finch, now working in website development and online marketing in her native Los Angeles. 'Dave was very cute, very kind and a very sweet person. He was shy and very charismatic, but humble too. I liked him from the start.'

Blessed with a sassy new girlfriend and a white-hot new band, memories of the misery of Scream's final tour faded quickly for Grohl. Nirvana's ten days in the UK were a blur of gigs, press interviews, practical jokes, food fights and passionate drunken fumblings. The trio cut a four-track radio session for long-time supporter John Peel at the BBC's Maida Vale studios, found themselves courted by major label A&R men and stood for *that* photo session with the *NME*'s Martyn Goodacre. Unable to keep a smile off his face the whole time he was in the UK, the excitable young drummer charmed everyone he met.

'The band took a definite step up when Dave joined,' Nirvana PR Anton Brookes told me in 2010. 'He took it beyond a level, it became ferocious. He just gave it that extra dimension. Nirvana became a serious contender.

'Kurt had sent me over a tape, recorded over a copy of *Bleach*, which had "In Bloom" and "Sliver" and "Dive" on it and a few other tracks that went on *Nevermind*, works in progress. And I remember thinking, "Wow, these are going to be massive, they're going to be able to sell out Brixton Academy!" Kurt told me that he had other songs that were going to be Top Ten singles. He totally believed it. He knew it.'

'We're changing a little bit,' Cobain admitted to Keith Cameron in his *Sounds* interview. 'The *Bleach* album is pretty different to what we're doing right now. We figured we may as well get on the radio and make a little bit of money at it.

'I don't wanna have any other kind of job, I can't work among people. I may as well try and make a career out of this. All my life my dream has been to be a big rock star – just may as well abuse it while you can.'

Lounge act

When Nirvana returned from the UK Dave Grohl moved in with Cobain at 114 North Pear Street in Olympia. He was quite unprepared for the squalor in which his friend lived: 114 North Pear Street made the scuzzy European squats where Grohl had laid his head during his days with Scream look like palatial Georgetown townhouses. The kitchen was *filthy*, covered in mould and littered with half-eaten corn-dogs, beer cans and putrefying take-away food. There was only one tiny bedroom, which Cobain had painted black. The living room was cramped and foul-smelling, the TV was broken, and the floor was barely visible beneath the detritus of Cobain's bachelor life. Half of the room was taken up by Cobain's stinking turtle aquarium, the other half by a couch which doubled as a spare bed. This was to be Dave Grohl's home for the next eight months.

'Kurt was an artist,' says Grohl, 'and as much as he was a brilliant songwriter, that passion and creativity made its way out of every pore of his body. The apartment we lived in was an experiment: you walked in and there was sculptures and paintings, there were turtles and medical books and Leonard Cohen records, it was chaos. But it was, like, "This is Kurt."'

Though he was new in town, Grohl had some familiarity with the neighbourhood in which Cobain lived. Four or five months before moving to Olympia, he had attended a party at the home of Cobain's next-door neighbour Slim Moon with his bandmates from Scream. It was not a night that held fond memories for the drummer.

'We'd played in some little art gallery space,' Grohl recalls, 'and after we played, Slim said, "There's a party over at my apartment, you guys should come." So we were like, "Cool! A party? Let's go get some beer and we'll come to this party." But our idea of a party was perhaps different from theirs …

'So we show up, the Scream guys, with a couple of racks of beer and it was Olympia, so the "party" was like kids in poodle skirts listening to Joni Mitchell. That shit was dead. And it was like "What the fuck?" And then a girl came out and played guitar and played a song that was kinda *alright*, but it wasn't good. And once that was over we were like "Fuck this!"'

Grohl went out to Scream's tour van, grabbed a cassette of the *Frizzle Fry* album by Frank Zappa-inspired San Francisco funk-rockers Primus, and cranked it up on Moon's stereo. His host and fellow partygoers could scarcely have been more mortified had he walked back into the apartment naked, crushing beer cans against his skull and helicoptering his penis.

'So I put on the Primus tape and suddenly I'm the epitome of uncool,' Grohl remembers. 'And I'm like, "What, I'm not the cool guy? You all are fucking nerds! Let's jam and get wasted!"'

'That scene ... Oh my God, they might as well have been fucking Mormons! As with most everything else in Olympia it felt like everyone was in a suspended reality that they were still 13 years old, that uncomfortable sexual tension of being that old, just past puberty. Everyone was so uncomfortable and nerdy, it just seemed odd. I told this story to Kurt the first time we spoke on the phone. I said, "Yeah, some girl came out and played some really lousy song and she wasn't any good ..." and he was like, "Yeah, that was my girlfriend, Tobi ..." I was like, "Fuck, I'm not getting this gig."'

Tobi Vail, Cobain's girlfriend, was a key player in Olympia's proudly anti-corporate indie-rock scene. The drummer in Calvin Johnson's minimalist, lo-fi rock band The Go Team, in 1990 she formed the fiercely confrontational feminist-punk band Bikini Kill with singer Kathleen Hanna, and coined the phrase 'Riot Girl' as a badge of identity for a movement of politically aware female activists starting their own fanzines, bands, record labels and galleries under the DIY punk umbrella. Alongside Calvin Johnson, his K Records co-owner Candace Pederson and a host of other young artists, musicians, activists and creatives, Vail lived at the Martin Building, Olympia's answer to Dischord House, and the hub of the Olympia scene.

'I liked Olympia, but it was sorta like Washington DC's retarded stepbrother,' says Grohl. 'There was a connection between the two cities because Calvin and Ian [MacKaye] knew each other, and maybe Calvin lived in DC for a time. But it was a weird scene. It was fun, and I would never say bad things about Olympia because some great things came from there, but I felt like an outsider for sure. The whole time I was in Seattle I felt like an outsider.

'I remember Slim Moon calling me "The Rocker". That was the first time anyone had called me that and I was like, "Really?" But I was from Scream, and Scream had long hair and tattoos, so they knew I wasn't some straight-edge Dischord kid who had gone to Georgetown University. But I'd never really thought about who I was. I wasn't a squatter and I wasn't a crusty or an indie guy – I was just a guy with long hair and a leather jacket who played the drums. But from my early days in Olympia I was "The Rocker".

'There was one band in town that I related to called Fitz of Depression: I could hang with those dudes because they were kinda scummy like me. But I was lonely. It didn't take long before I called LA and told Pete Stahl, "Hey man, I really miss you." Franz and Pete were both pretty fucking pissed off and I could understand that, but I had to do what I had to do. So I'd call down there and talk to Pete and Pete would say, "Hey Franz, do you wanna talk to Dave?" And there'd be this long silence and then Pete would say, "Yeah, he doesn't really want to talk to you." So it was a pretty lonely time. I didn't know anybody up there. I was up there all by myself with a bunch of strangers who, to be honest, were really weird.'

'I can only guess how out of it someone like Dave would have felt in Olympia after years on the road with the partying road dogs that were Scream,' says musician, activist and founder of Simple Machines records Jenny Toomey, a DC resident who lived in the Martin Building in the summer of 1990. 'Baileys Crossroads and Olympia are not a matched pair of cities. I really love Olympia, so I don't want to seem in any way snarky, but it was simultaneously one of the coolest and most fucked-up places I have ever been. When Dave says those folks were weird … they really were. They all dressed in 1950s and '60s clothes with kitty-cat glasses, they baked pies and made apple butter, they had dance parties and made mix tapes. Everyone was in a band, everyone crafted, everyone had a fanzine, everyone was everyone else's biggest fans … even when they were not. It was all sugar and cream with the dark ripple that can only come from living in a building with sixteen to twenty apartments inhabited by a handful of artists who had all slept together, broken up, picked sides and fermented mini wars while maintaining a façade of inclusiveness, openness and revolution. It seemed fitting that the second season of *Twin Peaks* began while I was out there. That show was so Pacific Northwest, with small-town values and dark, evil secrets. That was exactly the Martin apartments.'

'Because rent was cheap and there was a lot of support for the arty, bohemian lifestyle, and to some extent people could live a very adolescent life for a long time very easily there, there was a certain Peter Pan element to Olympia,' admits Slim Moon. 'To people from other parts of the country, people in Olympia might have seemed a little naïve. But they were Peter Pans who were pushing each other to do shit. People pushed each other to excel, to make art, to be in bands, to put on shows, whatever, to do their own thing and not just be consumers. It could be elitist, and maybe there was a secret set of rules that outsiders couldn't understand, and yes, it could be a mind-fuck. But even if Dave thought that these people are all just unrealistic snot-noses, I think that that little push that the whole subculture of that town gave musicians probably rubbed off on him in some way. Kurt came to love bands like The Raincoats and The Vaselines and even Leadbelly because of Olympia – before he came to town he was listening mainly to hard, heavy music like Scratch Acid and Flipper – so Dave would never have played on songs like [Vaselines'] "Molly Lips" were it not for Olympia. And maybe those influences bled into his songwriting when he started to do his own music.'

Grohl did work on his own music while under Cobain's roof, sketching out song ideas with an acoustic guitar on the singer's four-track tape recorder. But the priority, obviously, was Nirvana. The band had rented out a rehearsal space in Tacoma, essentially a carpeted barn with a PA, and Cobain insisted they practise every day. Grohl soon settled into his new routine, and in Tacoma new songs began to take shape.

'My day would start about three or four in the afternoon,' says Grohl. 'It was winter in the Northwest, and we'd wake up when the sun was going down. We would go to the AM/PM and buy corn dogs and cigarettes. Then we would go up to Tacoma and rehearse in the barn until about midnight, then drive back down to Olympia.

Lounge act

'We'd always start rehearsals with a jam, an open, free-form jam, and a lot of the songs came from that. At the time we were really experimenting with dynamic, with the quiet verse/loud chorus thing. A lot of it was derivative of Pixies and Sonic Youth. You just knew when the chorus was supposed to get bigger, and you just knew the point of the song where just when you think you can't take it any higher you *do* take it one step higher. From that came songs like "Drain You" and "Smells Like Teen Spirit". I didn't really think that much of "Teen Spirit" at first. I thought it was just another one of the jams that we were doing; we had so many jams like that, that we'd record onto a boombox tape and then lose the cassette and lose the song forever. But "Teen Spirit" was one we kept coming back to because the simple guitar lines were so memorable. That song definitely established that quiet/loud dynamic that we fell back on a lot of the time. And it became that one song that personifies the band.'

Grunge's national anthem actually started out as a cute little joke at Kurt Cobain's expense. Its title came from a phrase Bikini Kill vocalist Kathleen Hanna (whom Grohl briefly dated before Jennifer Finch) had graffitied on Cobain's bedroom wall: 'Kurt Smells Like Teen Spirit'. Cobain thought the phrase carried a certain poetry, alluding to the rebellious attitude he'd carried over from adolescence, but Hanna was in fact teasingly observing that Nirvana's front man was so smitten with her bandmate Tobi Vail that he was now marked with the scent of Vail's favourite deodorant. The song itself was written in anger in the weeks after Vail dumped Cobain in November 1990. Though laced with ennui, dissatisfaction, resignation and awkwardness, at its core lies a confused young man's heartbreak over a girl who's '*over-bored and self-assured*'. An early version of the song contained the lyric '*Who will be the King and Queen of the outcasted teens?*' Cobain had rather hoped it would be him and his hip, sassy and rather brilliant girlfriend. Just prior to the couple breaking up he had asked Grohl to help him ink a DIY K Records logo on his arm to impress Vail; now, in freshly penned new songs such as 'Lounge Act' and 'Drain You', he lamented the power his ex held over him. These scars would not heal so quickly.

This is a Call

As Christmas 1990 approached, Dave Grohl left his lovesick friend to return home to see his family in Virginia. In truth, he was glad to escape Olympia for a week or two: he'd taken on the role of house-husband at Pear Street, tidying up after Cobain, and even washing his clothes, so the idea of enjoying some home comforts back at Kathleen Place held a certain appeal. While back home, he also stopped over in Arlington to see his old friend Ian MacKaye.

'We were hanging out at Dischord House and Dave said, "Oh, I have a tape of the stuff we're recording," and I said, "I'd like to hear it,"' MacKaye recalls. 'So he played "Teen Spirit", just a rough mix of it. I said, "Wow, that is a fucking good song. This is going to be really popular." In 1990 my band Fugazi had put out *Repeater* which sold maybe 200,000 or 250,000 copies and Nirvana had sold about 40,000–50,000 copies of *Bleach*, so when I said this would be popular I was thinking it could sell like maybe, 80–100,000 copies. I remember saying to him like, "Wow, that's going to be a hit," but I didn't mean it like a hit in the Top Ten, just a hit within our filthy mass of punks.'

J. Robbins, who'd sat in with Scream for a US tour during one of Skeeter Thompson's AWOL periods, was also in Dischord House when Grohl dropped by.

'I remember hearing "Teen Spirit" from the other room and being like, "Woah, that is good!"' he recalls. 'Dave was really proud of it, and he was all excited. Everyone at Dischord that day was like, "Wow, Dave's new band is awesome."'

As Nirvana's new songs began to take shape, so too did the background team entrusted with the task of taking the band to the next level. In November 1990 the band signed a management deal with Gold Mountain, a high-powered Los Angeles firm founded by ex-Led Zeppelin publicist Danny Goldberg and the savvy, streetwise John Silva who then, as now, looked after Sonic Youth's business affairs. In his first meeting with the band, respectful of their relationship with Sub Pop's Poneman and Pavitt, Goldberg wondered aloud if the trio might be

156

interested in remaining with the Seattle label. 'Absolutely not,' Cobain responded instantly. The die was cast.

Cobain had reason to be bullish. Butch Vig's Smart Studio demo had created a buzz among the major label A&R community, and MCA, Capitol, Charisma, Columbia and Geffen records had all expressed an interest in signing the band. Even before negotiations began, both Nirvana and their management had a preference for Geffen, then enjoying a golden period commercially thanks to the phenomenal success of rejuvenated rock legends Aerosmith, their hungry, increasingly out-of-control young protégés Guns N' Roses, leathery English cock rockers Whitesnake and Cher. Of more immediate relevance to Nirvana was the fact that Geffen A&R man Gary Gersh had recently signed Sonic Youth … and Sonic Youth had Kurt Cobain's ear.

'You can't talk about Nirvana being on Geffen without talking about Sonic Youth,' says Mark Kates, then the promotions director at Geffen, and now manager of MGMT, The Cribs and Dave Grohl favourites Mission of Burma at Fenway Recordings. 'When we signed Sonic Youth Kim Gordon very specifically said to me, "The next thing you should sign is Nirvana." I bought *Bleach* and I listened to it, and it sounded really dense; I'm not sure I even heard "About a Girl" right away. But the first time I saw them at the Kennel Club in San Francisco with Tad in February 1990 I remember thinking that what they were doing wasn't as dense as that record sounded.

'But the show that really impressed me on a number of levels was when they played at the Motor Sports Garage. A bunch of us were in Seattle for the release of The Posies' *Dear 23* album, and to see a local band play to over 1,000 people was significant. There were plenty of people there from record companies, and our conversations [with the band] started not long after that – not necessarily because of that show, but that show certainly made the case for them being a somewhat commercial proposition.'

On 30 April 1991 Nirvana formally signed with Geffen. They received an advance of $287,000. As part of the deal, a further $75,000 was given to Sub Pop as a buy-out fee. In addition the Seattle label negotiated a deal whereby they'd receive a percentage of, and their logo on, the first two DGC releases, a canny move which ultimately secured their financial survival.

Whatever he may have claimed in later years, Kurt Cobain now had his heart set on making a big mainstream rock record. At home in Olympia, he drew up a list of possible producers for *Sheep* – among them Guns N' Roses producer/engineer Bill Price, Black Crowes producer George Drakoulis, Jane's Addiction producer Dave Jerden and Steve Thompson and Michael Barbiero, who'd worked on Metallica's ... *And Justice for All* album. This was music to Geffen's ears.

At the time, every major label in America was looking for a band who could span the gap between indie/alternative rock and hard rock/ heavy metal. Elektra had The Big F, a dense, challenging noise-rock trio from Los Angeles. Epic had New Jersey's Mindfunk, a groove-rock quintet fronted by ex-Uniform Choice frontman Pat Dubar and featuring ex-Celtic Frost drummer Reed St Mark and one Jason Everman on guitar. Atlantic had Kings X, a progressive rock-tinged power trio from Springfield, Missouri. MCA had the brilliant Dave Grohl-approved prog-thrash collective Voivod from Quebec. And Geffen themselves had LA dirtbags The Nymphs, fronted by provocative livewire Inger Lorre.

The traditional narrative outlined when discussing Nirvana's success in the early '90s is that Kurt Cobain's band represented a raw, visceral, more *real* alternative to heavy metal, specifically to the Aerosmith/ Zeppelin/Kiss-inspired LA 'hair metal' bands – among them Mötley Crüe, Poison, Ratt and Guns N' Roses – who dominated MTV and rock radio playlists in the wake of the breakthrough success of Guns N' Roses' incendiary 1987 début *Appetite for Destruction*. This, certainly, is part of the story, but it's not the whole story. For those prepared to look beyond the preening poseurs of Sunset Strip, metal in America was evolving, as was its fanbase. A new breed of bands had emerged with alternative/metal sounds than owed as much to Killing Joke and Joy Division as traditional metal touchstones. Awareness of these bands was not simply confined to underground metal circles either; the American music industry served notice of the new climate by including

Lounge act

Soundgarden's *Ultramega OK* and Faith No More's platinum-selling album *The Real Thing* alongside Metallica's single 'One' (from ... *And Justice for All)* in the nominations for the Metal category of the 1990 Grammy Awards.

It was Metallica who altered the playing field. Formed in Los Angeles in 1981 by vocalist/guitarist James Hetfield and drummer Lars Ulrich, and influenced by Motörhead, the New Wave of British Heavy Metal, the Misfits and nihilistic West Coast punk, the quartet began life as front-runners of the violent, chaotic Thrash Metal scene. Developing along parallel lines to the US hardcore scene, Thrash was a movement in which angry, alienated kids sang aggressive, anti-social songs to, for and about other angry, alienated kids, an underground community powered by fanzines, the trading of badly dubbed cassette tapes and a word-of-mouth, peer-to-peer buzz which was gradually amplified from a whisper to a scream. And it was Metallica who took this ferocious, flesh-stripping sound from suburban garages into the mainstream ... on their own terms. If, as Kurt Cobain defined it, punk meant 'musical freedom ... saying, doing and playing what you want', then by anyone's standards, in the first decade of their career, Hetfield and Ulrich's band were as 'punk' as any band on the underground circuit.

The quartet's début album *Kill 'Em All*, released in July 1983, had a relentlessly brutal kinetic force, which thrilled suburban teenage metal-heads looking for sounds darker and uglier than the pristine pyrotech-nics served up by Iron Maiden and Judas Priest. Aged 14, Dave Grohl bought the album on mail order via an advert in metal fanzine *Under the Rainbow*, and it soon became a soundtrack to his misadventures with Jimmy Swanson: 'I still listen to *Kill 'Em All* once a week,' he confessed 25 years later. In March 1986, Metallica's third album, the peerless *Master of Puppets*, gatecrashed the *Billboard* Top 30 and began a steady climb to one million worldwide sales without a single, a video or any significant above-the-radar media support at all. So anticipated was the band's self-titled 1991 album – known to fans as 'The Black Album' on account of its none-more-black artwork – that on 3 August 1991 their record label Vertigo hired Manhattan's legendary Madison Square Garden sports and entertainment complex to preview its twelve tracks over the venue's massive PA system to anyone who cared to listen. As the opening notes of the album's crunching opening track 'Enter Sandman' spilled across the arena, some 14,000 Metallica fans were in their seats to hear it; among them sat confirmed fans Kurt Cobain and Chris Novoselic. Within the record industry, heavy metal fans might have been regarded as uncouth, unclean and unsophisticated, but their passion, loyalty and intense devotion to their music were undeniable ... as was their financial muscle. There was a growing awareness within the industry that this was a demographic ripe for exploitation.

In 1990 no new band looked better placed to straddle the alternative rock/heavy metal divide than Geffen's politicised art-rockers Warrior Soul. Fronted by Detroit-born motormouth Kory Clarke and mentored by Metallica's hugely powerful management company Q Prime, the band's début album *Last Decade, Dead Century*, screamed on behalf of the disillusioned and disenfranchised. In April 1990, within one month of that album hitting the streets, Clarke was on the cover of *Kerrang!* magazine – then, as now, the world's biggest and most influential rock/ metal magazine – with his band being hailed as 'the hottest new band you'll hear all year!' Ultimately, record company mismanagement and Clarke's stubborn refusal to play industry games conspired against them, but lessons were learned in the process: by the time Nirvana inked their contract with the label, new strategies were in place and sussed, indie-savvy personnel such as Kates, ex-SST salesman Ray Farrell and former music journalist-turned-marketing manager Robert Smith had been added to the staff. There was a feeling in the company that if Nirvana could connect with what Kates calls the 'straightahead hard rock people' via traditional channels such as LA's influential KNAC radio and MTV's *Headbangers' Ball* then the band had a decent shot at matching or even surpassing the 200,000 sales racked up by Sonic Youth's major-label début *Goo*.

If the suits at Geffen required a template for such a campaign, they only had to look at the success achieved by another Seattle rock band, Alice in Chains, on Columbia records. Often written out of the history of Seattle rock – largely, one suspects, because neither Sub Pop, the hip

Lounge act

English music weeklies nor staffers at *The Rocket* could take any credit whatsoever for their breakthrough – the brooding, narcotically damaged quartet had shifted a cool 500,000 copies of their début album *Facelift* by the end of 1990 thanks to one killer hit single (the hypnotic 'Man in the Box') and a relentless touring campaign which saw them support acts as varied as Iggy Pop, Poison, Slayer and Van Halen. While much more overtly metal, and infinitely less 'credible', than Nirvana, Alice in Chains, like Soundgarden before them, established that there was a genuine market for 'alternative' rock, and helped kick down doors for the 'Seattle Sound' at college radio, rock radio and MTV alike. Anyone who says differently simply wasn't paying attention.

~

On 17 April 1991 Nirvana booked a last-minute afternoon show at the tiny OK Hotel club in Seattle with Bikini Kill and Dave Grohl's friends Fitz of Depression. Kurt Cobain's first words to the packed room were 'Hello, we're major-label corporate rock sell-outs.' Behind his kit, Dave Grohl couldn't help but laugh: the show had been arranged solely for the purpose of raising petrol money for the hard-up band's imminent trip to Los Angeles to record their new album.

Forty-five minutes into his band's set, Cobain introduced a new song. 'This song,' he said, 'is called "Smells Like Teen Spirit".'

The song clearly wasn't quite finished. Cobain sang the same lyric (*'Come out and play, make up the rules …'*) at the beginning of each of the three verses and fumbled his way inelegantly through an awkward guitar solo based on the song's melody line. But the manner in which 'Teen Spirit' switched from lilting nursery rhyme verses into its explosive, widescreen choruses sucked the air right out of the room. Before the song's second chorus had kicked in, crowd surfers were launching themselves at the stage from every corner of the room.

'The audience,' Dave Grohl recalls succinctly, 'went nuts. I don't know if it was the rhythm or the melody but people got caught on it pretty quick.'

Standing at the back of the club, Sub Pop's Jonathan Poneman looked on in disbelief at the force of nature his band had become.

'I remember going, "This is a really good song,"' Poneman told journalist Carrie Borzillo. 'And it's just cruising along and it's like, "Wow, this is a really catchy verse." And then it comes to the chorus and everyone went, "Oh my God, this is one of the greatest choruses of any song I've ever heard in my life!" I remember standing in the back of the room and looking around and there was this feeling of "What *is* this?"'

Sub Pop's publicist Nils Bernstein was also present that afternoon. Interviewed in 2004 for the *Classic Albums* series, he remembered the gig as a landmark in Nirvana's career to date, and a thrilling glimpse into their future.

'It was a *huge* show,' he noted. 'I remember seeing it, and it was like, "Okay, now it's all over, now they're actually writing huge, amazing songs."'

The man tasked with committing those 'huge, amazing' songs to tape, much to his own surprise, was Butch Vig. The producer was finishing up work on Smashing Pumpkins' *Gish* album in Madison when he received a call from Cobain asking if he was free to produce Nirvana's new album. As Cobain had crossed out every name on his shortlist of potential 'name' producers, his call to Vig was less a request than a demand: Geffen had already booked a studio – Sound City, in Van Nuys, Los Angeles, an area better known for churning out pornographic movies – and the band was due to begin tracking in just five days. After accepting the commission, Vig asked to hear the band's most recent material, and Cobain duly sent over a boombox recording Nirvana had made during one of their rehearsal sessions in a Tacoma barn.

'It sounded *terrible* because it was just completely distorted,' Vig recalls. 'But in the middle of all the white noise I could hear the "*Hello hello hello*" part of "Teen Spirit" and I could hear "Come As You Are" and it sounded great. After the first song I remember Kurt yelling into the boombox, "We have a new drummer, he's the best fucking drummer in the world!" and then there was a cymbal crash. I laughed … but as it turned out, he was right.'

In the final week of April, Grohl and Cobain left Olympia for the eighteen-hour drive down the I-5 highway to Los Angeles in Cobain's

Lounge act

Datsun B210; Chris and Shelli went ahead of them in their Volkswagen van. Within twenty minutes Grohl and Cobain were forced to pull over as the Datsun's engine was overheating. Ten minutes later they were on the side of the highway again, refilling the radiator. This process was repeated approximately every fifteen minutes. After five hours on the road, the pair had made it only as far as Oregon: 'It was like a nightmare where you're running but getting further away,' Grohl recalled. After calling Novoselic from a payphone, they made the decision to go back to Tacoma to get their Dodge van from outside the bassist's home. The journey back took just as long.

'We were so pissed off we pulled into a quarry and stoned the fucking car for half an hour,' Grohl recalled in his interview segment for the *Classic Albums* series. 'We busted out the windows … left it in front of Chris's house and then got the van and drove down.'

The band were booked into the Oakwood apartments, near Sound City, for the duration of their stay in Los Angeles: 'We called it "The Cokewoods",' recalls Vig, 'because it's where all the wannabe actors and rock bands stayed.' Fellow residents included the Swedish rock band Europe – in LA to record their *Prisoners in Paradise* album – and much amusement was had by Nirvana in the days ahead as they sat drinking cheap beer by the complex's pool, watching the big-haired, Speedos-clad Swedes frolicking with actresses in barely-there bikinis. But there was work to be done too. Before decamping to Sound City Vig booked the band into a rehearsal space in North Hollywood so he could hear the new songs properly and work on honing arrangements. The first song Nirvana chose to air for the producer was 'Smells Like Teen Spirit'.

'I remember pacing around the room going, "Holy shit, this sounds so fucking good."' recalls Vig. 'I said, "Wow, that sounded great, can you play it again?" Dave didn't have any mics on his kit, and Kurt and Chris had their amps at stun volume, but it just still sounded *perfect*. I called their manager and said, "I think we only need like two or three days of rehearsal, I don't want to burn them out." It was one of those things where you get out of the way, don't overthink it, go in and record *now*.

'That was the first chance I had to meet Dave. Chris had told me his name but I didn't know who he was or who Scream were; I didn't meet him until the day I flew into LA. But he just took those songs completely over the top. He was rock solid time-wise and he just hit the drums like a motherfucker. He's the best rock drummer I know, hands down. He really locked Chris and Kurt together; those songs are really powerful and a lot of that has to do with his drumming because he's just *on* it.'

Nirvana began recording at Sound City on 2 May 1991. The studio had a rich history: Fleetwood Mac had recorded tracks for their 1977 album *Rumours* there, and gold and platinum discs from the Jackson 5, Dio, Cheap Trick, Foreigner and legendary stunt king Evel Knievel lined its walls. It had a big live room, a vintage Neve mixing desk and its rates, by Hollywood standards, were cheap: the band were charged $500 a day from the album's allocated $65,000 budget.

Grohl opted to rent a drum kit for the recording session. On 2 May he hired a Tama Artstar II kit with a 16 by 24 inch bass drum, a 12 by 15 inch rack tom and a 16 by 18 floor tom from Drum Doctors on Sherman Way in North Hollywood. He also snapped up a brass Black Beauty snare drum, the heaviest snare drum in the shop, nicknamed 'The Terminator'. Metallica's Lars Ulrich had used a Black Beauty on *Master of Puppets* and Def Leppard's Rick Allen had used one on *Pyromania:* for Grohl, this was very much a luxury item.

Kurt Cobain's sole instruction to Butch Vig as the band began the session was crystal clear: 'I want to sound heavy,' he told the producer. The band would warm up for takes by hammering through versions of Zeppelin and Aerosmith standards; Grohl hit the drums so hard that he had to change the skins every other song. But the recording process was largely quick and painless. Vig would arrive at Sound City around lunchtime, and the band would bowl in around three in the afternoon; recording bass and drums first, they'd nail the basic tracks for two or three songs per day, and exit the studio around 11 p.m., leaving Vig to patch up the occasional bum note. Cobain was initially reluctant to lay down more than one guitar track or vocal per song – as with his very first recording session at his aunt Mari's house he was keen to keep things 'pure' – but Vig cajoled him into doubling up on parts by pointing out that John Lennon double-tracked his parts on The Beatles' albums.

'It was really fun making that record,' the producer says. 'There was no pressure. They'd just got an advance, so they finally had some money to go out and buy some records or buy another guitar … and they liked to party. Sometimes after the session they'd go out to Venice Beach in Santa Monica and take mushrooms or sit up and drink beer and listen to Beatles records and watch the sun come up. They were having fun, man. I could still see that Kurt would slip into these manic depressive moments where he would just sit in the corner and shut down for a while, and that happened at least once a day at some point: he would fall into this black hole and eventually he'd pull himself out. Sometimes he'd be recording and he'd just put his guitar down and leave and walk into the other room, and then an hour and a half later he'd walk back in and go, "Okay, cool, let's play," and they'd start playing again. So I had to sorta deal with those mood swings, but for the most part they were having a gas. Dave was very funny, he cracked up all the time.'

Recording at Sound City gave Grohl a new perspective on Los Angeles. He bought his first motorbike from a guy called Jeff for $800, and rode it around the Hollywood Hills at night, taking in the beauty of the city and dreaming of being in a successful band. Being back in LA also gave him the opportunity to reconnect with the Stahl brothers. Pete Stahl dropped by Sound City one afternoon and was blown away by the rough mixes he heard. Franz Stahl meanwhile assisted the band in their pursuit of 'fun': in an unsent letter in his journals Cobain wrote of scoring drugs at the Tropicana with Grohl and Stahl and almost stumbling upon a confrontation between the LAPD and local gangbangers. 'I don't remember that incident,' Stahl laughed when I mentioned it to him in 2010. 'I remember other incidents at the French Cottage in Hollywood, which was a real crack hotel. Had I been with Kurt at the Tropicana scoring drugs I was obviously very drunk and high …'

On the afternoon of 18 May, Vig found himself sitting alone at Sound City. When he called John Silva to enquire about the whereabouts of his band, he was informed that Novoselic had just been released from jail. The previous evening the producer had called time on the session early so that he and the band could attend a Butthole Surfers/Red Kross/L7 show at the Hollywood Palladium. Novoselic, who had celebrated his 26th birthday the previous evening, had driven the band to the show in his Volkswagen van, chugging from a bottle of Jack Daniels as he drove. After losing his friends at the show, Vig took a taxi back to his hotel; the Nirvana boys were not so smart. At around 2 a.m. that morning the LAPD pulled Novoselic's van over as he attempted to drive back over Laurel Canyon; the bassist was arrested for driving under the influence of alcohol and taken to jail. High on mushrooms, drunk and disorientated, Grohl and Cobain were left to walk seven miles back to their apartment. 'They were pretty wasted that night,' Vig recalls. 'Thank God nobody was hurt.'

The night was significant for another reason: it was the first real opportunity Kurt Cobain had to hang out with his new crush, Courtney Love, the 26-year-old lead singer and guitarist of LA-based alternative rock band Hole. Love, born Courtney Michelle Harrison, was best friends with Dave Grohl's girlfriend Jennifer Finch – the two had played together in a band called Sugar Baby Doll in the mid '80s – and a rising star on the indie rock scene: Sonic Youth's Kim Gordon had just recently finished recording the band's ferocious début album *Pretty on the Inside*. Love and Cobain had met before, when Nirvana played Portland's Satyricon club in January 1990, and there was a mutual attraction between the pair. Upon spotting Cobain at the Hollywood Palladium, Love punched him in the stomach and wrestled him to the floor, a primitive, but strangely effective, courtship ritual. Cobain, high on mushrooms and self-medicating with cough syrup, stayed under her spell for the remainder of the night.

Courtney Love was not an easy woman to ignore. Loud-mouthed, confrontational, sharp and sassy, the 26-year-old singer was, quite simply, a force of nature. Like Cobain, Love was the product of a broken home and an itinerant childhood. The daughter of former Grateful Dead tour manager Hank Harrison and therapist Linda Carroll, Love had bounced around between Los Angeles, Portland, Oregon and New Zealand in her early childhood, finally settling down with a friend of her mother's in Eugene, Oregon. There she fell in with a crowd of tough teenage girls and cultivated a reputation as a trouble-maker, a reputation she has yet to shed.

'I found my inner bitch and ran with her,' she cheerfully informed *Spin* magazine in 1995.

Love and her 'inner bitch' clocked up some serious air miles. She worked as a stripper in Japan, studied at Dublin's prestigious Trinity College, hung out with Julian Cope and Echo and the Bunnymen in Liverpool, fronted an early version of Faith No More in San Francisco ('She caused a whirlwind of shit,' bassist Bill Gould once told me approvingly. 'She was a magnet for chaos') and landed a bit part in British film director Alex Cox's *Sid and Nancy* in New York, all before her 22nd birthday. In 1989 she wound up back in Los Angeles on a mission to put together a band influenced by Sonic Youth, Big Black and Fleetwood Mac; as Nirvana were extricating themselves from their Sub Pop contract the label were making plans to release Hole's second single, the typically abrasive *Dicknail*. After hanging out with Love at the Palladium, Cobain began telling his friends that he had just met the coolest girl in the world. Five months would pass before the pair crossed paths again; from that day forth, their lives would be forever intertwined.

By the beginning of June, Nirvana's album, now titled *Nevermind*, was in the can. The recording budget had doubled from Geffen's original $65,000 estimate to over $120,000, but in everyone's opinion this was money well spent. As Geffen executives began to appear in the studio to hear Butch Vig's rough mixes of the album, word was already spreading around Los Angeles that Nirvana had created a monster. Grohl's old friend Barrett Jones was among those who heard early mixes of the record: he left Sound City 'blown away' by what he had heard.

'I remember getting chills just listening to playbacks in the studio,' he says. 'I thought it sounded so good. I told Kurt in the studio that they'd be on the cover of *Rolling Stone* before the year was out ... and I was right.'

'John Silva and I went to the studio to hear it when the mixing was finished at Scream in the Valley,' says Mark Kates. 'And it sounded like a really great, powerful, complete album. You're never going to get any of us to say that we could foresee what was going to happen – anyone who says that would not be telling the truth – but we felt they had accomplished the absolute maximum of what could have been expected from them.'

'As we were mixing the album, Chris and Kurt and I would take a tape of the songs and just drive around the Hollywood Hills listening to it,' Grohl recalled a decade on. 'That was something else. Like when "Smells Like Teen Spirit" first came through the speakers: the only demos we'd done of that song were on a boombox – we were used to hearing it sound like a shitty bootleg … all of a sudden you have Butch Vig making it sound like *Led Zeppelin IV*.'

Amid all the positivity surrounding the recording there was but one dissenting voice. Somewhat awkwardly for Dave Grohl, that voice belonged to his girlfriend.

'When I was in the studio hearing how those songs were represented I didn't like it,' admits Jennifer Finch. 'I thought the songs had got very watered down and very commercial. Dave and Kurt and I went to the first Lollapolooza festival together and we listened to the first version of the album together, Butch's mix of the record, and I was like, "Wow!" I don't think I said anything negative, but I was like, "Wow, this is really, really different," with that weird smile on my face. It's hard when you're dating somebody, you don't wanna be "the girlfriend that has the opinion", you know? But I wasn't a big fan of it at all, and I couldn't totally hide that. I thought that maybe they'd gone too commercial too quickly.'

'But, of course, at that point we didn't think *anything* was going to happen with the record,' says Grohl. 'It was like releasing a Jesus Lizard record or something. I thought "Teen Spirit" was another good song, and it might get on *120 Minutes* and allow us to tour with Sonic Youth or maybe headline Brixton Academy, but no one thought it was a hit single because a hit single was just unimaginable. There was no world domination ambition. Because that just couldn't happen. That wasn't *allowed* to happen.'

Smells like teen spirit

The promoter said, 'That guy is gonna come back with his friends and he's going to fucking kill you, so stay in here, and when I give you the secret knock, I'm gonna get you the fuck outta here and into a cab.' So we run outside: Kurt gets into the cab, Chris gets into the cab … and here comes the guy with all his friends so the cab pulls off …

Dave Grohl

Dave Grohl stands on the stage of Boston's Venus de Milo nightclub, choking back laughter as he watches Kurt Cobain smear thick white lard onto his best friend's bare ass. Standing on a plastic Twister mat, Chris Novoselic tugs his tiny black briefs back up over his skinny hips, and attempts to regain his dignity, or as much dignity as a six foot seven inch man wearing only his pants, a pair of white tube socks, half a tub of unctuous vegetable oil fat and a broad smile can hope to muster. Waiting to interview Nirvana for their first ever TV appearance, the nice lady from MTV isn't quite sure where to look.

'So what's going on here?' she asks breezily, as Novoselic begins massaging the Crisco vegetable fat into his nipples. 'What are you doing here?'

'We're playing Crisco Twister,' says Nirvana's bassist, as if this were the most natural thing in the world, as if this were standard practice for new bands being interviewed on MTV.

Spotting Grohl sniggering out of shot, Novoselic breaks away from his interviewer and hurls a fistful of lard across the stage in his direction. When Grohl gleefully lobs a wad of goo right back at the near-naked bassist, MTV's exasperated director has seen enough. At his signal, the cameras stop turning over and the microphone is cut dead. It's 23 September 1991 and Nirvana's first MTV interview is over before it has really begun.

A less patient man than Mark Kates might have thrown in the towel with his new charges at this point. Nirvana's stay in Boston was not exactly stress-free for Geffen's head of alternative music promotion. It was Kates's decision to schedule the first US date of the band's North American tour at the 1,000-capacity Axis club in his hometown that evening. The gig, at which Nirvana were to be sandwiched between Chicago's Smashing Pumpkins and local alternative rockers Bullet LaVolta, was a birthday bash for Boston radio station WFNX, and the Seattle band's participation was intended as Geffen's 'thank you' to station director Kurt St Thomas, Nirvana's first and biggest champion at radio. But upon learning that the WFNX gig was to be a 21+ event, Cobain promptly demanded that Kates arrange a second show at the venue, an all-ages gig, the following night, giving the promoters just 24 hours to shift 1,000 tickets.

That same evening Cobain met local singer-songwriter Mary Lou Lord at a Melvins gig at Boston's Rat club and – without flagging his intentions up to Grohl, Novoselic or Kates – promptly decided to blow out all his scheduled promotional duties (including a hugely important interview with the *New York Times*'s Karen Schoemer) so he could spend the day hanging out with his cute new friend. On the eve of the release of *Nevermind*, the album he hoped would make him a star, Cobain's disengagement from the process represented a pointed act of disobedience towards his new corporate paymasters, his own little foot-stamping punk rock declaration of independence.

Still, any irritation Kates might have harboured towards Cobain was swept away the moment Nirvana took the stage at the Axis on 23 September. Kates knew Nirvana were good, but their performance this night was something else – explosive, chaotic, life-affirming, transcendent. As wave after wave of stage divers tumbled through air stale with perspiration, Cobain slashed wildly at his guitar strings and howled like his battered Converse trainers were on fire. '*With the lights out, it's less dangerous. Here we are now, entertain us ...*'

At the climax of the set, Monty Lee Wilkes, Nirvana's tour manager, walked past Kates shaking his head.

'This tour,' he said, 'is going to get crazy.'

~

Nirvana began road-testing their new album just days after leaving Sound City. On 10 June 1991 the trio began an eight-date West Coast tour supporting J. Mascis's Dinosaur Jr, a group Cobain held in high regard, and one from whom his own band had drawn inspiration. But from the tour's opening night at the Gothic Theater in Denver, Colarado, it was painfully evident that the majority of those in attendance were more excited about seeing the opening band than the headliners.

'They were smoking Dinosaur Jr every night, just blowing them away,' recalls Franz Stahl, who'd landed a job teching for the trio on these dates. 'By the time Dinosaur Jr came on more than half the audience would be gone, people didn't even hang around.'

'It was prior to *Nevermind* coming out and so the band had all these cassettes with them with different mixes of all the songs, and they'd listen to them throughout the trip and talk among themselves about this, that and the other. I'd just be sitting listening to these songs going, "God, this shit is *great*." And Kurt would be going, "Er, it's alright ..." To be honest, I don't recall "Teen Spirit", that wasn't one of the songs that I thought was going to blow up, but I was like, "Guys, this tape is insane, this is amazing!" They'd be like, "Yeah, yeah ..." But I could see it, I could just see it. I'd talk to my brother and go, "Dude, this is going to be *huge*."'

'I heard "Teen Spirit" for the first time in that stinky van too,' says Nirvana sound engineer Craig Montgomery. 'We listened to it on the boombox and I remember that when it broke down into the quiet, chiming guitar part right after the intro, I said, "Wow ... Pixies." And Kurt said, "Do you think it sounds too much like the Pixies?" I said "No, no one is going to pick up on that ..." But it was kinda a logical progression from what they were doing live: Kurt was trying to incorporate more of that pop influence into the songs because that's what he was into at the time. After having spent a European tour in the van listening to Abba it wasn't surprising to me that more of a pop sensibility would show up in the music.'

Gold Mountain's Danny Goldberg saw Nirvana play live for the first time when the tour rolled up to the Hollywood Palladium in Los Angeles on 14 June. The music industry veteran remembers being 'completely overwhelmed' by his first sighting of his new act.

'Kurt had a mystical and powerful connection with the audience that took my breath away,' he recalled in his modestly titled memoir *Bumping into Geniuses*. 'After years of increasing cynicism about what rock and roll had turned into, I felt the naïve excitement of a teenager. Somehow Kurt Cobain was able to be both on the stage and in the audience, rocking the crowd out and yet also among them. It was only then that I realised that Kurt Cobain was not just a smart, quirky rock artist but also a true genius.'

'There are certain frontmen that don't even consider that concept for one second,' says Dave Grohl. 'There are some people – whether that's Ian Curtis or Bob Dylan or Kurt – whose message and lyrics and personality truly is bigger than a guitar and a stage and an audience. And that can be the most powerful thing. Some frontmen have a real powerful physical presence, like Henry Rollins or H.R. from Bad Brains, and then you have people that just have a huge emotional presence. I think Kurt had an incredibly deep and powerful emotional presence that made it so that he didn't have to take one step in any direction, because the sound of his voice and the intention of what he was doing onstage was enough to blow an arena full of people away. Coming from the hardcore scene where most of the singers were just fucking insane – they were on top of your head and doing backflips and they were bleeding and covered in glass and peanut butter – to see someone that could just stand and scream his throat raw and have that be enough was really something. I'd never been in a band with someone like that. And I never will be again, I'm sure.'

'It's funny how oblivious they all were to what was about to happen,' says Pete Stahl. 'I remember sitting with Dave and Chris in their van outside the Hollywood Palladium and talking about the record getting ready to come out and they were saying, "Wow, we'll never sell enough records to pay off this studio budget." But you could tell something was going on. From the time I watched Kurt sing in the studio there was definitely something going on.

'The next time they came back to LA, our band Wool opened up for them at the Roxy. And that was like a madhouse. I remember loading our gear out and someone came up to me and offered me like $200 for my wristband. I was like, "What the fuck is going on?" Things like that just didn't happen in our world.'

On 17 August, two days after the Nirvana/Wool show at the Roxy, Nirvana shot a video for *Nevermind*'s first single, 'Smells Like Teen Spirit', at GMT Studios in Culver City, California. Loosely based upon two of Kurt Cobain's favourite films, the Ramones' *Rock and Roll High School* and cult teen rebellion flick *Over the Edge*, the concept of the video, which involved the band lip-synching in front of an anarchic 'pep rally from Hell', was all the singer's own work. Cobain sketched out every single shot for the video in advance of the shoot: as an artist, he understood the power of visual imagery and the impact it could have.

'I saw this movie *Over the Edge*,' he told *Melody Maker* journalists the Stud Brothers in 1993. 'I remember leaving that theatre and almost everyone who was in there came running out screaming their heads off and breaking windows and vandalising and wanting to get high. It totally affected them and influenced them. It may not have been the intention of the person who made the movie, and it is a great movie, but that's what happened.'

With his meticulously plotted storyboard for the 'Smells Like Teen Spirit' video, Cobain's own intention was simple: he wanted nothing less than to provoke that same level of mayhem in every suburban neighbourhood in America.

Geffen chose unknown director Samuel Bayer, a recent graduate from New York's School of Visual Arts, to helm the promo. It was his first gig in the music industry, a fact that soon became transparent even to Dave Grohl, himself a video virgin.

'The director had a loud bullhorn thing,' the drummer recalled to *Newsweek* in 1999, 'and he was trying to explain the concept to the crowd, and saying, "Okay now, in the first verse you're supposed to look bored and complacent and unhappy. Just sit in your seats and tap your foot and look, you know, distraught, whatever." And then by the end of the song they're supposed to be tearing the place to shreds. When they got to the first chorus the crowd was completely out of control, and the director was screaming at the top of his lungs for everyone to fucking calm down and be cool, or they'll get kicked out. So it was pretty hilarious actually, seeing this man trying to control these children who just wanted to destroy.'

As the shoot dragged on, tensions on the soundstage mounted. Cobain had made no secret of his desire to direct the video himself, and as he swallowed mouthfuls of Jim Beam whiskey between takes, watching Bayer strut around like a bargain basement Cecil B. DeMille, his mood got uglier and his frustration more tangible. When he screamed his lyrics into the rookie director's lens, his anger was all too real. At the end of the evening, sensing that his own agitation was being mirrored among the increasingly restless teens watching the shoot, Cobain encouraged the extras to come down from the bleachers to thrash around his band as if they were at a real punk rock show. Cue mayhem.

In the edit suite, Cobain reasserted his independence by changing the ending of Bayer's cut of the video. Against the director's wishes, he inserted a closing sequence of his own face leering into the camera in close-up. It was a masterstroke. Throughout the video Cobain had come across as every inch the brooding, agitated misfit, his fine features masked by his lank blond hair. But here, at the video's violent, riotous dénouement, the mischievous expression on his handsome face offered an invitation to the dance, his eyes screaming 'JOIN US!' It was an invitation that would prove irresistible.

With the 'Teen Spirit' video wrapped, Nirvana did what so many American bands do in the summer, and came to Europe for the festival season. That August the trio interspersed festival appearances at England's Reading festival, the Monsters of Spex event in Cologne and Belgium's Pukkelpop, with one-off club gigs supporting their new label mates and management stablemates Sonic Youth. On 20 August they launched their European tour with an appearance at Sir Henry's in Cork; the following day they played the 500-capacity Top Hat club in Dún Laoghaire, a small seaside town south of Dublin. Grohl and Cobain were thrilled to be in Ireland: on his first morning in the country Dave Grohl phoned his mother Virginia and said, 'Mom, all the women here look like you!'

The Top Hat show was the pick of the two Irish dates. Twenty years on, one attendee, Colin Fennelly, then a schoolboy at St Kieran's College in Kilkenny, later the bassist of Kerbdog, whose 1998 album *On the Turn* stands up as one of the finest alternative rock releases of the decade, has vivid memories of the evening.

'Most of our gang were only there to see Sonic Youth,' he says, 'but my friend Cormac and I had been listening to *Bleach* in our house in Dublin over the previous year, and "Negative Creep" in particular was a big hit with us. We managed to get to the very front of the crowd with ease for the start of Nirvana's set, but as soon as they kicked into "School", their opening number, the whole crowd began to surge forward. I remember being blown away by the energy of the band, especially Dave: the way he just threw his body at the drum kit stays with me still. I can't remember much about Sonic Youth that night: afterwards the Nirvana set was all we could talk about."

'It was the first time I had seen an audience so enthusiastic,' Grohl told the *Irish Independent* in 2011. 'They were going fucking bananas. And that was just before *Nevermind* came out. I hate to say it was the calm before the storm because it was pretty fucking insane, but if you can imagine that being the calm, try imagining the storm.'

༒

Nevermind was released in the US on 24 September 1991, and one day earlier in the UK. 'There will not be a better straight ahead rock album than *Nevermind* released all year,' Everett True predicted in his *Melody Maker* review of the album. In truth, there would not be a better straight ahead rock album than *Nevermind* released all decade.

This is a Call

Twenty years after its release, Nirvana's second album remains an indecently thrilling body of work, a collection of breath-robbing, heart-pounding songs infused with such edge-of-darkness desperation, soul, humanity and raw, inchoate anger that it seems to stop the clocks. At once antagonistic and approachable, *Nevermind* distils four decades of rock 'n' roll history into twelve deathless shards of noise – part pop, part punk, part grandstanding classic rock – which switch back and forth between apathy and anger, self-loathing and sensitivity, humour and horror with such dizzying, quicksilver agility that the listener is never quite afforded comfort or security within its embrace. And yet one is drawn in time after time after time.

The first 'side' of the album is pretty much untouchable in critical terms, with 'Smells Like Teen Spirit' opening the record like an adrenaline spike to the heart. Cobain's attempt to nail the perfect pop song, Nirvana's most iconic anthem fuses Pixies' whisper/scream, soothe/slaughter dynamic and four breezeblock 'Louie Louie' powerchords in a lightning bolt pop moment which age cannot wither. 'In Bloom' follows, latterly interpreted as a condescending swipe at knucklehead jocks who'd lustily sing along to Nirvana's *'pretty songs'* though originally conceived as a sincere(ish) tribute to Dylan Carlson, it mixes nursery rhyme melodies with a lurching, seasick sway, driven by Grohl's head-caving rhythms. 'Come As You Are', Cobain's open-armed invitation to the marginalised and misunderstood, those 'outcast teens' he instinctively empathised with, appropriates the bass riff from Killing Joke's apocalyptic 'Eighties' for one of the album's most infectious hooks: from its subject matter to its playground melodies, it's the album's most unashamed tilt at an underground anthem.

Track four, 'Breed', originally demoed as 'Immodium' at Smart Studios, is darker and more gnarled, mixing scorched-earth guitar riffs with a thunderous, relentless rhythmic barrage which would weaken the most muscular air drummer. 'Lithium', originally mooted as the album's first single, is a fragmented take on Cobain's unhappy adolescence, piling disquieting images of depression, loneliness, insecurity and insanity against one of the sweetest melody lines on the album. On record, the song lopes along on a deceptively simple mid-pocket groove, but nailing the tempo proved to be a challenge for Grohl. In the end, the frustrated drummer reluctantly agreed to record to a click track for the sake of expediency, though the compromise rankled: 'When you tell a drummer "I think you should use a click track" that's basically like stabbing them in the heart with a fucking rusty knife,' he later commented.

The heartbreaking, graphic 'Polly' closes out the album's opening half. Sung in the first person from the rapist's perspective, it's an uncomfortable, unsettling listen, but arguably the most powerful track on the album. First demoed in Madison with Cobain playing a five-string junk shop guitar, its stark, minimalist vibe was considered impossible to recreate at Sound City, so the original recording became the only track from Nirvana's Smart Studio demo to be transferred intact to *Nevermind*.

If side two of *Nevermind* can't quite sustain the drama and drive of the album's opening 23½ minutes, it's not without strokes of genius. Recorded in just one take, 'Territorial Pissings' is a rudimentary, frenetic punk rock blitz upon male machismo, a theme which had obsessed Cobain lyrically since the Fecal Matter demo. 'Drain You', Cobain's bitter reflection on the break-up of his relationship with Tobi Vail, was originally conceived as a track for a Cobain/Grohl/Dale Crover side-band called The Retards, and demoed at Crover's home in San Francisco in 1990 with Grohl playing bass; quite why Cobain originally considered it unworthy of Nirvana is a mystery, as the version captured at Sound City is one of *Nevermind*'s stand-out moments. 'Lounge Act' is also about Vail: in an unsent letter to his ex Cobain once wrote, 'I don't write songs about you, except for "Lounge Act", which I do not play, except when my wife is not around.'

'Stay Away' (demoed at Smart as 'Pay to Play') and 'On a Plain' are the album's two least self-conscious tracks; they're also arguably the weakest moments on *Nevermind*, though Cobain's sweet melody on the latter and Dave Grohl's flat-out fucked drumming on the former merit repeated listens. The album concludes not with a bang, but with a whisper, with the haunting, fragile 'Something in the Way', Cobain's factually questionable but undeniably emotive tale of living under Young

Street Bridge in Aberdeen as a homeless teenager: 'It almost killed Dave to play so quietly,' Butch Vig later noted.

Nevermind also offered up one hidden surprise – 'Endless Nameless', a thirteenth track of buckling distortion and roaring feedback culled from a free-form jam at the end of one particularly frustrating take on 'Lithium'. Towards the end of the track, a furious Cobain can be heard smashing his black Fender Stratocaster into pieces, an appropriately committed way on which to end his band's punk rock masterpiece.

In the twenty years that have passed since its release, *Nevermind* has been routinely acclaimed as one of the finest rock albums of all time. History, and the countless analytical articles devoted to its creation in the intervening years, may have robbed the disc of some of its mystery, but upon its release, like *The Stooges*, *Never Mind the Bollocks* and the *Nervous Breakdown* EP before it, this intoxicating tangle of angst, attitude, screaming guitars and fragmented lyrical riddles invited one compelling question: Who are these people and what do they want?

'I had advance tapes of *Nevermind*,' says Anton Brookes, 'and it was bizarre, because whenever I went out to a gig I'd just get mobbed by people coming up to me going, "Oh, have you got a tape of that Nirvana album?" There was such a buzz about it. People would stop me in the streets sometimes and go, "Oh my God, so-and-so played me the Nirvana album, it's incredible." On the street *everybody* was talking about it.'

'I first heard *Nevermind* on a cassette that had the first song slightly clipped,' says Charles R. Cross. 'I honestly think I made one hundred dubs of it and those dubs went out to probably thousands: years later I would talk to people who also had ended up with a dub of a tape with the clip. *Nevermind* was more than a huge leap forward: in many ways it didn't even sound like the same band that made *Bleach*. Sonically it was a world apart. But it was the songs – 'Smells Like Teen Spirit', 'Come As You Are', 'Something in the Way' – that made it. One can't say enough about what a solid album it is. It may be the single last album that appealed to multiple genre lovers, and that everyone had in their collection. There hasn't been anything like it since.'

Smells like teen spirit

'I had a cassette copy of *Nevermind* because friends that booked them during the *Bleach* era were sent the advanced cassette of the album months before it came out,' Dave Grohl's future girfriend Melissa Auf der Maur, then a 19-year-old art student in her native Montreal, remembered in an interview for *Taking Punk to the Masses*. 'I put that thing on my tape player in my apartment and I cried. I invited every single person over and said, "Listen to this. The world is changed" … I was like, "Nobody is going to listen to anything but this record, because now the world has changed."'

'When you heard the first notes of the Nirvana record you just knew, you could just tell, that it was absolutely going to change *something*,' says Pearl Jam guitarist Stone Gossard, who had helped kickstart the 'Seattle Sound' with Green River. 'It was so obvious that it was the perfect balance of totally straight rock blues and punk rock. And sonically it had nothing to do with Mötley Crüe, which was so refreshing: as much as I loved the first Mötley Crüe record, I was ready for something new.'

Early reviews of *Nevermind* were overwhelmingly positive. In his 9/10 *NME* review, writer (and future broadcaster) Steve Lamacq called it 'a record for people who like Metallica, but can't stomach their lack of melody' and predicted the album would 'stand up as a new reference point for the future post-hardcore generation'. *Kerrang!*'s Gordon Goldstein (aka former hardcore promoter/fanzine writer Mike Gitter) awarded the album a maximum KKKKK rating and hailed it as 'a brutally frank record with a wounded soul'; *Rolling Stone* was more cautious, bestowing just three stars out of a possible five on the record (though a revisionist tweak on the magazine's website now suggests *Nevermind* was granted four stars), but reviewer Ira Robbins recognised the album as a landmark release for the American rock underground.

Geffen pressed up 46,251 copies of the album in the US and 6,000 copies in the UK and hoped for the best. In truth, their focus was elsewhere: that same week Guns N' Roses' epic *Use Your Illusion I* and *Use Your Illusion II* albums débuted at numbers two and one respectively on the *Billboard* 200 with first week sales of 685,000 for the first volume and 770,000 for volume two. Compared to the nation's favourite hard rock band, Nirvana were very much a cult concern.

❧

On the morning of 24 September, as part of their promotional campaign for the record, Dave Grohl, Chris Novoselic and Mark Kates visited Newbury Comics, Boston's hippest independent record shop. They didn't see a single person pick up a copy of the new Nirvana album. 'We were expecting to see a line around the block, but there wasn't,' admits Kates. 'There was no vibe whatsoever.' The following morning the band and crew rose early, climbed into their trusty Dodge van and set out for Providence, Rhode Island to resume their tour at Club Babyhead. Among the touring party the vibe was very much business as usual.

'The tour started in Toronto at the Opera House and it seemed like a fairly typical Nirvana gig,' says Grohl. 'There were maybe 500 or 600 people there. And to me you have to remember that was like making it – going from the 32 people who would usually come to see Scream in every city to like 500 people, I considered that to be the greatest success of my entire life. The capacities of a lot of the gigs that we were playing were low – we played a place in Portland, Maine or maybe Vermont where the legal capacity was 67, like a tiny little living room of a place, and it was chaotic. But when the video hit MTV it made a big difference.'

On 30 September MTV introduced the 'Smells Like Teen Spirit' video as a 'World Premiere' on its flagship 'alternative' show *120 Minutes*. Two weeks later the video was moved into the channel's 'Buzz Bin' slot, intended to showcase new talent: artists selected for the 'Buzz Bin' could expect to have their video aired between 12 and 30 times a day. With 'Teen Spirit' also riding high on the *Billboard* Alternative, Modern Rock and Top 40 charts, it was becoming increasingly difficult to avoid the Seattle trio.

'It didn't matter what time of day or night you turned on MTV, "Teen Spirit" was on,' recalls Anton Brookes. 'You'd walk down the street and you'd hear it on the radio. You'd walk into a shop or bar and it would be blaring out. Everywhere you went it was there. It was surreal.'

'I'd graduated from college and I was at home vacuuming and I heard this riff and I'm like, "I fucking love this!"' recalls Grohl's childhood friend Tracey Bradford. 'I turned off the vacuum cleaner and turned around to the television to watch MTV and I see this long-haired guy playing the drums with a Scream T-shirt on. And I'm like, "It's fucking David Grohl! Oh my God!"'

'My band Kyuss was on tour,' recalls Queens of the Stone Age / Them Crooked Vultures frontman Josh Homme, 'and I remember seeing the video on MTV at 3 a.m. in a hotel room. I was saying, "Man, this is so good, everyone should be into this music but they're not going to be, it's not going to get played because it's too good." About a week later I realised how wrong I was …'

'The video was probably the key element in that song becoming a hit,' says Dave Grohl. 'People heard the song on the radio and they thought, "This is great," but when kids saw the video on MTV they thought, "This is cool. These guys are kinda ugly and they're tearing up their fucking high school." We were touring and we'd go back to the hotel and turn on the TV and see our video and go, "That's so funny, we're on TV, and we've just played the 9:30 Club!" or whatever. And then with the video came more people and the clubs got bigger and bigger.

'The only indication that our world was turning upside down would be when you'd get to the venue. That's when it would be, "Holy shit, these people are fucking nuts." You'd show up to a 500-capacity gig and there were 500 *extra* people there. We were still in our little bubble – we were in our van, the three of us, Chris's wife Shelli, our monitor guy Miles [Kennedy], and Monte Lee Wilkes our tour manager – and it didn't seem like anything unusual was happening until we'd get to the gig and it was fucking chaos. And we started to notice there were normal people here. We were like, "What are they doing here? That guy looks like a jock, what the fuck is he doing here?" And it was like, "Oh, maybe that video thing is attracting some … riff-raff."'

This is a Call

On 12 October 1991 *Nevermind* entered the *Billboard* album chart at number 144. That same day Butch Vig drove down to Chicago from Madison to meet up with the band at their headline show at the Metro, the same venue Cobain, Novoselic and Chad Channing had played as a support band on the eve of their Smart Studio session 18 months previously. The drummer was astonished to find around 5,000 people waiting in line for the 1,100-capacity club.

'At that point there was a huge buzz in the air,' says Vig. 'People were calling me going, "Oh my God, the Nirvana record is amazing." And I knew there was this electricity in the air, that something was going to happen for them. I took an artist friend of mine, Bill Rock, to the show and he was like, "Who's Nirvana?" I said, "They're going to be the next Beatles." Right before the band came on they were playing the end of Smashing Pumpkins' *Gish* really loud over the PA and that ended right as Nirvana walked onstage so I was double proud in a way. And the second Nirvana walked onstage it was like Beatlemania, kids were just screaming and crying, and Bill was like, "Holy shit!" He didn't know any of the songs, he just saw them play and saw the crowd reaction and he said, "This is incredible." And it was. I was thinking, "Wow, this record has really affected people."'

By coincidence, Courtney Love was also in Chicago on 12 October. Hole's lead singer had blown into the Windy City to see her on–off boyfriend Billy Corgan from Smashing Pumpkins, but following an argument with Corgan, Love elected to hook up with Babes in Toyland drummer Lori Barbero for a trip to the Metro instead. Later that evening, she and Kurt Cobain had sex for the first time. Their coupling took place in the hotel room Cobain was sharing with Dave Grohl: after unsuccessfully attempting to block out the sounds of passion emanating from the adjoining bed, Grohl crept out of his own bed and sought refuge in soundman Craig Montgomery's room. He and Cobain would never be so close again.

Smells like teen spirit

The tour rumbled on. In St Louis, Missouri, the owners of the Mississippi Nights club called in the local police after Cobain, frustrated at the band's set being interrupted time and time again by over-enthusiastic stage divers, invited the entire 500-strong audience onstage. In Lawrence, Kansas the band hung out with 'Beat' legend William Burroughs, a hero to both Kurt Cobain and Dave Grohl's father, James. But in Dallas, Texas on 19 October the tour almost came to a sudden juddering stop, when bouncers at the Trees nightclub threatened to kill the band.

'We had a lot of fun on that tour,' laughs Grohl. 'In Dallas, Kurt smashed up the monitor board that belonged to the bouncer standing in front of him, and then jumped into the crowd and hit the guy on the head. The guy's head was spilling blood and he started to beat Kurt up. And Kurt was totally fucked up. Afterwards, the promoter said, "That guy is gonna come back with his friends and he's going to fucking kill you, so stay in here, and when I give you the secret knock, I'm gonna get you the fuck outta here and into a cab." So we run outside: Kurt gets into the cab, Chris gets into the cab … and here comes the guy with all his friends so the cab pulls off … And I have to jump back into the club all by myself. Then they get stuck in traffic and some guy breaks the window. Meanwhile, some chick takes me back in her car … and she gets into a car accident. It was insane.'

Promoting their new *Every Good Boy Deserves Fudge* album, Mudhoney were also touring US clubs in October '91. The two bands' itineraries were due to converge at the end of the month, with two co-headlining shows, at the Fox Theater in Portland, Oregon on 29 October, and at the Paramount in Seattle on Hallowe'en. When Nirvana arrived in Portland, they were informed by Geffen's regional sales rep Susie Tennant that *Nevermind* had passed the 500,000 sales mark, and would now be classified as a gold record by the Recording Industry Association of America. The notion of Nirvana and Mudhoney swapping headlining duties for the tour's remaining two dates was now deemed fatuous: Nirvana would headline both shows.

The band returned to Seattle as conquering heroes. It seemed that the whole of the Northwest music community was there to greet them. Though Geffen's decision to film the show for possible future release added a certain tension to the night, Nirvana pulled off a storming nineteen-track set which left no one in any doubt that their time as local underground heroes was at an end.

'Nirvana had never played in Seattle before with expectations,' says Charles R. Cross. 'All their other concerts had been them trying to get attention. Finally they came back in October '91 and everyone came to see them expecting them to be great. And they were.'

Among the crowd at the Paramount that night were Grohl's former Mission Impossible bandmates Chris Page and Bryant Mason, who had moved to Seattle the previous summer. After the show Grohl sought the pair out, and sat chatting quietly with them as the backstage area filled up with friends, family, media and peers.

'The backstage scene was absolutely mobbed,' recalls Page. 'You could tell things were starting to fly in directions that no one had expected. Dave made some comment like, "This is so crazy." He kept saying, "It's all happening so fast … it's all happening so fast."'

∽

On 2 November 1991, as Nirvana headed over to Europe for six weeks of headline shows, *Nevermind* broke into the top 40 of the *Billboard 200*, hitting number 35. The following week the album moved up to number 17. One week later it was at number 9: the next it sat at number 4. In the two months since its release the album had now sold 1.2 million copies in the US alone.

This unexpected success ensured Nirvana were now making headlines outside of the pages of music magazines. As *Nevermind* climbed up the charts, the *New York Times* dedicated the front page of its business section to an investigative analysis of Geffen's 'orchestration' of Nirvana's rise. 'We didn't do anything,' admitted DGC president Ed Rosenblatt. 'It was just one of those "Get out of the way and duck" records.' Interviewed in *Details* magazine, Mark Kates admitted that, rather than concerning himself with Nirvana's radio or TV spots at this stage in the campaign, his time might have been better spent driving copies of *Nevermind* straight from the pressing plant to record shops, such was the consumer demand for the record.

Smells like teen spirit

'I was at Geffen when [Guns N' Roses' hugely successful 1987 début] *Appetite for Destruction* was released,' says Kates, 'so I'd seen a phenomenon happen before. And in this job it's very helpful to have had that kind of experience, to be able to read signs and be able to see things that indicate far more than the specific nature of what they are. Let's just say you get an inner feeling that something is going on that not only can you not control, but also you wouldn't want to control.'

This inability to control the momentum around Nirvana may have been exhilarating for the suits at Geffen, but soon enough the three young men in the eye of the hurricane began to feel like their lives were no longer their own. Suddenly everyone wanted a piece of Nirvana – an autograph, an interview, a photograph, a handshake, an endorsement, an outrageous quote, a punk rock gesture. And Cobain, Novoselic and Grohl were expected to comply with every request, every demand.

For a dispiriting insight into the realities of the major label promotional treadmill, one could do worse than check out footage of Royal Trux – a band formed from the ashes of Pussy Galore, the DC outfit that so terrified Barrett Jones at Laundry Room in the autumn of 1985 – recording idents for 'alternative' cable TV rock shows during their brief period as an underground buzz band on Virgin Records in the mid 1990s. As co-vocalists Neil Hagerty and Jennifer Herrema drawl their way through dedications to 101 different programmes – 'We're Royal Trux and you're watching our latest video on *Over The Edge* ... on *Outrageous* ... on *Bohemia After Dark* ... on *Notes from the Underground* ... on *Rock 'n' Roll Circus Show* ... on *Subculture* ...' – you can actually see the blood drain from their faces and their will to live slowly ebbing away. Multiply Royal Trux's promotional commitments by a factor of one hundred and you will have a rough idea of Nirvana's schedule as their major label début climbed the charts.

In April 1984, shortly after their début album reached number two in the UK charts, The Smiths' guitarist Johnny Marr and vocalist Morrissey were cajoled by their record company into appearing on children's TV show *Charlie's Bus*. The programme saw the two punk-inspired musicians travel around London on an open-top bus with a group of kids, who were primed to ask questions of the duo; Morrissey and Marr's discomfort, and frustration at being talked into this embarrassing promotional chore, is written all over their faces. 'Where are we going?' one young lady enquires of the singer at one point. 'We're all going mad,' is Morrissey's pained, pithy reply. The first indications that the pressures engendered by the unexpected success of *Nevermind* might be having a similar effect on the mental health of the three musicians behind it came during Nirvana's winter '91 European tour.

In the UK, Geffen's decision to press up only 6,000 copies of *Nevermind* had ensured that the album barely scraped into the Top 40 after selling out completely in just two days – it actually débuted at number 36, two places lower than the chart début of Mudhoney's *Every Good Boy Deserves Fudge* one month previously – but with 'Smells Like Teen Spirit' firmly ensconced in the Top Ten, the buzz around the band was building daily. On 2 December 1991 journalist John Aizlewood from the strait-laced, earnest monthly music mag *Q* was dispatched to Newcastle-upon-Tyne, where Nirvana were due to play a sold-out show at the Mayfair club, to file an introductory feature on the band. When Aizlewood introduced himself to Cobain pre-show, the singer ignored the journalist's outstretched hand and stared at him in silence. Keeping his eyes firmly fixed on the writer, Cobain then climbed onto the table in his dressing room and began calmly and methodically throwing sandwiches from the band's rider onto the carpet beneath him. He followed this by scattering breakfast cereal atop the sandwiches, before pouring a carton of orange juice onto the mess. The singer then dived off the table top, executed a forward roll through the gunk on the carpet, and stood facing Aizlewood in silence, with sandwich spread, salad leaves and cold meat slices dripping from his clothes and hair. No one in the dressing room spoke a word as *Q*'s journalist and photographer slunk away in embarrassment. The interview never did take place.

Nirvana did not want for media attention during their time back in the UK, however, thanks largely to a trio of unforgettable TV appearances. On 8 November, on late night youth entertainment show *The Word*, Cobain prefaced an incendiary version of 'Smells Like Teen Spirit' with the declaration that Courtney Love, 'lead singer of the sensational pop group Hole', was 'the best fuck in the world'. On 27 November, booked to perform their Top Ten single on British TV institution *Top of the Pops*, Nirvana gleefully mocked the show's mimed performance format, with Grohl and Novoselic hamming up their out-of-sync performances and Cobain delivering his live vocals in a deadpan gothic drawl he later claimed was a tribute to Morrissey: 'Would you mind doing that again?' the show's unimpressed producers asked the singer afterwards. 'No, I'm quite happy with that, thank you …' Cobain answered. On 6 December, on Channel 4's *Jonathan Ross Show*, there was further mischief from the band, as they ditched their agreed performance of 'Lithium' in favour of a screeching, feedback-laced blast through 'Territorial Pissings'. As the trio set about destroying their equipment, the usually quick-witted Ross made a churlish quip about the band's availability for 'children's birthday parties and Bar Mitzvahs', making himself sound every bit as out-of-touch and uptight as Bill Grundy had appeared in haranguing the Sex Pistols on prime-time British TV 15 years previously. Above the whining feedback in the Channel 4 studio, one could hear the creak of a generation gap yawning.

The band's European tour ended on 7 December with a show at the TransMusicale Festival in Rennes, France. The set began with Dave Grohl taking lead vocals on an endearingly ramshackle cover of The Who's 'Baba O'Riley' – during which he changed the words to sing *'It's only a major label wasteland'* – and ended with the trio trashing every piece of equipment on the stage. Shows in Ireland and Scandinavia were immediately cancelled as the band flew home to Seattle tired, stressed-out and utterly bewildered at their changing fortunes. Their descent into what Grohl would later call 'a tornado of insanity' had begun.

'On that European tour I remember the introduction of anxiety into my life,' says Grohl. 'I had this fear of being alone, because I was so surrounded: I was being pushed and pulled to go do interviews, and go do TV and go say hello to these people and those people. We had no idea what it all meant then. I didn't have my own hotel room, I was sharing with Alex MacLeod, and when I got back home it became really hard to go to sleep at night if I was in a room by myself. I was so used to being surrounded by chaos that silence or solitude kinda flipped me out.

'But was I comfortable selling 10 million records and buying a house and finally being able to support myself playing music? Absolutely. I never had a problem with that, I have never, ever wished for less.'

'It was unbelievable,' Grohl told *Rolling Stone* in 2001. 'We went from selling amp heads and *Love Buzz* singles for food to having millions of dollars. Coming from Springfield, Virginia, I went from having no money at all and working at Tower Records to being set up for the rest of my life. I remember the first time we got a thousand-dollar check. We were so excited. I went out and bought a BB gun and a Nintendo – the things that I always wanted as a kid.'

'I was fortunate in that band that I wasn't the focal point, I was practically anonymous so I got to enjoy a lot of the good things without the hassle,' Grohl told me the following year. 'I'd go home to Virginia or back to Seattle and hang out with Barrett and watch TV and everything was absolutely normal.

'I didn't live an extravagant, decadent lifestyle, but shit, it was great. I didn't do drugs, I didn't get depressed; I saw the whole thing as a blessing. Being the person that wasn't in the spotlight I was left alone so I could live a normal life. But I could see how other people would have trouble with it.'

'One day we were this virtually unknown band who happened to have signed a major label record deal, the next everyone was telling us that we were the best band in the world,' recalled Chris Novoselic. 'I mean, how are you supposed to deal with that?'

It might have been prudent for Gold Mountain to pull Nirvana off the road at this point, to give the trio time to adjust to their new reality. But the company had already accepted a $10,000 per show offer for the band to support the Red Hot Chili Peppers on the West Coast leg of the Californian funk-rockers *BloodSugarSexMajik* arena tour, so on 27 December Cobain, Novoselic and Grohl were pushed back onstage once more. Though the reception afforded Nirvana each night bordered on hysteria – 'I remember getting shivers every night from the whole place going crazy,' says Barrett Jones, on the tour as Grohl's drum tech. 'It was the first time I'd ever seen an entire arena jumping up and down in sync' – the tour was not one Dave Grohl remembers fondly.

'That US club tour and the European tour that followed were Nirvana at our best,' he says. 'We were fucking smoking then, we were a jamming band at that time, way more so than later on. But the Chili Peppers tour was a strange one. Kurt was not in a good place on that trip, and we wouldn't see each other pretty much until the house lights went out every night. So that was kinda weird. And being in arenas was definitely like putting on some clothes that didn't fit yet. To be honest, it didn't ever really fit. And I always put that down to losing my concert virginity to Naked Raygun in a tiny club. It took me a long time to appreciate the grand gestures required for stadium rock: knowing what it felt like to play the old 9:30 Club or some of the closets we were playing in, and the intensity of a room that small with music that loud, is something that I don't think you can recreate in a building that holds 20,000 people. I don't think any of us were entirely comfortable with it.'

The strained atmosphere around the dates was exacerbated by the fact that the opening band on the tour was Stone Gossard's new band Pearl Jam, a band Cobain was constantly criticising in interviews for having what he perceived as a 'careerist' attitude, unacceptable in punk rock circles.

'That was a little weird,' admits Gossard. 'It was like hanging out with your ex-girlfriend's new boyfriend who hates your guts.'

The rivalry between the two bands added an edge to the tour. In San Diego, Pearl Jam frontman Eddie Vedder's hometown, the singer climbed 100 feet above the stage on a lighting rig during his band's set, as a watching Dave Grohl held his breath in genuine terror: 'We were playing before Nirvana, you had to do something,' reasoned Vedder a decade later. 'Our first record was good, but theirs was better.' In San Francisco, on New Year's Eve, Pearl Jam played the intro to 'Smells Like Teen Spirit' during their set, as Vedder told the crowd, 'Don't forget, we played it first.' The Nirvana camp were not amused. But they would have reason to smile soon enough. Later that evening a record industry associate walked onto Pearl Jam's bus to inform them that *Nevermind* was destined for the top of the *Billboard* chart.

༄

On 11 January 1992 *Nevermind* displaced Michael Jackson's *Dangerous* album from the top of the *Billboard* 200. Nirvana were now the nation's favourite, and most bewildered, new pop stars. That same weekend the band were in New York City to perform on *Saturday Night Live*, America's highest-rating TV programme, and the show on which Dave Grohl had first stumbled upon the existence of punk rock twelve years previously. It was a weekend no one in the Nirvana camp would ever forget.

On the morning of 11 January, Danny Goldberg received a phone call at home from Courtney Love, asking if he could deliver $5,000 in cash to her at the Omni Hotel in midtown Manhattan, as she and Cobain were of a mind to do some shopping before the *SNL* taping. Nirvana's manager dropped off the money in $100 bills later that morning. That afternoon Love and Cobain strolled down to 'Alphabet City' on Manhattan's scuzzy Lower East Side and scored a quantity of China White heroin, returned to their hotel suite and locked the door.

According to *Come As You Are*, Cobain and Love first did heroin together in Amsterdam during Nirvana's winter '91 European tour. Both had dabbled with the drug previously – Cobain started using on a casual basis in Olympia, while Love later claimed to have first shot up at a party at actor Charlie Sheen's house – but using together helped the couple spin their own little cocoon in which to shelter from an increasingly turbulent outside world. The next time they took drugs together, one week later in London, the pair decided to get engaged. Cobain would later maintain that he used heroin only as a painkiller to cope with debilitating stomach pains, but even his closest drug buddy could see that he was in denial about his habit.

'He was an oblivion seeker, a fucking lotus eater,' Courtney stated in 2010. 'I never wanted that. I was the kind of drug addict that just wanted to be comfortable in my skin. Escapism once in a blue moon, but it wasn't for me. Kurt would just go on until he dropped.'

Smells like teen spirit

As discreet as Cobain initially was about his drug habit, he wasn't always able to disguise the symptoms associated with heroin use. On 10 January 1992 the Californian music paper *Bam* ran an interview with the singer, conducted backstage at the Los Angeles Sports Arena two weeks previously, which alluded to the possibility that Cobain was using heroin. Writer Jerry McCulley noted that Cobain was 'nodding off occasionally in mid-sentence ...' and wrote, 'He's had but an hour's sleep, he says blearily. But the pinned pupils, sunken cheeks and scabbed, sallow skin suggest something more serious than mere fatigue. The haggard visage and frail frame make him appear more like 40 than 24.'

Nirvana's 'people' initially dismissed McCulley's story as tawdry gossip-mongering, but events in New York City that weekend were less easy to ignore.

In the early hours of 12 January, as Dave Grohl and his mother Virginia bonded with Wendy O'Connor at the *Saturday Night Live* aftershow party, Courtney Love woke up alone in her bed in the Omni Hotel. She had returned to the suite without her fiancé, as Cobain had a late-night interview scheduled with Kurt St Thomas at another Manhattan hotel, but the singer was now due back. Squinting into the darkness, to her horror Love found her husband-to-be lying face down on the hotel room floor, apparently lifeless. As Love slept, Cobain had returned to the suite, shot up heroin and overdosed. Keeping a remarkably cool head, Love attempted to resuscitate her lover, throwing water over his prone body and repeatedly punching him in the stomach until she heard a gasp of breath. Her actions saved Cobain's life.

Dave Grohl would not be told about the incident until the band returned home to Seattle.

'There were a lot of those ... incidents that you just found out about later,' he told me hesitantly in 2009. 'In a weird way, it just became this thing that nobody knew what to do about. If you've ever known someone who's battled something like that you just know that there's nothing you can do.'

It was in New York that weekend that Grohl woke up to the fact that his bandmate was a heroin addict. In one of the most powerful, graphic and affecting passages in *Come As You Are* the drummer recalled walking into the couple's suite at the Omni to be confronted with the grim reality of heroin use.

'I remember walking into their hotel room and for the first time really realising that these two are fucked,' he stated. 'They were just nodding out in bed, just wasted. It was so disgusting and gross. It doesn't make me angry at *them*, it makes me angry that they would be so pathetic as to do something like that. I think it's pathetic for anyone to do something to make themselves that functionless and a drooling fucking baby. It's like, "Hey, let's do a drug that knocks us out and makes us look stupid." It's stupid and gross and pathetic for anyone to take it to that point.

'I don't know when Kurt started doing it, but evidently he was doing it while we lived together,' Grohl told me in 2009. 'But I was oblivious to this. The way life was in the apartment, we would go up to Tacoma and rehearse in the barn until about midnight, then drive back down to Olympia. There was no TV, so we'd either go to a friend's house to listen to records and smoke, or we'd come back to the apartment and Kurt would go into his room, close the door and write all those journals that have been published. And I would sit on the other side of that door, on my couch, which was also my bed, and play guitar and write songs. There was a four-track in the room so sometimes I'd record, but I'd have to do it really quietly, so as not to wake him up. And I think that's maybe when he was starting to do some drugs.

'I joined the band on 23 September 1990, and we left to make *Nevermind* in April, so it wasn't until after *Nevermind* that Kurt started getting fucked up. I almost want to say that it was in Europe that it started happening, but I don't know, I just don't know, because honestly at that time I had no idea, you could be on heroin right now and I wouldn't know. Now I know, but then I had no idea.

'I was a kid. I didn't know anything about heroin. I barely knew anything about cocaine. My drug career was limited to heavy hallucinogenics and mountains of weed. I never did coke, I never did heroin, I didn't fucking need speed … But also, in Virginia, none of us had any fucking money to buy drugs anyway. It was like, "How am I gonna get high?" "You got any lighter fluid? Okay, put that on a fucking rag …"

That kind of shit. Even if we could have afforded heroin I can't imagine us affording the fucking needles.

'So around *Saturday Night Live* was a bad time. And then Kurt moved down to Los Angeles. And when he moved down here that's when it got bad …'

Cobain's overdose in New York meant that Gold Mountain could no longer ignore the fact that their prime asset was using heroin. Goldberg and Silva contacted the William Morris booking agency to tell them to book no further Nirvana shows until they figured out how to deal with the problem, scuppering a proposed US arena run. While they fretted as to how to address the issue, a spate of distracting legal issues surfaced.

The first involved the use of the name 'Nirvana' itself. Unbeknown to Cobain, a band called Nirvana already existed. The original Nirvana were a British psychedelic/progressive rock band who recorded for Island Records in the late 1960s; still touring under that name in the early '90s, the band undeniably had just cause to sue their Seattle namesakes. The case was settled out of court when Gold Mountain agreed to pay the British group $100,000, a settlement which enabled both bands to continue trading under the Nirvana name.

The second case involved a face from Dave Grohl's past. Shortly after Nirvana signed their record contract with Geffen, Glen E. Friedman got in touch with Gold Mountain to remind them that he still had Grohl under contract as a member of Scream. Friedman claimed that he had put $10,000 of his own money into financing the final Scream demo – essentially the tape that became 1993's *Fumble* album – and he wished to reclaim his investment. Gold Mountain initially dismissed Friedman's claim upon their artist and the dispute raged on for months.

Dave Grohl is now legally forbidden from speaking about this issue: when we spoke in Los Angeles in 2009, mention of Friedman's name caused Foo Fighters' frontman to ask me to switch off my tape recorder, the only time during a five-hour conversation that he made such a request.

Friedman himself did not respond to a request for an interview for this book.

This is a Call

If the dispute with his former manager was to prove a lesson in music business practices for Dave Grohl, it was as nothing to the storm heading his way. In April 1992 Kurt Cobain announced to Grohl and Novoselic that he wished to redraft Nirvana's publishing agreement. Up until this point, publishing royalties had been split evenly between the three band members: under the new arrangement proposed by Cobain, the band's publishing would be altered so that Cobain would receive 90% of monies due … and more contentiously, the agreement would be applied retroactively, dating back to the release of *Nevermind*. In effect, this agreement meant that both Grohl and Novoselic now owed Cobain money. The ensuing arguments nearly split the band.

'This is a sticky conversation,' Grohl told me in 2009, 'but yeah, let's just say that things changed. And I realised, "Okay, wait, this isn't three guys in a van any more." I kinda knew that, because my mom had a gold record on her wall, but that's when I started thinking, "You know, I don't know if I signed up for this, this isn't what I signed up for."

'When we signed our deal it was a three-way split. And sometimes that changes after you sell ten million fucking records, you know? So the publishing issue came up … and I got nothing. Close to nothing. Like nothing at all … My first reaction was, "Okay, yeah … I mean, like, how much do you need? I've already made enough money to buy a house … Holy shit! So that's not too terrible." And then I found out what it *really* meant. And I'm like, "Wait a minute, should I be punished because I didn't know what I was signing?" Because apparently nobody else did either. So that was a big one. I considered bailing out at that point. But I stayed …'

✽

While Nirvana lay low, seeking to deal with their internecine issues out of the glare of the world's media, the 'grunge revolution' gathered pace. No one had paid much attention at the time, but on the day *Nevermind* album reached the summit of the *Billboard* 200, another Seattle rock band had chalked up a modest, yet significant, chart success of their own. For Pearl Jam, news that their début single 'Alive' had broken into *Billboard*'s Hot Mainstream Rock Tracks chart at number 32 wasn't a cause for wild celebration in itself, but it demonstrated that four months on from the release of their début album *Ten* they still had impetus, still had momentum. And Nirvana's milestone achievement had laid down a new marker: 'I remember thinking, "Wow, it's on now," guitarist Mike McCready told one US journalist a decade later. 'It changed something. We had something to prove: that our band was as good as I thought it was.'

Five months later, on 5 May 1992, *Ten* was certified platinum in the US, as it passed the one million sales mark. By mid-July, when Pearl Jam and their friends in Soundgarden left their hometown to start the second annual Lollapalooza tour alongside the Red Hot Chili Peppers, Ministry and ex-N.W.A. rapper Ice Cube, both Chris Cornell's group and Alice in Chains had platinum albums under their belts too. Jumping upon the bandwagon somewhat belatedly, *Rolling Stone* and *Spin* began to hype Seattle as 'the new Liverpool', and scores of major-label A&R men descended wolfishly upon the community to strip it of its assets. In every down-tuned riff and misanthropic grunt emanating from the Crocodile Café, the Showbox and the Off Ramp the majors thought they heard 'The New Nirvana': Mudhoney duly left Sub Pop for Reprise, Tad inked a deal with Warners imprint Giant Records and Melvins signed to Atlantic. As former *Rolling Stone* writer Cameron Crowe was bringing the 'Seattle Sound' to Hollywood, with Matt Dillon (who portrayed troubled teen Richie White in *Over the Edge*) starring as disaffected rocker Cliff Poncier in the sappy Jet City-based, grunge-soundtracked romantic comedy *Singles*, a host of fame-hungry Californian rock bands were donning flannel shirts and cherry red Doc Martens boots and heading in the opposite direction, hoping to buy into the feeding frenzy enveloping the city. A generation of down-at-heel, ornery local musos were left wondering where it all went right.

In the midst of all this drama, noise and confusion, hardly anyone noticed Dave Grohl's first solo album emerge without fanfare on the tiny Simple Machines label run out of a suburban home in Arlington, Virginia by Jenny Toomey and her Tsunami bandmate Kristin Thompson. Released on cassette only, as part of Simple Machine's Tool Set tape series, *Pocketwatch* was packaged as the work of a band named Late!, but the cassette inlay card credits revealed 'all music and instruments' to be the work of one 'Dave G'. And here lay the foundations of a career of which the young multi-instrumentalist could not at this point have imagined.

Officially the *Pocketwatch* cassette was recorded in just two studio sessions: the opening six tracks were laid to Ampex tape with Barrett Jones at 'Upland Studios' aka Laundry Room in Arlington on 23 December 1990, while the remaining four tracks were recorded by Gray Matter man Geoff Turner at his WGNS studio in Arlington on 27 July 1991. There is some dispute about this chronology, however: Barrett Jones maintains that the ten tracks were actually comped together from a number of different studio sessions, while legendary DC producer Don Zientara also claims to have worked on the cassette with Grohl at Inner Ear. Whatever, the truth is that Grohl's burgeoning talent as a songwriter might never have been revealed at all, but for a crush on a pretty girl.

'Basically I'd been living in Olympia and there was a girl from Washington DC that I had a super crush on, this girl Jemmy Toomey,' Grohl told me in 2009. 'I always had a crush on her, she was so fucking cute, and I was secretly in love with her. She came over to the studio one day and I was recording with Barrett and she said, "Wow, this is really cool, we should put out a cassette." Up to that point the only people who'd heard anything I'd done were my mom, my sister, Barrett, Pete [Stahl] and my buddy Jimmy [Swanson] – they were my audience – but she heard it and liked it and wanted to do it so I was like, "Okay …" I was just excited that someone was excited enough to want to hear it.'

'My band was recording with Barrett too,' remembers Toomey, 'and either we found out that Dave was going to be there and so I dropped by to see what was going on, or it was just an overlap, like they were closing down what they were doing and we were loading our stuff in. But I remember really liking it and I asked him for a tape. Maybe I was crushing a little too, but I thought it was really good.'

'It was right around the time that PJ Harvey was beginning to do stuff, and you have these people like PJ and Dave who just come out of nowhere with this effortless creativity and this ability to synthesise all this stuff: there's just this bright, white light that comes out of them when they do what they do and it feels just effortless. I thought it was really interesting.'

While it's fair to say that without Nirvana and Foo Fighters Dave Grohl's *Pocketwatch* cassette would be of no more historical significance than Toomey's own short-lived Tool Set side-projects My New Boyfriend and Slack, its lo-fi production, warmth, wit and humour ensure that it has a naïve charm all its own.

The cassette's stand-out (and best known) track is 'Friend of a Friend', a stark, gently strummed meditation upon Grohl's early months in Olympia, finding his feet in a strange town with bandmates he barely knew. Written on Kurt Cobain's couch in the small hours of a bleak mid-winter, it's a sensitive, tender observation of the intimate friendship between Cobain and Novoselic, the songwriter who *'plays an old guitar, with a coin found by the phone'* and his more gregarious, sociable best friend who *'thinks he drinks too much'*. The first Dave Grohl-penned song written on an acoustic guitar, 'Friend of a Friend' would re-emerge in 2005, re-recorded by Grohl for the acoustic portion of Foo Fighters' *In Your Honor* double album: the events of the intervening years only serve to heighten the song's poignancy.

Pocketwatch also saw the first public appearance of 'Color Pictures of a Marigold', another gently unfolding, quietly voiced acoustic track Grohl held dear: though the version on *Pocketwatch* is credited to the Christmas 1990 session with Jones, Grohl demoed it again at Laundry Room on 16 February 1991, suggesting that he was not yet fully convinced he had the definitive recording on tape. Two years later he would cut the track again with Steve Albini, and it would achieve cult status as the only Nirvana song neither authored nor sung by Kurt Cobain, when it emerged on the B-side of the *Heart-Shaped Box* single with the shortened title 'Marigold'.

That the two best-known tracks on *Pocketwatch* are skeletal acoustic sketches does not paint an accurate representation of the album: for the most part, Dave Grohl's début solo album offers up the kind of fuzzed-up, driving alternative rock the singer would take to the bank with Foo

Fighters in later years. Among its noisier components, 'Petrol CB' (confusingly retitled 'There's That Song Again' when it emerged on vinyl on the 1992 Simple Machines' seven-inch box set *Neapolitan Metropolitan*) stands out; featuring a gnarled stop-start riff, harshly distorted vocals and a reverb-drenched, shimmering chorus, it suggests that Grohl, like many of his peers in the Alternative Nation in the early '90s, was taking some songwriting cues from My Bloody Valentine. 'Just Another Story About Skeeter Thompson' is memorable for entirely different reasons, as over a grinding, insistent crossover-punk riff Grohl delivers a humorous spoken word 'tribute' to Scream's mercurial bassist: he recalls how, while staying at his friend Tos Nieuwenhuizen's house in Amsterdam during his second European excursion with the band from Bailey's Crossroads, he was interrupted while reading *Maximumrocknroll* (*'or Flipside ... one of those punk things'*) by Thompson holding out his penis for examination, asking, *'Does that look like pus to you?'* Delightful.

Future Foo Fighters B-side 'Winnebago', the hoarse-throated Hüsker Dü-esque 'Hell's Garden' and the dynamic DC hardcore-flavoured instrumental 'Pokey the Little Puppy' are enthusiastic rather than enthralling, but their characterful crunch measures up nicely against the strains of corrosive alt-rock delivered by contemporaries on the Amphetamine Reptile, Trance Syndicate and Matador labels in the early 1990s. As with Nirvana's *Bleach*, *Pocketwatch* merits respect rather than reverence, and its full significance would be measured by events that lay ahead, but it remains an engaging blueprint for Grohl's signature songwriting style.

With Grohl loath to promote *Pocketwatch* in any way – the drummer being anxious that the album might be viewed as a crass cash-in on the popularity of *Nevermind* – as Jenny Toomey remembers it, "no one really noticed" the cassette for the longest time. When word of its existence finally went overground, Simple Machines almost buckled under demand for the tape, not least because Toomey had to dub every single copy from Grohl's second-generation demo tape by hand in her bedroom: 'People don't ever think about this in relation to labels, but indie labels don't get in trouble when they're not successful, they get in trouble when they have one artist that's more successful than they can keep up with,' she points out.

'Eventually we just took it off the catalogue, because it was just too much,' she admits. 'I don't bear any ill-will to Mr Grohl, and I haven't really seen him much over the years, but there were several times when we literally just begged him to let us put it on CD, not just because wouldn't it be nice to have a "little engine that could", that helped us pay for the other records, but also because it was a pain in our ass to dub them five at a time! But whatever, we respected him, and we were certainly very proud to have put it out. I was always amazed that Dave ever second-guessed it: he seemed fairly modest about his skills for a long time.'

∽

The release of the *Pocketwatch* tape had the unexpected side effect of spurring Nirvana back into action. Impressed by Barrett Jones's production on the cassette, Cobain booked a one-day session at the new Laundry Room Studio – in the basement of the West Seattle house Jones and Grohl had been sharing since July '91 – to hammer out some new material. Convening at Grohl's house on 7 April 1992, the band snapped back into high gear immediately, recording one-take performances of future B-side 'Curmudgeon' and 'Oh, The Guilt' (set aside for a future split single with Touch and Go records' brilliant Jesus Lizard) and treating themselves to two runs through a cover of 'Return of the Rat' by seminal Portland garage rockers The Wipers (destined for release on the singles box set *Eight Songs for Greg Sage and The Wipers*, which also featured contributions from Hole and the heavyweight Portland hardcore crew Poison Idea).

'We got to the point where we could just crank out songs,' Chris Novoselic later stated. 'Kurt would be improvising, and we were so good at playing we'd just pick up the song; the second time we'd play the song we'd record it. That's what happened with those B-sides we did at the Laundry Room.'

With Cobain understandably preoccupied with looking after his now pregnant wife in Los Angeles, it would be a further two and a half months before Nirvana properly returned to action. In the interim, Grohl took advantage of his free time to add bass, guitar and drums to Melvins' mainman Buzz Osbourne's solo EP *King Buzzo* at the Laundry Room, displaying both a wry wit and a shrewd knowledge of punk rock history by adopting the pseudonym 'Dale Nixon' on the record credits, 'Dale Nixon' being the same name Greg Ginn had employed when covertly laying down the bass parts on Black Flag's *My War* album. The EP featured a re-working of 'Just Another Story About Skeeter Thompson', now simply titled 'Skeeter'.

In mid-June Nirvana regrouped to return to Europe to make up the dates they had cancelled at the back end of 1991. Old problems surfaced almost immediately. Three days into the tour, following a superb 22 June show at the King's Hall in Belfast, Northern Ireland, which this writer was privileged to attend, Cobain collapsed at breakfast in the city's Europa Hotel. The official line given to UK journalists covering Nirvana's 'comeback' was that the singer had a 'weeping ulcer': 'It's because he eats a lot of junk food,' deadpanned PR Anton Brookes. In reality Cobain was suffering from methadone withdrawal. When a news journalist from *Melody Maker* queried the official diagnosis, bluntly asking the PR man directly whether there was any truth in the rumour that's Cobain's collapse was the result of a heroin overdose, Brookes was forthright and bullish in his dismissal of the story.

'Everyone's been saying that, but there's nothing in it,' he countered. 'I mean, how many times did Kurt supposedly die in car crashes last year? Some people claim he started the LA riots! It's all bullshit. It's just cos they're the most copy-worthy band in the world right now.'

It was an admirable performance by the PR man, but few were convinced. The paper's decision to run their story under the headline 'Nirvana Star Rushed to Hospital with "Mystery Stomach Bug"' hinted at both their own heavy scepticism and the deeper, darker problems they intuitively knew were bedevilling the Seattle three-piece.

'You had to say and do a lot of things to keep face for the band,' Brookes subsequently admitted. 'I did that out of loyalty, not because they were paying me, but because they were friends. Everything had changed. Nirvana had become a multi-million-pound industry. To management and everyone else, it was still the same close-knit family, but I remember we all went around together then – the band, crew, [support band] Teenage Fanclub – everybody except Kurt and Courtney, who stayed in their hotel room. It became them and everyone else.'

For all the PR man's skills, however, the cracks in the Nirvana camp could not be papered over forever. With rumours circulating that Nirvana's proposed August headline slot at Reading festival was likely to be cancelled, in July writer Keith Cameron, one of Nirvana's most loyal, supportive and trusted confidants in the media, and a man who had shared floor space with Dave Grohl at the Novoselic's Tacoma home less than two years previously, was flown to Spain to interview the band for *NME* to set the story straight. This he did, but not in the way in which Nirvana's management or PR people had envisaged.

When he arrived in Spain, Cameron found the atmosphere enveloping the Nirvana camp to be poisonous, with both the crew and indeed the band's rhythm section walking on eggshells to avoid upsetting Cobain and his six months pregnant wife. After being made to wait for two days for an audience with the singer, on 3 July Cameron was bemused to see Cobain being led meekly into the subterranean dressing rooms at Palacio de los Deportes de la Comunidad de Madrid by Love, who loudly and sarcastically trumpeted, 'Here he is! Here's everyone's little investment!'

When Cameron finally sat down with his old friend, Cobain flatly denied that he was using heroin – going so far as to demand that the writer check his arms for traces of needle marks. But the perceptive Cameron quickly surmised that the real story of the tour lay not with the singer's personal problems, but with the attitude of his heavily pregnant wife.

Musing upon how Nirvana could go from 'nobodies to superstars to fuck-ups' in the space of six months, Cameron's verdict was damning:

'Spend two days in tour fatigues with this new, arena-compatible Nirvana production machine – "I don't know the names of most of the crew," admits Dave – and it dawns on you that the overriding issue here is not that Kurt Cobain is on heroin (or isn't, or was, or is and is trying to get off) but that his wife is a grade A pain in the arse,' he wrote.

Cameron's hard-hitting story was filed under the brilliant headline 'Love Will Tear Us Apart'. 'This is serious shit,' he wrote, 'and it's no wonder some people are freaking and saying Reading will be it. Game Over. The End.'

Around the same time *Melody Maker*'s Everett True wrote a more sympathetic account of the state of the Nirvana nation. The final section of his article was given over to Dave Grohl, who seemed to have retained an excellent sense of perspective amid what he would later term as the 'tornado of insanity' enveloping the band.

'Any musician would be lying if they said that they didn't want people to appreciate their music,' he stated carefully. 'But something on this scale is just too perverse and too bizarre to accept sometimes, especially for us. We definitely aren't the ones who wanted this. I just don't want this fiasco to ruin my life.'

In the weeks leading up to the Reading festival, Anton Brookes was forced time and again to deny that Kurt Cobain's ill-health would compel Nirvana to withdraw from the bill. One of Brookes's Bad Moon press releases testily concluded with the words 'Nirvana are playing fucking Reading.' But in truth no one really knew whether or not the gig would happen: not Brookes, not John Silva, not Dave Grohl, and quite possibly not Kurt Cobain himself.

In the first week of August Cobain and Courtney Love checked into the Cedars-Sinai Medical Center in LA; Love to prepare for the imminent arrival of the couple's first child, her husband to receive treatment for narcotics addiction. At 7:48 a.m. on 18 August Love gave birth to a baby girl, weighing in at 7 pounds and 1 ounce; the couple named her Frances Bean, after Frances McKee of The Vaselines. But even on this happy occasion there were dark clouds overhead. In a 1995 interview with *Spin* magazine's Craig Marks, Love claimed that Cobain summoned a drug dealer to the hospital that same day, and had the dealer inject drugs into his morphine drip, after which he OD'd: 'He like totally died,' she said. In an interview with *Rolling Stone*'s David Fricke in 1994 Love also claimed that her husband brought a gun to the hospital on 19 August, and the couple weighed up the pros and cons of a suicide pact. Clearly these were troubled times.

On Friday 28 August Dave Grohl and Chris Novoselic showed up at the Richfield Avenue site to check out John Lydon's Public Image Ltd, and noisy New Yorkers Cop Shoot Cop and The Lunachicks; of Kurt Cobain there was no sign. On the Saturday night, 29 August, the band had a fraught, uncomfortable rehearsal in London, and it slowly dawned on Grohl that this might be the end of the line.

'We rehearsed once, the night before, and it wasn't good,' he recalled. 'I really thought, "This will be a disaster, this will be the end of our career for sure."'

Reading 1992 was to be more than just a gig for Nirvana. Not only was it the biggest payday of their career – the trio commanding a $250,000 appearance fee as the final band on the final night of the festival's 20th anniversary staging – but the entire main stage bill on Sunday 30 August had been built around them, a measure of just how much power and respect they commanded at the time.

'It was just all our friends!' Grohl recollected. 'Who's on first? The Melvins. Who else played that day? L7. Screaming Trees. Teenage Fanclub. Mudhoney. And [Abba tribute band] Bjorn Again playing "Teen Spirit" at 3 in the afternoon? That was fucking awesome ...'

This was not just a gig. This was to be a coronation.

'But we were wracked with nerves,' Grohl remembered. 'Before the gig everyone was saying, "Will they make it? Are they in rehab? Are they dead?"'

'The hype about us cancelling was so huge that even our friends in other bands were surprised when we turned up. It was a bad time for the band and then we had to step up in front of 40,000 people. And luckily something special happened. We expected it to be the biggest disaster of the year, but it turned out to be one of the greatest things in my life.'

Just after nine o'clock that evening, as darkness descended on the royal county of Berkshire, Everett True, the journalist who had first propelled Nirvana into the spotlight, pushed a wheelchair carrying a hunched figure in a white hospital gown and blond wig into the middle of the broad festival stage.

'You're going to make it, man,' said Chris Novoselic, stooping down for a handshake.

'With the support of his friends and family, he's going to make it,' the bassist told the crowd.

Clinging onto the microphone stand for support, Kurt Cobain pulled himself out of the wheelchair with exaggerated effort and stood before 40,000 expectant faces.

'*Some say love it is a river …*' he sang weakly, then toppled backwards onto the stage.

As cheers, laughter and whirring feedback rang around the site, Dave Grohl hammered out the opening fusillade of 'Breed' and the most talked-about gig of Nirvana's career was underway. Twenty-four songs and 90 minutes later, as Cobain brought 'Territorial Pissings' screeching to an end with a strangled, horrendously off-key rendition of 'The Star Spangled Banner' – a playful nod to another iconic Seattle musician's most legendary festival performance – Grohl exited to his left with a broad smile splitting his face.

'It was an incredible night,' remembers photographer Charles Peterson, who had flown over from Seattle especially for the show. 'You had 40,000 people standing with steam rising from them and you had Kurt standing in front of them in his white smock with the light shining down upon him … he looked like Jesus. Having seen Nirvana in clubs playing to next to no one just a few years previously you can't even imagine how surreal and special that felt. It felt like a victory.'

'We pulled it off,' Dave Grohl later noted humbly. 'We proved we weren't useless pieces of shit.'

I hate myself and I want to die

There are certain people in your life that you just know, they're not gonna make it. So in the back of your mind you emotionally prepare yourself for something like that to happen … not that it makes it easier, but so that when it does happen your world won't collapse completely …

Dave Grohl

On the morning of 23 July 1993 Courtney Love heard a resounding thud from inside the bathroom of her suite in New York's Omni Berkshire Place hotel. She opened the bathroom door to find her 26-year-old husband lying on the floor, with his eyes wide open and a syringe sticking out of his arm. Kurt Cobain wasn't moving. He wasn't breathing. And, unless his wife acted quickly, he wasn't going to see the sun rise and fall over the Manhattan skyline ever again.

Keeping a cool head, Love picked up the phone and called the hotel rooms of Frances Bean's nanny Michael 'Cali' DeWitt and Cobain's friend, and British press officer, Anton Brookes, asking for assistance. When the pair arrived, they jolted Cobain back into consciousness by throwing water on his face and punching him repeatedly in the stomach. Brookes then dragged the dazed, groggy singer out into the muggy Manhattan morning and forcibly marched him up and down the street until Cobain was able to walk for himself. The PR man then quietly returned to the couple's suite, picked up Cobain's heroin baggies off the floor and flushed them down the toilet.

This is a Call

Courtney Love's admirable calm under pressure betrayed a grim reality: saving Kurt Cobain's life had become a depressingly routine affair for Hole's lead singer. This was her husband's second overdose in as many months. On 2 May Cobain had returned to the couple's rented home at 11301 Lakeside Avenue in Seattle after shooting up heroin at a friend's house; according to the Seattle Police Department Incident Report filed later that evening, he then locked himself in his room, where 'his physical condition gradually deteriorated to the point that he was shaking, became flushed, delirious and talked incoherently'. Investigating police officer George noted that the singer was conscious but 'impaired to some degree'. 'This type of incident had happened before to Cobain,' his report concluded.

Cobain's mother Wendy O'Connor and his sister Kim were in the house with Courtney Love at the time of the incident. And as events unfolded, Love dragged O'Connor upstairs to show her the mess Cobain was in.

'I'm like, "This is your fucking son,"' Love recalled two years later. 'He just looked at her and said, "I'm not on drugs, mom, I'm not on drugs."'

Twenty-four hours after his overdose in Manhattan, sitting at a table in the boardroom of the Omni Berkshire, Cobain trotted out the same line to visiting English journalists from *Q* and *Melody Maker*, who were blissfully unaware of the drama of the previous day.

'I think people who glamorise drugs are fucking assholes and if there's a hell they'll go there,' the singer told *Melody Maker* writers the Stud Brothers. 'It's really bad karma.'

If, with the benefit of hindsight, Cobain's cautionary words rang somewhat hollow, his cynicism was understandable. He himself had learned a harsh life lesson the previous year, in regard to the music industry's capacity to bury its head and wilfully ignore the inconvenient realities of drug addiction when it suited key players to do so. While Cobain was detoxing in Cedars-Sinai in Los Angeles, Danny Goldberg was asked if Nirvana might consider playing the MTV Awards in the city on 9 September. Goldberg pointed out that as the band's lead singer was in rehab, this would be unlikely.

I hate myself and I want to die

But Goldberg had been long enough in the game to recognise the risks inherent in making an enemy of a powerful media corporation. Reluctantly, and with a heavy heart, he placed a call to Kurt Cobain in hospital and asked if the singer might discharge himself early, to take one for the team. 'Kurt agreed right away,' noted Goldberg in *Bumping into Geniuses*, 'but the melancholy in his voice was unmistakable.' On 9 September Nirvana and their dope-sick singer obediently painted on smiles and performed 'Lithium' at MTV's marquee event; the fact that on that same evening the band was awarded gongs for winning the categories of Best New Artist and Best Alternative Video (for 'Smells Like Teen Spirit') was but a happy coincidence obviously.

Dave Grohl may have had such corporate chicanery on his mind when he spoke to *Q*'s Phil Sutcliffe at the Omni Berkshire the following July. Freshly returned from a two-week US club tour with his old friends in Scream, who had reunited to celebrate the long-overdue release of their excellent *Fumble* album on Dischord, Grohl's punk rock soul and conscience had been reawakened: 'Humping our own gear into CBGB's and sleeping on friends' floors restored my faith,' he commented.

No longer a punk rock naïf, Grohl's growing distaste for the reality of life within the major-label record industry was evident in his short conversation with Sutcliffe. The music business, he opined, was full of 'arrogant people, people who have no shame, people without a shred of decency, people who are just out for money, money, money'. Grohl himself had long since taken to removing himself from discussions of Nirvana's financial or business affairs; his stock response when questions were raised was to shrug, smile and say, 'I'm only the drummer.'

'I'm fine as long as I can just get up onstage and play drums with Krist and Kurt,' he told the man from *Q*.

In truth, Grohl had not been afforded much opportunity to indulge in the simple pleasure of jamming onstage with his friends in the wake of their triumphant Reading festival headline show. In the 11 months that had passed between that already legendary August night at Richfield Avenue and the band's appearance at New York's Roseland Ballroom on 23 July 1993 (in the same week in which *Nevermind* finally dropped out of the *Billboard* 200 after 92 weeks in the chart) Nirvana had played a grand total of just eight shows. But at the most recent of these, in April 1993 – a San Francisco benefit concert for Bosnian rape victims organised by Novoselic who had by now reverted to using his Croatian birthname, Krist – the trio had aired no less than eight tracks from the much-anticipated follow-up to their phenomenally successful major-label début. Finally, after months of drama and gossip and bullshit and hype, Nirvana were getting back to the business of being a working, creative rock band once more.

1993 had started in inglorious circumstances for the trio, with two decidedly lame performances at stadium gigs in Brazil, arranged as part of the inaugural Hollywood Rock Festival. The band were under-rehearsed and Cobain was under-the-weather: after mixing pills with alcohol before the first show, staged on 16 January at the 80,000 capacity Estádio Cícero Pompeu de Toledo in São Paulo, he was barely able to play his guitar, a farcical situation which led Krist Novoselic to walk offstage 30 minutes into the proposed 90 minute set, hurling his bass at Cobain as he exited. When the bassist was persuaded to return by Nirvana's crew, who were mindful that the band would lose out on a huge pay cheque if they didn't play for at least 45 minutes as contracted, the trio swapped instruments, with Cobain taking Grohl's spot on the drum stool, Novoselic switching to guitar and Grohl taking on bass and vocal duties.

What followed was either punk rock nirvana, or an embarrassing shambles, depending on your point of view, as the world's most critically respected rock band hamfistedly bashed their way through a succession of bar band cover versions – Iron Maiden's 'Run to the Hills', Zeppelin's 'Heartbreaker', Queen's 'We Will Rock You' and Kim Wilde's 'Kids in America' among them – to the utter bemusement and increasing irritation of their audience. Nirvana's stint as a rock 'n' roll jukebox climaxed with a shirtless Grohl singing off-key lead vocals on ragged versions of Terry Jack's syrupy 1974 MOR standard 'Seasons in the Sun' and Duran Duran's 'Rio'; by this point a sizeable minority of their audience had walked out in disgust. Fugazi's Ian MacKaye, who'd been invited along to Brazil as part of L7's road crew, remembers the trip being 'bonkers': 'I went along and thought, "Hmmm, well, this is what not to do,"' he later told me. Speaking to MTV News later in the year, Novoselic likened the show to a 'mental breakdown'.

'I felt this big,' Grohl admitted to Phil Sutcliffe, holding his thumb and forefinger one centimetre apart. 'You just think: "What the fuck are we doing? What is this about?"'

'It was still fun,' Grohl insisted to me in 2009. 'It wasn't as fun as it was when we were on tour with Urge Overkill in 1991, playing places that held 700 people, but we were still the same people; it's just that everything else around us had changed, our environment had changed. And unfortunately Kurt had a hard time with drugs. I was lucky, I could walk away from each show and disappear. No one fucking knew who I was, I could stand in the front row of one of our shows and people still didn't know who I was. I was fortunate enough to experience all of the good things and avoid a lot of the bad things. Whether I was smart or it was just dumb luck, that's how it went.'

Their brace of shambolic gigs aside, the trip to Brazil did have some positive benefits for Nirvana. As the trio had a free week between the 16 January São Paulo show and the concluding date of the Hollywood Rock festival at Praça da Apoteose in Rio de Janeiro on 23 January, Cobain booked the band into the BMG Ariola Ltda studio in Rio for three days to demo tracks for the eagerly awaited follow-up to *Nevermind*.

Nirvana's last recording session had been a waste of both time and money. Inspired by their no-frills session at Laundry Room in April 1992, Cobain had scheduled a session in Word of Mouth studios in Seattle – better known by its former name Reciprocal Studio – with *Bleach* producer Jack Endino on 25 and 26 October 1992. Cobain had been stockpiling material for Nirvana's third album even before the band started recording *Nevermind* – written in the Pear Street apartment he and Grohl shared, 'Pennyroyal Tea' had been premiered at the band's OK Hotel show on 17 April 1991; rudimentary versions of 'All Apologies' (then titled 'La La La') and 'Radio Friendly Unit Shifter' (originally titled 'Nine Month Media Blackout') had been demoed with their sound engineer Craig Montgomery at Music Source in Seattle on New Year's Day, 1991; and 'Dumb' was first committed to tape for a

John Peel radio session on 3 September 1991 – so the expectation was that the band would demo the lion's share of their new album in two days with Endino. But on the first scheduled day of recording Cobain simply didn't show up at all; Grohl and Novoselic's calm acceptance of this fact told its own story. On day two the singer surfaced without a word of apology, and the band set to recording, completing six basic tracks and one half-hearted vocal take – for the mordant 'Rape Me' – before the arrival of Courtney Love and two-month-old Frances Bean effectively ended Cobain's interest in the session. Compared to the industry and focus Nirvana had displayed when recording 'the Dale demo' and *Bleach*, for Endino the session was a disappointing, and indeed troubling, non-event.

'It did seem odd to me that Kurt would show up a day late for a session, and more worrisome that everyone else took this as "expected" behaviour,' the producer told me in 2010. 'It seemed to me at the time like "rock-star" behaviour, but clearly in hindsight it was just junkie behaviour. Once he actually showed up, he was as focused as ever, but the whole session was slightly strange to me.'

In an echo of the garage session that yielded Dain Bramage's *I Scream Not Coming Down*, the most memorable incident at Word of Mouth saw the Seattle police department arrive at the studio door following up a noise complaint, as Dave Grohl's ferocious drumming inside the soundproofed live room was so loud that it could be heard echoing throughout the surrounding neighbourhoods. 'I said, "You know, I've got Nirvana in there, they're this huge band,"' Endino recalls. 'This cop just said, "I don't care who you've got in there, you have to turn it down." That was the first time that had happened with that particular studio in five or six years.

'But in the end no one from the label or band ever asked me for the tapes or even for rough mixes to listen to,' the producer admits. 'It left me wondering why they even bothered with the session.'

In stark contrast, at BMG Ariola Ltda from 19 to 21 January Nirvana were on point, sharp and focused. With Craig Montgomery manning the mixing console once again, the trio cut seven new tracks – 'Heart-Shaped Box', 'Scentless Apprentice', 'Milk It', 'Very Ape', 'Moist

I hate myself and I want to die

Vagina', 'Gallons of Rubbing Alcohol Flow Through the Strip' and the sarcastically titled 'I Hate Myself and I Want to Die', earmarked by Cobain as the title of the band's third album) and two playful cover versions ('Seasons in the Sun' and a solo Dave Grohl take on cult Swedish underground metal band Unleashed's 'Forward into Countless Battles') in three days. The low-key but productive session fired their drummer's enthusiasm for the album sessions proper.

'It was really raw,' says Grohl, 'but the songs were so bizarre that I was excited because I didn't know what kind of album we were going to make.'

Kurt Cobain, though, knew exactly what kind of album Nirvana were going to make. Or perhaps more accurately, he knew exactly what kind of album his band *weren't* going to make. From the moment that *Nevermind* started selling, but, significantly, not before that point, Cobain would tell anyone who'd listen that he hated the sound of the album, that it was too polished and clean; Nirvana's next album, he promised, would be rawer, more primitive and more punk rock.

'I don't listen to records like [*Nevermind*] at home,' he told English journalist Jon Savage airily, on the eve of his band's July 1993 Roseland Ballroom concert. 'I can't listen to that record. I like a lot of the songs. I really like playing some of them live. In a commercial sense I think it's a really good record, I have to admit that, but that's in a Cheap Trick sort of a way. But for my listening pleasure, you know, it's too slick.'

Even as Nirvana were demoing new material with Barrett Jones, Jack Endino and Craig Montgomery, Kurt Cobain had a fixed idea of the producer he wanted to helm Nirvana's third album sessions. And that choice, in itself, would be a punk rock statement.

The liner notes Steve Albini penned for Big Black's posthumous live album *Pigpile* may have referred specifically to that band's *modus operandi* but they're as good a guide as any to the basic principles which have informed Albini's life's work, from his days as a fanzine writer in Evanston through to his career as a musician and producer. 'Treat everyone with as much respect as he deserves (and no more),' Albini wrote in 1992. 'Avoid people who appeal to our vanity or ambition

211

(they'll always have an angle). Operate as much as possible apart from the "music scene". Take no shit from anyone in the process.'

As both a music critic and musician, Albini's name was synonymous with uncompromised integrity, brutally straight talking and harsh, unconventional and fiercely intelligent rock music. That reputation carried through to his work as a producer, to the extent that Albini actually refuses to accept the term 'producer' in connection with his studio work with bands: he sees his role as being that of a sound engineer, and focuses upon rendering the sound of a band playing live in the studio to tape – *always* to tape – unfiltered and untreated. Whether Albini actually likes a band's music is irrelevant – 'It's not my place to be the arbiter of culture and say, "No, you do not deserve to make a record,"' he told me in 2002. 'If I feel like a band's motives are genuine, then the question of whether I like their music artistically becomes immaterial' – and he has no interest in offering guidance on arrangements, lyrics or song choices. Bands seeking a motivational hype man capable of sprinkling magic dust on half-formed ideas would be advised to look elsewhere for a studio collaborator, but with his reasonably priced rates (as late as 2002, when his CV included work on albums by industry heavyweights such as Page & Plant, Cheap Trick and PJ Harvey, Albini's base rate for working with independent label bands was just $300 per day) and his refusal to adhere to the industry standard practice of taking percentage points on album sales, Albini's professional services remain well within the reach of most working bands.

In 1992, when Kurt Cobain was asked by *Melody Maker* to nominate ten records that changed his life, he listed The Breeders' *Pod* and Pixies' *Surfer Rosa* as his number one and two choices; Steve Albini had produced both records. Albini had also recorded the first four albums by Cobain favourites The Jesus Lizard, the unhinged, unnerving Chicago-based quartet formed from the ashes of Scratch Acid; in their terrifying squall Cobain heard a purity of expression that he'd been seeking since his earliest experiments with sound recording at his aunt Mari Earl's house. The singer became convinced that only Albini could coax out the demons within his own head. He knew too that Albini

possessed the strength of character to stonewall record company interference in the project, however unpalatable the results might prove to
be. And yet, typical of Cobain's passive-aggressive approach to communication, the singer didn't approach Albini to invite him to work with
Nirvana until the producer had been moved to write a letter to a British
music weekly denying that he'd asked to work upon the record. When
Cobain finally plucked up the courage to call, Albini asked for a little
time to consider his answer. The producer wasn't playing mind-games:
his reticence stemmed from the fact that he was possibly the only music
industry professional in America who hadn't yet heard *Nevermind*, so
he felt it only polite that he should familiarise himself with the band
before committing to the project.

'I knew Nirvana *existed*, but I wouldn't have considered myself a fan,'
he told me in 2010. 'I wasn't a big fan of a lot of the Seattle stuff. I
thought Mudhoney had a good single, and I liked the band Tad: Tad
Doyle was an interesting character and I thought that band's approach
was a little bit more thuggish and interesting. But not many of the Sub
Pop bands appealed to me that much. But after working with Nirvana
for a while I developed an appreciation of them that I'm pretty sure I
wouldn't have developed on the outside.'

The key players at Geffen were determined to give Nirvana time
and space to work at a leisurely pace upon their third album. To
facilitate this (and to exploit the band's newly engorged fan-base) the
label released the rarities, radio sessions and demos collection
Incesticide in December 1992. But Albini had his own firm opinions
as to how the next Nirvana record might be made. He insisted that if
the band should decide to work with him, they should record as they
had done pre-*Nevermind*, quickly, efficiently and without external
distractions; he proposed a working schedule of just two weeks to
make the record. Furthermore, he suggested that Nirvana should pay
the $24,000 fee for the recording session themselves rather than rely-
ing on record-label funds; this, he argued, would ultimately give the
band greater independence over the process. In addition, Albini
drafted a contract between himself, the record label and the band,
asking that all parties acknowledge that whatever record Nirvana

should make with him would be released without interference, and without further adornment. Tellingly, no one from Geffen was prepared to sign this contract.

'Our A&R man at the time, Gary Gersh, was freaking out,' Grohl told Phil Sutcliffe in 1993. 'I said, "Gary, man, don't be so afraid, the record will turn out great!" He said, "Oh, I'm not afraid, go ahead, bring me back the best you can do." It was like, "Go and have your fun, then we'll get another producer and make the real album."'

On 12 February 1993 Kurt Cobain and Krist Novoselic flew from Seattle to Minneapolis–St Paul International Airport, where 23-year-old Brent Sigmeth was waiting to drive them to Pachyderm Recording Studio, a residential recording studio located in the tiny town of Cannon Falls, Minnesota. Drummer Dave Grohl flew in from Washington DC the following day. Nirvana had been booked into the studio under the name The Simon Ritchie Bluegrass Ensemble – a little punk-rock in-joke, as John Simon Ritchie was Sid Vicious's real name – but the arrival at Pachyderm on 11 August of a truck laden with flight cases stencilled with the words 'Nirvana, Seattle' rather gave the game away.

The choice of studio was Steve Albini's. Albini had recorded The Wedding Present's *Seamonsters* album at Pachyderm in 1991, and had returned to the facility to make PJ Harvey's *Rid of Me* in December 1992; he liked the studio's live room, liked working its vintage Neve 8068 recording console – previously housed in Jimi Hendrix's Electric Ladyland Studio – and liked the fact that Cannon Falls was in the middle of fucking nowhere, providing zero distractions to visiting musicians. Gold Mountain approved: their priority was to keep Cobain away from anywhere with a drugs subculture, to prevent predatory heroin dealers latching on to their artist. Located in a 50-acre private forest, overlooking a spring-fed trout stream, Pachyderm was ideal. The isolated studio didn't get a whole lot of passing trade at the best of times, much less in the depths of a harsh Minnesota winter.

When Nirvana arrived, Albini asked Pachyderm's chef Carter Nicole Launt, who was dating engineer (and Shellac bassist) Bob Weston, to make dinner. While the food was being prepared he put an unusual proposition to the band.

'We'd never met Albini before and, of course, he's a legend so we were all a little nervous and in awe of this guy who'd made some amazing records that we'd worn out on our turntables,' says Grohl. 'He had this reputation of being a dastardly asshole, the biggest cynical prick, but he was nothing but nice. But right off the bat he said, "OK, I do this with every band. If you beat me at a game of pool, I'll make your album for free. If I beat you, you pay me double." We were paying him $100,000 to make that record. Anyone who's got the stones to gamble something that large must be an amazing pool player so everyone said, "No." Plus he had his own stick, so we didn't want to fuck around with that.'

'I'm not a particularly good pool player,' shrugs Albini, 'but I can make a fair game, and I feel that that's a perfectly reasonable proposition; double-or-nothing on a fair game. But I think they were a little more risk averse than I was.'

Work on Nirvana's third album began on Valentine's Day 1993. The band set up their own equipment, Albini positioned his microphones and recording of the basic tracks began immediately. True to Albini's purist methodology, almost every song was recorded in one or two takes. Dave Grohl relished the challenge.

'When you record with Steve,' he says, 'he turns on the machine, hits the red button and says, "OK, go." You play the song, and then when it's over he hits stop and says, "What's next?"'

'When we talked to him before recording he made a point about, "Are your songs prepared? Are you going to come into the studio and fuck around for two weeks? Are you going to write in the studio?" We said, "No, no, no." We set up and recorded.'

'I was pretty impressed when the three of them all got set up and started playing these songs,' says Brent Sigmeth, now Pachyderm's in-house producer, but then a rookie studio assistant. 'It was really fast and really raw and really cool. It kinda seemed like I was going to witness something really unique, and that's how it turned out.'

'The sessions went really smoothly,' says Albini. 'None of it was difficult. They'd sent me their demos from Brazil and they were pretty skeletal – there were really only a couple of proper songs there – so I was a little bit surprised that when they got to Minnesota it seemed like things had fleshed out quite a bit. I thought they were all excellent musicians, particularly Dave, who is an absolute monster of a drummer. I know Dave is highly regarded as a drummer, but I still think he's underrated as a drummer.'

'When Dave arrived and set up his drums and started playing in that room, Bob Weston and I kinda looked at each other and said, "Oh my God, we gotta get out of here or we'll have hearing damage,"' says Sigmeth. 'We literally walked out of the room and went, "Wow, okay, he plays *loud*." I was just trying to stay out of the picture, but I was really enjoying it.'

'We knew that Albini didn't wanna deal with some big-time rock band or have to coddle some half-assed musicians,' Krist Novoselic told Keith Cameron in 2001. 'So, we knew how to rock! We'd been rockin' for years, we had our licks down. I remember Albini standing there by the tape machine with his arms folded, bobbing his head, and we would just pop 'em out one after the other. "Well, that sounded good. Let's do this song."'

Grohl finished his drum tracks for the album in just three days. He then sat around with nothing to do but watch TV for days on end. One afternoon, bored senseless, the drummer poured some of the studio's tape-head-cleaning alcohol on his baseball cap, set it alight and walked into the lounge where Albini was sleeping, screaming that his head was on fire. Albini opened his eyes, looked at the drummer's blazing head, sighed and promptly fell back asleep. Grohl's singed baseball cap took pride of place in Pachyderm for the next decade.

'Dave probably felt quite cooped up,' says Brent Sigmeth with some understatement. 'He's kind of a hyper dude. He wanted to go ice fishing and he wanted to go snowmobiling, but time went so fast that I couldn't pull it off for him. He ended up watching Steve Martin's *Planes, Trains & Automobiles* more times than is healthy.'

After just one week at Pachyderm, a total of 17 songs had been recorded. Among these, though not earmarked for inclusion on the album, was a new version of 'Marigold' aka 'Color Pictures of a Marigold' from Dave Grohl's *Pocketwatch* tape.

As the second week of recording in Minnesota began, an unexpected visitor arrived at Pachyderm: Courtney Love had decided to pay Cobain a surprise visit. Love's presence rather upset the harmonious vibe of the process; Grohl actually retreated to his room for the remainder of the session after one particularly heated argument with her. Brent Sigmeth freely admits that Love 'terrified' him, while Steve Albini later called her a 'psycho hose beast'. These days he is a tad more circumspect.

'I don't like spending any energy thinking about or talking about Courtney Love, but when she turned up things did slow down,' the producer told me in 2010. 'I don't know if the band said anything to her, but I never took anything she said seriously. I don't know if she tried to have an influence on the sessions, but she certainly didn't on me.'

Despite the disruption caused by Love's visit, Nirvana wrapped the recording of their new album one day ahead of schedule. Wine and cigars were dispensed to all present, and a mood of contented accomplishment prevailed. Against all odds, Nirvana had pulled together a collection of songs every bit as powerful and passionate as *Nevermind*: regardless of how well the album sold – and Albini boldly predicted, 'I don't think that all the pussies and wimps who liked the last album will ever like this one' – the trio were convinced they had created their masterpiece.

'I love that record,' said Grohl. 'I like it more than *Nevermind* because there was nothing in between the band and the tape. Nothing at all. We weren't nervous to make it, we had a collection of songs that we thought were challenging and interesting and powerful and beautiful. That album is about as pure as an album can be.'

The band left Pachyderm in high spirits. They would soon be brought crashing down to earth. Just two weeks after leaving Cannon Falls, Kurt Cobain phoned Steve Albini to tell him that his A&R man Gary Gersh hated the record.

'When we turned that record in to the record company, the first listen they called back and said, "Are you guys fucking kidding me? Is this a joke?"' recalled Grohl. 'We're like, "No, that's our record." They're like, "No, no, no, no, no, no, this isn't your next record. That's a joke." We basically said, "We are Nirvana. That is our new record."'

This bullishness on Nirvana's part didn't last. Some weeks later, Steve Albini received a second phone call from Kurt Cobain. This time Cobain was rather more sheepish.

'He said they were starting to believe that they were unhappy with the record and they wanted to remix some stuff,' Albini recalls. 'And I said, "Okay, well, I'll give it a listen and if I feel I can do any better or if I feel like there's specific stuff I can change then I'll be happy to give it a shot." And so I listened to the master again at home in Chicago and I really felt pretty strongly that I couldn't improve on what we'd done. And after doing that, I called Kurt back and said, "Well, what exactly did you want to do, like how many songs and what did you want to do?" And he said, "Well, basically everything." And at that point I knew that there was something going on other than them actually being dissatisfied. Like somebody had put a bug in their ear about something. Kurt might have been in a vulnerable state at that point – I don't know if his drug use kicked back in or if he started to fear for his pension or whatever, I have no idea what happened – but as soon as he said that I realised that there was something up and that it didn't have anything to do with whether or not they were actually satisfied with the record.'

On 19 April the *Chicago Tribune* ran an article by writer Greg Kot titled 'Record Label Finds Little Bliss in Nirvana's Latest'. In Kot's story Albini baldly stated that Geffen hated the record he had made with the band: 'I have no faith this record will be released,' he said. Kot backed up Albini's comments by quoting unnamed sources at Geffen who claimed the album was 'unreleasable'. The article was seized upon by media outlets across the world, including *Newsweek*, *Billboard* and *Rolling Stone*, with every story drawing attention to what was perceived as corporate interference in Nirvana's art. Such was the furore surrounding the album that on 11 May Geffen felt compelled to issue a press release refuting the now commonly held belief that they were going to bury the record.

I hate myself and I want to die

By this point R.E.M. producer Scott Litt was already remixing two songs from the album – prospective singles 'Heart-Shaped Box' and 'All Apologies' – at Heart's Bad Animals Studios in Seattle.

'Up to the point where we finished the mixes on that record I had a pretty good time working with Nirvana,' says Albini, 'and it remains a pretty good memory for me. After that – once the management company and record label started turning the heat up on the band and they started dropping shit into the press – it got really ugly.

'I have to admit, though, I was surprised at how devious their record company people were, doing really bizarre shit, like planting lies about me in the press. I didn't expect them to be that petty. In my view the whole thing was being done just as a way to manipulate the band. It wasn't that they were genuinely dissatisfied with the record, the record stands on its own merits, but it was made in a way away from their comfort. It was kinda seen as a dangerous thing if a band was allowed to make a record on their own terms like that. And so the record label people tried to scuttle that effort however they could, because they were afraid that a record made unconventionally might be successful and then they would have to allow that into their paradigm.

'I don't harbour any bad feelings towards the band,' Albini insists. 'It was people external to the band who were pulling this bullshit. I've said this before, and I still think this, the three guys in the band were perfectly reasonable and easy for me to deal with, but literally every other person involved in that record was an asshole.'

Asked in 2007 how the recordings that Nirvana took from Pachyderm compared to the version of *In Utero* that hit record stores worldwide on 13/14 September, Dave Grohl said the two were 'pretty similar'. This both is, and isn't, true, as can clearly be heard when the Albini mixes (later released unofficially on the Small Clone label) are played alongside Geffen's version of the album. While 'Heart-Shaped Box' and 'All Apologies' were the only two tracks remixed – with Scott Litt doubling Cobain's vocals, cleaning out some of the distortion and feedback, compressing the guitar lines and adding reverb to Grohl's snare – the mastering of the album served to put an entirely new sheen on Albini's natural, atmospheric recordings.

And it's arguably Grohl's drum sound which suffers most, most noticeably on the album's heavier tracks – 'Radio Friendly Unit Shifter', 'Milk It', 'Scentless Apprentice', 'Serve the Servants' – where the drums are backed off to allow Cobain's vocals more space to breathe. While Albini didn't bury Cobain's vocals as deeply as he customarily buried David Yow's vocals on The Jesus Lizard's albums (where Yow yelps, slobbers and moans like a man being strangled while drowning in quicksand), on his original mixes Cobain sounds more desperate, urgent and anguished as he struggles to be heard above the instrumental swamp; on the mastered version there's more clarity, more separation and less audible distress.

It would be too simplistic to say that, with the final version of *In Utero*, Nirvana bowed to commercial forces – 'Radio Friendly Unit Shifter' and 'Tourette's' in particular are no one's idea of crossover hits – but the fact remains that given the opportunity to deconstruct the radio-friendly sheen of *Nevermind*, as Cobain always maintained was his intention, the band took a conscious decision to step back from the raw ambience captured by Albini to present a more conventional, less challenging version of the recordings to the world. Just as Cobain was careful not to tip the album too far into noise territory – the 'pop' moments outweigh the more abrasive 'punk' tantrums seven to five – so the final version of *In Utero* offers a sound knowingly compromised for public consumption. Given the constant conflicts and contradictions in Cobain's attitude to success, such a stance could hardly have surprised those who knew him best.

Beyond the specifics of mixing and mastering, however, *In Utero* ultimately stands or falls upon the strength of its songs, and in terms of craft and composition Cobain's songwriting here eclipses anything in his past. Knowing just how much scrutiny would be placed upon the opening track of the follow-up to *Nevermind*, his decision to introduce *In Utero* with the lyric '*Teenage angst has paid off well | Now I'm bored and old*' is truly fearless. 'Serve the Servants' also packs Cobain's thoughts on the media's demonisation of his wife, his memories of childhood neglect and his reflections upon his new-found celebrity status into four scathing minutes: it is a bravura performance. 'Scentless

Apprentice', based on Patrick Süskind's 1985 novel *Perfume* and built around a gnarled, ascending Dave Grohl-authored guitar riff and earthquake drumbeat, is the album's second undeniable *moment*, and although Cobain later haughtily dismissed the central riff as 'a cliché grunge Tad riff' it's the most memorable guitar line on the whole album. But it's 'Heart-Shaped Box' that is the album's undisputed artistic high-point: the darkest of love songs, it incorporates familiar Cobain lyrical themes – entrapment, dependency, addiction – into an achingly beautiful meditation upon obsessive, consumptive love.

In truth, *In Utero* is a profoundly confused and conflicted album which is neither the unlistenable career suicide note many feared nor in truth a set of songs leaving grunge formulas in the dust. As writer John Mulvey noted in his superb analysis of the album in *NME*, *In Utero* sounds like the work of a band looking for a direction they can psychologically deal with. For every petulant punk rock hissy fit – the lyrics of the scouring 'Tourette's' are listed simply in anagram form as '*Cufk Tish Sips*' – there's a moment of sublime, delicate beauty, from Cobain's cracked, tender vocals on 'Pennyroyal Tea' through to the gorgeous simplicity of 'Dumb'. Amid the dark, brooding anger there are moments of levity: 'Very Ape' is a wonderful swipe at the competitive one-upmanship found within indie rock circles – and ushering in the scabrous 'Rape Me' with the chords of 'Smells Like Teen Spirit' is brilliantly knowing. But overall a pervasive sense of ennui and listlessness weighs heavily. It was an album that raised more questions than it answered about Cobain's state of mind.

Reviews for the album were mixed. *Melody Maker* noted that 'Nirvana's hungrily awaited third album is not quite the rubbed-raw, confrontational, fan-alienating catharsis it's been talked up to be', but concluded, 'we still need people who can speak the truth like this'. *NME* said the album was 'a mess, but a bloody entertaining one'. Writing in *Rolling Stone*, David Fricke said, '*In Utero* is a lot of things – brilliant, corrosive, enraged and thoughtful, most of them all at once,' while observing, 'None of this unrepentantly self-obsessed rant & roll would be half as compelling or convincing if Nirvana weren't such master blasters.' As anticipated, *In Utero* débuted at Number One in both the UK and US album charts, but the band's management, record label, music critics and fans alike were fully aware that this was but a prelude to the real story: the world was waiting to see how Kurt Cobain would cope with operating in the spotlight once again.

〜

Autumn 1993 found Nirvana doing something they hadn't done in two years – a US tour. When the band stepped onto the stage of the Veterans Memorial Coliseum at the Arizona State Fairgrounds in Phoenix, Arizona on 18 October they did so as a four-piece, with former Germs guitarist Pat Smear newly installed in the line-up. By then Dave Grohl had already declared – and withdrawn – his intention to leave the band.

Amid the many dark, disturbing images in Anton Corbijn's acclaimed, arty video for *In Utero*'s lead-off single 'Heart-Shaped Box' there's a tender human moment which went largely unnoticed that autumn. Three minutes into the promo clip, Krist Novoselic gently wraps his right arm around Dave Grohl's shoulder and draws the drummer closer; Grohl reaches up and clasps the bassist's hand in his own. The sickness at the heart of Nirvana was taking its toll upon both men. The elation Grohl and Novoselic felt as they left Pachyderm with the masters of their new album had long since dissipated. The summer months had been filled with drama – overdoses, allegations of domestic violence (charges that both Cobain and Love flatly denied), band arguments and veiled threats – and tensions within the band were mounting: that Pat Smear was recruited as Nirvana's second guitarist without Cobain bothering to flag his decision up with the band's rhythm section was symptomatic of the lack of communication within the unit at the time. And even as preparations for the tour got underway Grohl became aware that his position in the band was under review. On a flight from Seattle to Los Angeles the drummer made up his mind to walk away from the madness.

'We got on a plane,' he recalls, 'and Kurt was kinda fucked up. And I heard him talking about how shitty a drummer I was. He was two rows back from me and I overheard him and I got off the plane and said to

Krist, "Hey, what was that all about?" He was like, "Oh man, it's nothing, he was just saying he thinks you should get a smaller drum set and
play more like Danny [Peters] or something." And I was like, "Oh,
yeah? Okay." I mean at this point the two camps had done this ...' here
Grohl spreads his arms wide to indicate the widening gulf between
Cobain and Love on one side and Novoselic and himself on the other
'... and back at the hotel I called our tour manager Alex and said, "You
know what? I'm out, dude ... that's it. Stop booking shows. I'll finish
the shows, but I'm out, I don't want to fucking do this any more, I don't
need this, people are insane. I just want to fucking play music, I don't
want to have to deal with any of this craziness." It was not fun. But then
he talked me back into it.

'We were the most dysfunctional fucking band you could possibly
imagine. We were all so terribly passive. Kurt was not a confrontational
person. If he had a problem with you, you could feel the vibe, but it's
not like he would scream at you for doing something wrong. I don't
remember ever seeing him do that, once, to anyone, ever. And Krist and
I were sorta the same way. It was eggshells, for sure. So a lot of those
conflicts were just either ignored, or resolved quietly. There wasn't a
whole lot of band meetings. It was very weird.

'But I stayed. And that was my own decision. My responsibility was
to Krist and Kurt, my job was to be there for them. There was never
anyone telling me "You have to ..." anything. Everybody else worked
for me, I knew that, right out the gate. I knew that the first time I tried
to quit. "Fuck you people, don't you fucking tell me what to do! Fuck
you! I need to do this? I don't need to do this. I *like* working at Furniture
Warehouse ..." You feel a responsibility to your audience and your fans,
but not so much that it would fucking kill me.'

Nirvana's new guitarist did much to improve the atmosphere in the
camp. Born Georg Ruthenberg on 5 August 1959, Pat Smear was a
punk rock lifer, with a wry sense of humour honed on the early
Hollywood punk scene with his band The Germs, a band Dave Grohl
remembers as 'the baddest motherfuckers in the world'. Formed in
1977 by Queen/Alice Cooper/Runaways fan Ruthenberg and his teenage best friend, the brash, bold and provocative Paul Beahm, aka Darby

Crash, The Germs set out to be Los Angeles' most notorious, contro-versial and talked-about band: after just one show at the Orpheum on Sunset Boulevard they'd pretty much achieved their aim, with *Raw Power* fanzine dismissing them as 'the biggest joke of the year'.

'None of the Germs could play their instruments whatsoever,' the fanzine noted. 'They took an hour to get set up and then played for two minutes. The lead singer smeared peanut butter all over his face and everybody's in the group, and they were all spitting on each other until they were kicked off. You can bet they won't be back either.'

'We went out of our way to say things and do things that most people would never say or do,' recalled Smear to rock writer/Hollywood punk rock man-about-town Brendan Mullen for his superb, highly recom-mended Germs biography *Lexicon Devil*. 'It was like, "We're gonna fucking start a band, and we're gonna change our names, and we're gonna fucking be this thing – we're gonna really be like that, 24–7, we're not going to fake it! … and we're never gonna puss out! Whatever it is we're gonna be, we're gonna be the most – if we're gonna be punk, then we're gonna out-punk the Sex Pistols! If we're gonna be the worst band ever, then we're fucking gonna be the *worst* band ever!'

Smear's first appearance with Nirvana came at the band's *Saturday Night Live* taping on 25 September 1993. By Hallowe'en his efferves-cent personality had raised morale in the camp to the extent that Nirvana took to the stage of the University of Akron on 31 October in fancy dress – Cobain dressed as the kids TV dinosaur Barney, Smear dressed as Slash, Grohl appearing as a mummy and Novoselic as a black-faced Ted Danson, a reference to a controversial appearance by the comedian at a 'roast' dedicated to his then-girlfriend Whoopi Goldberg.

The following week *Nevermind* passed the five million sales mark in America. Danny Goldberg told *Newsweek* that credit for pushing album sales to this landmark figure should go to MTV: Gold Mountain had already accepted the network's invitation to have Nirvana play on its high-rating *Unplugged* show.

The band taped their *Unplugged* performance at Sony Studios in New York on 18 November 1993: their 14-song set was filmed in a

single take. Shunning his best-known songs – 'Come As You Are' was
the only *Nevermind*-era single aired – Cobain opted instead to flesh out
the set with cover versions from David Bowie ('The Man Who Sold the
World'), The Vaselines ('Jesus Don't Want Me for a Sunbeam'),
Leadbelly ('Where Did You Sleep Last Night') and no less than three
songs by SST's Meat Puppets ('Plateau', 'Oh Me' and 'Lake of Fire').
Augmented by cellist Lori Goldston, Nirvana had never sounded more
desolate, desperate or chilling: this was a punk rock performance in the
same way that Bruce Springsteen's *Nebraska* is a punk rock record. On
a stage resembling a funeral rest home, Cobain sang of death, deliver-
ance, betrayal and rejection; when the set emerged as *MTV Unplugged
in New York* one year later every word would carry an additional
emotional charge.

〜

'1994 was a bad year right out of the gate,' says Dave Grohl. 'Things
had changed a lot. Kurt had struggled through a lot of stuff and we
were trying to come to terms with being this enormous band, I guess.
That whole year is blurry for me because of how lost I was the whole
time.'

The year started with Kurt Cobain on the cover of *Rolling Stone*
magazine. In an open, emotional interview, sensitively handled by
David Fricke, Cobain addressed the nature of fame, marriage and
fatherhood, and spoke of his ongoing battle with drugs and the future
of his band in stark, unflinching terms. He admitted that his drug use
had caused problems between himself, Novoselic and Grohl and stated
his belief that, creatively, Nirvana were 'stuck in a rut'.

'Krist, Dave and I have been working on this formula – this thing of
going from quiet to loud – for so long that it's literally becoming boring
for us,' he admitted. 'It's like, "OK, I have this riff. I'll play it quiet,
without a distortion box, while I'm singing the verse. And now let's turn
on the distortion box and hit the drums harder." I want to learn to go
in between those things, go back and forth, almost become psychedelic
in a way but with a lot more structure. It's a really hard thing to do, and
I don't know if we're capable of it – as musicians.'

Yet even as Cobain was decrying the use of this songwriting formula, he was working on a new song, 'You Know You're Right', that stuck rigidly to the template. From 28 to 30 January, just prior to the first leg of the band's European arena tour, Gold Mountain booked the band into Robert Lang Studios in Shoreline, Seattle – a facility ten minutes' walk from Dave Grohl's home – to record the song. Once again, Cobain failed to turn up for the first scheduled day in the studio. There was no sign of the singer on 29 January either. But on the afternoon of 30 January he finally appeared … minus his guitars and amps. It was not a good omen. But in just three takes, the song – classic whisper-scream purgative punk with a brutally succinct one-word chorus – '*Pain*' – was committed to two-inch tape. The band promised to return to the studio after the European tour to complete the session. Circumstances would conspire to break this promise.

'The last time we'd toured Europe we were still Nirvana, from Seattle, now we were *NIRVANA!*' says Dave Grohl. 'Things had changed. We had the Buzzcocks and then Melvins out with us and I was really excited about that, and we were having good shows, but by the time we got to Germany I don't think Kurt wanted to be there any more. I remember on that tour, I think it was the first time I felt depression, one of the only times I've ever felt depression, like "can't get out of fucking bed" depression. It was in Milan, and I so badly wanted to be home. I'd never felt that way. I don't think I'd ever missed something where it just makes you collapse. I couldn't get out of bed. And that was a pretty good indication that I wasn't happy and didn't want to be there. But I had made the commitment of doing it and I didn't want to let anyone down. But it wasn't long after that until I think Kurt felt the same way …'

On 1 March 1994 Nirvana played their final show at Terminal Einz in Munich, Germany. There was no place for 'Smells Like Teen Spirit' in the band's 23-song set. When he walked offstage, Cobain asked the band's agent Don Muller to cancel the remaining dates as he was too sick to perform.

'Kurt wanted to go home,' says Grohl, 'so I think he intentionally blew his voice out, so that any doctor in his right mind would look at his throat and go, "It's kinda inflamed." He intentionally blew his voice out so that we could all go home. I had to stay another day to make a video for the *Backbeat* soundtrack and then the next day I flew home, via Heathrow and San Francisco. So finally I get home, put the bags down, and collapse in bed. And I wake up at five in the morning to an emergency phone call.

'And it's some guy, going, "Dave? Is this really Dave Grohl?" And I'm like, "Yeah, who is this?" And he's like, "I'm John, I live in Boston and I'm a huge fucking fan, and I just wanted to say you guys are great." So I'm like, "How did you get my phone number?" and he said, "I just told the operator it was an emergency." So I'm like, "Okay, that's cool, just don't phone back ..." Five minutes later the phone rings again and someone goes, "Dude, turn on CNN ..." And I see Kurt, in Rome. So, that's when I knew, "Oh no, it's over ..."'

It was 4 March 1994, and Kurt Cobain was in a coma in Rome's Policlinico Umberto Primo hospital after swallowing 50 to 60 Rohypnol pills in the suite he was sharing with his wife at the Hotel Excelsior.

'I woke up at, like, four in the morning to reach for him, basically to fuck him, 'cause I hadn't seen him in so long,' Courtney Love later told *Spin* magazine. 'And he wasn't there. And I always get alarmed when Kurt's not there, 'cause I figure he's in the corner somewhere, doing something bad. And he's on the floor, and he's dead.'

In his right hand Cobain held 1,000 American dollars. In his left hand was a suicide note. 'Like Hamlet, I have to choose between life and death,' it read. 'I choose death.'

'So I see that [on CNN] and I'm like, "What the fuck?"' says Grohl. 'And so Krist and I get on the phone. And then someone says, "He's okay, he's just in a coma, he's not dead." It was so chaotic and crazy. I mean, there are certain people in your life that you just know they're not gonna make it. So in the back of your mind you emotionally prepare yourself for something like that to happen ... not that it makes it easier, but so that when it *does* happen your world won't collapse completely. But it was so weird, and surreal, that 28 hours ago I was hanging out with these people. But then someone called and said that he died, and I lost it, I just fucking lost it. This was just twenty minutes later. And then someone rings up again and goes, "Oh, no, he didn't die." It was bad.

'And then he came home, and we talked on the phone. And I told him, "Man, Kurt, fuck …" I didn't tell him that someone had told me that he'd died, but I told him that I was terrified and so worried. And he was really apologetic, like, "So sorry, I was partying and drinking and I wasn't paying attention to what I was doing." And I said, "Listen, I don't think you should die!" And then, I think, well, then, you know what happened …

'From there on out it wasn't long until he died. It was a weird fucking thing. I was totally non-emotional. I don't even know if I was in shock, I was just shut down. I remember trying to make myself cry and I couldn't.'

The circumstances of Kurt Cobain's last days are still somewhat confused. On 18 March Courtney Love called the Seattle police out to her family home, telling them that her husband had locked himself in a room and was intent upon killing himself. The following week, together with Danny Goldberg, John Silva, Gary Gersh, Krist Novoselic and other close friends, Love staged an intervention to convince Cobain to go into rehab in Los Angeles. On 1 April Cobain jumped over the wall of the Exodus rehab clinic and caught a flight back to Seattle. Four days later the singer barricaded himself into the greenhouse of his Lake Washington home, shot up 1.52 milligrams of heroin, placed a shotgun against his head, and pulled the trigger with his thumb.

When Dave Grohl talks about Kurt Cobain's last days his body language and speech patterns change. The bounce disappears from his voice, and his recollections are delivered haltingly. When we spoke in November 2009, he slumped almost horizontal on the couch in his suite at the Sunset Marquis, with his head in his hands and tears in his eyes.

'It's hard for me to even talk about,' he said finally. 'It was just so nuts, I don't even know how to explain it. The time leading up to that … I can't talk a lot about it. I can't talk about it too much because a lot of fucked-up shit went down that nobody knows about. And Krist and I have always kept quiet about a lot of what happened because it's a personal issue. People know that there was an intervention. People know that he was sent to Los Angeles. People know that he split rehab and that he disappeared. And I know just about as much as everybody else does.

'But there's some other things that happened long before any of that stuff that made it clear that maybe we weren't going to be a band forever. And I think maybe at that point it was time for everybody to back away from it. I'd had enough before he'd disappeared, I think Krist and I had both had enough of it.

'One of my favourite lines in a Nirvana song – which is fucking dark and I didn't realise its weight until I sat in my house in Seattle playing Ian MacKaye the first mixes of *In Utero*, without a lyric sheet – is the line on "Scentless Apprentice" where Kurt sings, "*You can't fire me because I quit*." Ian heard that and he goes, "That's fucked up." And I realised, "Wow, that is fucked up." So to me if there's one line in any song that gives me the chills it's that one. Maybe all those things that people wrote about him painted him into a corner that he couldn't get out of.'

As news of Kurt Cobain's death reverberated around the world, Grohl locked the doors of his Shoreline home and retreated into grief with his fiancée Jennifer Youngblood. One day, weeks later, a letter arrived. It had been sent to Grohl by his friend Nick Christy, the frontman of Nameless, Grohl's first band. Christy offered Grohl his condolences and tried his best to empathise with his friend's loss. And at the conclusion of the letter Christy tried to shine some light into the darkness.

'Dude, you're awesome, you're great at what you do, you're talented and I'm sure you're going to land on your feet,' he wrote. 'You're a special person and I'm sure God has a plan for your life. And I know you'll do fine.'

I'll stick around

After Kurt died … the way that I thought about, and listened to, music changed forever. All that bullshit, which I tried so hard to avoid, all of that fucking 'cool', all of that fucking guilt, just went away. I just thought, 'You know, it's so useless.' Why am I here in the first place? I'm into music. Do a lot of people enjoy it? Of course. Do I care if they think I'm cool? No, I just wanna fucking play …

Dave Grohl

From the outside, with its red brick walls, arched doorways and slanted red slate roofs, Robert Lang Studios in Seattle resembles an enchanted castle. Perched on a hillside affording spectacular views of Puget Sound and the Olympic Mountains, it's an imposing structure, with an impressive client list and a truly fascinating back story.

In the early 1970s Lang and his best friend Dubby had a dream of building a recording studio in Seattle. In 1974 they realised that dream, opening a small facility in Richmond Beach in the Shoreline area. The studio was compact and bijou – early clients jokingly christened it 'Munchkin Studios' due to its minuscule dimensions – but to its owners it was every bit as magnificent as Abbey Road or Ocean Way, a sonic temple in which magic might be plucked from the air. In 1979 Dubby passed away, but not before informing his friend that he had a sum of money buried in the ground near the property. The following year Lang found his friend's stash – a little under $100,000 in $100 bills – and vowed to honour his departed friend's memory by fashioning a world-class recording facility on the very ground in which Dubby had secreted his life savings. In the years that followed, Lang literally carved a studio space out of the hillside to create a cavernous live room, which he lined with granite, marble and wood. While the project was ongoing Lang could sense his friend's spirit guiding him: to this day he believes that Dubby's spirit 'runs wild' around the property. That notion would be easier to dismiss had numerous clients not experienced unexplained paranormal activity, from full body apparitions to equipment randomly switching itself on and off, while using the facility.

On 28 June 1993 Lang was cutting a slab of Chinese marble for the floor of his studio, when a blinding flash of light interrupted his work. When he set to his task once more, he noticed what appeared to be a human form newly present in the stone's white veins: on closer examination he identified the figure as that of the risen Jesus Christ, framed by a halo, holding a flaming torch to the Heavens, an image of resurrection and renewal. A man sees what he wants to see and disregards the rest, to misquote Paul Simon, but the image is undoubtedly striking, and to Lang, a charming, level-headed and rational man, it is further evidence that his studio is a special, spiritual place.

It was in this studio, the following summer, that Dave Grohl took his first steps towards creative rebirth.

In the weeks and months that followed Kurt Cobain's April 1994 suicide, Grohl found himself void of direction and motivation; he was lost, untethered and drifting aimlessly.

'After Kurt died,' he told me in 2009, 'honestly, it was maybe the next morning, I woke up and I thought, "Holy shit, he's gone and I'm still here: I get to wake up and he's gone." And then my life completely changed forever.'

As he struggled to make sense of a world without Cobain, Grohl sought solace in the arms of his girlfriend Jennifer Youngblood. Just weeks after Cobain's passing, the pair decided to marry. But even as he celebrated life as a newly-wed, Grohl was keenly aware that he remained estranged from the one thing which had always provided him with succour, security and support: the simple act of making music.

'After Kurt's death I was about as confused as I've ever been,' he admitted in 1995. 'To continue almost seemed in vain. I was always going to be "that guy from Kurt Cobain's band" and I knew that. I wasn't sure if I had the desire to make music any more.'

But even here, at what was undoubtedly the most disorientating and darkest point of Grohl's life to date, the musician still maintained at least some sense of perspective. 'As much as I missed Kurt,' he said, 'and as much as I felt so lost, I knew that there was only one thing that I was truly cut out to do and that was music. I know that sounds so incredibly corny, but I honestly felt that.

'The way that I thought about, and listened to, music changed forever,' he said. 'All that bullshit, which I tried so hard to avoid, all of that fucking "cool", all of that fucking guilt, just went away. I just thought, "You know, it's so useless." Why am I here in the first place? I'm into music. Do a lot of people enjoy it? Of course. Do I care if they think I'm cool? No, I just wanna fucking play …'

Grohl's sense of perspective was brought into sharp focus by words that came addressed to him on a postcard sent by the Seattle punk group 7 Year Bitch. The band had themselves been forced to confront the harsh realities of life when in 1992 guitarist Stefanie Sargent succumbed to a fatal heroin overdose, and two years later the surviving members felt sufficiently moved by Grohl's circumstances to send him a message wishing him well, a message that provided a light which beamed from the murky present into a more settled future. The words on the postcard read, 'We know what you're going through. The desire to play music is gone for now, but it will return. Don't worry.'

'That fucking letter,' Grohl later confessed, 'saved my life.'

Just two months after Kurt Cobain's name appeared in the obituary columns of the world's press, Grohl made his first post-Nirvana public appearance. On 4 June 1994 the drummer was reunited with Thurston Moore, Dave Pirner, Greg Dulli and friends as the Backbeat Band for a breathless, sometimes chaotic sprint through The Beatles' 'Money (That's What I Want)' and Little Richard's 'Long Tall Sally' at the MTV

Movie Awards in Los Angeles. With his hair in a ponytail and his face somewhat obscured by a baseball cap, Grohl attacked his instrument with an almost psychotic abandon as the *ad hoc* collective imbued these classic slices of rock 'n' roll history with a messy punk edge of which their authors would surely have approved. A one-off, never-to-be-repeated performance, the night sealed the Backbeat Band's hallowed, almost mythical, status within the alternative rock world.

Just over a month later, on 12 July, Grohl was reunited onstage with Krist Novoselic in Olympia, when alongside Yo La Tengo guitarist Ira Kaplan the pair joined forces to provide the musical backing for ten-year-old Simon Timony at the fabulously named Yo Yo A Go Go festival. Timony, the stepson of Half Japanese frontman Jad Fair, had been the driving force behind *The Stinky Puffs* EP, a four-track recording released on a small Texan indie label in 1991 which the youngster had posted to a delighted Kurt Cobain. Half Japanese opened for Nirvana on the band's autumn 1993 tour, and Timony had met Kurt Cobain, Chris Novoselic and Dave Grohl for the first time at New York's Roseland Ballroom in November 1993. Shortly before the Yo Yo A Go Go festival the youngster had written to Novoselic asking if he might consider accompanying him onstage for his show on 12 July. On the night of the show Grohl was also on hand with Mark Kates, and made the spontaneous decision to join in.

Though their appearance was unannounced, the media present for the opening night of the festival ensured that this brief re-formation of Nirvana's rhythm section became global news. 'One journalist said that Simon had performed a mass healing,' Fair told writer Gillian Gaar. 'And that's really how it felt.' The Stinky Puffs set, which included a song for Cobain titled 'I Love You Anyway', was recorded and released the following year.

Later that same summer Grohl and Novoselic were reunited once more, this time in the live room of Robert Lang Studios. Grohl had been introduced to ex-Minutemen/fIREHOSE bassist Mike Watt at the MTV Movie Awards in June, and the legendary punk rock lifer had asked the drummer if he might consider lending his talents to the recording of his début solo album, *Ball-Hog or Tugboat?* Signed to

This is a Call

Columbia Records in the post-Nirvana gold rush, Watt had already recruited no less than *fifty* guest musicians (among them Eddie Vedder, Thurston Moore, J Mascis, Beastie Boy Adam Horowitz, Frank Black, Henry Rollins, Circle Jerks' bassist Zander Schloss and Jane's Addiction drummer Stephen Perkins) for the project, one its creator likened to a creative 'wrestling match'. In terms of authenticity, if not commerciality, *Ball-Hog ...* would be a tough act to top: Grohl did not require a second invitation.

He contributed drums to two tracks on *Ball-Hog or Tugboat?* – 'Big Train' and 'Against the 70's'. While the former is a filthy-sounding blues rumble with a lyric so nakedly suggestive it might make Mötley Crüe blush (*'Big train, big train, do you wanna ride my big train?'*), it is on the latter track that Mike Watt's début album comes closest to magic. *'The kids of today should defend themselves against the 70's,'* sings Eddie Vedder, Pearl Jam's frontman, with just the right combination of sincerity, determination and annoyance. *'It's not reality,'* he adds, *'it's just someone else's sentimentality.'* The song was a minor hit single on US college radio: hearing it at the time, it was hard not to wish Nirvana's rhythm section could be reunited on a more permanent basis.

Beyond highlighting its creator's impeccable punk rock credentials, Watt's *Ball-Hog or Tugboat?* has one outstanding legacy: it was the catalyst to re-ignite Grohl's own creative urges.

'After we went to Robert Lang's and did a couple of songs with Watt, I thought, "Okay, I'm gonna get my shit together and demo some stuff at home and then book a session, for myself,"' Grohl told me in 2009. 'So I booked six days with Barrett. It was some cathartic thing: I needed to punch through this place I'd been trapped in for a while and I thought this would be the best therapy for me.'

Grohl revisited the various recordings he had made with Barrett Jones in the basement of their Bellevue home and selected twelve songs to re-record. In addition, he had penned and home-demoed three new songs in the aftermath of Kurt Cobain's passing – 'I'll Stick Around', 'Oh, George' and 'This Is a Call': these too he would redo at Robert Lang's soundproofed bunker. 'Before at Barrett's I'd record songs in fifteen minutes, so I was planning on recording three songs per day this time,' he recollected. 'I'd already sequenced the album in my head before recording it, so I went and recorded them in order.'

And so between 17 and 22 October 1994 Grohl committed fifteen songs to tape with Barrett Jones at the studio located minutes from his front door. 'This Is a Call' was recorded first, in two takes, totalling 45 minutes of studio time. From there, the pace and tone of the session were established.

'The first four hours was spent getting sounds,' Grohl revealed in the first Foo Fighters' press release. 'This was a cinch for Barrett, whom I'd asked to produce since he was the one person in the world I felt comfortable singing in front of. By five o'clock we were ready to record. Over the past six years Barrett and I had perfected our own method of recording. Start with drums, listen to playback while humming tune in head to make sure arrangement is correct, put down two or three guitar tracks, do bass track and move on to next songs, saving vocals for last. This time, though, it became sort of a game. I wanted to see how little time it could take me to track fifteen songs, complete with overdubs and everything. I did the basic tracks in two and a half days, meaning I was literally running from instrument to instrument, using mostly first takes on everything. All vocals and rough mixes were finished on schedule: one week.'

It is tempting with hindsight to ascribe too much order to the period that followed Grohl's recording of these tracks and their subsequent release in the form of an album. But life is rarely as ordered as it may appear to outside eyes, a truism that applies to an even greater degree when it comes to bands, musicians and the music industry. Happy accidents are common, and the axis upon which decisions that subsequently come to be seen as pivotal turn is often precarious indeed. While there can be no doubt that as the days of 1994 grew shorter and colder Dave Grohl had in his mind an idea for a creation that would soon enough become Foo Fighters, the notion that he had mentally mapped out a route from basement tape to platinum albums and international acclaim is fanciful indeed. For while the demise of Nirvana provided Grohl not just the obvious visitation of grief and even trauma, it also sounded a quieter note that sounded something like emancipation: Grohl was young, wealthy and suddenly free to follow his instincts as never before. And so when, in early November 1994, the drummer received an invitation from Tom Petty's management to join Petty's legendary band The Heartbreakers for a taping of *Saturday Night Live*, Grohl leapt at the opportunity, temporarily parking thoughts of his own project.

'My first reaction was, "What the fuck? He couldn't find a real drummer?"' Grohl laughed in 2011. 'Of course I jumped at the opportunity. Because I've always loved Tom Petty. Even when I was a stubborn, cynical, punk-rock asshole, I still loved Tom Petty. Because I felt like he was a stubborn, cynical, punk-rock asshole too.'

In 1994 Tom Petty was enjoying one of the peaks of his artistic life. During the previous two years the Gainesville-born singer-songwriter and all-American icon had been squirrelled away at Los Angeles' Sound City and Ocean Way Recording studios with producer Rick Rubin creating *Wildflowers*, his second solo album without long-time backing band The Heartbreakers. Released in November of that year, the fifteen-song, 62-minute set can be considered not far short of a masterpiece. Invited to perform two tracks from the album – 'Honey Bee' and 'You Don't Know How It Feels' – on *Saturday Night Live*, Petty was able to call upon the services of the thrillingly capable Heartbreakers once more, but that well-drilled unit were without a drummer, having just lost the services of the always mercurial Stan Lynch. Hence the call placed to Dave Grohl.

'Right when the thing with Stan Lynch happened, we were already booked to go on *Saturday Night Live*, so that left us high and dry,' Petty told *MOJO* in 2009. 'So we thought, first of all, who's a great drummer? Dave Grohl is our favourite drummer right now and he isn't doing anything. So I called Dave's office. He phoned back and was really keen to do it. I didn't get that deep with him about Kurt Cobain. What I did talk to him about was joining the Heartbreakers. He thought about it but he was torn. He told me he'd just completed [what became] the first Foo Fighters album on which he'd played everything, so the idea of actually being in a band really appealed to him. But I told him that with that going on, and with a deal, he would be unhappy with us.

I'll stick around

We're an older bunch of guys and I thought he would be happier doing his own thing.'

Even as he was respectfully declining Tom Petty's invitation to keep the beat for his Heartbreakers, in the autumn of 1994 rumours abounded regarding Grohl's employment status. It was suggested that the drummer might join forces with ex-Misfits frontman Glenn Danzig in the muscular, dramatic *noir* rock collective Danzig, replacing none other than Chuck Biscuits, one of his teenage heroes. Even louder came the rumour that Dave Grohl was to join Pearl Jam, a notion put to Virginia Grohl by one of her high school students in Alexandria, and duly passed along to her son. 'I don't know where the fuck these rumours came from,' was Dave's response, not strictly speaking in itself a denial.

But while in 1994 the world at large still viewed Dave Grohl as simply being a drummer – albeit a terrifically accomplished, A-list drummer – the man's perception of himself was changing. Awake to the possibilities afforded by his brand new demo tape, Grohl quickly came to realise that in those few days in October he had put his name to something that was possessed of both quality and potential. Or, more to the point, he *hadn't* put his name to it, for if there was one thing above all Dave Grohl desired for his own music at this point, it was anonymity and protection from the complicated shadows cast by the ghost of Nirvana. Even so, word regarding the tape was beginning to spread.

'One of the DJs from a Seattle radio station came up to Barrett's studio to hear something else and Barrett played him a demo of "I'll Stick Around",' Grohl told me. 'And actually, when I'd demoed that song with Barrett, when I heard it back for the first time, mixed, I actually had an anxiety attack because I finally realised that this was good, whereas everything else I recorded over the previous six years I thought was crap. I just thought, "Oh shit, this is real. Oh no! Now I have to pursue this ..."'

Grohl took his demo to a cassette copying facility in Seattle, and emerged with 100 copies of his fifteen-song tape. Inspired by former Police drummer Stuart Copeland's decision to release his earliest solo material under the pseudonym Klark Kent, the drummer decided to title the demo with a fictitious band name, just as he had done when issuing the *Pocketwatch* cassette as Late! The name he chose was Foo Fighters.

In 1995, in his band's first press release, Grohl explained the origins of the band name thus: 'Toward the end of the Second World War, U.S. Air Force flyers patrolling the German skies would encounter a number of strange aerial phenomena in the area between Hagenau in Alsace-Lorraine and Neustadt an der Weinstrasse in the Rhine Valley. Similar to modern reports of UFOs or so-called "flying saucers," these objects would come to be referred to as "Foo Fighters" ("Foo" being slang for the French *feu*, fire).' In 2009 he told me simply, 'I wanted to call it Foo Fighters because I didn't want people to know it was me.'

In his bid to create music anonymously, making multiple copies of the Foo Fighters demo Grohl would later acknowledge as being his 'first mistake'. His second? 'My blind generosity,' he said. 'That fucking tape spread like the Ebola virus, leaving me with an answering machine full of record company jive.'

Originally Dave distributed his Foo Fighters demo to a select group of friends, including Chris Novoselic, former Nirvana tour manager Alex MacLeod, Gary Gersh and Mark Kates. Another recipient of the tape was Kurt Cobain's guitar tech (and later Grohl's own guitar tech) Ernie Bailey, who tells a lovely story about receiving the demo in *Taking Punk to the Masses*.

'At one point Dave phoned me and said that he had this demo tape, y'know, that he wanted me to hear,' Bailey recalled. 'I remember feeling awkward about that, y'know, it's really tough when friends present you with their demo tape. So he said he was going to swing by. I remember him ringing the doorbell. I think I told him on the phone, "If I'm not here, just pop it through the mailbox," and so I waited for him to pop it through the mailbox and then after he drove off I went and got it and listened to it. And I wanted to phone him straight away and say, "Hey, this is really good!"'

Another impressed Seattle music scene luminary was Eddie Vedder. So impressed was Vedder, in fact, that on 8 January 1995 Pearl Jam's

I'll stick around

frontman gave the world its first listen to Foo Fighters: in the third quarter of his four-hour DIY 'Self Pollution Radio' show Vedder aired the tracks 'Gas Chamber' – a cover of the opening track on *Back to Samoa*, the Angry Samoans album Grohl had picked up at lacrosse camp a decade previously – and 'Exhausted'. Speaking on air about the music, Vedder introduced the songs thus: 'This is a rare opportunity to play this stuff to you. It's two songs by Dave Grohl. As far as I know he's played everything on these songs, he's playing all the instruments, and he played it to me a while back … We ended up recording a song or two with Mike Watt … I'm just going to let these songs fly … They're real good.'

Word of this most underground of musical projects was slowly bubbling its way to the surface. At the tail end of 1994 *Kerrang!* was able to exclusively reveal that Dave Grohl's latest excursion would be known as Foo Fighters, with the magazine stating that the former Nirvana drummer would henceforth be singing and playing guitar. A 'music industry source' was quoted as claiming the Foos to be 'a great band in their own right'.

In truth, at the time the story ran, in early December, Foo Fighters could not yet be legitimately referred to as a 'band'. For while the songs of Foo Fighters existed on a cassette tape, now swirling around the underground as second- and third-generation copies, much like the tapes dedicated to thrash metal and hardcore punk bands traded by Grohl a decade or more earlier, as late as December 1994 Foo Fighters as a band did not exist. In a recording studio it was possible for Grohl to play each of the instruments heard on his tape; live it was not. If its creator wished to take Foo Fighters beyond the realms of recorded music, and into the great wide open, he needed a band.

And so, without fuss or fanfare, he went out looking for one.

◡

The first, or at least second, part of Foo Fighters' puzzle came in the form of 26-year-old bassist Nate Mendel. Born and raised in Richland, WA, on the eastern side of the Cascade mountain range, a locale he later described as 'a weird place to grow up', the thoughtful, laid-back

Mendel was introduced to punk rock at age 14: if finding punk rock records in eastern Washington was a struggle, finding any semblance of a 'scene' was even tougher.

'I played in a punk band called Diddly Squat, and we were out in the middle of the desert, on the other side of the mountains from Seattle,' the bassist told me in 2009. 'There was a developed punk rock scene and an infrastructure in the bigger cities, but where I lived there wasn't any of that. So I took it upon myself to find places where we could play. There was a place called The Hoedown Center and I'd ring up and ask to play a little music show, and I'd bring in bands from out of town. There was no place to go and no bands to see so we just made it happen on our own.'

'*Maximumrocknroll* was the *New York Times* of the punk rock scene. So you'd get your name in there, and when it came time for bands to book tours they might see that you booked shows and give you a call. It was a great way to experience music growing up. No one had any money or a place to stay, so, like, bands would stay at my house. I'd wake up in the morning and Fat Mike from NOFX would be getting served pancakes by my mom.'

One Mendel-booked show, on 24 October 1987, saw Diddly Squat open for DC hardcore legends Scream. It was then that Mendel first met his future musical collaborator Dave Grohl.

'I remember very little about that show,' the bassist admitted to me, 'but I must have shook Dave's hand at the very least. I can't remember being impressed by his playing, but then at the time I wasn't a musician guy paying attention to the ability of different musicians, I just wanted to dance around and slam-dance and just go nuts.'

The following year, Mendel relocated to Seattle. Here he spread his wings musically, playing with a reformed version of DC punks Christ on a Crutch, while also jamming with teenage guitarist Greg Anderson in Galleon's Lap and the straight edge band Brotherhood. Christ on a Crutch contributed one track ('Off Target') to the 1989 Dischord compilation *State of the Union* and released a handful of independent singles locally before falling apart in 1993; Mendel then fell in with another local outfit, the fabulously named Chewbacca Kaboom, where he struck up an instant friendship with livewire drummer William Goldsmith.

Born in Seattle in 1972, the affable, outgoing Goldsmith had first started messing around on the drums as a pre-pubescent fifth grader. A freestyle player too inattentive to focus on the sheet music handed out by his school's music teacher, the teenager received many a detention for cluttering his playing on the school's drumkit with rolls and fills. His elder brother later introduced him to Led Zeppelin, The Who and the worlds of punk, New Wave and classic rock. 'All I wanted to do,' said Goldsmith, 'was be Keith Moon, with the kick drum foot of John Bonham.'

Soon enough, Chewbacca Kaboom morphed into Sunny Day Real Estate, a less 'hardcore', but more dextrous and emotional outfit, fronted by songwriter Jeremy Enigk. The group's 1994 début album, *Diary*, released on Sub Pop, received substantial underground acclaim: at one point it was the second biggest selling album in Sub Pop's catalogue, second only to Nirvana's *Bleach*. Intense and impassioned, the album has since been recognised as one of the releases that laid down the blueprint for the punk rock subculture dubbed 'emo', a resurrection of the word first applied to bands such as Rites of Spring and Embrace during DC's Revolution Summer. In common with their spiritual DC forefathers, Sunny Day Real Estate were not long for this world, things heading south for the group when their frontman 'found' Jesus and suggested to his bandmates that Sunny Day Real Estate's music should henceforth follow a Christian path. Nate Mendel's reaction to Jeremy Enigk's proposition was distinctly un-Christian: 'I wanted to fucking murder him,' said the bass player.

Around the same time, Mendel met Dave Grohl for a second time at a Sunny Day Real Estate concert in Seattle. On seeing the drummer backstage, the bassist remembers saying, perhaps to himself, 'Hey, it's that guy from Nirvana.'

'I'd never really met someone in a famous band before,' he told me in 2002. 'But he seemed cool and friendly, and I knew because of his DC hardcore roots he'd probably be okay … I guess those first impressions were pretty accurate.'

It just so happened that Jennifer Youngblood was a friend of Nate Mendel's girlfriend, a connection that led to the bassist being invited to *chez* Grohl for Thanksgiving dinner in November 1994. The host declined to tell his guest that he believed his Shoreline dwelling to be haunted. After the meal, the party sat down to a session at an ouija board, a session that drew the attentions of an 'uninvited guest' that displayed its displeasure to the others in the room by banging on the dining room table. Grohl recalls that the bassist 'freaked out'; Mendel's reaction is unprintable.

The following month, Sunny Day Real Estate themselves gave up the ghost. At the end of a month-long tour with Dischord prog-punks Shudder to Think and New Yorkers Soul Coughing, the quartet bowed out with a show at the Black Cat in Washington DC on 16 December 1994. At the climax of the band's set, Enigk turned his back on the audience and, to his bandmates' visible disgust, started quietly praying.

'This was exactly the big, huge rift that made everybody feel so uncomfortable,' Soul Coughing frontman Michael Doughty later told *Magnet* magazine. 'Nate just threw his hands up, put his bass down and left the stage. Dan [Hoerner, SDRE guitarist] just started drowning everything in feedback. The club got so hot they'd opened a door behind the stage, and Willie, who had worked so hard during the show – as the cold air poured in, steam is pouring off his body. He was so pissed off, just venting this incredible rage, staring at Jeremy, the steam exploding off him.'

As chance would have it, Dave Grohl had caught the quartet's final hometown show just weeks previously. It was then that he realised that he might not need to cast too far from his own home for a rhythm section for his new band.

'Around that time my friend Tracey said, "Have you heard of Sunny Day Real Estate?"' Grohl told me. 'And I'd heard of them but not *heard* them yet. When I mentioned them to Barrett he said, "Yeah, they sound like they're from DC." So then Tracey said, "They're playing their last show tomorrow night," so I went down to see them. And I watched Will and thought, "Shit, if that guy's not gonna be in a band tomorrow, he's gonna be in *my* band tomorrow."'

I'll stick around

On 16 December, Grohl left a message for Goldsmith at the Black Cat, a club he actually co-owned, asking the drummer to call him.

'I called him back,' Goldsmith remembered four years later, 'and he said, "So your band's in the shitter, huh?" And I said, "Yeah." And he said, "Well, do you and Nate want to do a band with me and Pat [Smear]?" And I said, "Sure, I guess."'

Since Kurt Cobain's death, Pat Smear had been living the life of a virtual recluse, sitting at home in Los Angeles smoking cigarettes and channel surfing through whatever television programmes happened to be airing that day. 'After you've been in the coolest band ever, what do you do?' he later pondered, not unreasonably. While in Los Angeles on posthumous Nirvana business, Grohl dropped his demo tape off at Smear's house, hoping that the guitarist would like it. As it turned out, Smear's enthusiasm for what he heard stretched further than mere approval.

'I listened to the tape while he was gone and I was just blown away,' Smear told me in 2009. 'I thought, "Oh shit, this is so great, I want to do this." And so about an hour after listening to the tape I walked down to the club where Dave was hanging out and said, "I love it, I wanna be in your band."'

'I knew that the band would need two guitars, but didn't think that Pat would want to commit to anything,' Grohl admitted in 1995. 'To my surprise, not only did he like the tape, he expressed interest in joining up.'

Dave Grohl's Foo Fighters were now officially a band.

～

From the moment that Eddie Vedder premiered Foo Fighters on 'Self Pollution Radio', major label A&R men began calling Grohl at home. Grohl had dealt with the corporate record industry before with Nirvana, of course, but now he was no longer 'just the drummer', happy to sit on the sidelines while deals were struck: with Foo Fighters, even after the recruitment of Smear, Mendel and Goldsmith, he was effectively 'The Band'. Two years previously, in a brilliant, if typically controversial, essay titled 'The Problem with Music', Steve Albini had laid bare the machinations of the major label world, exposing the myriad ways in which seemingly lucrative record contracts could come back to haunt artists; his article calmly concluded, 'Some of your friends are probably already this fucked.' It was an essay that resonated throughout the underground rock community, and one Grohl could not have failed to notice. Somewhat spooked by the deluge of messages cluttering up his answering machine, in the opening days of 1995 Grohl turned to John Silva for advice. The wily music business veteran suggested that the drummer speak with his lawyer Jill Berliner before contacting anyone else. And Berliner gave Grohl the same advice that Phil Spector had passed on to Andrew Loog Oldham when the Londoner was shopping around Rolling Stones demos to major record labels in 1963.

'I got on the phone with Jill Berliner, who's a fucking amazing woman,' Grohl told me, 'and she said, "Here's what you do: you start your own record company – you own the record, you put it out and you just distribute it through a record company."'

Before one could say 'Fuck the Man!', and before the advent of his 26th birthday, the young musician who created Foo Fighters had also formed his own record company on which to release his music. The company was named Roswell Records, after the secret location in New Mexico that housed the supposed wreckage of alien spacecraft discovered by the United States government. And in true independent, even socialistic, style, with one fell swoop, and for the first time in his professional life, Dave Grohl claimed ownership of the means of production, and became master of his own destiny.

'Every single thing that Foo Fighters have ever done, I own – the entire catalogue,' he said, explaining the mechanics of the situation to me in 2009. 'I license it to the record company and say, "You can have it for six years; after six years you have to give it back. And if you want to keep it some more, then you have to fucking pay." So ultimately, every two years, another one of the albums is up for renegotiation; so the idea is to have your catalogue behind you every two years. I only sign for one- or two-album deals – I'm not locked into ten-album deals – so every time it's time to sign a new deal …

Writing the set-list for the final show of the *Foo Fighters* album tour, 19 July 1996, at the Phoenix Festival at Long Marston Airfield, Stratford-upon-Avon.

Meeting Grohl backstage at London's Brixton Academy, 23
November 1997.

Skin and Bones: Foo Fighters in the hot tub at the U2-owned Clarence
Hotel, Dublin, July 2002.

Opposite: Looking suave on the 'Monkey Wrench' video shoot at the
Ambassador Hotel, Los Angeles, March 1997.

Laying down apocalyptic thunder in LA for the *Killing Joke* album.

With QOTSA's Josh Homme and Nick Oliveri at the Troubadour, Los Angeles.

In corpse paint for *Kerrang!* magazine, London, November 2003.

Opposite: Handsome Devil: Grohl invokes The Great Horned Beast for *Tenacious D in The Pick of Destiny*.

Up close and personal with wife Jordyn at the 2006 Grammy Awards after-party at the Roosevelt Hotel, Los Angeles.

Bonded by Blood: With lifelong friend Jimmy Swanson at The Forum, Inglewood, California, 6 March 2008.

Rock God: Grohl onstage at Wembley Stadium, London, June 2008.

Family Man: Getting down at the Yo Gabba Gabba! Live! There's a Party in My City! event in Los Angeles, 27 November 2010.

Foo Fighters with *Wasting Light* producer Butch Vig in Dave Grohl's garage in Encino, California, 17 November 2010.

I'll stick around

'The best part is that no one ever tells us what to do,' he said with a smile. 'No one has ever told us who to record with, where to record, how to make a video, what video to do, when to go on tour. Because I am the President of Roswell Records, at the end of the day I'm in charge.'

Grohl was now starting a whole new game, and at square one. Soon enough it was time to unveil his new band. Foo Fighters' first live appearance was at a Seattle keg party: 'It wasn't too bad. But it kind of was,' Grohl later recalled. The band's first show in a regular club – at the Jambalaya Club in Arcata, California, on 23 February 1995 – came as a support act for the Unseen, a group of sharp-dressed and musically astute teenagers. Prior to this show Grohl bought second-hand T-shirts from a local thrift store and, with the aid of a homemade stencil, spray-painted onto them the name of his band, a move which turned out to be almost as big a hit with the audience as the set itself. The following month Foo Fighters graduated to the status of headliners, with an appearance at the Satyricon Club in Portland, Oregon, the first major city one reaches when travelling south from Seattle. In the audience on the evening of 3 March was one Jerry A, the frontman with celebrated local hardcore punks Poison Idea. Writing of what he witnessed in the pages of *Kerrang!*, Jerry said that Grohl possessed 'a well-developed singing voice which he put to good use with pleasant, heart-felt harmonies in a similar style to his former band, minus the hard edges'.

'But compared to Kurt,' he wrote, 'Grohl has neither the charisma nor the entertaining stage presence.'

The following day Foo Fighters headed north to Seattle to make their first headline appearance in their hometown. Appearing at the Velvet Elvis club, the group performed a nine-song set to an audience containing rather too many familiar faces, ensuring that the blue touch-paper remained unlit. Still, their display was convincing enough to draw a positive review from *Kerrang!* journalist Kevan Roberts. 'It turns out that Dave Grohl's been the best-kept secret in rock,' he wrote.

Really, though, this brief spate of appearances was merely the exhibition game that prepared the ground for the regular season to come.

This is a Call

Following the release of *Ball-Hog or Tugboat?*, in the spring of 1995 Mike Watt was to embark on a solo tour of the United States. His original idea for his solo tour was to invite along Dave Grohl and Eddie Vedder to be a part of his group – a proposal to which the pair gave their consent so long as each man could also perform in a supporting capacity prior to Watt's own headline turn. Eddie Vedder would appear as a member of Hovercraft, the art-rock project he founded with his wife, Beth, while Grohl would take his Foo Fighters out on their first national excursion. And so it was that the most intriguing alternative tour of the year came to fruition.

'I was shitting a pecan log about that tour, man,' Mike Watt later told me. 'With the Minutemen, D Boon [the group's singer, now deceased] was like Kurt in that he pushed up the other two guys, so I was never really a background guy, but I was never the front guy either. So that was really scary for me. And I could see how it might be scary for Dave too. But it was cool. It was a tour like the old days. And I don't think the guys wanted the hype, but it kinda got strange because with the hype there was so much attention on them.'

Foo Fighters embarked on the tour in a manner in which the headliner would surely approve. They travelled not in a tour bus, but in a van; Nate Mendel read the American political journal *Harpers* while the band listened to Queen and the soundtrack album to Andrew Lloyd Webber's *Jesus Christ Superstar*. From time to time William Goldsmith would employ his frontman's camera in order to take pictures of his own genitalia. These were happy, uncomplicated times.

'Dave had an amazing amount of enthusiasm, and a great attitude about what this band could be,' said Mendel. 'We approached everything with the idea that we'd make every show and everything we do an exciting adventure. And that's what we concentrated on. There was no sitting down and making a ten-year plan. I wasn't surprised that there was attention from the start. But the main challenge for us was to establish our own identity and not use Dave's past as a crutch.'

From the start the tour was a success, playing to packed rooms of between 400 and 800 people each night. Onstage each evening Dave Grohl looked out from his new vantage point at the front of the stage

246

and saw before him an assortment of Nirvana shirts, a sight about which he was philosophical and even sanguine: by definition those gathered were familiar with the traditions of underground music the tour was seeking to uphold, and were both curious about and support- ive of Dave Grohl's latest venture. And while the frontman himself may have downplayed and in some cases even dismissed his abilities as a performer able to command attention from the centre of the stage, footage from this period shows a man the world viewed as being a drummer to be possessed of enough charm and charisma to project himself and his music to the back of the small rooms in which he found himself.

'When I first started singing for Foo Fighters, never in my life had I ever considered becoming the front man of a band,' Grohl would tell me some fifteen years later. 'I was perfectly comfortable being the drummer and I didn't ever aspire to being the person out front in the spotlight. But when Foo Fighters started I realised I'd been thrown into that position and it was incredibly uncomfortable for me: I might be something of a jackass in real life, and love to be the life of the party, but the responsibility of being someone larger than life seemed too much for me.

'To me what makes a good front man is that the person I'm watching perform is entirely themselves, and not a character, not an act. I've always gravitated towards music and musicians that are real: I can appreciate a Bowie and a Marilyn Manson or a Gene Simmons or an Alice Cooper but there's something about a Neil Young or a Paul McCartney or an Ian MacKaye that I relate to the most. I like the guys that become the show and become the entertainer and ringleader with- out having to put on a costume. That, to me, is pretty bad-ass. That's like John Wayne shit right there.'

Every journey begins with one step, and Foo Fighters' tour with Mike Watt represented their own faltering baby steps on a journey that would eventually deliver them to the arenas of their home country and the stadia of England. But at some point at the end of each evening from 12 April to 20 May Grohl was able to return to his more familiar position behind the drumkit, keeping the beat for the tour's headliner.

He did so with his customary flair – Watt himself told me, 'Dave was something else to play with. His sense of timing, his musicality was amazing' – secure each night in the knowledge that his own band was gelling better than he could ever have hoped, and playing better than he could ever have dreamed.

'All four of us in the band came from bands that had stopped prematurely so that first tour and everything that came along with it was almost like comfort food in a way for us,' he told me fifteen years on. 'We got a van and built a platform in the van and we went on tour with bands we liked and it wasn't like a contrived grab at bringing back the good old days, it was just where we felt most comfortable. And it was nice that way, because we functioned like a band and we played like a band, and it was fucking great. But I didn't do it to forget about everything that had happened before: I did it because I wasn't finished. There was more to do.'

∽

When the Foos' tour with Watt drew to a close in San Diego on 20 May, the band were given two weeks to prepare for their début appearance on foreign soil, at the tiny King's College student union hall in London on 3 June.

The gig drew rave reviews from those in attendance. But, really, for those paying attention the advent of the summer was not so much about appearances in small clubs in large cities as about the forthcoming début album from the band in question. Two months earlier, in April, *Kerrang!* had been played each of the fifteen songs that comprised Grohl's demo tape recorded the previous year with Barrett Jones, and had judged the music to be 'awesome'. By July, shorn of three songs – 'Winnebago' and 'Podunk' would be used as future B-sides, while the rather excellent 'Butterflies' would remain to this day unreleased – Foo Fighters' eponymous first album was ready to drop.

Released on Dave Grohl's own Roswell Records, distributed by Capitol Records and featuring artwork by Jennifer Youngblood, *Foo Fighters* was released to the world on 4 July 1995, perhaps tellingly a date known to Americans as Independence Day. Advance press was warm and supportive. *Rolling Stone* awarded the twelve-song set four stars, with the reviewer, Alec Foege, shrewdly observing that 'Dave Grohl could turn out to be the '90s punk equivalent of Tom Petty.' *Melody Maker* hailed the album as a 'play-loud Summer blast' while its sister paper the *NME* countered that Dave Grohl's band had recorded a set that was 'massively important', praise indeed from a magazine that viewed itself in much the same terms. *Kerrang!* awarded the album a maximum KKKKK rating, predicting that this was a collection that would 'sell by the millions'. *Q*, as was its habit, was rather more sniffy. 'Too much may be placed upon Foo Fighters, expectations which Grohl, never regarded as a songwriter or vocalist, hardly deserves or needs,' wrote John Aizlewood. 'These expectations may prove to be his undoing, but, just as likely right now, they may yet be his making. He's done what he can.'

Foo Fighters is a superb statement of intent. Early in 2011, discussing his approach to songwriting in *Guitar World*, Dave Grohl said this: 'I approach every song trying to write the biggest chorus I possibly can. But then what I'll do is use that as the prechorus and go ahead and write an even bigger fucking chorus.' This formula runs right through *Foo Fighters*, most effectively on three brilliant singles – 'This Is a Call', 'I'll Stick Around' and 'Alone + Easy Target' – which fuse The Beatles, The Beach Boys, Hüsker Dü and *Trompe Le Monde*-era Pixies into irresistible, fizzing distorto-pop gems. The last of the three shines with such incandescent brilliance that Kurt Cobain actually considered claiming it for Nirvana.

'I recorded "Alone + Easy Target" at the tail end of 1991,' Grohl told me. 'Barrett and I were now living together, and I recorded songs like "Floaty" and "Alone + Easy Target" and maybe "For All the Cows" in our basement. I told Kurt that I was at home recording and he was staying in a hotel in Seattle at the time, as he was living in LA, and he said, "Oh, I wanna hear it, bring it by …" So I went over to his hotel and I played him "Alone + Easy Target". He was sitting in the bathtub with a Walkman on, listening to the song, and when the tape ended he took the headphones off and kissed me and said, "Oh, finally, now I don't have to be the only songwriter in the band!" And I said, "No, no, no, I think we're doing just fine with your songs." But it was funny, because Nirvana would play the "Alone + Easy Target" riff at sound-check sometimes. I think he liked the chorus.'

Cobain, of course, would not have the opportunity to hear the other two standout tracks on *Foo Fighters* as both 'This Is a Call' and 'I'll Stick Around' were written after his death. The latter song is arguably the most controversial song on the record. Seeking references to Grohl's painful recent history, fans and critics alike seized upon the song's incendiary chorus – '*I don't owe you anything*' – and jumped to the erroneous conclusion that the track was about Nirvana's late frontman, an interpretation which both embarrassed and irritated Grohl. In real-ity, with lyrics such as '*How could it be I'm the only one who sees your rehearsed insanity?*', the song is about Courtney Love, though Grohl denied this for years. 'I don't think it's any secret that "I'll Stick Around" is about Courtney,' he finally admitted to me in 2009. 'I've denied it for fifteen years, but I'm finally coming out and saying it. Just read the fucking words!'

'This Is a Call', the album's searing opening track, is harder to deci-pher. Written in a Dublin hotel room while Grohl and Jennifer Youngblood honeymooned in Ireland, the song's verses contain unfath-omable references to fingernails, Ritalin and acne medication Minocin, before exploding into a widescreen chorus – '*This is a call to all my past resignations*' – which sounds suspiciously like a kiss-off to the drama of the Nirvana years.

'I intentionally wrote nonsensical lyrics, because there was too much to say,' Grohl told me. 'I mean, with "This Is a Call" the verse is just bullshit, it's nothing, I wrote it in a bathroom, but the chorus on the other hand means a lot to me. This was me finally saying goodbye to my past.'

Elsewhere, though, *Foo Fighters* is clearly indebted to Grohl's past, or rather to his teenage record collection. The breezy and beautiful 'Big Me' owes a debt to early R.E.M., the punk-ish 'Wattershed' – titled in tribute to Mike Watt's role in setting Grohl back on his feet – could have been lifted from *Back to Samoa*, while 'X-Static' (which features a guitar cameo from Greg Dulli) nods towards the glistening dream-pop soundscapes of My Bloody Valentine. But it would be churlish to suggest that *Foo Fighters* is wholly in thrall to the '80s: the warmth and wit of the lounge jazz-meets-hardcore fuzz live favourite 'For All the Cows' and the slow-burning, blissed-out drawl of 'Exhausted' display a new openness and experimental edge to Grohl's songwriting which suggested he had both the chops and the chutzpah to stride away from familiar formulas and ghosts of the past.

That said, however, in 1995, without exception, each reviewer of the début Foo Fighters collection contextualised the album by referencing Nirvana. This, perhaps, was inevitable. But when it came to discussing the songs on the album, their author proved unwilling to buy into the process. That journalists desired to ask questions regarding not only the music of Grohl's previous band, but also its messy conclusion, was to be expected, but Foo Fighters' frontman's refusal to comment on such matters – for reasons that were probably as political as they were personal, at least in terms of attempting to position his new group as far away as possible from Kurt Cobain's headstone – ran counter to the expectations and wishes of magazine editors.

'I understand that people want to know this, but there has to be a line drawn,' Grohl told *Rolling Stone* firmly. 'Because the day after your friend dies and *American Journal* wants to talk to you and [ABC news anchor] Diane Sawyer wants to do an interview … It made me so fucking angry. It made me so angry that nothing was sacred anymore. No one could just stop, not even for a day or a year or the rest of our lives, and just shut the fuck up. So I decided that I was just going to be the person to shut the fuck up.'

But while all over the world journalists' heads were banging against a Dave Grohl-shaped brick wall, over their heads things were going swimmingly. In the UK, *Foo Fighters* débuted at number three in the national albums chart; in the US it entered the *Billboard* Top 200 at number 23. Beyond such bald statistics, more satisfying for Grohl was the idea that those who had bought Foo Fighters' début album seemed to concentrate on what it was rather than it what is was not, and to accept the group on the terms its creator wished for – as a band in their own right, and not an adjunct of Nirvana.

Evidence of this came late in the summer of 1995, in what would become one of the most famous stories in Foo Fighters' file. The final weekend of August found the band at Reading festival, the site at which Nirvana had headlined to more than 70,000 people three years earlier. Perhaps wishing to avoid comparisons to this event – one that had quickly attained the status of great cultural significance – Dave Grohl decreed that Foo Fighters' first appearance at the Berkshire site would be not on the main stage but rather in one of the marquee tents that lay on the fringes of the site. And so it was that on Saturday, 26 August, Grohl's new band appeared in the wholly unsuitable confines of the *Melody Maker* tent, a facility designed to hold just a few thousand people but which, here, had attracted the attentions of tens of thousands of festival goers, all desiring their first glimpse of Foo Fighters. The set was witnessed by English music journalist Paul Travers, who remembers the occasion well.

'Whoever decided – and it appears it was Dave Grohl's idea – that a band with as much ready-rolled interest and anticipation as Foo Fighters should play one of their first-ever UK shows in a smallish tent at Reading needed their head examined,' he says. 'Half an hour before they were even due in the tent and its surrounding environs were already jam-packed and it took some serious elbow work to get within sight of the stage. When they did arrive, the place exploded. The walls and ceiling became slicked with sweat and people were passing out from the heat. Others started shinning up the huge supporting pole in the middle of the tent and scrabbling up any climbable bit of structure around the sides. A few made it, to huge applause, to the rigging that started about 15 feet up the central pole and continued straight up to the ceiling. When the power was pulled and Dave announced that he'd just been told the show would be cut if people didn't get down, it looked for a moment like things might go either way. Thankfully, the most prominent climbers did eventually descend into the waiting arms of security, the power was restored and a potential riot was averted.'

But if Foo Fighters' appearance at the Reading festival was the most remarkable live appearance the group made in support of their début album, it was far from the only one. In the time between the release of the band's début and the final date of the tour to support that release, the Foos played no less than 151 concerts worldwide. While some of the dates were glamorous in terms of their profile – on 14 and 15 November 1995 Grohl fulfilled his October 1990 dream of playing on the stage of London's Brixton Academy not once, but twice – other shows, such as that staged at Paris's cosy Bataclan theatre, were bookings made by a band willing to work for their audience and earn their wings. This strategy worked, and worked well. Through perspiration as much as inspiration, Dave Grohl's insistence that Foo Fighters were more than an excursion, and were in fact a band that were here to stay, became a self-fulfilling prophecy. By the time the quartet returned home from the road more than twelve months after the release of *Foo Fighters*, they had to their credit almost two million album sales. Not bad work for a group Grohl feared would be viewed as nothing more than the folly of 'that guy from Kurt Cobain's band'.

'I remember there being a lot of emphasis put on the meaning of that album, or what that album represented,' he recalled, speaking to me some fourteen years after the fact. 'I would read reviews and it seemed like to a lot of people it was more than just a demo tape that was recorded down the street, that it was some sort of token continuation, and as with most things I do, I try not to over-think things, or think too much about something like that. I knew what it meant to me to be able to go down and make music. After Nirvana, it was hard for me to even listen to music for a while after Kurt died. So to go into a studio and take thirteen or fourteen songs that I liked the most and book fucking six days, which I considered an eternity, to record those songs, was a big deal to me: it was important that I did that at that time in my life. But I remember there were people that really resented me for having the audacity or gall to fucking keep playing music after Nirvana. It was the most ridiculous thing. I was fucking, what, 25 years old? I was a kid, man. I wasn't finished.'

'No one has every said anything to my face, like "You were a fucking asshole for doing this,"' Grohl told writer Tom Doyle in 1996. 'But every so often you sense a tinge of resentment. I'm sure that the thing

This is a Call

I was supposed to do was become this brooding, reclusive dropout of society and that's it. Nirvana's done, I'm done, that's the end of my life. Fuck that. It was a blast. I miss Nirvana with all my heart; I listen to live bootlegs because I miss it so much. I miss Kurt. I dream about him all the time – I have great dreams about him and I have sad, heart-wrenching, fucked-up dreams about him. I miss it all a lot. But if you're dealt a fucking hand you deal with it. And I'm not about to drop out and stop living.

'When Nirvana ended, I wasn't finished. I'm still not fucking finished.'

My poor brain

Because my life was fucking going down the toilet I would sit at night in my sleeping bag in the back room of Pete Stahl's house and I would list out all of my problems, like: 1. Homeless. 2. Divorced. 3. No access to a bank account … Because if I thought of all those things at once I surely would have had a complete nervous breakdown …

Dave Grohl

Advance promotional copies of the Foo Fighters' second album *The Colour and the Shape* were doled out to journalists, radio pluggers and other small but necessary cogs in the music industry machine in April 1997 as a cassette tape, glued inside a cheap portable player. Though the era of digital file-sharing was still in its infancy – 18-year-old tech geek Shawn Fanning's revolutionary peer-to-peer sharing platform Napster would not be launched until 1998 – Dave Grohl and his record label were aware that the band's follow-up to the two-million-selling *Foo Fighters* was one of the year's more anticipated rock albums, and were wary of copies appearing online in advance of its scheduled mid-May release. There was also a more stubborn logic at the root of the decision to preview the album via this rather antiquated and unwieldy distribution channel: making the album had cost Dave Grohl his marriage, half his band and, on occasion, his sanity, so after all the arguments, tears, tantrums and sleepless nights bound up in the process, he figured that those graced with early copies of the album could damned well put in a bit of effort on the listening side too.

Though he still had a clutch of unreleased solo compositions gathering dust on the shelves of Barrett Jones's Laundry Rooms studios – 'Butterflies', the slow-burning 'Mountain of You' and the Cheap Trick-meets-Replacements buzz-saw pop of 'Make a Bet' among them – Grohl was determined that Foo Fighters' second album should be a unified group affair, built from the ground up. From their earliest rehearsals in William Goldsmith's basement in Seattle, the quartet had begun writing new material, songs that crackled with positive energy and bristled with taut post-punk power. These had been teased apart, retooled, honed and buffed during pre-gig soundchecks from Minneapolis to Manila across their fifteen-month touring schedule, and Grohl felt confident that his band had it in them to make an album both ambitious and liberating. Having taken on the world with a demo tape recorded in five days, the Foo Fighters' frontman was now of a mind to push his band's sound into more lavish and expansive territories.

'I've made punk rock records,' he explained, 'and they're fun and great and it's quick and there's passion. But I did that with the first record. I've never made a big, proper rock record before, so why not? People just don't seem to do it any more, so we might as well take a shot.'

To help realise his grand vision, Grohl called upon the services of the talented English producer Gil Norton. With his lush, widescreen production work on classic albums such as Echo and The Bunnymen's *Ocean Rain*, Catherine Wheel's *Chrome* and Throwing Muses' self-titled 1986 début, Norton had a reputation as an innovative studio technician, but it was his masterful work with Pixies, specifically on their 1991 album *Trompe Le Monde*, which truly captured Grohl's imagination. 'I love it for the way you can hear the band falling apart, getting scattered, shooting off in a million different directions,' he commented in 1997. 'Because of that it's their most extreme LP: the noisiest, the quietest, the poppiest, the weirdest.' The album had a deep personal resonance for Grohl too: it was the soundtrack to the beginning of his romance with photographer Jennifer Youngblood.

Norton was finishing up work on Counting Crows' *Recovering the Satellites* album when Grohl approached him about working on the second Foo Fighters' record. The producer was delighted to sign on for the project.

'When I first heard the first Foo Fighters album I got the sense of a really accomplished songwriter, and I really liked the raw power of it,' he told me in 2010. 'And I loved the demos that Dave had done for the new album, so I knew we had a great batch of songs.'

The first sessions for the second Foo Fighters album began on 18 November 1997 at Bear Creek Studios, a 1,750-square-foot converted dairy barn situated on a ten-acre horse farm in the sleepy, rural neighbourhood of Woodinville, Washington. As he was in the habit of doing with Black Francis prior to Pixies' recording sessions, Norton spent several days alone with Grohl beforehand in a nearby hotel, stripping back his songs to their basic components, and challenging the songwriter to pinpoint the essential truths underpinning each one. Only then were Smear, Mendel and Goldsmith invited to join the sessions for two weeks of extensive pre-production, after which the process of tracking to tape began. Schooled in the art of punk rock, where attitude and aggression took priority over technique and timing, the quartet had no idea just how intense and challenging the sessions would be. Not all of them would make it through the other side.

'Gil has a reputation as being a real taskmaster in the studio,' says Grohl. 'He cracks the fucking whip, and anyone who's ever worked with him will say the same thing. He accepts nothing but absolute perfection in what you do – whether that means dissonant, noisy chaos or a perfect pitch, perfect performance pop song, he needs it to be the best. So working with him was Really. Fucking. Hard.'

For a time it seemed that nothing the quartet laid down for Norton met the producer's exacting standards. The Englishman demanded take after take from the young musicians, citing faults with tunings and tempos and intonation and harmonies, to the point where Grohl, Mendel, Smear and Goldsmith began to seriously question their own abilities. In the *Back and Forth* documentary, William Goldsmith says that Norton referred to Mendel and himself, the band's acclaimed engine room, as 'the rhythm-*less* section' ('which was encouraging,' Goldsmith added in a voice dripping with sarcasm) and morale and confidence within the unit began to wilt. As the session became increasingly tense and fraught, Goldsmith began to feel that he was being unfairly singled out for criticism and he started to buckle under the pressure.

'Dave had me do 96 takes of one song, and I had to do thirteen hours' worth of takes on another one,' the drummer told the *Miami New Times* in 1998. 'It just seemed that everything I did wasn't good enough for him, or anyone else. I think that everyone at the label wanted Dave to play drums on the record. The producer wanted him to play drums on the record, and it felt like everyone was trying to get me to quit.'

'When you're a producer the aim of the game is to extract the best performances, the best songs and the best album at the end of the day,' counters Norton calmly. 'It's not like I'm *trying* to be a hard taskmaster. I want them to be very proud of what they've done at the end of it. Doing any album is quite emotional, and with any artist recording new songs your nerve ends are out more than at any other time: in the creative process it can be hard work.

'Me and William got on really well during the album,' he adds. 'We used to go out, and I love William: the problems were just in his own head really. He suddenly started over-thinking it and got insecure, and no matter what you did it wasn't making him feel any better. From my point of view, you always want a musician to get through the recording process; it wasn't ever that I was thinking, "I don't want William playing on this."'

'I think William was intimidated by Gil,' says Grohl, 'and I'm sure that he probably felt weird about me being a drummer and being in the studio. It was a big deal and there was a lot of pressure to make it great. We were all trying really hard.'

As if proceedings at Bear Creek were not already sufficiently tense, in mid-December Grohl was served with divorce papers at the studio. His marriage to Jennifer Youngblood had been on the rocks for some time, indeed their fracturing relationship had inspired much of the lyrical content of the album on which he was working, but the timing was unhelpful, to say the least. Calling upon the same reserves of stoicism which served his mother so well at the time of her own divorce, Grohl kept his focus upon his work – 'He didn't get overly emotional about it with me, and I didn't see him crying or anything, but obviously it was a big part of his life and a concern at the time,' says Norton – but with work at the studio falling far short of his lofty expectations, it soon became evident that pressing the 'pause' button on the session might be to everyone's advantage. As he was given to do at times of stress, Grohl headed back home to Virginia to his mother's house, perplexed as to where exactly his grand vision for the album was falling down.

'I took the tape home and listened to it,' he recalls, 'and I remember having a conversation with Pat, saying, "You know, it *has* to be better than this, it really has to be better than what it is."'

Depressed, bored and lonely back in Virginia, Grohl sought refuge in Geoff Turner's WGNS studio in Arlington, where he began playing around with two new riffs that he'd written at Bear Creek. Within an hour he had completed two new songs, bruised love songs both. The first, 'Walking After You', centred around a lyric about a '*heart cracked in two*', is gossamer-fine and haunting: the second, 'Everlong', is the most pure, perfect love song Grohl has ever written. Based around a naggingly insistent riff Grohl initially considered a Sonic Youth rip-off, it builds and climbs towards a heart-stopping chorus that tumbles forth breathlessly, all innocent, lovesick and yearning. It remains Grohl's most beautifully affecting universal love song.

'I knew it was a cool song but I didn't think it would be the one song by which most people recognise the band,' Grohl admitted in 2006. 'And I think it was the first time people had ever quoted lyrics to me, like, "That song is beautiful! That line where you say, '*Breathe out, so I can breathe you in …*'" Chicks would come up and recite that to me. That song's basically about being connected to someone so much that not only do you love them physically and spiritually, but when you sing along with them you harmonise perfectly.

'My marriage wasn't going well and we'd just split up and I'd just got my divorce papers at the studio, and of course that's when I started writing!' he told me three years later. 'I got married in 1994 to Jennifer: we'd been dating for two or three years and the day she moved out to Seattle I asked her to marry me. We were kids and honestly we just shouldn't have done it; even in the time we were engaged I think we both realised that we probably shouldn't get married. And then Kurt died and our whole world was turned upside down, and so in a way I think I clung to that engagement and the marriage as like my last piece of stability. It was something to hold on to. And then it was gone too ...'

'It wasn't a surprise to me when Dave came back from Virginia with two good new songs,' says Gil Norton. 'We had a great bunch of songs for the record, but Dave never stops, his brain never switches off and he's constantly trying to better the work that he's got. But when I heard "Everlong" it was just like, "*Oh ...*" It made the whole album whole. It was the catalyst that brought it all together.'

With the dawning of the new year it was decided that the Foos needed a fresh start on the record. Leaving behind the tranquillity of Bear Creek, operations shifted to Los Angeles, to Grandmaster Recorders in Hollywood, a plush facility located in the old Bijou silent movie theatre on Cahuenga Boulevard, which had hosted sessions by everyone from Stevie Wonder and David Bowie to the Red Hot Chili Peppers and the Black Crowes in days past. After listening anew to takes recorded in Washington, Norton encouraged Grohl to think about re-tracking certain songs. As an experiment, Grohl recorded a new drum track for one of the album's key cuts, the driving 'Monkey Wrench': the result, according to Norton, was a take 'ten times better' than the version of the song captured at Bear Creek. It made sense, then, to put some of the other recordings under the microscope too. In the days that followed, Pat Smear and Nate Mendel were summoned to Grandmaster to redo their parts on track after track: they quickly realised that they were, in fact, remaking the album from top to bottom. Equally obvious was the fact that in this process the presence of William Goldsmith was not required. Unsure as to what this meant for the future of the unit, Mendel and Smear opted to say nothing. When Goldsmith found out, the shit hit the fan.

'I had this idea that I was going to play drums because we were running out of time and William was having difficulty recording,' says Grohl. 'So I thought, "Okay, well, just to save time, I'm going to record these new songs, I'll do the drums and stuff on this, and then we'll have Will redo the other stuff." And then Will caught wind that I was going to do drums and basically just said, "Well, I don't agree and I don't want to be in the band." And I begged Will to stay in the band. I went up to Seattle and sat with him and said, "Please, stay," but he said, "No." Most people are under the impression that I kicked him out of the band, but he absolutely quit. And I absolutely sat with him and said, "Dude, I want you to stay in the band, what do I do? Do you want me to help you with drumming? Whatever I can do, let's do it, so you can stay in the band." And he just said "No."'

'We talked,' Goldsmith told *Back and Forth* director James Moll in 2010, 'and Dave said, "You know, I still want you to tour the record you know." And I was just like, "Dude, as it is now I have to rebuild my soul, refind it ... So thanks but no thanks."'

'I know that William will never forgive me for playing drums on that record,' Grohl admitted to Moll. 'I know it. And I wish things were different. But I felt like this was what I had to do in order to make this album happen.'

In *Back and Forth* Dave Grohl is asked to re-examine his treatment of William Goldsmith in the weeks which saw *The Colour and the Shape* put to bed. It's an awkward moment for the Foo's frontman, who visibly squirms as he searches for the right words. 'It was a really weird time and I was young ... What the fuck ...' he finally mumbles, then his voice tails off, his head droops and his eyes lower to the floor. James Moll's camera remains trained on him for a few seconds longer, but Grohl has nothing more to say.

❧

While the original Foo Fighters line-up was slowly disintegrating behind closed doors in Hollywood, two new albums bearing Dave Grohl's name emerged with little fanfare.

Released on Barrett Jones's own Laundry Room Records imprint, *Harlingtox Angel Divine* is the sole fruit of a one-off 1990 studio project involving Grohl, Jones, Scream's Dutch booking agent Tos Nieuwenhuizen (also the guitarist/vocalist in heavyweight Dutch punk/metal trio God) and Bruce Merkle, frontman of Washington DC's wired post-punk troupe 9353.

'How did this occur?' read the liner notes to the album. 'The Harlingtox story was hatched in Washington, DC in the spring and summer of 1990. It's very 1990-like. It reeks of Bush/Quayle annoyances and growing pains in general. Harlingtox was never a band, there has never been a Harlingtox show. It was musically arranged by Dave and Tos, probably first conceptualised in Europe during a Scream/God tour the previous year.'

Existing midway between the unhinged death rattle of Unsane, the thudding claustrophobia of Barkmarket and the low-slung, stream-of-consciousness psychosis of early Clutch, *Harlingtox Angel Divine* is splendidly queasy listening, but not for the faint-hearted. With Merkle gabbling and babbling in tongues, adopting a variety of deranged voices from 'oleaginous game show host' to 'faeces-caked serial killer choking upon wok-fried human entrails', the quartet lurch and lunge around the fringes of punk, metal and industrial noise, offering a nightmarish vision of a society teetering on the brink of collapse. Opening with the unnerving 'Treason Daddy Brother in Crime Real Patriots Type Stuff', a two-minute public service announcement from the messed-up and marginalised ('*We're all gonna score. Fuck your drug war!*'), the five-track album never deviates from the wrong side of the tracks, slamming through bleak art-metal ('Orbiting Prisons in Space'), creepy, churning sludge-rock ('Recycled Children Never to Be Grown') and stuttering post-hardcore ('Obtaining a Bachelors Degree', wherein Merkle gleefully drools '*I have always been a stupid fucker.*') before concluding in the marginally more accessible, though still relentlessly unpleasant, 'Open Straightedge Arms'. For the sake of the sanity of all involved, it is perhaps best that *Harlingtox Angel Divine* was strictly a one-shot deal.

By comparison, Grohl's original soundtrack for *Touch* – a quirky, pitch-black comedy/thriller starring Christopher Walken, Skeet Ulrich and Bridget Fonda and adapted by Paul Schrader (*Taxi Driver / American Gigolo*) from an Elmore Leonard novel – is a likeable, laid-back and rather charming affair. Recorded at Robert Lang Studios in the summer of 1996, just days after Foo Fighters closed out their inaugural world tour at the Phoenix Festival in the picturesque English village of Stratford-upon-Avon, the thirteen-track collection afforded Grohl the opportunity to stretch and experiment. Only one song, the fizzing, perky 'How Do You Do', resembles Foo Fighters; elsewhere Grohl marries Californian surf music with DC hardcore dynamics (on the staccato Dick Dale-meets-Fugazi instrumental 'Bill Hill Theme') indulges in lazy back-porch country blues ('Making Popcorn', 'Remission My Ass') and throws down some slinky, white-boy funk on the *noir* grooves of 'Outrage'. John Doe, the frontman of seminal LA punks X, provides vocals on the down-home country 'n' western shimmer of 'This Loving Thing (Lynn's Song)', but his guest spot is rather eclipsed by Veruca Salt vocalist Louise Post's sensuous, smoky turn on the gorgeous, drifting 'Saints in Love' and the dreamy duet 'Touch', a sweet, mesmerising ballad given an extra frisson by rumours that Grohl and Post were conducting an illicit affair at the time. Asked about his reported relationship with Post in the summer of 1997, Grohl simply said, 'That's a big no-no. Next question': that September, during Veruca Salt's first Australian tour, Post announced from the stage of St Kilda's Prince of Wales hotel that Grohl had just broken up with her and had started dating actress Winona Ryder.

Kerrang! was one of the very few magazines to review *Music from the Motion Picture Touch*. Writer James Sherry noted, 'Not only is *Touch* a great album, it's also a major personal achievement for Dave Grohl and a valuable insight into what he may turn his musical hand to once he's tired of touring in a rock 'n' roll band. The future should be interesting.'

Grohl's own assessment of his first foray into the soundtrack world was typically modest: 'I had no idea what I was doing and I faked it and it worked,' he said. 'It's important to break out from behind the dunce throne they call the drum set and do things that are challenging.'

With William Goldsmith's exit from Foo Fighters, Grohl now faced the task of finding someone to occupy the 'dunce throne' in his own band. Enter Taylor Hawkins.

An engaging mix of Californian pothead and lithesome all-American surfer dude, Oliver Taylor Hawkins was born in Fort Worth, Texas on 17 February 1972. Growing up in Laguna Beach, California, Hawkins was given his early musical education by his older brother Jason, who introduced him to FM radio staples such as Boston, The Eagles and Aerosmith, but it was two idiosyncratic English bands, Queen and The Police, who first truly captured his imagination. Like Dave Grohl, Hawkins started out playing guitar, but inspired by the flailing energy of Queen's drummer Roger Taylor and The Police's Stewart Copeland, soon enough he switched his affections to drums. At the age of 10, in his next-door neighbour Kent Kleater's Laguna Beach garage, Hawkins sat behind a drum kit for the first time; within weeks he was able to play along to Queen's *News of the World* album. 'And then,' he admitted in 2005, 'my life became drums, drums, drums.'

Hawkins's first 'serious' band was Sylvia, an experimental, psyche-delic rock group featuring vocalist/guitarist Riz Story, guitarist Sean Murphy and bassist Jauno. The drummer later remembered the band as 'awful'; Story and Murphy would go on to enjoy moderate success in the rock band Anyone. In the summer of 1994 Hawkins turned to session work, landing a gig with the British-born, Montreal-raised singer Sass Jordan; the following year he jumped ship to another Canadian singer/songwriter, 21-year-old Alanis Morissette, who had just released her third studio album *Jagged Little Pill*. By October 1995 Hawkins's new boss was the world's most talked-about new artist, with a *Billboard* Number 1 album: *Jagged Little Pill* would go on to sell a staggering 33 million copies worldwide.

Grohl and Hawkins met for the first time on 17 December 1995 at a KROQ Almost Acoustic show at Los Angeles' Universal Amphitheater, where Foo Fighters shared a billing with Morissette, Sonic Youth, Radiohead and Butch Vig's Garbage. A fan of both Nirvana and Foo Fighters, Hawkins relished the opportunity to bro down with Grohl, a drummer whose style, power and touch he greatly admired. For Grohl, meeting the easy-going, live-wire Hawkins for the first time was like staring into a mirror. 'We got along like brothers from the second we met,' he recalls. 'We were best friends from that instant.'

'I was just this little dork playing in Alanis's back-up band and the first thing that struck me was that Dave was really nice, and really fun to hang out with,' Hawkins told me in 2009. 'I'd met some other people from big bands, musicians that I'd looked up to, and when I met them the vibe was, "Oh, you're not important," but I walked away from Dave thinking he was a cool guy. I had so much respect for him mainly because of that first record, which I really loved and still do. And it was just an instant rapport, like, "Oh my God, you're so much like me!"'

In summer 1996 Foo Fighters and Alanis Morissette had occasion to play several European festivals together, giving Grohl and Hawkins the opportunity to bond further over hard liquor and hard rock. In spring 1997, when Grohl phoned to ask if Hawkins knew of any good drummers looking for a new gig, Hawkins's response was immediate.

'He said, "Fuck yeah! I'll do it,"' Grohl recalls. 'I reminded him that we weren't selling out stadiums like Alanis and he said, "I don't care, man, I just want to be in a fucking rock band."'

Hawkins made his début with Foo Fighters on 19 April 1997 at a secret club gig at the Alligator Lounge in Santa Monica, California. The show passed smoothly enough, but the preceding week had not been without its stresses: on the first day Hawkins showed up to rehearsals, guitarist Pat Smear announced his intention to quit the band.

'We had a European tour booked,' recalls Grohl, 'and on the first day of rehearsals Pat said, "Hey guys, can I talk to you?" And he very calmly and politely says, "You know what? I'm gonna leave the band. You guys should be a three piece." And we were like, "Pat! What the fuck, dude? We leave in ten days! What do you mean?" and he said, "I'm sick of touring. I don't want to go on tour any more."'

'I just remember I was just sick of it,' Smear told me. 'From the minute we started it was just non-stop and I think I'm just lazier than the rest of them! It was crazy the amount of things we did in a year. I just got burnt: we came on so strong for so long and I just wanted it to stop.'

'The most touring Pat had ever done before Nirvana was I think maybe … none,' says Grohl. 'So that first record really freaked him out a lot. And then there were some … personal things. But honestly I was on my knees fucking crying, begging him to stay, I really was. But he just said, "No, I don't want to, I don't want to."'

'Everyone was kinda mixed up and crazy at the time. I was sleeping in Pete Stahl's back room and because my life was fucking going down the toilet I would sit at night in my sleeping bag in the back room of Pete's house and I had a journal for when I was writing lyrics and just keeping a journal, and I would list out all of my problems, like – "1. Homeless. 2. Divorced. 3. No access to a bank account. 4. I'm sleeping in a sleeping bag! 5. Pat quit the band. 6. William quit the band …" Because if I thought of all those things at once I surely would have had a complete nervous breakdown. So I would list them and think, "Okay, well, let me try to figure out each one of these things by going down the list." Like, "Homeless … I really need to find somewhere," you know what I mean. It was not a good time. My ex-wife was mixed up in it and she was not being cool at all. I was just trying to stay the fuck out of everybody's way, just to finish what I'd started.'

The stresses involved in the breakdown of Grohl's marriage led the singer to see a therapist for the second time in his life. Unlike the sessions he had endured as a wayward teenager, as an adult Grohl found the experience positive and rewarding: 'Everyone could do with a little therapy now and again,' he later told me.

'The best thing about therapy is reassurance,' he said, 'having someone talk back and give you a response that makes you feel like you're not alone, and that what you're going through is understandable. Therapists may have a better understanding of human nature than your best friend who deals pot and works in a gas station.

'But I had a bad experience with a therapist once where he basically told me that because I tour and live in hotel rooms and don't have a "normal" job my life is just not reality. And I thought it was time to get the fuck off the couch, because this *is* my reality.

'I'm not opposed to having therapy again,' Grohl added at the time (indeed he would later revisit therapy on several occasions when life

seemed 'overwhelming'), 'but that time it was like, "If you don't understand my world that's fine, but don't tell me it doesn't exist."'

Despite the trauma and instability of both his private and professional life, Grohl hid his problems from the public gaze. Having secured
a promise from Smear that the guitarist would remain by his side until
a suitable replacement could be found, on 2 May 1997 Grohl was back
in London, performing 'Monkey Wrench' on Channel 4's Friday night
entertainment show *TFI Friday*, with his trademark beaming smile
fixed firmly on his face. As Foo Fighters hit the promotional trail for the
release of their second album, to the outside world at least, Grohl
appeared ready to take on the world.

$\backsim$

The Colour and the Shape was released on 20 May 1997, to somewhat
mixed reviews. Cutting-edge electronica, as supplied by The Prodigy
and the Chemical Brothers, was now the flavour of the month among
music critics, and rock bands touting glossy, shiny rock anthems aimed
squarely at the mainstream were considered decidely *déclassé*. Jessica
Hopper's review of the album in *Spin* encapsulated the patronising tone
of many of the initial notices received by *The Colour and the Shape*: in
her six out of ten critique, Hopper pegged Grohl as 'a simple rock guy
in a simple rock band who occasionally manages to write some really
good songs'.

'He'll probably never come up with a godhead masterpiece,' Hopper
concluded, 'but then again, he already played drums on one.'

Rolling Stone too referenced Nirvana in their review, noting that Foo
Fighters' eponymous début album had been 'hungrily received by a
nation of Nirvana fans looking for a substitute'. For writer Christina
Kelly, the second Foo's album was 'over-produced', with a 'big, radio-
ready, modern rock sound': 'Screaming can get boring,' Kelly noted
tartly, 'but it's what Grohl does best.'

Many of the album's UK reviews were equally ambivalent. 'At it's
worst,' wrote *Select*, '[the album] puts remarkably little distance between
Foo Fighters and any run-of-the-mill band with tattoos, big shorts,
bleached hair and a bug up their ass.' 'There is a touch of desperation

about the album,' wrote Andy Gill in the *Independent*, 'as if Dave Grohl and his cronies realise that there's not that much mileage left in this kind of lumpen, overwrought American rock.'

In May 1997 I reviewed *The Colour and the Shape* for *Kerrang!* magazine. Awarding the album a maximum 5K rating, I celebrated it as 'one of the most captivating and sublime collections of songs you'll hear this year.' Fourteen years on I stand by those words.

The album can be read as a quest, one lost soul's attempt to make sense of a world crumbling beneath his feet. It opens with Grohl whispering, '*In all of the time that we've shared I've never been so scared*' ('Doll'), then descends into the noisy rush of 'Monkey Wrench', a song dealing with the exhilaration that comes with overcoming feelings of entrapment, claustrophobia and suffocation. The track concludes with Grohl singing, '*I was always caged and now I'm free*,' and from this point on the album is in freefall, as the singer tries to take stock of his changing world. There are songs about love and obsession ('Everlong', 'Up in Arms'), about insecurity and betrayal ('Walking After You', 'February Stars') and about childhood dreams and adult responsibilities ('Hey Johnny Park', 'My Hero'). Throughout Grohl flits between rage and reconciliation, but the album closes (on 'New Way Home') on a positive note, with the newly empowered, emancipated singer screaming '*I'm not scared*' as he faces up to an uncertain future.

An artistic triumph, *The Colour and the Shape* was also a confirmed commercial success. The album reached number 10 on the *Billboard* 200 and peaked at number 3 in the UK; the album also reached the Top Ten in Australia, Canada and New Zealand. Looking back, Gil Norton hails the album as 'a big, bold statement'.

'It really elevated Dave to where he should be,' says the producer. 'It helped established Foo Fighters as a new band and gave Dave the platform to go on to do what he's done. I'm proud of what we achieved.'

Following a homecoming show of sorts in the parking lot of Tower Records in Rockville, Maryland, Grohl took his new-look Foo Fighters out on the road. Following a UK theatre tour, the band embarked upon a small-scale American club tour, then hit the global festival circuit, appearing at Japan's FujiRock festival, Germany's Bizarre Festival,

My poor brain

Lowlands in Holland, Pukkelpop in Belgium, England's V97 festival and Ireland's Feile. The shows were strong and, despite the clock ticking on Pat Smear's tenure in the band, morale was high, due in no small part to the effervescent Hawkins. 'I think I helped bring Dave out of his shell a bit,' says the drummer. 'We were young bachelors at the time and I remember saying to Dave, "Hey man, you were the fucking drummer in Nirvana, get rid of your punk rock ethos and let's go find some chicks!" On a personal level it was easy to fit in.'

On 29 August, at the start of Labor Day weekend, the quartet returned to Seattle to play the 27th annual Bumbershoot Festival at the city's Memorial Stadium. It would prove to be an emotional, historic night.

Opening his band's set with 'This Is a Call', Grohl told the 75,000 strong crowd that Foo Fighters were now 'officially associated with stadium rock!' The quartet then tore through a fifteen-song set, climaxing with 'New Way Home', with Seattle's adopted son drawing huge, appreciative cheers as he sang of driving to his Shoreline home past '*the boats and the King Dome*'. Those cheers were just fading when Krist Novoselic walked onstage holding his bass guitar. With Grohl on drums and Pat Smear on vocals, the trio launched into covers of 'Purple Rain' by Prince and Led Zeppelin's 'Communication Breakdown'. The final song carried a certain amount of irony, for unbeknown to the crowd this would be Pat Smear's last full show with Foo Fighters for nine years.

'When he left I was kinda happy to see him go, to be honest,' recalls Grohl. 'In those few months shit went really south with Pat and I, it was not a good few months. And it took a while for Pat and I to talk again – I don't know how long, it was a few years. He had finally got the paperwork [confirming] that he was officially out of Foo Fighters and he sent me a very sweet letter that said, "I'm sorry that it all went down that way, and whether you like it or not we'll forever be connected by these things, Foo Fighters and Nirvana, and I love you and I hope you're doing well. And here's my phone number ..." And I immediately called him because I missed him so much. He answered the phone and I think for the first five minutes we just laughed, we didn't even say anything, we were just laughing at the absurdity of it all. And now he's back in the fucking band again!'

On 4 September 1997 Pat Smear officially announced his (initial) retirement from Foo Fighters. He did so in the most public way imaginable. The quartet were booked to play outdoors on the balcony of New York's iconic Radio City Music Hall for MTV's Video Music Awards; after a storming run through 'Monkey Wrench', Smear stepped up to the mic and declared that he was leaving the group.

'The last song we played was my last song with the band,' he said. 'I'd like to introduce you to Franz Stahl, who'll be taking over. Rock on, guys!'

∽

Franz Stahl had been tipped off by his brother Pete that he might get a call about joining Foo Fighters. While his older brother was tour managing Dave Grohl's band, Franz Stahl was in Japan, playing guitar with Jun 'J' Osone, bassist of the hugely successful J-Rock band Luna Sea, then just striking out as a solo artist. When the call from Grohl came, Stahl immediately accepted his old friend's invitation to join the band. On 3 September the guitarist bade farewell to his Japanese friends and flew from Tokyo to Los Angeles and then on to New York to meet up with his new bandmates; the following day, as his father and brother looked on from the street, he was playing 'Everlong' in front of a TV audience numbering tens of millions. 'It was crazy,' says Stahl, 'but I couldn't have been more happy.'

'When Pat decided to leave I knew we should ask Franz [to join],' Grohl told me. 'I'd been in a band with him before, and we'd grown up playing music together and I knew he was a great player and we came from the same place: how could it not work?'

There was precious little time for Stahl to adjust to his new surroundings: two weeks after he joined Foo Fighters, the band kicked off a six-week American tour at the Huntridge Theatre in Las Vegas. *Kerrang!*'s Lisa Johnson, a long-time friend of the group, was invited along to rehearsals to see how the new boy was settling in. She found the band, and their new guitarist, in ebullient spirits.

My poor brain

'Had Franz not been in Wool at the time, he would've been Foo Fighters guitar player when we started the band,' Dave Grohl disclosed. 'But he was, and Pat's awesome and he was a friend, so …'

It would be eleven months before Foo Fighters paused to draw breath again. On the evening of 29 August 1998 Grohl's band brought down the curtain on their *The Colour and the Shape* world tour with a main stage performance at England's Reading festival. The weekend was a special one for Dave Grohl, surrounded as he was by familiar faces. His friend Greg Dulli's Afghan Whigs had a main stage slot on 28 August on a bill topped by ex-Zeppelin duo Page & Plant. Washington DC's Girls Against Boys, featuring former Lünchmeat men Scott McCloud, Johnny Temple and Alexis Fleisig, were to open up the main stage on 30 August, on a day headlined by Butch Vig's Garbage. But even as he enthused to friends about his fourth appearance at the legendary weekender, Grohl's mind, typically, was racing ahead.

'Now I'm looking forward to our next record more than I ever have been,' he said. 'For a while I was thinking, "God, what are we gonna do for our next record?" But Taylor plays piano and guitar and writes songs and sings. Nate writes stuff. It's just gonna be the freak-out record. And now with Franz I just know it'll be this big, strong … rock opera! We have to do it. It's time for our version of The Beatles' *White Album*.'

～

It was spring 1999 before Foo Fighters regrouped to make their third album. By now Grohl had tired of living the bachelor lifestyle in Los Angeles and had relocated to Virginia, where he purchased a family home at 1800 Nicholson Lane in Alexandria, just minutes from his former high school. It was in the basement of this house that the third Foo Fighters' album was created. But before the band arrived at this stage, Grohl had some painful housekeeping to attend to.

Issues with Franz Stahl began to arise as soon as the quartet reconvened to begin writing for the new album. Grohl had booked the band into Barco Rebar, a small rehearsal space in Falls Church, Virginia, just minutes from the site of his very first Scream audition with Stahl, but the sessions were stilted and unproductive … or at least they were when the band jammed as a quartet.

'We didn't have any songs so we had a rehearsal space in Virginia and everyone would fly out and we'd jam for a week or two and write, and then break off for a month and then come back and do it again,' Grohl recalls. 'And in those rehearsals Taylor, Nate and I really started to click, we really started to play together, and it was the first time our band started to feel like a band, where everyone was contributing and it was starting to sound like Foo Fighters. There's a song off that third record called "Aurora", which is still one of our favourite songs, and it means a lot to us because that was one of the first songs we wrote for the third record and it just came out of nowhere: the three of us pulled it together and it really seemed like a new beginning for the band, so that I didn't feel responsible as the composer any more. I was like, "Wow, this is a band, we could do beautiful things together."

'But Franz had a really hard time finding his way into that equation. He was having a hard time jamming with us and he was having a hard time remembering the things that we'd been jamming on; he's a fucking amazing player but for whatever reason it just wasn't really jelling with us. And we did one rehearsal session and then we came back after a month and had another rehearsal session, and again Nate and Taylor and I were locking in pretty well and Franz was still having a hard time fitting in. And so I was on the phone with Taylor after we did another two weeks of writing and I said, "Yeah, I don't know what's wrong with Franz but I'm sure he'll get it, and I'm sure it'll all pull together." And Taylor said, "Well, actually dude, Nate and I, we're not really so sure it's working out with him." And my heart kinda sank, like, "Oh fuck, okay, let's talk about this."

'And then the three of us started talking about it. And we decided we were going to go in and make the album as a three piece. And so we had to tell Franz. And that was another fucking drag, because here were our options: Franz was living in Austin, Texas at the time and we could have either flown to Austin under the guise that we were just going to hang out with Franz, which would have seemed unusual, or we could have Franz fly all the way to Virginia so that we could fire him and fly him all the way back. Or we could all have a conference on the phone and call him and tell him. And we decided that we were going to call him.

'This didn't happen quickly, this happened over the course of a few months, of really thinking about what to do and talking about it. And so we called him and we told him that we didn't know if it was working out musically. And he was really fucking upset.'

'I remember being up in my studio upstairs taking the call and I just couldn't even believe what I was hearing,' says Stahl. 'I was like, "What do you mean? What are you talking about?" Everything that they were saying to me, there was just no validity in any of it. It was complete bullshit. I couldn't believe that I was having this conversation and I couldn't believe that this phone call even existed. I just remember at the end, assuming that I could talk to them later, going like, "Yeah, alright, I'll talk to you later." And I remember hanging up and going downstairs and lying on the bed next to my wife going, "You wouldn't believe what just happened," and then explaining to her what had happened. So then I caught the first plane I could, flew up to DC and banged on the door at his house to ask for an explanation.

'They were fucking *completely* surprised. They couldn't believe that. They answered the door and I was like, "What the fuck's going on?" and they proceeded to give me the biggest load of bullshit I ever heard. And I just broke down in tears, man, I couldn't believe it. I could not believe it.'

'It sucked,' says Grohl flatly. 'Again, here's this person that I love, this person that I've known my whole life, and I have to make a decision like this, which is based on music more so than the history of our friendship, to preserve or take care of the reason why we're here, which is the music. And I've really tried to explain that to him. But I don't think he understood where I was coming from … because still to this day we don't talk.'

'It's awkward, it's very awkward,' Stahl admitted to me in 2010. 'To be honest, I've never really had any closure on the whole affair and there's a lot of it that I've kinda had to blot out of my mind and out of my memory. I came into the band and was thrown right into this tour which lasted forever, and then all of a sudden it's like, "Okay, let's try to write stuff." And I don't think anybody had really decompressed from that tour. In hindsight, I was the new guy and maybe I should have voiced my opinion more, but at the same point I was really hesitant to step on anybody's toes: it's Dave's band and he writes the songs, so I held back. I was just wary of forcing my ideas, so I really didn't come up with too much stuff.

'By the second time we'd gotten together we had changed everything. And then I left to go home to Austin and I was going to come back up. I thought we'd be working on it deeper, and I thought everyone would go home and figure some things out. So I kept asking Dave to send me a tape because I didn't have a copy of the new stuff. But I didn't get one. And so when I came up there the next time I was kinda lost, because I'd be like, "Okay, that's right, shit, we changed it to that …" And so I ended up looking kinda like an ass. I don't know why he never sent me the stuff, but in hindsight I think maybe the rumblings started back then, because why wouldn't he send me the stuff? I mean, I'd been in a band with him years before this, we'd written whole records together, and it wasn't like they were under any deadline either. So I think there were other variables involved leading to my departure, I don't think it was because of that. And even if it was, why wouldn't he talk to me about it? Dave was my bro, who I'd known and been in a band with … That was one of the things that always bugged me about the whole thing: it's like, if you've got an issue with me or anybody, just come and talk to them, and say, "Listen, this or that, and if we can't work this out then here's the door." But I wasn't even afforded that …'

With the situation with Stahl unhappily resolved, it was then Nate Mendel's turn to drop a bombshell of his own: he too wanted to quit the band.

In 1998 the members of Mendel's old band Sunny Day Real Estate had started speaking to one another once more. The arguments that had caused such bitter conflict in 1994 no longer seemed so important, and soon enough old friendships were rekindled, creative sparks were re-ignited and the quartet had written a clutch of beautifully intense new songs. Jeremy Enigk, Dan Hoerner and William Goldsmith were keen to give the band another go; so too was Mendel, but doing so would necessitate leaving Dave Grohl's side. 'We waited about a year for him to do it,' recalled Goldsmith, 'and finally he did.'

'I had this kinda high school crush irrational attraction to that project,' Mendel admitted in *Back and Forth*. 'And I was tortured. And I called up Dave ...'

'I was pissed,' Grohl admitted. 'I think I told him, "Okay, you know what, *you* call up everyone and tell them you quit, I'm gonna go fucking get drunk ..."'

The following day, a hungover Grohl got a call from Mendel at his mother's home in Kathleen Place. The bassist apologised for his rash resignation and asked if Grohl might take him back to the band.

After all this drama, the making of what became *There Is Nothing Left to Lose* was an absolute breeze.

'The three of us moved into my house in Virginia,' Grohl recalls, 'the three of us, my buddy Jimmy and our producer Adam Kaspar. We bought a mixing desk from Nashville, put it in my basement, bought a 24-track machine, put it in the corner, bought three or four compressors and ten microphones, put sleeping bags on the walls for sound-proofing and started recording.

'It was springtime in Virginia; all the windows were open, there was beer and BBQs and we would record all night and sleep until noon, listen to what we'd done the night before and maybe re-record it. It was the most relaxed and simple and perfect recording session I've ever been in in my life. It was everything you would want making an album to be. When I listen to that record I honestly think it's my favourite Foo Fighters record because of all of those things: every one of those songs feels that way to me. It's such a relaxed, honest, organic and real album, and it was a really good experience for all of us. It was fucking great.'

While living *chez* Grohl, Foo Fighters made a short documentary film about the making of *There Is Nothing Left to Lose*. There's one brilliant scene in the film where Grohl, clutching a bottle of whisky, pretends to drunkenly berate one of the studio engineers about the sound of the recordings.

'Don't tell me how to make a record!' the singer mock slurs. 'I was in Nirvana! I was in the greatest rock 'n' roll band of the nineties! We changed the course of rock music!'

Ironically, the inspiration behind *There Is Nothing Left to Lose* came not from the punk rock which had informed Nirvana's game-changing rage, but largely from the AM radio hits Grohl, Mendel and Hawkins first heard blasting from their parents' car stereos in the 1970s – the music of The Eagles, Fleetwood Mac, Wings and Peter Frampton, ironically the very music against which the original punks were so keen to rebel. This was a punk rock gesture in itself, and Grohl was wholly unrepentant.

'Having grown up in that punk rock scene, I've been so inspired by so many people, so many different bands and so many different experiences,' he told me in 2009, 'but one of the things I refuse to subscribe to, or buy into, is the guilt that most people are tortured by in that scene, the musical guilt.

'I think about it sometimes. I think about the reasons I fell in love with punk rock when I was 12 or 13: it was because of the music – the sound of what these people were doing was so fucking powerful that it moved me and totally changed my life. I didn't even need to know their intentions, I just loved the feeling that I got when I listened to the Bad Brains or when I listened to AC/DC, it was the same energy. But, along with that punk rock background or foundation comes this obligatory guilt. I guess when you state your intentions so clearly early on it becomes hard to negate that if you move in another direction.

'Personally, I don't feel like I've ever moved in another direction. I joined Freak Baby because I wanted to fucking jam, and we turned into Mission Impossible because if I played the drums it would sound better than Freak Baby. I joined Dain Bramage because I wanted to play more. I joined Scream because they were fucking amazing. I joined Nirvana because of *Bleach* and because there was no more Scream. But the guilt that a lot of those people from that scene still carry with them – musical guilt, does that make any sense? Fuck no! I should be able to do what the fuck I want to do!

'And so the only thing from that whole experience that breaks my heart is that that musical guilt kept people from doing some of the things they could have done. I understand, like, the political boundaries that the punk rock scene had, but for me that was never the idea; maybe it was being from Virginia, and not being from Washington DC, but my motivation was much more musical than anything. And I feel like our band has always remained true to that ideal, just to do whatever satisfies us musically. If it feels right and instinctive at the time, then we should do that and not have anything keep us from it. Because that guilt, that fucking guilt, is what killed Kurt.'

Though its sound might be rooted in the past, at its core *There Is Nothing Left to Lose* is a record about new beginnings – new relationships, new ambitions, new dreams. Dave Grohl once described the inspiration behind the album's first single, the soaring, elevating 'Learn to Fly', as being informed by 'the search for something real, something that's going to make you feel alive'; that mood echoes throughout its eleven tracks. On the Foo Fighters' most organic, unified record, there's only really one song – the fuzzed-up opener 'Stacked Actors' – rooted in anger and disillusionment; elsewhere there are songs of hope and contentment, love and aspiration, making *There Is Nothing Left to Lose* the most romantic, accessible album in the Foo's canon.

In terms of tone then, 'Stacked Actors' might be a red herring, but it's a startlingly effective introduction to the album. Riding in on a filthy, ultra-distorted riff, it lashes out against fakes, phoneys and wannabes (*'Line up all the bastards, all I want is the truth'*) in a lyric the author admitted touched upon his fraught relationship with Courtney Love, but more broadly concerned the vacuous nature of fame and celebrity in Hollywood.

'Nothing seems sacred here,' he raged at the time. 'Music is something real and beautiful, and it *is* sacred, but it's just being dragged through a trench of shit right now. The whole thing here in Hollywood about fame and beauty and the glorification of the celebrity just made me want to go fucking crazy and kill everyone.'

Standing in stark opposition to Grohl's apoplectic anger at the outset of the album, the shimmering 'Aurora' is *There Is Nothing Left to Lose*'s most beautiful, affecting song. Named after the road leading from downtown Seattle to Grohl's former marital home in Shoreline, Washington – a road lined with strip malls, gun shops, thrift stores and porn shops – it's a song displaying Grohl's capacity to find magic and wonder in the most mundane of surroundings. Its creator would later hail it as 'probably the greatest song we've ever written'. Elsewhere Grohl expanded upon the country-blues sound he first explored on the *Touch* soundtrack with the twanging 'Ain't It the Life', 'Breakout' takes a tongue-in-cheek look at a dysfunctional relationship and 'M.I.A.' is a rather sweet plea for space and solitude from a man who's spent the greater part of his life in the public eye.

With the album in the can, at the tail end of the summer Grohl and his bandmates returned to Los Angeles to hold open auditions for a new guitarist. They were initially dismayed by the calibre of the musicians who turned out: one unfortunate soul wasn't even capable of taking his guitar from its case before being gently led from the room. Finally, as they were abandoning hope of finding a suitable candidate, Chris Shiflett walked in through the door.

Born on 6 May 1971 in Santa Barbara, California, Christopher Aubrey Shiflett first picked up a guitar at age 11: by 14, his first band, the cutely titled Lost Kittenz, were playing garages and backyard parties in the wealthy beach town. Originally a fan of Kiss, Dio and the sleaziest rock 'n' roll bands strutting on Sunset Strip, by his mid-teens Shiflett had discovered punk rock; one of his early bands, Rat Patrol, actually supported Scream in Santa Barbara. The guitarist landed his first 'serious' gig in rather fortunate circumstances: he was working in the San Francisco office of Fat Wreck Chords, the punk rock imprint owned by NOFX mainman Fat Mike, when he heard that guitarist Ed Gregor from No Use for a Name, one of the label's most popular acts, had quit the band; one noisy audition later Shiflett was a professional punk rocker. Four years on, he heard a similar rumour about Foo Fighters.

'I was a huge Foo Fighters fan,' says Shiflett. 'My friend had a cassette of the first album way before it was even out, and I loved it.

And when the second record came out I was an even bigger Foo Fighters fan. Of all the big rock bands of that era they were by far my favourite. In the summer of 1999, No Use for a Name had just made a new record and we were getting ready to go on tour, when I heard from a friend that Foo Fighters were looking for a guitar player. I was like, "Dude, you *gotta* get me an audition." He knew somebody that worked at their law firm and he actually managed to get me an audition. Then I just sat down in my room and played along with those first two records for a week.'

One week after his first audition, Shiflett received a call from Dave Grohl inviting him back down to Los Angeles for a second try-out. That evening he joined the band at the Sunset Marquis hotel to drink into the small hours. The following day he received a second phone call from a hungover Grohl.

'Say goodbye to your friends,' said Foo Fighters' frontman. 'You're going on tour.'

With Foo Fighters dates in Australia, Canada and the USA under his belt, Shiflett had clocked up significant air miles even before *There Is Nothing Left to Lose* dropped. Released on 2 November 1999, the album débuted in the Top Ten in both the United Kingdom and United States, and in the Top Five in Australia and Canada. Not everyone was taken by the band's new blissed-out atmospherics, however. 'The artist formerly known as Grunge Ringo remains stuck in the generic grunge mediocrity mire,' snipped *NME*. *Kerrang!* was rather kinder: 'Grohl has seemingly discovered where his biggest strength lies – tugging at heartstrings rather than slashing at powerchords.' Falling somewhere between the two, *Rolling Stone* rather meekly commented, '*There Is Nothing Left to Lose* is distinguished by its punky guitar-bass-drums directness. In almost every way it is a more modest effort than its predecessor.'

But of all the words devoted to weighing up the band's latest offering, the most significant piece of writing around *There Is Nothing Left to Lose* appeared not in a magazine or newspaper, but rather came inked on the neck of the Foo Fighters' inspirational leader. Chosen to adorn the cover of the album, the simple 'FF' logo inked by Londoner Lal Hardy was Dave Grohl's own subtle way of asserting that, for all the tumult and tension of the past years, his band was here to stay. He was not to know that the Foo Fighters' most challenging years still lay ahead.

Disenchanted lullaby

When Taylor overdosed that was the first time in my life that I ever considered quitting playing music. Because it had got to the point where I wondered if music just equalled death. *Really?* Because I'm in it for the fucking music, but I don't want to do it if everyone is just going to die all the time ...

Dave Grohl

On the eve of Dave Grohl's 32nd birthday, Foo Fighters brought the curtain down on their fourteen-month-long *There Is Nothing Left to Lose* world tour in front of 200,000 fans at the Rock in Rio festival in Rio de Janeiro. As he blew out the solitary candle on the birthday cake presented to him mid-set by his new girlfriend, 28-year-old former Hole/Smashing Pumpkins bassist Melissa Auf der Maur, Grohl had every reason to believe that 2001 would be for him a vintage year, both personally and professionally. John Silva already had his schedule for the upcoming twelve months loosely mapped out. The first half of Grohl's year was to be given over to the writing and recording of the fourth Foo Fighters album, the summer months would see his band swing into Europe for their by-now-traditional high-profile festival shows, and the back end of 2001 would see the quartet return to arenas worldwide once again. By Grohl's own workaholic standards, it was hardly the most punishing itinerary.

After embracing his girlfriend and saluting the cheering crowd with a heartfelt 'Obrigado!', the birthday boy restarted the Foo Fighters' set with the apposite 'Next Year'.

This is a Call

'Into the sun we climb,' he sang. *'Climbing our wings will burn bright. Everyone strapped in tight, we'll ride it out. I'll be coming home next year.'*

At the time, Grohl could not possibly have known just how prophetic those lyrics would turn out to be.

〜

After a little time off to reacquaint themselves with the faces of family and friends, and following a band outing to Los Angeles' Staples Center on 21 February to pick up a brace of Grammy awards for *There Is Nothing Left to Lose* (Best Rock Album) and 'Learn to Fly' (Best Short Form Music Video), it was with no real sense of urgency that Foo Fighters regrouped in early March at Taylor Hawkins's home in the Los Angeles suburb of Topanga Canyon to begin recording demos that they hoped would form the basis for their as-yet-untitled fourth album. Despite Grohl's avowed aversion to the trappings of Los Angeles, and of Hollywood in particular, *chez* Hawkins provided a setting that was very different from the neon and the nonsense of 'The Strip'. Arguably Los Angeles' foremost bohemian enclave, Topanga Canyon had in the past provided the inspiration for Neil Young's deathless 1970 album *After the Gold Rush*, as well as Joni Mitchell's *Ladies of the Canyon* collection, released the same year; a generation on the neighbourhood was still providing both shelter and muse for many of Southern California's artists, musicians and performers. Hawkins's own home, a three-bedroom property he shared with his two dogs Bud and Pharia, afforded views of both the winking, glistening Pacific Ocean and the canyon. Like its owner, the house had a laid-back, chilled-out feel: visitors to the property were invited to swim in the outdoor pool, bounce skywards on a circular trampoline in the garden or simply stretch out on a hammock slung between two poplar trees to take in the awe-inspiring views. Inspired by Dave Grohl's decision to install a 24-track recording studio in his home in Alexandria, Hawkins had followed suit by assembling a similar set-up in his own garage. In this setting, playfully dubbed 'Pussy Whipped Studios' by the drummer, the working environment came to be informed by 'vibe' and ambience as much as it did work rate, notes and melodies.

Disenchanted lullaby

'This place is like our own little boot camp,' Grohl told LA-based writer Joshua Sindell for a studio report filed in *Kerrang!* magazine. 'The whole idea of building a home studio is just to be in complete control of everything. I will never work another way again. There's just no way. There's no clock on the wall, it's your fucking house, which also means that you're allowed to decide who's allowed to come by the studio and who's not.'

Free from the constraints of the professional recording studio, as well as the considerable expense of making music in such facilities, Foo Fighters demoed their new material at a relaxed pace.

As the days of 2001 grew warmer and longer, Grohl, Hawkins, Mendel and Shiflett committed to tape rough versions of ten to fifteen songs that they hoped would make the grade. Working titles for the new material included 'Tom Petty', 'Knucklehead', 'Spooky Tune', 'Full Mount', 'Lonely as You' and the mildly amusing 'Tears for Beers'. In contrast to the laid-back, FM radio vibe of their previous recording, initial reports from the sessions promised a new album high on energy and volume: 'A lot of the stuff we've been writing now has been written with everything [turned up to] eleven,' explained Grohl, channelling the spirit of Spinal Tap's Nigel Tufnel.

Tapping a similar vein, Grohl delighted in playing visitors to Hawkins's home recordings he had made with Hollywood actor/comedian Jack Black's new tongue-in-cheek project Tenacious D. He would also preview a clutch of heavier recordings he himself had laid down for a project the world would come to know as *Probot*. But his focus, he maintained, was very much on Foo Fighters, and a collection of songs he considered as strong as any he had recorded in his career to date.

'There's freaky time signatures, it's fucking fast, it's loud, and some of it's even tuned down really low, but it also has a great melody to it,' he revealed. 'Taylor said to me that this new stuff is the kind of music he's always wanted to play in a band.

'I was talking to Taylor about how I think it's a good idea that we really take our time on this record,' he added. 'But we've been on a roll. It's just coming so quickly that we're all really satisfied.'

With the benefit of hindsight, that quote should perhaps be filed under the heading 'Famous Last Words'.

Summer 2001 gave Foo Fighters the opportunity to spread their wings and flex their musical muscles on the European festival circuit. With their star in the ascendant, the quartet flew to Germany to play a fifteen-song Friday night set at the Bizarre Festival in Weeze, Germany, on 17 August, before touching down in the UK for appearances at the V Festival. On 18 August the band performed eleven songs for more than 50,000 people gathered in the Weston Park in Staffordshire, and then again the next day to a similar number of faces gathered at Hylands Park in Chelmsford. In the days that followed, the quartet were slated to appear at the hard rock Ilha do Ermal festival in Portugal, as well as in the more intimate surroundings of London's Forum in Kentish Town and Edinburgh Corn Exchange. Their working holiday in the Old Continent was set to finish at the beautiful Slane Castle estate outside Dublin on 1 September, with an early evening slot warming up a 80,000-strong crowd for the arrival of local heroes U2. But a sudden, shocking turn of events ensured that Foo Fighters would not fulfil the final four bookings of that summer's tour.

Following their appearance at the Chelmsford leg of the V Festival, the quartet travelled the short distance to London, where they were booked to stay in the stylish Royal Garden Hotel, just off Kensington High Street in the city's western quarter. The precise details of exactly what transpired in the early hours of 20 August remain somewhat clouded to this day, but what is known, though, is that prior to their morning bus call Dave Grohl was informed that his band's drummer had overdosed, and had been rushed to the private Wellington Hospital in St John's Wood in North West London. In the 2011 Foo Fighters documentary film *Back and Forth* Chris Shiflett refers to Hawkins's hospitalisation as being the result of a heroin overdose, though this has always been strenuously denied by Hawkins himself. Whatever, in the summer of 2001 the seriousness of what had transpired remained largely hidden from public view. A statement released to the press was short and succinct. 'Foo Fighters drummer Taylor Hawkins was hospi-talised yesterday [Monday] morning after having apparently overindulged during festivities following the V2001 festival in Chelmsford, UK,' it read. 'Hawkins is reported to be in a stable condition. Foo Fighters' remaining UK and European dates, including the Ilha do Ermal festival in Portugal and a support slot with U2 at Dublin's Slane Castle, have been cancelled.'

When Dave Grohl could bring himself to talk about the incident, he revealed that Hawkins had fallen into a coma that lasted for 'maybe ten or twelve days'. Hawkins's own estimation was that he was without consciousness for around 48 hours. What is certain, though, is that in the days following an event the other three members have come to label 'Taylor's little nap', the drummer's life was very much in danger.

Speaking to me in 2009, Grohl described his friend's misadventure in London as being an event that 'changed everything'.

'That was the first time in my life that I ever considered quitting playing music,' he admitted, 'because it had got to the point where I wondered if music just equalled death. *Really?* Because I'm in it for the fucking music, but I don't want to do it if everyone is just going to die all the time. It just didn't seem worth it. I would walk back from that hospital to my hotel every night and talk to God, out loud, as I was walking. I'm not a religious person, but I was out of my mind, I was so frightened, and heartbroken and confused, like, "How could that possibly happen?" It was just not fair, it just wasn't fair.

'When that happened to Taylor, I just told everyone that I don't even want to hear the word Foo Fighters for a long time, until *I'm* ready to fucking say it again. And thank God Taylor survived. So when we brought him back to the States the most important thing from that moment on was that everyone be healthy and happy. Fuck the band, fuck Foo Fighters. And still to this day it's that way. I love everything about what I do, but the most important thing to me is that people live happily ever after. So then we had this conversation within the band: "Whenever you're ready, Taylor, you let us know, and we can start working."'

Speaking for the first time publicly on the subject of his mishap in spring 2002, Taylor Hawkins denied that what had happened in his hotel room in London was the result of the misuse of either cocaine or heroin, but was in fact caused by an addiction to painkillers. Pressed as to what kind of painkillers, the drummer snapped at his interviewer, and said, 'Just fucking painkillers, okay?'

'It doesn't matter what they were,' he insisted. 'All that matters is that I had a problem with them. It was a situation that had gotten out of control for me. That's all. And last summer I took too many of them and I went into a coma for two days. It was very serious. I've been into rehab and cleaned up. It's all in the past. It's over now and I've come through what happened. End of story.

'Believe me, I'm not proud of what happened,' he added. 'I don't want to celebrate it and I don't want to dwell on it. I'm happy to clear up what happened, but that's it. It ends there. It was such a cliché. Member of a rock band – the drummer of a rock band, no less – takes too many drugs, becomes ill, has to go into rehab. If you spell it out it's just so embarrassing. It's so obvious.'

Speaking to me in 2009, some eight years after the event, Taylor Hawkins had this to say about the events of that August morning:

'It was a very difficult time for me. That was when I had to decide if I wanted to be a kid for the rest of my life or to grow up and be a man. I had to let go of … [pauses] There was a lot of things going on in my life personally at the time, and it just sorta culminated in that. But that was my battle, that was my thing to deal with. Dave was there, and everybody was there, and everybody talks about, you know, it was tough for them. But it was no tougher for anybody than it was for me … That was the end of my youth and my stupidity of thinking I was bullet proof. And hopefully I've grown up a lot since then.'

Having returned from the United Kingdom to the United States, Dave Grohl, Nate Mendel and Chris Shiflett afforded their bandmate the time and space he needed to at least begin to address his medical and mental needs. By the time summer had given way to autumn, both parties felt the time had come where work on Foo Fighters' fourth album could recommence. By the autumn the group was reunited in Grohl's basement studio in Alexandria, recording new material once more. With hindsight, both Grohl and Hawkins now recognise that their desire to see business returning to normal – as if establishing a working routine was all that was required to draw a line beneath the unpleasantness of that summer – as a decision made in haste. It was a mistake from which they were able to repent at painful leisure.

'I think honestly what happened is that we started working too soon on the record,' is Grohl's admission. 'We just weren't ready to do it. We started in on it again before we were ready, before Taylor was ready, before the songs were ready: we felt obligated, in a way. That's kinda the difference between the first album and the fourth album. In a way they were both made for the same reason – the first album, unconsciously – but the fourth album was a conscious attempt at healing the band. And it didn't work. It had the opposite effect.'

'We just weren't ready,' Hawkins agrees. 'We were almost forcing ourselves to make that record. And it just wasn't right.

'I think that I just wanted to stay busy. I wasn't quite at home with my new lifestyle yet, so I didn't know anything other than "I should be working." But looking back, I probably could have used three or four months to get my head together.'

Perhaps adhering to the maxim that creativity is 90 per cent perspiration and only 10 per cent inspiration, force themselves to make an album is exactly what Foo Fighters did. Ensconced in Grohl's home on Nicholson Lane with producer Adam Kasper and recording engineer Nick Raskulinecz, throughout November and much of December 2001 the musicians fought to regain their creative mojo, and struggled to recapture the sense of unity and creativity that had informed their previous sessions at 606. Each day Grohl would bring into the studio the bare bones of a song – he had 20 or so such sketches that he hoped would serve as the framework onto which he and his colleagues might graft a completed composition – and at the end of each day these ideas would have amounted to naught. As time ticked on, stagnation set in. By the time Christmas 2001 had become the new year of 2002, the band's plan to record their fourth album in a homely and organic setting in Virginia had been ditched. Instead, the band shifted their operational HQ back to the West Coast, to Conway Studios, a state-of-the-art facility set in tropical gardens on Melrose Avenue in West Hollywood. Conway had previously played host to sessions by

Soundgarden, Beck, Fleetwood Mac and U2, and was considered one of the most luxurious, and expensive, studios in the city, a far cry from Grohl's humble set-up at 606. But in going from chalk to cheese Foo Fighters also went from bad to worse.

'Nothing was being accomplished,' Grohl told me. 'The songs lacked any sort of life, they were just weird carbon-copy versions of songs that they were meant to be. It's hard to explain. And then someone would come in and record half a track and go, "Okay, I gotta go see my acupuncturist, I'll be back later," and meanwhile we're paying $4,000 a day for this room …'

As if things could hardly have been any more complicated, or disheartening, for the principal players, into this scenario stepped Queens of the Stone Age, a band having a little local difficulty in the studio themselves in 2001. Formed from the ashes of cult Palm Desert stoner/psychedelic riff monsters Kyuss, and piloted by that band's guitarist Josh Homme – a man whose effortless cool earned him the nickname 'The Ginger Elvis' – and his mercurial wingman Nick Oliveri, by 2000 the 'robot riff' collective already had two stellar albums to their credit, 1998's self-titled début and *Rated R*, released two years later. During the early part of the 2000s one would have been hard pressed to nominate a more critically acclaimed or creatively vibrant rock band.

'We had Queens of the Stone Age on tour with us for a really long time in 2000,' says Grohl, 'and instead of putting "Queens of the Stone Age" on their dressing room door we used to put "Critic's Choice" because they were the coolest band in the world. And honestly, we thought that too.

'I first met Josh in 1992, at a show at the Off Ramp in Seattle as Kyuss were touring with Pete Stahl's band, Wool and The Obsessed. This was the first time I'd seen Kyuss and I was blown away, they were fucking great. They seemed like us, like kids who grew up in the suburbs listening to rock 'n' roll records, doing petty crime and drugs, just little vandals from the middle of nowhere.

'So in 2000, as we were touring with Queens of the Stone Age, someone asked me what was my biggest regret of the year 2000 and I said it was that I didn't get asked to play on the Queens of the Stone Age *Rated*

Disenchanted lullaby

R record. So Josh said, "Dude, if you want to come and play on a couple of songs on this new record why don't you do it?" So we went in and recorded a couple of songs – an early version of "Little Sister" and the song "… Millionaire", the first song on the record – and then I split. Then Taylor wound up in the hospital, and we came back and Josh called me and said, "Hey dude, what are you doing?" I was driving up the Pacific Coast highway going to the beach, so I said, "Just heading up to the beach." He said, "Dude, things aren't working out with our drummer. Do you want to play on our whole record?" And I said, "Absolutely. I'll be there at eight o'clock." I made a U-turn and went straight back to the studio, a studio that was owned by the producer Eric Valentine in Hollywood. And we recorded the drums for the *Songs for the Deaf* album in like, ten days, maybe two weeks.

'And so then I told them I would help them find a new drummer. I said, "So what about [former Kyuss drummer] Brandt Bjork? Let's get Brandt, man, fuck, that'd be amazing, the three of you together again? That would be unbelievable." So I get on the phone with Brandt, and I say, "Dude, have you heard the stuff?" And he's like, "Yeah, I've heard it, but …" I don't remember how the conversation went, but he wasn't into it. And then there's this other drummer, [former Page & Plant sticksman] Michael Lee, so I'm like, "Josh, there's this guy Michael Lee, you're gonna freak out, he's perfect, he's fucking unbelievable, let me call him." So I called up Michael Lee. And once Michael Lee was interested I thought, "Uh-oh, that guy is the most amazing drummer in the world, so maybe I should do one show with Queens of the Stone Age before Michael Lee does." And so we set up a show at the Troubadour in Los Angeles, and we started rehearsing for it.

'At night I'd go rehearse in a closet with Queens and I'd be in the best band in the world. And then I'd come back to Foo Fighters studio and be totally dismayed by the apathy and lack of any sort of passion. So things started getting tense in the studio.'

With work on Foo Fighters' forthcoming album understood to be nearing an end – and recording costs now sailing towards a cool one million dollars after two months in Alexandria and almost three months at Conway – in March 2002 the Foos invited the world's press into their lair. Unaware of the tensions behind the scenes at Conway, RCA, the group's record label, flew English journalist Ian Winwood to Los Angeles to write a cover feature previewing the album for the readers of *Kerrang!*

'Even the most dysfunctional bands are loath to air their laundry in public, at least not at the time that it's happening,' says Winwood, reflecting back on the experience almost a decade on. 'There's also a tendency in journalists, especially journalists with less experience, which would have been me at the time, to want to believe the best of a given situation, especially with a band as likeable as Foo Fighters. So at first glance it seemed that everything at Conway Studios was just fine. Dave was commanding company, cracking jokes and telling everyone how he'd just spent many thousands of dollars on a gun-metal BMW M5. He also played a selection of new songs through the speakers in the studio's console room. Looking back on the occasion, and knowing what I now know about what life in the camp was like at that time, it seems quite obvious to me that there were signs that all was not well, signs that I should really have picked up on.

'I remember being with Taylor Hawkins in one of the rooms, and him asking me what I honestly thought of the songs that I'd just heard. It's always difficult listening to new songs in the company of the people that wrote and recorded them – even if you really like the material you sound like a sycophant when you try and find a way of articulating this – but the truth is that Foo Fighters songs I'd been played hadn't really made much of an impression on me at all, so I was more concerned with couching my answers in diplomatic terms without betraying myself or telling an outright lie. It seems obvious now that had I been listening properly to what I was being asked I would have sensed that the reason Taylor was asking me what I really thought of the songs was because Taylor himself wasn't at all sure about them. No one in the band was.'

Winwood, though, didn't know the half of it. As Grohl and Hawkins posed in Conway's smart garden area, pulling faces for photographer Tony Wooliscroft, the pair's expressions showed no trace of the argument that had taken place away from prying ears just moments before,

Disenchanted lullaby

an argument that had potentially taken Foo Fighters to the point of fracture.

'I remember getting into a fight in the control room with the *Kerrang!* people outside,' Grohl recalls. 'It wasn't even a fight, just people making little jabs and little comments here and there. And I said, "Okay, do you want me to go and tell those guys that we're going to break up right fucking now? Because I will. We can if you want." And then the room was kinda silent. We did our photo shoot and we did our stuff and then I played the show with Queens of the Stone Age.'

By all accounts, Dave Grohl's live début with Queens of the Stone Age was a magical evening: *Kerrang!* later hailed it as 'a classic, once in a lifetime show, one of those rare nights that seems to last forever and yet is over all too soon'. Billed as 'An Evening of Communion and Fellowship', it took place on 7 March 2002 at the Troubadour club at 9801 Melrose Avenue in Los Angeles. It was Dave Grohl's first full live set behind a drum kit since Nirvana's 1 March 1994 show in Germany.

The choice of venue also came steeped in history. Since opening its doors in 1957, the Troubadour has provided the setting for early performances by artists such as Elton John, Fleetwood Mac and Tom Waits; it was here, too, that the 'hair metal' scene brought to international prominence by Mötley Crüe and Guns N' Roses in the 1980s was incubated. With its black walls and claustrophobic interior the venue may rightly be described as a toilet, but it is a toilet with hundreds of famous signatures on its walls.

Dave Grohl saw many friends descend on the legendary Los Angeles club on the evening of 7 March. One notable comrade, however, was conspicuous by his absence: the man at whose hospital bedside he had sat for day after day the previous summer.

'It was the first time I'd played a show on drums since Nirvana,' says Grohl. 'It was a big deal for me, it had been a long time. There were people in the audience I'd known for five or six years, close friends, that had never seen me play the drums before. It was a part of me that I hadn't revisited in a long fucking time. And the one person who wasn't there was Taylor. And that really hurt me. It was like him not turning up for my wedding or something.'

'I can see why that would be hurtful,' Taylor Hawkins admits. 'The funny thing is Dave and I have never discussed this, but I can guess we can discuss it here. Now that we've all gone off and done other things it's not as big of a deal, but at that time that was the first time any of us had gone off to do something else and the band was at a point where we were not really looking good. And to me, going to see Dave play with Queens would have almost been like going to see your girlfriend fuck some other dude. I know he wasn't trying to hurt me, he was just out doing what he wanted to do and enjoying what he wanted to do, but I think if he gave it real thought to what was going on at the time with the band, he'd have to understand that him playing with someone else and us being at the point where our band was falling apart was a little hurtful to me.

'It was a tough time, and I wasn't really interested in going to see Dave play with another band when our band felt like we were breaking up. He's never even said anything about this to me really, but I understand. While on one hand I was excited for Dave as a friend – as a friend I'm always excited for Dave playing with someone else and enjoying flexing his musical muscles – but on a band level, on our little family level, I was upset. I wasn't exactly over the moon that Dave was enjoying his rise with Queens of the Stone Age, because to me that spelt out the end of this.'

'Me and Dave get along the best,' Hawkins once told me, 'but we don't get along the best either, do you know what I mean? Because we're more like brothers. He can really hurt my feelings worse than anybody else. I'm not just talking about the music or whatever, he knows how to fucking make me feel like shit if he wants to. And I know how to fucking press his buttons too, I know where his weaknesses and insecurities are. And that can be a hard thing for us. He doesn't like too many people to know too much about him.'

With communications in his own band at all-time low, on 24 April Grohl returned to the Troubadour for a second time with Homme and Oliveri. This time, joined by A Perfect Circle guitarist Jeordie White (formerly known as Marilyn Manson sidekick Twiggy Ramirez) the trio took to the stage as the cast of Oliveri's side-band Mondo

Generator. This too was a truly remarkable night, a gig I count myself fortunate to have seen. Officially Oliveri's ragtag collective were playing in support to local punks Amen, but the fact that a good 80 per cent of the paying audience filed back out into the muggy LA night air as soon as Mondo Generator finished their set told the real story of the evening.

For Grohl, the camaraderie, spontaneity and slightly unhinged nature of the gig brought his own band's current malaise into perspective, too much fucking perspective as Spinal Tap once pithily observed. It was at this point that he decided that the desperate circumstances in which his band found itself required drastic actions as a means of, if not redemption, then at least stopping the rot. With his band having authored music that for the most part they did not care for, and certainly did not believe in, Grohl took the executive decision to take what had been recorded thus far and simply toss it in the bin. When one considers the notion of artistic integrity – or perhaps the concept of what it means to be 'punk rock' – the willingness of a band to put its money where its mouth is to the tune of something like one million dollars is a hard gambit to top.

'I remember getting a promotional schedule for that album, looking at it and thinking, "Wait a minute, I don't even like this music, how am I supposed to promote it? How can I tell anyone I'm proud of this when I'm just not?"' the singer recalls. 'And to be honest, the last thing in the world the band wanted to do was [for us] to be in the same room as each other. So I thought, "Fuck it, okay, I'm going to play with Queens of the Stone Age for a while, and if the other guys want to be in the band again, then we can be in the band. But right now nobody wants to be in the band."

'It's nice to know that we always have that emergency switch, that we don't have to be in this band, we don't have to do anything that we're doing,' Grohl told me when the dust had settled. 'We make commitments and we honour those commitments, but at any time we could always say, "Nah, fuck it, let's stop." And we know that, and it's great. Honestly, I don't feel obligated to anyone but the other guys in the band, and if the day comes where we all look at each other and say,

"Nah, fuck it and fuck you," it'll be easy just to pull the switch. And that was about to happen then.'

In switching his attention from his own band to Queens of the Stone Age in 2002, Dave Grohl didn't so much 'pull the switch' on Foo Fighters as press the 'Alarm' button.

'My first thought was, "Man, I'm not even going to get to make a record with these guys? Are you kidding me?"' says Chris Shiflett. 'Bands are funny organisations: lines of communications tend to be pretty bad, but you tend to fumble your way through it. But when I heard we'd postponed the album it made me very nervous. Very nervous indeed.'

Temporarily released from the pressures of being bandleader for Foo Fighters, Grohl instead revelled in finding himself once more working in the engine room of a powerful rock band. To prepare for the tour the drummer worked out; on the road he guzzled Crowne Royale whisky, smoked cigarettes, drank coffee and ate pungent cheese as an alternative to the QOTSA-approved list of narcotics eulogised in their crowd favourite, 'Feel Good Hit of the Summer'. Tiring of journalists continually enquiring as to the future of his own band, Grohl turned down most of the interview requests that came during the time of his busman's holiday, all of which meant that he was free to do something that it seemed he'd been unable to do for some time – take pleasure in the simple act of making music.

'Around the time I started playing drums with Queens I got these two red tribal symbols on my arms,' he told me in 2009, rolling up his T-shirt sleeves to exhibit his tattoos. 'At the time I didn't think too much about it, but I think I had these tattoos done because I was getting my arms back. There's a reason why I'm here, and it's not my voice, it's because these arms taught themselves how to play drums by listening to punk rock albums and Led Zeppelin. And so in a way it's like I have these tattoos as a way to say, "Don't forget what you're here to do!"

'When I joined Queens I think it's the first time that I've ever felt truly confident and strong in a band. After doing that Troubadour show we walked offstage and [sometime QOTSA collaborator] Mark Lanegan said – and this was one of the few things that Mark Lanegan ever said to me – "You know, it'd be a shame just to do that only once." So my decision was purely musical and motivational: I was now playing drums in the best band I'd ever been in.

'Being in Queens was one of the greatest experiences of my life without question. If you can say that you were a member of Queens of the Stone Age that's like wearing a patch on your chest that says "I am a badasss" for the rest of your life, because the only people that get to play in Queens of the Stone Age are badass motherfuckers, and that's the truth.

'Walking through the backstage area of a festival with Queens is like the moment in a Western where the saloon bar doors swing open and the piano player stops playing and everyone just stares. You have Josh, Lanegan, Oliveri and me walking in a straight line and it's like being in the coolest gang. We never had a bad show, every show just got better and better.

'Playing drums in Queens was like ESP – we barely talked about music, we just made it. It was like the perfect fuck – like fucking the hottest fucking porn star – something that memories and legends are made of. That precise musical connection is something you search for your whole life.'

It was, though, surely inevitable that Dave Grohl's happy world of escapism with Queens of the Stone Age would soon enough come crashing against the realities that were his obligations as a Foo Fighter, both to his bandmates and to the music that they made together. Like a warning sign flashing on a motorway, the weekend of 27/28 April 2002 must surely have been present in his mind. This was the date of the annual Coachella Music & Arts Festival in Indio, California. The bill for the year in question included The Prodigy, The Strokes, Oasis and Bjork; also booked, albeit on separate days, were Foo Fighters and Queens of the Stone Age.

It was during rehearsals for their appearance at Coachella that unspoken tensions and resentment in the Foo Fighters camp came noisily to the surface.

'The whole band had a big blow-out,' explains Grohl. 'We were trying to write a set list and that turned into a petty, ridiculous little argument where then I thought, "Okay, I think this is probably going to be the last show." But I didn't say anything. We started rehearsing, but the vibe was so bad that Chris said, "Hey guys, maybe we should talk this out …" And then it just exploded.'

'There was finger pointing and yelling and, honestly, I thought that would be the last show. And it would be a good way to go.'

'I was being an asshole,' says Taylor Hawkins with disarming honesty, 'so it was mainly Dave and I shouting. I felt that Dave was elsewhere at the time. We had a huge argument, but it did clear the air. That was when Dave let everyone know, "I'm leading this band." The argument was kinda a bit like, "Don't question me, everyone can have their opinion, that's fine, but I'm the leader, I'm gonna have the final word, I'm gonna make the decisions and I'm gonna essentially write the songs." So that's when everyone went, "Okay, well, now I understand where we're at, it's Dave's band and Dave's ideas and if you don't like it that's okay, we can agree to disagree, but that's the final word." The dynamic changed a little bit then, but in a way it made things easier, it got rid of any lingering questions. Now we know who's driving the ship. I'm not saying Dave's a total control freak, because he's not, he's interested in everyone's opinions and he wants everyone to enjoy what they're doing, but at the same time if he feels strongly about something there's not much to be discussed.'

In Dave Grohl's mind, Foo Fighters' Coachella performance on 28 April 2002 saved his band, "turned everything around". It was a show that convinced him that Foo Fighters were a powerful, vital band in their own right, and a show that convinced Shiflett, Mendel and Hawkins that Grohl's focus was unwavering.

Watching from the sidelines, Josh Homme was able to see the situation for what it was, rather than for what it appeared to be to its panicked combatants.

'I always knew that Dave was going to go back to Foo Fighters, and I knew this was just a classic moment for us,' he told me in 2009. 'I was always trying to intimate that this wasn't something the other guys needed to worry about, but that's kinda impossible. Band people, and I mean this in a very blanket way, are very easily rattled: many bands don't last and they're such an unpredictable animal, so it's easy to get your confidence rattled. Dave might even have had a moment or two wondering what he was going to do, but I knew. And what was great about that time was that Dave did go back, and that said that it's possible to have a musical mistress. It would have been terrible if Dave had stayed in Queens, because it would have eliminated and killed the suggestion that you can do multiple things. In a rare moment it proved that having multiple personalities isn't a bad thing for someone playing music. Once you feel you can do anything in music, that's when you get closer to God ...'

Never mind being closer to God, in spring 2002 Foo Fighters would have settled for being closer to completing their troublesome fourth album. Prior to taking the decision to consign the work recorded in Virginia and at Conway Studios to the bin, Grohl had played a selection of songs for former guitarist Pat Smear. The response from the usually positive guitarist was lukewarm at best.

'He was the only person to say he didn't like it,' says Grohl. 'He said, like, "I don't know, it's not your best." And we were like, "Fuck you! What are you talking about?" But he was correct. And then of course we threw that in the trash can and fucking did it again.'

In truth, Pat Smear wasn't the only one harbouring reservations. In his role as engineer on the project, Nick Raskulinecz hadn't felt it his place to speak out loud regarding his concerns about the quality of the music Foo Fighters were recording, but such concerns did exist. Eventually, at Grohl's prompting, his true feelings were brought out into the light.

'I knew it wasn't as good as it could have been,' says Raskulinecz, 'but I wasn't the producer at that point, so it wasn't really my job in the recording to make those comments. My job was to make it sound good. But Dave called me up point blank one day and asked if I thought the record was as good as it could be and I said, "No, I thought it could be better …" And then he asked me if I thought I could produce it, and we went back to Virginia and tracked the whole album in two weeks.'

'It took about four months to do those Million Dollar Demos, and that's far too long for a rock record,' says Hawkins. 'Unless you're doing *A Night at the Opera*. When we went back in, me and Dave had done some demos for five or six new songs, three of which – "Low", "Times Like These" and "Disenchanted Lullaby" – made it on to the record. And fuck, if those songs weren't on the record …

'"All My Life" we had for a long time, not necessarily with all the lyrics, but the basic structure. The same with "Have It All". But we ended up making them better when we re-recorded them, because we did it without all the technology and ProTools, and went for more of a real human feel, as opposed to this quantised Limp Bizkit version. So when we went back we were just planning on recording these five songs, and adding them to "Have It All" and "All My Life". But we ended up rearranging a lot of them. "Come Back" is completely unrecognisable from the old version, "Lonely as You" is completely unrecognisable, "Overdrive" is … recognisable, but we put a big line of cocaine on top of it, we did it in an early Police record fashion, as opposed to the sterile "Learn to Fly" fashion that it was originally. And "Burn Away" was completely different. So basically we rearranged a lot of them.'

Even with the foundations for the album laid down in just thirteen days – a work rate that equalled a day for each month Foo Fighters had wasted on recordings that were deemed unfit for purpose – the sessions for the album that would become *One by One* were far from routine. For one thing, time was of the essence, with more Queens of the Stone Age shows crowding the horizon and the start of the summer festival season hovering into view. But necessity being the mother of invention appeared to light a spark that had previously been missing from Foo Fighters' efforts to make music in the twenty-first century. From 6 to 18 May Grohl and Hawkins hammered out the nuts and bolts of their band's fourth album with something approaching ease; later in the month, with Grohl back on the QOTSA tour bus, Mendel and Shiflett were trusted to lay down bass guitar and lead guitar parts with Nick Raskulinecz in the absence of their band leader. The recording process may have been unorthodox – Shiflett later described the experience as being a 'weird, broken way of making a record', while Hawkins admitted the process was 'a little bit shoddy' – but with the band now hundreds of thousands of dollars in hock to their record company the time had clearly arrived to paint in broad strokes rather than to obsess over finer details. And as unorthodox as the process may have been, ultimately it ensured the band's survival.

'There's that cliché, "What doesn't kill you makes you stronger," and that absolutely applied,' says Nate Mendel. 'Stumbling on that record was tough: it was the first time it was hard and it frustrated us, to know that it wasn't good enough. So what do you do? And then the record came out good and it really crystallised the idea of what we do, it made us realise that we had something valuable that we'd created for ourselves.'

And in the midst of all this activity, to the outside eye at least Foo Fighters still exuded the easy-going confidence of one of the world's coolest gangs. While just weeks previously the future of the group was very much in doubt, even to certain members within the group, Grohl's habit of maintaining a unified front when it came to his band's public face meant that no cracks were discernible to the naked eye. On the contrary, a look at the quartet's summer itinerary pointed towards a group whose mobility still charted an upward trajectory. In Scotland and the Republic of Ireland Foo Fighters had climbed the bill at the T in the Park and Wittness festivals respectively, while on the last weekend of August the group headlined the prestigious sister festivals staged at Richfield Avenue Park in Reading and Temple Newsham Park in Leeds. Playing to 140,000 people and more, over two nights in Berkshire and West Yorkshire, the former date surely held a special resonance for Dave Grohl. A decade earlier this had been the site of Nirvana's now legendary headline appearance at the Reading festival. Although with a different band, and playing a sixteen-song set that featured not a single Nirvana composition, the drummer turned frontman could hardly have looked out at the sea of faces before him and not feel assured that his standing in the musical present, and not just his place in musical history, was secure.

This is a Call

'I was actually pretty excited, more excited than nervous, because it was really an honour to be at the top of the bill,' he told me one week later, as we travelled together on a Eurostar train bound for Paris. 'The other guys in the band were pretty nervous. I had to give them a pep talk, give them the "Hey ho, ra-ra, we should be at the top of the bill because we've been a band for eight years and we're better than we ever have been and we can do this, we can fucking do it, I know we can." Then we did it, just like I said we would.

'I just felt like the whole evening was magic. I mean, for something that started with a fucking demo tape recorded at a studio down the street from my house to hearing 40,000 people scream the lyrics to my songs was a huge accomplishment, it was a huge emotional deal. My family was on the side of the stage crying, it was like I'd won a gold medal or something. It was really a lifetime achievement, it was fucking awesome, insane. I get choked up talking about it.

'I had a profound revelation as I was staring at my mother and my sister on the side of the stage: that I wrote a song on the back of a fucking AM/PM receipt, and now 60,000 people are singing it. I honestly felt like the luckiest guy in the world.

'It felt great, it felt like, you know, we'd arrived.'

∾

But if on that weekend Dave Grohl finally emerged from Nirvana's shadow, in the eyes of the alternative rock community at least, the smoke from that band's embers continued to engulf him. In September 2001 Courtney Love had filed a suit in Los Angeles Superior Court against Grohl, former Nirvana bassist Krist Novoselic and the group's record label, the Universal Music Group, in an attempt to wrestle control of Nirvana's master tapes. Along with this, the plaintiff also sought to dissolve the LLC (Limited Liability Corporation) she had founded with Grohl and Novoselic in 1997 in order to oversee the correct handling of all posthumous Nirvana releases.

Courtney Love's contention with her business partners – what news journalists refer to as 'the blood and guts' of the story – concerned the unreleased Nirvana song 'You Know You're Right', the composition recorded by the group at Robert Lang's Seattle studio in January 1994. Grohl had previously described the song as 'a trip', as 'weird', as both 'beautiful and disturbing'.

'It doesn't really give you a sense of closure,' he stated. 'In fact, it makes you feel worse about the whole situation.'

Although the warring parties were agreed on their desire that the song be made available to the public, the format on which 'You Know You're Right' would appear was a source of contention. While Grohl and Novoselic were of the opinion that the song's rightful place should be as part of a Nirvana box set, Kurt Cobain's widow desired that the track take pride of place on a more commercially enticing single-disc 'greatest hits' compilation.

The battle lines for this skirmish were initially drawn even earlier than the suit filed in California in September 2001, when on 11 June 2001 Courtney Love submitted a memorandum filed in the State of Washington, an addition to the case of *Courtney Love Cobain, et al., versus David Grohl, et al.* The document laid out the nature of the disagreement, the divide between those who wanted the song to emerge as part of a box set and those who wished it to appear on a more affordable one-disc release, and in one telling sentence surely revealed the true nature of the dispute. 'All parties believe,' came the revelation, 'that the recording, which has never before been released, has the potential to be a significant hit.'

For the most part, the arguments that followed were conducted behind closed doors. In interviews Grohl was relatively tight-lipped on the dispute, not least because of the legal ramifications that would be triggered were he to freely express his feelings. It was a surprise then for this writer to see Grohl label Love an 'ugly fucking bitch' from the stage of Ireland's Witness festival in July 2002. When I expressed my surprise to Grohl two months later, Foo Fighters' frontman was more circumspect.

'It's so easy to have the excuse of legalities so as not to talk about anything, but yeah there are times when you're pissed off,' he conceded. 'It's inevitable that there'll be days you feel like you want to pop. It happens to the lawyers, it happens to Courtney, and it happens to Krist and I. I've been pretty reserved about my feelings towards all of this for years, but it popped out of my mouth a few times. You know, it's only natural for someone to get to their boiling point.

'But this lawsuit is not the end of the world to me,' he added. 'Fortunately I have something now that's productive and positive. I'd probably be more concerned and more upset about this whole business if I didn't have this band, but why focus so much on that when I have something like this?

'When you're onstage headlining the Reading festival you're not wondering how the court case is going to settle, you're revelling in the moment of one of the greatest nights of your life.'

Perhaps surprisingly, given the explosive nature of the argument, the two warring parties never faced a public day in court. Indeed the dispute ended with a whisper rather than a scream. After months of wrangling it was agreed that 'You Know You're Right' be included on a single-disc compilation of Nirvana songs, simply titled *Nirvana*, while Kurt Cobain's solo acoustic demo of the track was included on the *With the Lights Out* box set in 2004. You could say that, ultimately, music was the winner. But the smile on Courtney's face might just have been a little broader.

Nirvana was released in the United Kingdom on 28 October 2002, and entered the national album chart at number 1. As coincidence would have it, the album that it replaced at the top of the charts was Foo Fighters' *One by One*.

∽

Preceded by the hit single, *All My Life*, and its blockbusting video, shot at the Great Western Forum in Inglewood, California, *One by One* landed like a bomb on both sides of the Atlantic. In the United States the eleven-song collection, featuring a beautifully understated piece of artwork inked by the inimitable Raymond Pettibon, débuted on the *Billboard* album chart at number 3, while the CD-buying public in the Republic of Ireland and Australia joined listeners in the UK in bestowing upon Foo Fighters the honour of a number 1 album. *One by One* also earned itself a Top Ten first-week placing in six other countries. To date, the album has sold well in excess of a million copies in the United States, and an impressive 700,000 copies in the United Kingdom.

Along with emphatic commercial success came much critical kudos. *NME* wrote of the album that 'everything [Foo Fighters] had, they still have – but now every note is ten times more focused and urgent'. *MOJO* hedged its bets slightly by reporting that although the Foos 'may have just failed to make a Great Rock Album – though it has many moments of greatness – they have unquestionably become a Great Rock Band'. Meanwhile in the United States the trade bible *Billboard* wrote that '*One By One*, in all its thunderous angst and desperate expressions of hope, represents a full on exploration of the Foo's '70s influence', while *Rolling Stone* was of the opinion that this was 'rock that draws power from its determination to struggle onward'.

Not all of *One by One*'s notices were positive, however. *Blender* and *Q* both damned the album with faint criticism and even fainter praise. But it was Paul Rees, then Editor of *Kerrang!* – a title which up until that point had dedicated more pages to Foo Fighters than any publication in the world – who aimed, and landed, the most stinging rebuke. On the positive spin that claimed that the album's hectic final recording push was the result of a creative burst, Rees observed that what appears on disc 'sounds more like a desperate attempt to simply finish the damn thing ...' before going on to state his opinion that while 'advance word from Planet Foo has also touted this as some sort of classic, the best Foo Fighters album yet. In reality, it's not even the third best Foo Fighters album.' The review concluded with the shortest of shrifts in the form of the claim that '*One By One* will do a job of providing perfectly acceptable background music for the masses. What it won't do is excite, thrill or challenge anybody, least of all its creator. "Dead on the inside I've got nothing to prove," sings Grohl on "Come Back". He's changed nothing here.'

The most damning criticism that can be aimed at the shoulders of *One by One* is that rather too much of it is mediocre and unremarkable. Although Dave Grohl at the time talked the album up positively, as Dave Grohl is wont to do, it wasn't too long after the release of his group's fourth album that he was admitting that the album contained, in his opinion, only four good songs.

'We rushed into it and we rushed out of it,' he admitted. 'Too many of the songs on that record just weren't good enough. It was just a question of getting it done and getting it out … I don't consider it to be our proudest moment.'

Hardcore Foo Fighters fans may find reasons to disagree with Grohl's brutal assessment of the album, but the tracks he nominates as its 'four good songs' are pretty easy to identify. In 2011 only the singles 'All My Life' and 'Times Like These' remain constant in Foo Fighters' epic live sets, and indeed just one year after the release of *One by One* the filthy, down-tuned 'Low' and the rather beautiful 'Tired of You', which featured delicate, soaring guitar harmonies from Queen's Brian May, were the only other cuts which could be considered staples of the show.

In the *Back and Forth* documentary Chris Shiflett nominates 'All My Life' as being his favourite Foo Fighters song to play live, a number capable of pushing a good show to greater heights and rescuing even the most disappointing of nights. From the moment Dave Grohl's throttled guitar opens the track, this is a song that has 'fan favourite' stamped through it from front to last. Charged with dynamism and a febrile sonic energy, it sparks with an energy that seems to suggest its creators, stymied by months of tension and creative inertia, had in one exhilarating rush finally released the pressure that had been building within them. Had the rest of the album from which 'All My Life' emerged followed this pattern then all the positive spin emanating from the mouth of Dave Grohl may have amounted to more than wishful thinking. 'Times Like These', meanwhile, is an effervescent slice of power pop that arrives as breezy and carefree as a holiday weekend, its seemingly effortless nature informed by a charming lightness of touch. Elsewhere 'Have It All', the album's fourth and final single, almost qualifies as an underrated gem, its fizzing and bouncing rhythms underscoring a melody that manages to be neither obvious nor anonymous. Most striking of all is 'Come Back', the 7 minute and 49 second song that closes the album in a manner that is both restrained yet commanding, the work of musicians who understand the truth in the cliché that power is nothing without control.

Too often, though, the work contained on *One by One* is anonymous and unengaging, not least because its creators seemed themselves to be unengaged with the music. It may be that the tales of struggle that surrounded the Foo Fighters' camp in 2001 and 2002 have bestowed upon this album a sense that the music itself is mired in difficulties, but either way much of the album is informed by a sense of joylessness and frustration; ironically a leaked clip of a much more energised early version of the listless 'Lonely As You' suggested that perhaps the original 'Million Dollar Demos' may not have been quite the disaster Grohl believed it to be in spring 2002. Whatever, at a time when the group as a unit lacked cohesion, it seems unsurprising that the album to which they put their name would be similarly lacking in direction.

෴

But if *One by One* carried with it an air of compromise, and the sense that, at least in part, these were songs fashioned for a job of work rather than a labour of love, elsewhere Dave Grohl was able to stretch his limbs in the pursuit of making music purely for the joy of doing so. As well as recording the bold and brilliant *Songs for the Deaf* with Queens of the Stone Age, 2002 also saw Grohl play guitar on the David Bowie song 'I've Been Waiting for You', from the Thin White Duke's *Heathen* set. The following year he provided backing vocals for The Bangles' comeback album *Doll Revolution*, played drums on the Garbage track 'Bad Boyfriend' from their album *Bleed Like Me* (produced by Butch Vig, also Garbage's drummer) and, perhaps most memorably, fulfilled drum duties on Killing Joke's largely terrifying twelfth album, which, like that band's fabulously toxic 1980 début, was a self-titled set.

'I'm biased,' said Grohl, 'but I think it's one of the best Killing Joke records they've ever made. I listen to those songs and think, "Wow, you know, I bet you that someone who likes [nu-metal superstars] Linkin Park would like this record." After a minute I thought, Oh my God, if every kid who likes Linkin Park bought a Killing Joke record the world would be a fucking scary place.'

This is a Call

In February of that year Foo Fighters frontman joined Bruce Springsteen, Elvis Costello and Steven Van Zandt onstage at the Grammys at Madison Square Garden for a breathless run through The Clash's 'London Calling', a tribute to the late, great Joe Strummer who had died two months earlier. But if his night out at the music industry's foremost awards ceremony primarily concerned itself with eulogising a punk rock hero – and there was also the small matter of picking up another Grammy, for Best Hard Rock Performance for 'All My Life', quite possibly the only song with a chorus about eating 'pussy' ever to receive a golden gramophone trophy – the greater part of Dave Grohl's 2003 was devoted to the pursuit of another love: that of heavy metal.

The gestation period of the project that would eventually become the *Probot* album was even longer than that for *One by One*. Back at 606 in Alexandria, in 2000 Dave Grohl had placed a call to Adam Kasper with an idea for a project: he would write and record a number of instrumental pieces that would be sent out to various vocalists from the world of underground metal, and these men would unleash Hell atop the backing tracks. The idea was not dissimilar to Black Sabbath guitarist Tony Iommi's 2000 solo album, *Iommi*, which featured contributions from artists including Ozzy Osbourne, Smashing Pumpkins' mainman Billy Corgan, System of a Down's Serj Tankian, Mr Brian May and Dave Grohl himself. But Grohl's vision for *Probot* would feature the presence not of metal's most famous voices, but its unsung heroes, men who had inspired Dave Grohl prior to his arrival in the mainstream with Nirvana. Work began on the album in the most relaxed of surroundings, with Grohl simply writing and playing riffs through a Peavey practice amp while elsewhere in the room the television relayed its images to no one in particular.

The first decade of the twenty-first century was notable for the manner in which modern metal manoeuvred its way into the mainstream of popular culture. Dave Grohl himself played a vital role in this transition, both with Nirvana opening doors for 'heavy' bands to seep onto radio playlists, and also in his willingness to associate himself with acts who a generation earlier had belonged in a ghetto that was derided and even despised by most other musical subgenres. Foo Fighters frontman may have headlined festivals in the 'noughties' dressed in a Venom T-shirt, or spoken of the carnage that he witnessed at Slayer's 4 December 1986 show at Washington's ornate Warner Theatre on that band's Reign in Pain tour (where the group's fans gleefully destroyed the venue's beautiful velvet-cushioned seats), but with few exceptions – the critical acclaim afforded to Metallica being the most notable – the 1980s were a period when the world of metal did not share house room with any other type of music. Instead, it lived in the doghouse. Even as a teenager Grohl instinctively understood that the music made by Voivod had much in common with that produced by Bad Brains – indeed, he would later speak of going to see both of these bands on consecutive weekends in the DC area – but for the public at large those that populated the community of underground and thrash metal lived in a neighbourhood that existed on the wrong, for which read 'stupid', side of the tracks. What's more, in hitting the jackpot with Nirvana Dave Grohl was seen, by magazines with an anti-metal agenda of their own to push, as being a member of a group that not only had nothing in common with metal, but actually provided an antidote to this barely housetrained school of music. Speaking to *Kerrang!* magazine in 2003, Grohl gave such a notion the short shrift he felt it deserved, noting, 'Nirvana were not just a punk band in the same way that Motörhead were not just a metal band.'

But if metal itself in the 1980s was separated from the rest of the musical universe, there were also divisions in its own ranks, between those who simply wished to play as fast and as loudly as they possibly could, seemingly with no eye for commercial gain, and those who longed to exploit metal's broad fanbase with what amounted to little more than bubblegum pop songs with manicured distortion. The damage Nirvana inflicted on metal and hard rock's terrain occurred in the latter camp rather than the former.

'Those bands were something neither me nor my friends had anything to do with,' Grohl explained to *Kerrang!* in 2003. 'For one thing they weren't any good. I never listened to the radio when I was young because I never liked the music that was played on it, even rock radio – especially rock radio. And I'd never watch MTV because you never saw anything on there that was any good. It was Metallica that opened doors for me, to bands like Possessed and Exodus. And it was a very grassroots thing, it was tape trading and digging and searching around for music in the underground. It was about community, about not having it handed to you on a plate. I didn't want it and I didn't want it comfortable. I didn't see the point in liking music you were supposed to like and that it was safe to like.

'In Nirvana we never made it our mission to be the poster boys of the alternative revolution or to make it our priority to destroy heavy metal. That was never something we were really concerned with. And I think the music that died when Nirvana became popular did prove itself to be unimportant, whereas bands like Slayer and Voivod continued to exist, because they came from a scene not unlike the underground punk scene, which is why it survived, just as the punk scene survived. It was built from something that mattered. But when you're talking about bands like Winger and Warrant, well, that just wasn't part of our world. It was too ridiculous to consider a reality, which is why it died. And I'm glad that it died. It stopped meaning something to people. But I think that's why people looked to Nirvana, because they thought we were human beings, that we were real people. And it was time for that.'

In this spirit, *Probot* was an album that was teeming with contributions from 'real people'. Following the tour in support of Foo Fighters' *One by One* album, Dave Grohl found the time to properly record the tracks he planned to send out to various leading lights from the metal underground of the 1980s. With the help of Zwan guitarist Matt Sweeney, a man who was able to act as the bridge between *Probot*'s creator and the artists he wished to enlist to provide vocals for the pieces he had created, Grohl contacted such figures as Lemmy from Motörhead (the one contributor whose profile was known to the mainstream music fan), Max Cavalera from Soulfly, Venom's Cronos, D.R.I.'s Kurt Brecht, Trouble frontman Eric Wagner, Cathedral mainman Lee Dorrian, Corrosion of Conformity's Mike Dean, Snake from Voivod and Maryland music legend Wino, then of Spirit Caravan, to name just a few.

Disenchanted lullaby

The recording sessions for the self-titled album were also unusual. With the exception of Lemmy's track, 'Shake Your Blood', which was recorded in Los Angeles with Grohl present (with the party later decamping to a nearby strip club) the music for each of *Probot*'s eleven listed tracks reached each individual vocalist via the Federal Express courier service. In receipt of these tracks each performer would then record their own vocal, as they saw fit, before returning the completed song, or songs, to Dave Grohl. It has been reported that most of the album's costs came in the form of payments to Federal Express.

'When I started recording this stuff, and it was four years ago, remember, I didn't think for a moment that it would become a record,' Grohl said in November 2003. 'I just wanted to record something for fun. But then it started to turn into something, and I decided to speak to people to take it further. But I was so nervous about contacting some of these guys. Wino is a god to me, as is Eric Wagner ... And here I was calling up Eric Wagner in Chicago and saying, "Hi, I'm Dave from Foo Fighters – would you like to sing on a metal song that I've written?" What the fuck was he likely to say to that? But it turns out that he was excited by it, it turns out that everyone was excited by it. I can't tell you how much it means to me to have the luxury of this opportunity. Not only *Probot*, but all the opportunities that success allows me. It's important to extend yourself to other types of music. It's good for your fucking soul, for your fucking heart.'

If Dave Grohl was honoured that the musical heroes of his noisy youth consented to involve themselves with his *Probot* enterprise, so too were the invitees honoured to have been asked.

'I think it's fucking amazing the way it turned out,' is the opinion of Cronos, the bassist and vocalist with vastly influential Geordie black metallers Venom, who contributed vocals to the song 'Centuries of Sin'. 'I mean, I was sent just the raw music for pretty much all of the songs and it was kinda a bit of a nail-biter on which one was mine, because there was quite a lot of them where I was like, "I don't know what to do with this," because it was so not like what I'd done before. So when Dave actually said, "Track three is yours," I was so relieved because that was the one I wanted. I was buzzing because that was my favourite one on the album anyway. I actually wrote three sets of lyrics: one was like a sleazy, red-light area, "going out for a whore" kinda song, another one was about young guys going out for a fight and drinking on the town, and then I also wrote the "Centuries of Sin" track, which was the Venomous one. But he went, "I just want you to do your thing on it. Don't think about Dave Grohl, don't think about Foo Fighters and Nirvana, think as if you were doing a Venom song." And I was like "Brilliant!"

'I could see where he was coming from. This stuff was not Foo Fighters, this stuff was not Nirvana, this was Dave taking a chance: either he was going to alienate every single Foo Fighters fan in the world and absolutely destroy his career or people are going to understand it and put it in perspective, which is absolutely how it ended up.'

'To me Dave Grohl is no different from a lot of guys I knew back in the 1980s,' says Cathedral frontman Lee Dorrian, who sang on *Probot*'s 'Ice Cold Man'. 'He's still got the same mentality, but obviously he's a lot more famous now. Most kids who grew up in that punk scene, that was their education. Someone like John Peel was the teacher you never had at school, and the scene was your family. I think the punk scene was a really good grounding for anyone who's young and getting into music and culture and is trying to figure the world out.'

Probot finally saw the light of day in February 2004. The album was released through the underground record label Southern Lord, owned by Greg Anderson, the same Greg Anderson Grohl had met outside the International Motor Sports Garage back in 1990. Earlier in the process Grohl had meetings with various major labels, and at each meeting he would ask those present if they knew who Cronos was, or who King Diamond (another of the album's personnel) was. When the answers came back negative, as invariably they did, the musician explained to the record company executives present that they were wasting one another's time. Even a meeting with the metal record label Roadrunner – home to Slipknot and Machine Head, among many others – did not provide *Probot*'s creator with the impression that his labour of love would be going to the right home. And so it was, having exhausted the more obvious avenues of release, that *Probot* met its waiting public on the reassuringly obscure Southern Lord label.

'I'd started the band Goatsnake with Pete Stahl so I'd run into Dave now and again, and every time I'd see him we'd sequester ourselves in a corner and talk about metal,' says Anderson. 'He was this giant pop star in my eyes but all he wanted to know about was what cool metal records he should go out and buy, and I thought that was cool. Dave would mention to me that he was putting together these songs and he mentioned Lemmy and Cronos, so it was just kinda talk, he never, ever mentioned business to me. And then the way I heard the story from Pete Stahl was that one day Dave was playing Pete songs from it and saying, "What the hell should I do with this stuff? I don't feel like a major label will understand," and Pete said, "Well, what about Anderson's label?" I laughed about that and thought nothing would come of it, but then Dave called me and said, "Hey, I wanna talk about this *Probot* record."'

And, so it came to pass that, in one 52-minute swoop, Dave Grohl introduced some of underground metal's leading lights – and the cult Southern Lord label itself – to a brand new audience.

'I've been told by several people that *Probot* was their gateway to check out Wino's band, or COC for the first time,' says Anderson. 'It was like an introduction to this music, like "Dave recommends ..." We got a lot of attention and the label profile as a whole was really elevated. And having that record in our catalogue was a great foot in the door for us.'

Towards the end of 2003, on the promotional trail for *Probot*, Grohl and Anderson found themselves in London, with both men desiring of a night out. Enlisting the services of Lee Dorrian as host for the evening, the party met in Kensington and headed north to Notting Hill Gate in order to visit the Death Disco club, run by Creation Records impresario Alan McGee, figuring that the instantly recognisable Grohl would be ignored by the club's hipster clientele.

'I thought, "Well, everyone is too cool for school there,"' recalls Dorrian. 'If Keith Richards walked in everyone would pretend not to notice, so I thought, "Dave won't be hassled." The doorman was being arsey, so we had to queue for 45 minutes to get in, and as soon as we got in literally everyone from the bar staff to the cloakroom attendant were all jumping on him. I was like, "Shit, sorry, man." But he just stood there drinking Absinthe and having a good time. He just dealt with it and humoured everybody. I couldn't deal with it; it'd weaken me. But he has such a good personality that he can handle it.'

'Each person had their own story about what a certain band or a certain song meant to them,' remembers Greg Anderson. 'And I'd be like "Fuck man!" I was getting worn out. But Dave would sit with every single person until they were done talking. And I asked him, I said, "Dude, does this bother you?" And he said, "No man, I actually really love doing this, it's part of the whole thing. And I just like talking to people." I was blown away. He's the real deal.'

If Dave Grohl is the real deal, then so too is *Probot*, a treacherously heavy collection instantly identifiable as a genuine labour of love. *Probot* has about it a heft and a greasy gravitational pull that is nothing if not authentic, that is nothing if not the sound of a kind of music made simply for its own sake. It is also something that cannot be bluffed. The point of underground metal, or of thrash and hardcore punk, was that its tonality and totality was such that it discouraged the attentions of the poseur. This was a world populated by people who genuinely loved the music, and the love of this music fostered a community that amounted to much more than a mere 'scene'.

More than anything, *Probot*'s most striking characteristic is that it is able to bring this notion of community, of fraternity, to life on a five-inch CD. Despite its number of different vocalists, this is an album that stands proud as a single body of work, of a celebration of an artistic mindset that spares no thought for commercial ends. Cronos might be over-egging the pudding slightly with his belief that this project might prove sufficiently extreme to 'destroy' Dave Grohl's career – in truth, most Foo Fighters fans politely ignored this raw, savage and only moderately successful outing – but as an addition to Grohl's CV this is an album that has no thought for long-term consequences, just like the genres it celebrates. Whether it takes the form of the hectic aggro-punk of the 1 minute 24 second 'Access Babylon' (sung by Corrosion of Conformity's Mike Dean), the super-heavy sludge of 'Ice Cold Man', the deathlesss rattle 'n' roll of Lemmy's 'Shake Your Blood' or the relentlessly ominous thud that propels the Max Cavalera-helmed 'Red War', this is a set that throughout sounds deliciously unclean and militaristically committed to its cause. It is the work of men who know what it is like to taste blood, and to find themselves with puke on their shoes. But in truth *Probot* came and went with little noise or ceremony. It was noticed by those who care about such music – and given approving looks from those who believe it is their job to judge the authenticity of underground metal – while the rest of Foo Fighters' constituency waited patiently for the band to return to active service. Which soon enough they would do.

As it was the purchase of D.R.I.'s eponymous 22-track seven-inch single on 3 July 1983 that propelled Dave Grohl into this musical netherworld, it seems only appropriate that the last word on this chapter of Grohl's life should be given over to that band's vocalist Kurt Brecht, who guests on the rumbling 'Silent Spring'. When I spoke to Brecht in 2010, his verdict on the *Probot* album, and indeed Grohl's career to date, was simple and perceptive:

'It seems to me,' he said, 'that Dave Grohl has got what every musician wants: freedom.'

When Grohl returned to his day job, and the creation of Foo Fighters' album number five, his aim would be to demonstrate exactly that.

Home

I want to be a band that can do fucking anything. Because we can do fucking anything …

Dave Grohl

The date of 7 July 2007 was an occasion when the well-fed and well-paid members of the world's musical communities were given cause to feel pleased with themselves. Just shy of five months earlier, failed US Presidential candidate Al Gore and promoter Kevin Wall staged a press conference in Los Angeles in order to announce a series of worldwide summer concerts organised to raise awareness of the issue of global climate change. Fashioned after the Live Aid concerts of 1985 (organised to raise money to combat famine in Ethiopia) and the Live 8 spectaculars of twenty years later (an octet of open-air shows staged to highlight the issue of Third World debt) this upcoming stable of musical events would be known as Live Earth. Happenings were set to take place at such locations as Giants Stadium in East Rutherford, New Jersey, the Coca Cola Dome near Johannesburg and the Makuhari Messe in the Tokyo suburb of Chiba; there was to be a free show held on Rio's iconic Copacabana Beach too.

But the brightest stone in Live Earth's glistening cluster of diamonds could be found in London, albeit in a not particularly attractive part of the city. The suburban borough of Brent may be as far removed from the lights and landmarks of Westminster as Staten Island is from Times Square, but this rather grey neighbourhood was the home of the then brand new Wembley Stadium. The original venue, built in 1923, became the grand old lady of European stadia: the place where in 1966 England won football's World Cup, the location of Bob Geldof's Live Aid spectacular and the setting for showcase football finals and concerts by iconic rock acts such as the Rolling Stones, Queen and U2. Rebuilt from the ground up in 2000, the second Wembley Stadium may have taken seven years to complete and cost more than a billion pounds, but with its 133 metre tall supporting arch and its inner bowl of 90,000 fire engine red seats, the second largest stadium in Europe could hardly have been more impressive.

The new Wembley Stadium branded itself, rather smugly, as 'The Venue of Legends'. But on the first Saturday in July such a claim amounted to a good deal more than hubris. Gathered in North-West London on that bright day were some of the biggest and most storied names in popular music, artists such as Madonna, Red Hot Chili Peppers, Genesis, Metallica, Beastie Boys, Duran Duran and the mighty Spinal Tap. Dave Grohl's Foo Fighters sat among this stellar bill of performers who had never before publicly uttered a single word on the subject of climate change, and have been largely mute on the subject ever since. Opening the show, Genesis singer and drummer Phil Collins told the crowd that in plugging in their instruments his band had made the global warming problem worse, while Metallica frontman James Hetfield – whose band would headline Wembley Stadium the very next day, and who provided the stage on which Live Earth's many acts performed – subsequently said of the occasion, 'I really avoided talking to the press around the Live Earth day. I didn't quite agree with what was going on there.' Meanwhile, performing his open-air show in the grounds of the Tower of London on 7 July, one-time Dave Grohl collaborator Elvis Costello made a point of joking to his own crowd that a slight frog in his throat had been caused by 'all the hot air coming from Wembley Stadium'.

When the performers playing at 'The Venue of Legends' received the running order for London's Live Earth concert, a running order not announced in advance of the day itself, the Foos found themselves below only Madonna on the bill: Metallica were appearing in a teatime slot that the BBC, broadcasting the event live to homes across the United Kingdom, opted only to air in part. Two days previously, on 5 July, Foo Fighters had played a secret show at the tiny 500-capacity Dingwalls club in London's Camden Town, an event attended by Queen drummer Roger Taylor. Grohl took the opportunity to ask Taylor what the new Wembley Stadium was like. 'Too big,' came the answer. 'Fucking huge.'

'And when someone from Queen says a place is too big,' Grohl told me in 2010, 'that means it's really fucking big.'

As if the occasion wasn't pressurised enough, on the evening of 7 July, as the sun was dipping below Wembley's iconic arch and his charges were about to step onstage for their most high profile show ever, Foo Fighters' manager John Silva approached Dave Grohl with a simple injunction.

'Okay, I just need you to do one thing,' he said. 'I just need you to be better than Metallica.'

Grohl looked at his manager and thought, 'Are you fucking insane? That's impossible. That's the most ridiculous thing anyone has ever said to me in my entire life ...'

But then again, maybe not. All day, a 'kinda strange day' as he remembers it, Dave Grohl had been watching the bands come and go on the Live Earth stage; he sensed from most of them a lack of any real connection between themselves and the 80,000 people gathered inside the stadium. And he made the decision that, in his own allotted stage time, Foo Fighters would go for the jugular.

The five songs that Grohl selected for Foo Fighters' set were 'All My Life', 'My Hero', 'Times Like These', 'Best of You' and 'Everlong', each one a tried-and-trusted arena rock anthem. Inspired by his memories of Queen's legendary set at Live Aid a generation earlier, his intention was to reach out to every single person gathered within the vast bowl, as well as those watching on television all over the world, not least on network television in the United States. And in doing this, and in doing it with considerable grace, charm and heart, the profile of Dave Grohl's band changed. Foo Fighters went from a band who were known to hundreds of thousands of their own fans but remained something of a well-kept secret to the wider world, to being a truly mainstream concern. All in just 25 minutes' work. In the week following their set, a two-year-old song, 'Best of You', appeared once more in the UK's Top 40 singles chart on downloads alone.

'I felt like I was being challenged by all of the bands before me,' Grohl recalled after the event. 'I'm not a competitive dude, but I thought, "Okay motherfuckers, watch this." I had my wife and my daughter at the side of the stage. I was standing there behind the curtain with a guitar in my hand, after four beers, and thought, "Fuck it, this is going to be good."'

Three years after his game-changing first appearance at Wembley Stadium, Dave Grohl told me that he felt that his band's Live Earth set marked his first true moment as a frontman.

'We showed up that day to Wembley, and we thought, "Oh God, how can we possibly entertain this size with this many people?"' he said. 'And then I looked at the line-up and saw that we were after Metallica, we were after the Chili Peppers and the Beastie Boys, and after the Pussycat Dolls, and I just couldn't imagine how our band was going to stand up. But I realised that we had five songs and 25 minutes, so we'll play the five songs that everyone knows the chorus to, and I'll get them to sing along with me. And in those 25 minutes I became the frontman. And every concert since then has been a little bit easier.'

Grohl may be being slightly disingenuous here when he says this. To those who had followed his band from their earliest days it appeared that Grohl always seemed comfortable behind the microphone, has always striven to make those in attendance feel like guests in his home rather than customers in his shop. And for five years prior to their appearance at Live Earth Foo Fighters had been headlining festivals to tens of thousands of people in the United Kingdom without Grohl giving anyone the impression that he was a frightened rabbit frozen at the front of the stage. But this was a band whose circumstances *were* changing, and for the better. From a band who in 2002 were at their wits' end and struggling to cobble together the songs that would comprise *One by One*, by the middle part of the decade the group seemed to be comfortably growing into their own skin. And the same could be said of their leader.

In August 2003 Dave Grohl took his marriage vows for the second time, on this occasion to MTV producer Jordyn Blum, whom he had met one evening in 2001 at Hollywood's chic Sunset Marquis hotel. Grohl was there that day only to make up the numbers for Taylor Hawkins, who'd snagged a date with one of the hotel's pretty barmaids, but he ended up writing 'you're my future ex-wife' and his phone number on a piece of paper he handed to Blum, there to support her friend, Hawkins's date. Prior to their marriage, as the couple's courtship grew more serious, so too did Grohl's relationship with, and commitment to, the city in which he'd met his partner.

'I went back and forth to Los Angeles for years and I basically used it like a dirty fucking whore,' he says. 'I took it and I dragged it around and I fucked it and I drank it under the table and I left it lying in the middle of the road, and then I would be like, "Okay, I'm done with this place, I'm going home now." It all changed when I met my beautiful Californian wife, Jordyn, and I figured, "Well, I can't take a born and bred Angelino out of Los Angeles. It's just not what you do."'

Jordyn Blum became Mrs Dave Grohl on 2 August 2003. The wedding itself took place that afternoon on the tennis court of Grohl's new home in Encino. Having decided that he no longer wished to treat the Los Angeles metropolitan borough like 'a dirty fucking whore', Grohl had decided to put down both money and roots in order to live full time on the West Coast. For his and Jordyn Blum's nuptials, Dave Grohl enlisted the services of Krist Novoselic as best man, with the job of usher being shared by Taylor Hawkins and Jimmy Swanson. Following the wedding ceremony, the 250 or so guests invited to share the happy couple's day were able to dance the night away to the sound of The Fab Four, a top notch Beatles tribute act.

But if domestic life was providing Dave Grohl with happiness and stability, domestic politics certainly was not. Since the election of Barack Obama – a man whose oratorical brilliance and melting-pot ethnicity made him a dream candidate for liberal America – much has been forgotten about the febrile atmosphere of the US body politic and the popular arts in the middle part of the first decade of the twenty-first century. But as George W. Bush prepared to run for a second term as President of the United States, and with that country's armed forces mired in unpopular conflicts in both Afghanistan and Iraq, the artistic community kicked up in protest in a way that hadn't really been seen since the days of the Vietnam War. Green Day released the Bush-baiting *American Idiot*, and sold 14 million copies of a set that spoke to people who wished not to be part of 'a redneck agenda'. Filmmaker Michael Moore released the film *Fahrenheit 9/11*, a documentary which stopped just short of labelling Bush and his cronies as being war criminals. Similarly disruptive was the Rock Against Bush movement, NOFX mainman Fat Mike's campaign (which enlisted the help of many of his punk rock pals, including Foo Fighters, to contribute songs that ended up on one of two Rock Against Bush compilation albums) to unseat the incumbent President.

But while the queue to hit the Bush-shaped piñata with a stick stretched from Pennsylvania Avenue to the Pacific Coast Highway, there was a marked reluctance among the great and good of the music industry to join their voices in song with Bush's political opposition. John Kerry, the Democratic Party's nominee for the 44th President of the United States, may have had all the easy-going charm of a six and a half foot ironing board, but in his endless rallies around the American heartlands the Massachusetts-raised Vietnam veteran was accompanied by musical support only from Jon Bon Jovi and Bruce Springsteen. That was until the campaign trail hit the Midwest, whereupon the New Jersey superstars were joined in a number of cities by Dave Grohl and his Foo Fighters, stung into action by the news that the Republican party was using the Foos' own everyman anthem 'Times Like These' to soundtrack George W.'s rallies.

'I was personally offended that George Bush was using "Times Like These",' Grohl explained the following year. 'We were trying to think of a way to get him to stop, like, "Fuck man, I'm gonna send the President a cease-and-desist order." I wrote that fucking song. I know what I'm singing about and it basically mirrored what John Kerry's campaign was trying to represent.

'I went out on the John Kerry campaign and tried to help them out because I really believed in getting Bush out of office. And it was really inspirational because you'd see tens of thousands of people gathered together with the common idea and will to make things better. We did a lot of stuff with the campaign, just travelling around through Middle America and seeing people who really needed to be rescued.'

It was this time spent on the fringes of Presidential politics that led Grohl to author a collection of songs for the next Foo Fighters album inspired by the experience.

'Every day before Kerry got up to speak, I'd go play acoustic music,' he explained. 'And the audiences weren't Foo Fighters audiences. The front row was World War II veterans and teacher unions and blue-collar workers. I came back from that so inspired by the people and the real emotion and the feeling of a small community all coming together for an honourable reason. But rather than write an angry Rage Against the Machine record, I wanted to give them a sense of hope and release and faith.'

※

With Dave Grohl moving to California it made sense that Studio 606 should follow. But rather than install a studio within the grounds of Grohl's family home – or at least not yet, anyway – in 2004 the band invested $750,000 of its own money to set up their own studio on neutral ground. Buying a large, anonymous-looking commercial property somewhere amid the sprawling nothingness of the suburban San Fernando Valley, an area infamous as the epicentre of the American pornographic film industry, the quartet went about equipping the facility to their exact requirements. The group's members even dirtied their hands themselves with a touch of heavy lifting.

On the ground floor of the 606 complex is the recording studio, modelled upon Stockholm's Polar Studios, the Abba-owned facility where Led Zeppelin committed their *In Through the Out Door* album to tape in the winter of 1978. Todd MacFarlane Metallica figures sit atop a workbench. There is ephemera celebrating Motörhead and Mötley Crüe. On the wall hangs a black and white print of Dave Grohl with Elvis Costello, Bruce Springsteen and 'Little Steven' Van Zandt, each man deep in concentration as they practised The Clash's 'London Calling' backstage at Madison Square Garden. There are framed posters advertising Black Flag's *Nervous Breakdown* EP, as well as the American punk record label Slash. There are cushions fashioned from Grohl's old concert T-shirts, lovingly handmade by Virginia Grohl. And in the hallway hang scores of gold and platinum discs for albums featuring Grohl in some capacity or other – from drummer in Nirvana, and for Queens of the Stone Age and Tenacious D, to bandleader with Foo Fighters. At the time Foo Fighters began work on *Echoes* ... the discs represented CD sales of somewhere in the region of 50 million, and suggested that in whatever guise he made music Dave Grohl did so with something of a Midas touch.

Despite the bespoke nature of their new studio, initial reports emanating from the latest 606 were not unduly encouraging. Speaking to *Kerrang!* in 2005 Dave Grohl admitted that for a time the notion of a fifth Foo Fighters album was just that, a notion.

'There was a moment when I thought, "Well, that was fun and we've had a good run at the thing,"' he said. 'I've always thought that bands shouldn't last forever, there's always an expiration date. So, yeah, for a moment I thought that we should call it quits and end it on a high note.'

Speaking to the *NME* in the spring of 2005, the frontman admitted that he never imagined that his group's success would reach such a point, and revealed, 'When it happened it got me thinking.'

'About what?' he was asked.

'About what it meant for us,' he responded. 'We'd reached a certain level and it meant something. It was just a question of what. Did it mean it was time for us to split up? Did it mean it was time for us to take one of those four-year breaks? Or time to try something different?'

When pressed on the viability of splitting up as being a realistic option, Grohl answered, 'Well, yeah, that was one of the things I wondered about. I did think about going out at the top.'

But after considering the three options of breaking up, of embarking on a four-year hiatus, or else simply trying something different, Foo Fighters opted for the last. Stretching their creative limbs, as well as flexing a little corporate muscle, the quartet decided that their fifth album would in fact be a double album, with one CD dedicated to the *Sturm und Drang* of the group in full-blown rock mode, and the second disc comprised of more reflective, acoustic-based numbers.

'It didn't make a lot of sense not to try and challenge ourselves this time out,' explained Grohl just prior to the album's release. 'It wouldn't have made any sense at all just to go in and make another record. That would have been boring for us. So we decided to do something that would challenge the band. I've always known that we were capable of producing an album like the acoustic record, but it never made sense to try and incorporate that into a rock setting. So this time we attempted to eliminate a lot of the middle ground. So we made a rock album that rocks as hard as possible and we tried to go completely the opposite way with the acoustic record.

'When I listen to some bands who have been around for ten or fifteen years like, God bless 'em, the Ramones or Green Day or AC/DC – those bands have made a career out of making music that wrestles with one dynamic. But fuck that, I don't want to be that band. I want to be a band that can do fucking anything, because we can do fucking anything. There's a song on the record that [jazz chanteuse] Norah Jones sings on: how nuts is that? But fuck it, why not? We should do whatever the fuck it is we want to do. Because when we do follow our instincts, when we do follow our hearts, it ends up sounding really good. My ambition is for people to ask us what kind of music we play and for us to answer, "Just music." Not, "Oh, rock music," but "Just music." I think with this album we've taken a step toward that happening.'

With sessions taking place at 606, work on the acoustic half of the album came together like a dream. The group originally had a list of dozens of artists they hoped would contribute to the songs; as things turned out, sessions came together so quickly that the authors hardly had the time to recruit many of the names on their wishlist. Even so,

Home

alongside Norah Jones (on 'Virginia Moon'), the quieter half of *In Your Honor* features appearances from, among others, Josh Homme (who plays additional guitar on 'Razor'), as well as songs starring The Wallflowers keyboardist Rami Jaffee, double-bass contributions from co-producer Nick Raskulinecz, that and the sound of mandolin and piano – on the songs 'Another Round' and 'Miracle' respectively – played by the hand of erstwhile Led Zeppelin bassist John Paul Jones.

'I ran around the room screaming,' said Dave Grohl of receiving a call from Jones saying that he was willing to play on the album. '"Guess who I fucking got a call from?"' When the Englishman arrived at 606 to record his parts, Foo Fighters' frontman reported, 'I tried to be cool, but I'm sure I looked like a total fucking idiot. I was shitting my pants. Full diaper.'

On his motivation for recording an album's worth of acoustic material, Grohl told me, 'I'd originally been thinking about making an album on my own. I've always thought about making an album on my own, because I enjoy recording by myself, and it might be something that you wouldn't expect. So I'd written a lot of really beautiful acoustic music and I thought, "Maybe what I could do is find a film that needs a score and make an album on my own, and sorta disguise it as a film score so it doesn't seem like a pretentious solo effort." Like with Tom Petty's *She's the One*, like an album of songs that are yours entirely but not meant to prove that you can do it on your own, if that makes any sense. And then I had a revelation at some point, thinking, "Wait a minute, this should be the next Foo Fighters album. Fuck rock music, let's really take a hard left on everyone and change up the game a little. Wouldn't that be nice?" So I considered it, but then I thought, "Wait a minute, I can't not make a rock album, so let's do a double."

'Meanwhile I was moving the studio out of Virginia and looking for a studio in Los Angeles, and that whole process was fucking long and crazy; I'm glad we did it, but holy shit – to write and record a double album in a studio that you built from scratch? We'd start with the contractor and the construction team at the warehouse and then go back down to rehearsal and writing and demoing and then at night come back to the studio to fucking staple insulation to the ceiling. And that was every day for six months. We were still building the studio as we recorded …'

Recorded from January to March 2005, *In Your Honor* was given its worldwide release that June. The double album entered both the US and UK album charts at number 2 (kept from the top spot in both countries by the release of Coldplay's third album, *X&Y*), selling 311,000 copies in the United States, and almost 160,000 copies in Great Britain, a jump of nearly 70,000 first-week sales from predecessor *One by One*. Foo Fighters' fifth album also débuted in the top five of album charts in thirteen other countries, and attained Top 40 status in six more. Reviews were also kind, although sometimes in a way that suggested damnation by faint praise. *Spin* wrote that 'both these records chronicle the mental and physical graffiti of figuring how to emerge from some very large shadows, including his own, with nerve and power'. The *New York Times* was of the opinion that 'the rock CD overpowers the acoustic one. Yet among the quieter songs, there are enough supple melodies and hypnotic guitar patterns to suggest fine prospects for a follow-through album that would dare to mix plugged-in and unplugged.' Others, though, were less charitable. *MOJO* claimed that *In Your Honor*'s rock disc was merely 'grunge-punk-metal boiled down to mere energy – and calories don't rock'. Across the Atlantic, *Blender* put it even more baldly when it wrote, 'Let's face it: Foo Fighters are dull.'

But it was perhaps the website Cokemachineglow that came closest to summing up a fan's eye view on Foo Fighters' fifth album. 'Lurking somewhere in its spotty 80+ minutes there lies an excellent 40-minute album, one of the best Foo Fighters have ever done,' noted reviewer Matt Stephens. 'As it is, though, with its heaps of filler, dated production, and needless separation of rockers from ballads, it may actually be their weakest.'

In Your Honor isn't Foo Fighters' weakest album – that dubious honour must go to its predecessor – and some of the reviews it attracted were perhaps unduly harsh (as a rule, the music press tends not to like it when it praises an album, as it did with *One by One*, that its creators subsequently dismiss out of hand). But the notion that its finest moments are harder to find for being obscured by tracks that aren't as remarkable as they might be is justified comment. *In Your Honor* opens and closes with some of the finest material Grohl has ever authored, but for all the admirable ambition and ability the band display, keeping the whole enterprise airborne across 21 tracks proves to be too much of a strain.

The title track provides a stirring opening to this epic endeavour. Over martial beats and guitars which soar skywards and beyond, Grohl's own fanfare for the common man is delivered with an intensity and raw passion that cannot fail to prickle the skin: '*Mine is yours and yours is mine / There is no divide / In your honor I would die tonight,*' Grohl sings. Only the hardest of hearts could fail to be moved. 'No Way Back' fizzes with an invigorating vigour, and 'Best of You' shrugs off a chest-beating opening which sounds like a pumped-up US military recruitment ad to blossom into an open-hearted everyman anthem capable of filling the biggest of stadiums. 'The Last Song', meanwhile, like 'Enough Space' on *The Colour and the Shape*, seems written with the express design to cause festival crowds to bounce, while its punchy call-and-response chorus – '*This is the last song that I will dedicate to you*' – is a gloriously uninhibited declaration of independence. There is art and craft too in the likes of 'DOA' and 'Resolve', but even amid their well-honed melodies there is still the nagging feeling that this album's noisier half has been somewhat taken for granted.

On the second half of the band's first double album too there are songs which shine with an incandescent brilliance. The reflective, delicate 'Friend of a Friend', reprised from the *Pocketwatch* cassette, is moving in its own right, even without the knowledge that the song was written in Kurt Cobain's apartment in Olympia some fifteen years earlier. Elsewhere, the gently rolling 'Cold Day in the Sun', voiced by Taylor Hawkins, flies by on a jaunty beat and the strength of its own breezy melody, while 'Miracle' sounds like the perfect song to accompany a cold beer and a last cigarette at the end of a stressful and taxing day. And tucked in the middle of this disc is the undeniably beautiful 'On the Mend', a touching tale of love and brotherhood written by

Grohl in a London hotel room in August 2001 as he wondered whether his comatose friend Taylor might live or die.

There is here a subtlety and poise not always displayed in the album's rather self-consciously 'rocking' opening disc.

The tour in support of *In Your Honor* saw the band's tour buses pull up to the backstage doors of some of the world's largest indoor venues. And festival season found the Foos taking star billing at some of the most prestigious events on the circuit – among them Japan's Fuji Rock Festival, Denmark's Roskilde, Holland's Lowlands, Belgium's Werchter, Scotland's T in the Park, Ireland's Oxegen and, once again, the Reading/ Leeds double-header.

But if evidence was required that Foo Fighters' profile was expanding beyond even that of festival headliner, such evidence came the following summer, when on Saturday 17 June 2006 the quartet headlined an outdoor show at London's Hyde Park. Ironically, the site of the Foos' greatest triumph to date took place less than a mile from the spot where they endured their darkest hour following Taylor Hawkins's overdose almost five years earlier. But in headlining a concert at London's most prestigious royal park, Dave Grohl's band were joining a roll-call of rock royalty. In 1969 the Rolling Stones performed a free gig on the site, just two days after the death of guitarist Brian Jones. Seven years later Queen followed suit with their own free show. More recently, the Red Hot Chili Peppers and Simon & Garfunkel were just two of the acts that had filled the air of one of London's most exclusive quarters with music.

Dave Grohl told the audience gathered in the greenery just off Park Lane that when the idea of playing Hyde Park was put to him he thought that maybe 30,000 people might turn up. As it transpired, a crowd of some 85,000 people enjoyed a day in the sunshine watching Juliette Lewis & the Licks, Angels & Airwaves, old friends Queens of the Stone Age, the redoubtable Motörhead, and then, finally, Foo Fighters. As if this wasn't proof of popularity enough, the next night the band headlined a show at Lancashire County Cricket Ground in Manchester, supported by The Strokes, Angels & Airwaves, The Subways and Josh Homme's side band The Eagles of Death Metal. And although Foo Fighters' fanbase was blossoming all over the western world, it was still the people of England that were carrying the brightest torch, and who had been carrying it the longest.

'It was the same with Nirvana,' observed Grohl. 'We exploded in England before we did in America. I think the UK's always had a pretty good idea of what's about to break. If it blows up in England, it's only a matter of time before it blows up everywhere else. Even so, I never imagined something like Hyde Park would work.'

But work it did, and spectacularly well. Featuring not just a selection of Foo Fighters favourites – 'Stacked Actors', 'Everlong', 'Monkey Wrench' and 'Breakout' among them – the set also found space for a *Probot* song ('Shake Your Blood', sung, as on its parent album, by Lemmy) as well as Queen's 'We Will Rock You' and 'Tie Your Mother Down', songs which saw Queen guitarist Brian May and drummer Roger Taylor emerge from the wings to join Foo Fighters onstage. By any measure, this was rock played by A-list musicians.

Prior to his band's headline set in front of 85,000 people, though, Dave Grohl could be found backstage barbecuing for friends, just as he had done when the insanity around Nirvana threatened to spill out of control, just as he had done when recording *There Is Nothing Left to Lose* within a stone's throw of his old high school in Virginia. Amid the sizzle of steaks and the chatter of friends and family, you could have been forgiven for thinking that Dave Grohl had not a care in the world.

'It didn't feel like the most important show of our career,' he later admitted. 'It was more like I was hosting a barbecue for 85,000 people. It just felt like the biggest party I've ever had.'

❧

Asked around the time of the release of *In Your Honor* if Foo Fighters planned to incorporate an acoustic set into their otherwise fully electric live show, drummer Taylor Hawkins laughed and answered in the negative, the reason being that 'people would throw piss'. But by 2006 the group had enough confidence in its quieter side to embark on a tour of theatres armed not with Marshall amps but with hollow-bodied guitars and, that most telling sign of a band in quiet reflection, stools. Towards the end of the summer the quartet appeared live at the Pantages venue in Los Angeles for a three-night stand that would be recorded for release as a live album. The core musicians were joined by players such as Rami Jaffee, percussionist Drew Hester, violinist Petra Haden, harmonica player Danny Clinch, as well as a familiar beaming face, guitarist Pat Smear.

A selection of songs from these performances was collated for Foo Fighters' first live album, titled *Skin and Bones*, released on 28 November 2006. Featuring imaginative reworkings of such staples as 'Times Like These', 'My Hero', 'Friend of a Friend' and 'Everlong', the fifteen-song set showed just how confidently the group had grown into their acoustic selves. Evidence of this came with the fact that, by definition, an acoustic live album from Foo Fighters would be compared to the similarly reflective Nirvana live album, *Unplugged in New York*, released in 1994. And while *Skin and Bones* was never likely to equal the majesty of that album, an album which is now recognised as one of the finest of its type, if not *the* finest, there is anyway something rather fanciful, perhaps even fatuous, about such a comparison. *Unplugged in New York* is the work of an entirely different band playing entirely different songs in an entirely different era. On its own terms, those Foo Fighters had since set for themselves, *Skin and Bones* is a worthwhile and enjoyable addition to its creators' *œuvre*.

In the same month that the Foos' first live album found its way into record shops, the group in its acoustic form accepted an invitation to tour Canada with the legendary Bob Dylan, then touring his acclaimed *Modern Times* album. There was something rather fitting about this partnership. In 1965 Dylan had outraged his supporters by 'going electric', playing a UK tour that saw his show split into two halves, one acoustic and one electric. Audiences did not take kindly to the latter section, with one ticket holder at Manchester's Free Trade Hall exclaiming that the night's headliner was a 'Judas'. Five time zones east, at that summer's annual Newport Folk Festival acoustic protest singer Pete Seeger reacted to Dylan's plugged-in performance with such displeasure that he threatened to sever the power cables leading to the stage with an axe.

Home

'We don't usually jump on other people's tours because we're out doing our own thing,' Grohl told *Uncut* magazine. 'But being asked by Bob Dylan to go on the road with him is like being knighted or something. How could we say no? We were asked by the man who turned rock 'n' roll from boogie-woogie into bad-ass. Respect and honour, and for us it was a once-in-a-lifetime opportunity.'

In the weeks immediately before the trek, Grohl and his bandmates pumped keyboard player Rami Jaffe, who had previously played with Dylan's son Jakob's band, The Wallflowers, for some insider knowledge on the old master.

'We all spent weeks asking him, "How's Bob? What's he like, man?" Grohl recalled. He said, "Bob's the coolest guy in the world. He's totally fucking chilled. But here's the deal, though. If he's got the hoodie on with the sunglasses, don't even fuckin' think of talking to him. If the hoodie is down and the sunglasses are off, it's fair game to go and say hello." That's the best advice anybody has given me all year!'

The tour was in Canada when Grohl received a message in his dressing room that Mr Dylan wished to see him. With some trepidation, Grohl headed for the door.

'So I walk out,' says Grohl, 'and I came around the corner and he's standing like a silhouette in a dark corner – black leather boots, black leather pants, black leather jacket. He said, "What's that's song you got, the one that goes, '*The only thing I ever ask of you is you gotta promise not to stop when I say when?*'" I said, "Oh, yeah, 'Everlong'." He said, "Man, that is a great song, I should learn that song."

'So I don't give a fuck what anybody else thinks,' Grohl laughed. 'Bob Dylan likes one of my songs. That right there is enough for me.'

⌇

Always an evolving entity, by the time Foo Fighters came to prepare themselves for their sixth studio album the participants opted for a more fluid approach than that taken on the *In Your Honor* set. Whereas that album had rather uniformly separated its electric and acoustic elements, with an unplugged tour underneath their belts it seemed that in re-entering 606 to record their next collection of songs the band felt more confident in mixing things up somewhat. Reunited with Gil Norton, Grohl, Mendel, Hawkins and Shifflet secluded themselves in their $750,000 bespoke recording studio in the San Fernando Valley and set to work. Their efforts amounted to the most supple and dexterous Foo Fighters album to date.

'You know, at some point you turn [the] warning light off,' said Grohl at the time. 'At this point, having done it for as long as we have, it becomes a little more introverted. As a musician you need to do the things that satisfy yourself. One of the great things about our band is that we've built this little world with our own studios and our own label and directing our own videos and finding our own producers and producing ourselves ... We were able to walk into our fortress, Studio 606, and lock the door and turn everything outside off, and I think that's helped us survive this whole time. So at some point you can turn that off. I mean, of course I hope the people enjoy what we do, but it's not a main motivation for doing it. It's a challenge.'

The group emerged from 606 with a dozen well-rounded songs, songs that would gather under the rather portentous title *Echoes, Silence, Patience & Grace*.

'It's always been a challenge to name any of our albums ...' admitted Grohl. 'I picked through the lyrics and found a lyric from the last song, "Home", which says "*Echoes, silence, patience and grace, all of these moments I'll never replace.*" I thought it was nice because it's open to interpretation and I think it's a beautiful title and I think the album is beautiful in its diversity and its melody and its musicality. It goes from delicate acoustic moments to the heaviest shit we've ever done.'

Indeed it did. From the opening dynamite blast of 'The Pretender' – the album's lead-off single, a track that spent a then record eighteen weeks atop the *Billboard* Alternative/Modern Rock Chart – to the fabulous Paul McCartneyesque pop roll of 'Long Road to Ruin' to the quite gorgeous closing track, the stately piano-led 'Home' – which its author described as 'the kind of song I can't imagine singing live because it's going to be too much' – *Echoes, Silence, Patience & Grace* is the culmination, and a seamless culmination at that, of everything Foo Fighters had been experimenting with since they decided to move away from only practising the type of loud rock music heard on the *One by One* album.

'Dave has always had the ability to write a great riff,' believes Gil Norton, the album's producer. 'He's prolific. We were joking about doing a website called Spare Riff at one time, because he just comes up with a million riffs all the time. But obviously he has slightly different subject matter now: he's older, he's got a family ... With the last album the whole sonic palate had increased and that sort of helped with the writing, because it just gave him more scope atmospherically.'

Released on 25 September 2007, *Echoes, Silence, Patience & Grace* débuted at number 1 in Australia, Canada, New Zealand and the UK. In the US, Foo Fighters' sixth studio album entered the *Billboard* Top 200 at number 3, with 168,000 first-week sales, a sizeable drop from the 311,000 sales racked up by *In Your Honor* on its first seven days in shops.

Critical reception to the album was, as ever, mixed. *Kerrang!*'s Ian Winwood was generous in his praise, writing, 'The fact that this is a record that doesn't sound like it was hard work means that it's good work. In fact, it's good enough to remind you just why you turned your ears towards Foo Fighters in the first place.' *NME* believed that the set was 'as consistent a record as Foo Fighters have ever made'. Not everyone, though, was as kind as they might have been. *Spin* said of the new album that it was 'another quality entry in a fantastically average career'.

Still, being a critic's band doesn't always pay the bills – being a 'fan's band' does. And Foo Fighters were definitely the latter, as they proved beyond argument in the summer of 2008. Almost a year on from their show-stealing performance at Live Earth, the band's agent Russell Warby booked the band as headliners at Wembley Stadium for the evening of 7 June 2008. They gave themselves almost six months to sell the 86,000 tickets required to completely fill the national stadium; as it turned out all the seats were sold in a few hours. A second date was pencilled in for 6 June; this, too, quickly sold out, adding up to 172,000 tickets purchased in a matter of days.

For six months prior to the first of the two concerts, Dave Grohl would ask himself just what his band had up its sleeve in order to rise to the challenge of filling this vast space with both his band's music and, just as importantly, its personality.

At approximately 10.30 p.m. on the evening of 7 June Grohl brushed his hair away from his eyes, looked out across the expanse of Europe's second-largest stadium and pronounced the night 'the greatest fucking night in our band's lives'. As he spoke, a smiling grey-haired man in a khaki army shirt holding a sunburst Gibson Les Paul walked onstage from his left, while another familiar face appeared stage right.

'We knew from the beginning that this wasn't going to be just any other show,' said Grohl. 'We've been planning this shit for six months, a long time. We knew that this country, you guys, you made us the band that we are today. So we'd like to invite a couple of very special guests, Mr Jimmy Page and Mr John Paul Jones from Led Zeppelin ...'

Seven months earlier, Grohl had sat three rows behind me at London's 20,000 capacity O2 Arena, as the reunited Led Zeppelin played the most hyped gig of the decade, as a tribute to late Atlantic Records mogul Ahmet Ertegun. So frantic and full-on was Grohl's air-drumming that night, mirroring every snare, tom and kick drum beat hammered out onstage by Jason Bonham, the late John Bonham's son, that he was literally shifting the air above my head.

At Wembley Stadium, Grohl finally realised his life's ambition to play drums for Zeppelin. Strictly speaking it wasn't Led Zeppelin – with the greatest respect, as a vocalist Taylor Hawkins is no Robert Plant – but, as Grohl began thundering out his hero John Bonham's instantly recognizable intro to 'Rock 'n' Roll', it would have taken a brave soul indeed to tell the man of the hour that he *wasn't* actually playing with Led Zeppelin. As dreams come true go, this one was going to take some beating.

In the early hours of 8 June, Foo Fighters' party retired to the newly opened Whiskey Mist club in London's up-scale Mayfair district, a club which soon enough would play host to England's royal princes, Hollywood's party-loving A-listers and the young, beautiful and bored scions of the world's wealthiest dynasties. Here, surrounded by his oldest friends, Grohl stood in quiet conversation with Jimmy Page, the pair now looking less like master and student than two dignified peers

Home

and equals. But even as he sipped slowly from a bottle of beer, even as he observed the animated, laughter-filled conversations of family, friends and colleagues, even as the post-gig adrenalin rushed around his body, there must surely have been one question uppermost in Dave Grohl's mind, a question not for tonight but for the months and years ahead:

Where now and what next?

These days

It's time for us to go out and be a rock band again. Someone has to do it, right?

Dave Grohl

4 July 2009. It's Independence Day weekend, and America is in the mood to party. The moon is shining down upon Washington DC and the Black Eyed Peas' hit single *Boom Boom Pow*, sitting pretty at the summit of the *Billboard* Hot 100 for a twelfth consecutive week, blasts from every shop-front, souvenir stall and boombox in the nation's capital. The stately tree-lined avenues around the National Mall are a bustle of colour, movement and noise, as tens of thousands of tourists and DC metropolitan area residents jockey for the best vantage points for the evening fireworks display.

Dave Grohl stands on the South Lawn of the White House, flashing a big bad wolf smile as he gently strums ringing open chords on his 1965 Pelham Blue Trini Lopez Standard guitar. In the distance he can see the lights on the Washington Monument blink red against a cloudless dark blue sky. Before him, seated at tables festooned with red, white and blue ribbons, are a battalion of US military personnel and their families, guests at 1600 Pennsylvania Avenue this evening for a barbecue dinner honouring their service to the nation. And in front of the troops, discreetly flanked by Secret Service minders, sits their

These days

Commander-In-Chief, Barack Obama, the 44th President of the United States of America, and his wife Michelle, the First Lady, their eyes fixed upon the stage as they wait for Foo Fighters to launch the night's pre-fireworks entertainment.

'Well, well, well,' says Dave Grohl, slowly taking in the vista before him. 'Who'd have thunk?'

∽

'Okay, so here was my day, two days ago. I started my morning at a Hollywood Walk of Fame ceremony for a smooth jazz artist called Dave Koz. Jordyn's cousin is an agent here in Los Angeles and he used to represent Dave Koz, so Dave's been a friend of Jordyn's family for, like, 20 years and he's a great dude. Anyway, he got a star on the Hollywood Walk of Fame, right in front of Capitol Records, so I started my day at this ceremony. And I'm hanging out with Barry Manilow, Dave Koz, Kenny G and Johnny Mathis, and those guys knew who I was! So Barry Manilow is like, "Hey man, how are you?" And I'm like, "Are you kidding me? Wow! I saw you in the airport in Dublin once and I almost fainted!"

'So then I go practise with my band … and it's good. From there, I go home and have dinner with my beautiful family and then I get a call to go to the studio and record an instrumental with [former Guns N' Roses duo] Slash and Duff [McKagan]. So the three of us sit in a room, we run through the arrangement, hit 'Record' and do it in one fucking take, and it's bad-ass: I'm sitting on my drum stool watching Duff and Slash try to figure out an arrangement, and my face just curls into a smile because I'm like, "Wow, these guys, they've both died like fifteen times and they're still friends, and this is great." And then I call my friend Nick Raskulinecz who's right up the street mixing the new Deftones record and I go up and listen to the new Deftones. That was *one day*. So as I was riding home on my motorcycle, that I love, I think, "Really? This is my life? I get to do this every fucking day? Cool."'

It's September 2009, and Dave Grohl and I are having lunch in his suite at the Sunset Marquis, West Hollywood's most laid-back, immaculately styled, rock-star-friendly retreat. Sprawled on a couch, all elongated limbs, gleaming teeth and fading prison-styled tattoos, Grohl is in excellent form: he's a blur of constant motion, tapping out beats on his thighs, bouncing upon his heels, excitably jabbing the air with his fingers, his every riff and yarn punctuated by explosive, highly expressive swearing.

The telephone rings, and he excuses himself to answer it.

'No, François, I'm good ...' he says quietly. 'No, really, I'm fine. Honestly. Thank you, François. Thank you.'

'I haven't stayed here in ten years,' he laughs as he returns to the table, 'but last time I stayed here I'm sure I didn't have a butler.'

Over the course of the next four hours Grohl would have occasion to revisit many more memories – some pleasant, some poignant, some evidently still raw and painful – as he retraced his journey from the basement punk rock clubs of Washington DC to that Independence Day performance on the White House lawn in an interview timed to coincide with the release of Foo Fighters' *Greatest Hits* album.

By his own exhausting standards, 2009 had been a relatively low-key year for Grohl. A self-imposed career sabbatical had afforded him the opportunity both to enjoy some genuine downtime with his family – expanded in April with the arrival of his second child, Harper Willow Grohl, a sister for three-year-old Violet Maye – and to take stock of his own life. And as he bounded down memory lane on that balmy September afternoon, it was clear that the 40-year-old musician could himself scarcely believe how his life less ordinary had unfolded. The kid who learned to play guitar by playing along to The Beatles' Red and Blue albums could now count Paul McCartney as a personal friend; the authority-baiting punk rock rebel was now on first-name terms with the President; the homeless drummer who scribbled song lyrics on the back of supermarket receipts now had his words screamed back into his face by stadium crowds. To paraphrase Talking Heads, there must have been days when Grohl found himself in his beautiful house with his beautiful wife and asked himself, well, how did I get here?

'Man, I never thought *any* of this was possible,' he admitted. 'But at the same time I'm proud of a lot of the shit I've done. I feel so lucky and – for lack of a better word – blessed that I've got to do all of these things, and accomplish this much. And do I think it's luck? No. Do I work fucking hard? Yes. Am I fucking good at what I do? I think so. But am I gonna tell everybody in the world that I think I'm the greatest songwriter and I'm an amazing drummer and I'm a fucking huge star? No, that's not my fucking style. That would mean that I care too much about how what I do is perceived. And there's a part of me that takes pride in my disregard of other people's ideas of who I am or what I'm all about.'

In a previous interview with Grohl, conducted almost a decade earlier, I had suggested to him that his outgoing, open and gregarious nature had, somewhat ironically, ensured his privacy; that the perennial cliché of Grohl as 'The Nicest Man in Rock' allowed the 'real' Dave Grohl to remain hidden in plain sight, unknown to all but his closest friends. It was an analysis with which he did not take issue.

'I don't know why, but I don't open up to many people,' he admitted at the time. 'You just don't give a piece of yourself to everyone. I don't understand the need for someone to expose themselves entirely to the world. I think that's odd. If there were two million people that knew me really well that would be kinda weird. There's only a handful of people that know me really well, and then there's a whole lot of others that know me enough.'

In 2009 I put it to Grohl that, for all his band's upward mobility and his own increased media profile, little had truly changed in this respect.

'I don't consider myself a loner, but it's just not important to me to be everyone's best friend,' he conceded. 'Maybe it's a defence mechanism. It would take a long time for anyone to get to know me. Definitely after the Nirvana thing exploded it changed the way I relate to people – not in a bad way necessarily, in a lot of good ways I'm sure, but fuck yeah, I want to keep a lot of me for me.

'It might have something to do with growing up in such a small family. There was my mom, my dad, my sister and I, and our cousins and grandparents lived far away, and I had two best friends, and that's all I fucking needed. I'm a horrible fucking pen pal, I never answer my phone, I would much rather stay at home and hang out with my daughters and mother and wife than go out to a bar on a Friday night. And I already get to hang out with my best friends Taylor, Nate, Chris and Pat for a living.

'And, like, the "Nicest Man in Rock" thing … it's cool, but it's funny to me because the guys in my band would probably tell you otherwise. There's a side of me that's so territorial that certain things make my fucking claws come out, and turn me from the trademark quote "Nicest Guy in Rock" to a very difficult person. Because I do have borders and boundaries. There are certain things where I'm like, "Man, don't even fucking go there." I have no problem going up to a paparazzi and going, "Are you fucking kidding me?" Which I've had to do a few times. The most important thing for me is my family, and my health and happiness, and making sure everyone's cool.

'But honestly, of all the things I've accomplished on my own and with different bands … it's overwhelming sometimes to me,' he admitted. 'I can't even imagine where to go from here.'

Even as he spoke, though, a whole new chapter of Dave Grohl's life was unfolding. That very afternoon Grohl was due to resume tour rehearsals with a new band, a heavyweight rock supergroup he had willed into existence during an interview with *MOJO* magazine some four years earlier. Asked then by writer Stevie Chick whether he had any new musical collaborations in mind, Grohl stated, 'The next project that I'm trying to initiate involves me on drums, Josh Homme on guitar, and John Paul Jones playing bass. That's the next album. That wouldn't suck.' Four years on, with Grohl behind the drum kit once again, that band would take flight as Them Crooked Vultures.

'At the time I wasn't entirely serious,' Grohl admitted to me that September afternoon. 'It was more wishful thinking, a "Here's what I hope happens next" thing. John Paul Jones had played on the *In Your Honor* record, and that was the first time I'd met him. He's a sweet guy, a great player and a brilliant musician. So when I was asked what I'd like to do next that was the first thing that came to mind, to be in a band with John, and Josh, who I have a connection with musically that I just don't have with anybody else: as a drummer, playing with him, we share this direction, this frequency. It's unspoken and intangible, almost like ESP. And we work well together, because he likes Black Flag and bad disco and so do I. I like shit to have groove but I like it to be heavy, and that's what we did together with Queens. After I went back to the Foos, I always hoped that I'd play with Josh again; I just didn't know when or how.

'So then last year it got to the point where both of us were tired of touring with our bands, and tired of being in our bands. The responsibility of these two bands that we've created could be sometimes overwhelming. I don't know about Josh's situation, but with Foo Fighters it still amazes me that we've taken this thing from a fucking demo cassette made in five days to selling out two nights at Wembley Stadium: it's crazy and it was never the intention. So you get there and it would be very easy to say, "Alright, let's fucking pack it up, pack it in, that's it, we don't need to do anything else, what more can we possibly accomplish?" So rather than do that, you have this sort of pressure release valve that you can hit and keep everyone from losing their fucking mind. And those are the side projects that we all have – Taylor with the Coattail Riders, Shiftlet with Jackson United and Nate with Sunny Day Real Estate – those are the things that keep Foo Fighters from breaking up.

'So back then, in 2005, I had mentioned that because I needed another release, an "In Case of Emergency Break Glass" band, because if it gets to the point where I fucking hate Foo Fighters I better have a very good band to be in outside of it, in order to keep Foo Fighters from breaking up. And honestly, as a drummer, I can't think of two people I'd rather play with. Josh is my favourite guitarist and John is my favourite bass player, so I had a hunch that the three of us together would make a great band. And I was fucking right.'

Grohl, Homme and Jones met for the first time to discuss their new musical project on the evening of 14 January 2009. They did so not in a Los Angeles record company boardroom, flanked by lawyers and management representatives, as might have been appropriate considering their lofty profiles within the music industry, but rather in the Anaheim branch of the Arthurian-themed restaurant chain Medieval Times. It was the night of Grohl's 40th birthday – an occasion he later hailed as 'the fucking greatest midlife crisis a man could possibly have'

– and as knights jousted for the entertainment of his 200 invited guests, Grohl, Homme and Jones, each wearing a paper crown, pulled apart hunks of roast chicken and glazed ribs with their bare hands and swapped ideas about what (im)pure fun their new project might be. A few days later the trio met up again at Homme's Pink Duck studio in Burbank, plugged in and began to jam. 'And within three minutes,' says Grohl, 'I realised that this was going to be the best fucking band that I've ever been in.

'It was not unlike a blind date,' he said, 'where you cross your fingers and hope it's not awkward. Because jamming with the wrong person can feel just as awkward as fucking someone you don't like. But we started playing and we didn't stop, at all, for maybe 30 minutes. The first jam was long and it was fun and everyone had smiles [on their faces]. And it sounded fucking great. So we did that for a few days and then looked at one another and said, "Well, should we be a band?" And that was that.'

'As soon as the Queens thing ended we were looking for an opportunity to do this again,' admits Josh Homme. 'I can't stand people who embrace mediocrity in music, and every time I've played with Dave he has absolutely gone to the limit of his abilities. Dave's goal is exactly like mine, to keep recharging your battery and finding new ways to stay creative. He's a really happy person in a sea of people who can't stand themselves.'

Unusually in an industry where there are very few genuine secrets, the trio managed to keep details of their new venture under wraps until July 2009, when Homme's wife, Brody Dalle, acknowledged the existence of the project in an online interview for her new band Spinnerette: 'I'm not at liberty to talk about it ...' she said, '[but] the thing ... which I'm not supposed to talk about is pretty fucking amazing. Just beats and sounds like you've never heard before.'

The following month, at the stroke of midnight on 9 August, Them Crooked Vultures made their global début at the 1,100-capacity Metro club in Chicago, premiering a hard-driving, classic rock 'n' roll sound Homme classified as 'perverted blues'. Two weeks later, in keeping with the clandestine nature of their 'career' to date, the trio (augmented by live guitarist Alain Johannes from Spinnerette) strolled onto the stage of London's Brixton Academy to play an unannounced hour-long set as support to the Arctic Monkeys, whose new Josh Homme-produced album *Humbug* had been released that same week. And three months after that, without very much hype or hullabaloo at all, the band's own self-titled début dropped.

Given the three musicians' impeccable CVs, and the fact that Grohl and Homme's previous collaboration, Queens of the Stone Age's *Songs for the Deaf*, had been roundly acclaimed as the finest hard rock album of the decade, expectations for *Them Crooked Vultures* were sky high. Early reviews only added to the hype. '*Them Crooked Vultures* flouts the supergroup manual,' wrote *MOJO*. 'It doesn't sound like the work of rich men on holiday, but rather three serious individuals looking to prove themselves over again.' The *Sunday Times* hailed the album as 'thrillingly, breathtakingly odd'. The *Washington Post* was equally captivated. 'When rock bands swarmed Earth 40 years ago, they seemed otherworldly – hirsute tribes clad in kaleidoscopic garb, brandishing their guitars like medieval weapons,' wrote Chris Richards. 'But over time, these mongrel hordes and their misshapen songs assimilated into American culture so seamlessly, they practically vanished into the normalcy of popular music. Today, our guitar heroes reside mostly in video games. In that sense, supergroup Them Crooked Vultures makes for an evocative throwback, recalling an era when riff-hurling rock troupes felt dangerous. And bizarre. And totally worth listening to.'

The key reference points for *Them Crooked Vultures* are Led Zeppelin, ZZ Top, Cream, Foghat, Masters of Reality and, perhaps most significantly, the stress-free, narcotics-friendly Desert Sessions collaborations Josh Homme has presided over at Rancho de la Luna in Joshua Tree, California since 1997. Like The White Stripes' superb 2003 collection *Elephant*, *Them Crooked Vultures* reeks of sin, sweat, sex and bad-ass braggadocio: swinging and swaggering, it's very much the (dirty) work of grown men old enough to know better, but stubborn enough not to give a rat's ass. Opening with the lewd, lascivious, cowbell-accented stomp of 'No One Loves Me' ('*I told her I was trash, she winked and laughed and said, "I already know, I got a beautiful place to put your face"*'), the trio invoke the unholy trinity of sex (on the steamy Southern Gothic swamp-blues 'No Fang'), drugs (on the nightmarish, woozy, wonky, acid-trip-gone-horribly-wrong 'Interlude with Ludes') and violence (almost everything else), with the drawling Homme portraying his renegade posse as *unwanted strangers, exploited and dangerous* on the cock-and-balls strut of 'Elephants'. This desperado gang vibe seeps through every move TCV make, which might seem a tad silly if the trio didn't have a fearsome arsenal of white-knuckle riffs to back up their lairy, priapic strut: the occasions where Homme, Jones and Grohl lock telepathically, and thrillingly, into extended driving grooves are reminiscent of Zeppelin at their most testosterone driven. Them Crooked Vultures might not be breaking new ground, but few bands shake the foundations with such muscle and majesty.

One week into the band's début US tour, I caught up with Dave Grohl backstage at Boston's House of Blues. Them Crooked Vultures' hard-hitting drummer was in playful mood, describing the tour as 'awesome'.

'We did the Austin City Limits festival and melted a few faces down there,' he beamed. 'Then we kicked Nashville in the balls. Then we went to Columbus, and beat them up for a little while, then went to Detroit and smacked them around a little bit. Then we went to Canada, and held them upside down by their feet. It's been fun, really good.'

On 17 December the TCV bandwagon rolled into London for the first of two sold-out nights at the famous Hammersmith Apollo, formerly known as Hammersmith Odeon, and one of the capital's most storied venues. In July 1973 David Bowie killed off Ziggy Stardust on the stage of the Odeon, in November 1976 a chunk of Thin Lizzy's *Live and Dangerous* album – arguably the greatest live rock album of all time – was recorded in the same venue. In the mid-1960s The Beatles sold out no less than 38 shows over 21 nights in the 5,000-capacity room, and on 18 December 2009 Paul McCartney returned to the venue to show his support for Grohl, with whom he had become firm friends in the wake of their onstage collaborations at McCartney's 2008 Liverpool Sound concert and at the Grammys in 2009. Discreetly tucked away on the left-hand side of the stage, McCartney and his girlfriend Nancy

Shevell stood smiling and bopping as rock's latest fab four delivered a thunderous masterclass in elemental grooving, controlled power and wall-shaking volume, a display which marked out Them Crooked Vultures as a vital force in their own right.

Later that night, the Vultures and various family and friends took over a charming Italian restaurant in West London for an end-of-tour party. Against a wholly incongruous soundtrack of Slayer, Metallica and Pantera, Grohl and Homme held court with grace and humour, occasionally breaking off from chatting to their guests to indulge in spontaneous, sporadic bursts of air guitar thrashing and/or air drumming. Grohl, temporarily relieved of the weight of carrying Foo Fighters, Inc., on his broad shoulders, had rarely looked more content or at ease.

'I now have three loves,' he told me as the party wound down. 'My family, the Foos and the Vultures. Shit man, the position I'm in right now, where I get to be in this band with two of my favourite musicians of all time and then I get to be in a band with my friends and family and play festivals and stadiums? That's a good thing, it's fucking great. John is already asking me when we're going to do a new Vultures record, and that will happen one day, and it'll be amazing. But right now I think it's time for me to return home.'

In May 2008, one month prior to Foo Fighters' brace of Wembley Stadium headline dates, Grohl was asked by *Kerrang!* magazine where he saw his band heading next.

'How could it get any bigger or better than it is?' he mused. 'We've never had a Number One record in America, and I remember Pat [Smear] saying once, "I never want a Number One record because, after that, what do you do?" So thankfully we've never had a Number One record in America.'

Three years later, on 20 April 2011, Foo Fighters' seventh album *Wasting Light* débuted at Number 1 on the *Billboard* 200.

Advance press on *Wasting Light* centred largely around the fact that the album had been recorded to analogue tape in Dave Grohl's garage.

That the process merited such attention speaks volumes about the sterile state of the music industry in 2011. In 1999 Foo Fighters had recorded *There Is Nothing Left to Lose* to tape in Dave Grohl's basement in Virginia without Pro Tools technology and without any real fanfare, but by 2011 the idea that rock music *should* be pristine and polished was so endemic in the recording industry that the notion of making a record in any other way was considered heretical. On the same November evening that photographer Lisa Johnson and I dropped in upon Foo Fighters' *Wasting Light* sessions at Grohl's Encino home, I interviewed San Diego pop-punks Blink 182 at their North Hollywood studio as they toiled upon the creation of their sixth studio album; in conversation with the band's vocalist/guitarist Tom DeLonge I mentioned the manner in which Dave Grohl's band were working with Butch Vig elsewhere in the city. DeLonge looked dumbfounded.

'Why would you do that?' he gasped. 'That would be like you carving your article into tablets of stone instead of using a computer!'

In truth, this mindset had only recently been banished from Foo Fighters' own sessions.

'The first song we recorded, we get a drum take and Butch starts razor-splicing edits to tape,' Grohl recalled to *Electronic Musician* magazine. 'We rewind the tape and it starts shedding oxide. Butch says, "We should back everything up to digital." I start screaming: "If I see one fucking computer hooked up to a piece of gear, you're fucking fired! We're making the record the way we want to make it, and if you can't do it, then fuck you!" Nobody makes us do what we don't want to do. "What if something happens to the tape?" "What did we do in 1991, Butch?" You play it again! God forbid you have to play your song one more time.'

Sessions for *Wasting Light* actually began in a more traditional manner in the autumn of 2008, using state-of-the-art digital recording technology at Grandmaster Recorders studios in Hollywood, the same facility in which three-quarters of the original Foo Fighters line-up completed the recording of *The Colour and the Shape* in 1997. The band had been writing and rehearsing new material in soundchecks while touring *Echoes, Silence, Patience & Grace*, and Grohl's original plan was that Foo Fighters should record a new album and release it quickly and quietly without committing to any touring, press interviews or promotional activity at all. With Butch Vig handling production, songs such as 'Wheels', 'Word Forward' and 'Rope' were laid down in a conventional fashion, but Grohl could see that his band were burnt out after a solid year's touring, and in the back of his mind he knew the songs weren't quite ready. Mindful of past mistakes, he called a halt to the session. Within three months he was back in the studio, but this time with John Paul Jones and Josh Homme.

'The Vultures did a lot more than I originally expected it to,' he told me as we sat in the studio control room at his home in Encino in November 2010. 'At first it was just an idea that Josh and I had to play together and not have to tour, and not have to do all the things that we were tired of doing with our other bands, and then I asked John to come jam with us and within five minutes I wanted it to be more than just a studio project. Because we were good – we were good in the room, we were good on tape, we were good onstage, we were just *good*. It was obvious within the first few weeks that it was going to be a good record and that we were going to be a fucking blazing live band. So it was just a series of challenges: write the first song, record the first song, record all the songs, release the album, perform in front of people, perform *everywhere* in front of people. And it just started snowballing …

'We could have done much more, but by New Year's I realised that if I waited any longer to do Foo Fighters' thing, there's going to be a really big gap between our last album and this one now. And, ultimately, this is where I belong. But it was a hard decision to make because I was in a band with John Paul Jones, who's one of my heroes, and Josh, who's one of my best friends, and I was playing better than I've ever played before and having the time of my life. But I wanted to be here in Foo Fighters at the same time. So in January I called Taylor and said, "Okay, let's start working on some ideas."'

On 16 August 2010, just two weeks after Them Crooked Vultures closed out their world tour onstage at the Fuji Rock festival in Naeba, Japan, Foo Fighters regrouped to restart work upon their seventh studio album. Inspired by the purity of the Them Crooked Vultures experience, Grohl now had a new vision for the album: his band would record to analogue tape, in his garage, and have a documentary film crew record the process.

'The process I think comes out in the music,' he said. 'When I listen to the second record [*The Colour and the Shape*], it's kinda complicated: there's some things that I like to listen to and some things that I don't, because I know what was happening at the time and what I was singing about. And then there's an album like the third album [*There Is Nothing Left to Lose*], which we made in my basement in Virginia which was just nothing but fucking good vibes, it was a pleasure to make that record, and when I listen to it, it sounds that way to me, just a nice, laid-back album because that's the way we felt at the time. So I feel like this whole process, you can actually hear it in the album. And it's been pretty fun.

'I know that whenever I listen to these songs in 20 years from now I'll remember recording "These Days" and having Violet tapping me on the shoulder the whole time I'm doing my guitar track. Or a song like "Miss the Misery" and I look down and Harper has got her pinkie in her mouth and she's dancing along. The kids are part of the album in a way, they're part of the memories for me.'

As photographer Lisa Johnson and I drove away from Grohl's home that November evening, the man of the house was already back at work, framed in the light in his studio control room, cradling a guitar. But before we said our goodbyes he had this to say about his band's forth-coming album:

'With the last album we were too concerned with being *musical*. When we went out and did that acoustic tour it made us feel like a band of musicians, like we were doing something a lot more than just turning on a fucking DAT machine and bouncing around to lasers, so that had a lot to do with the last album, making it more than just four-chord shit. But it seems like every album we've made is a result of the one that came before it, or a response to it. And we haven't made a really heavy, full-on eleven-song rock record in a long time. There are a few bands that later in their career have made one album that kinda defines the band: it might not be their best album, but it's the one people identify the band with the most, like [AC/DC's] *Back in Black* or the *Metallica* record. It's like you take all of the things that people consider your band's signature characteristics and just amplify them and make one simple album with that. And that's what I thought we could do with Butch, because Butch has a great way of trimming all the fat and making sense of it all. And I think that's what he's done with this shit. We have a tendency to over-complicate things. But now it's time for us to go out and be a rock band again. Someone has to do it, right?'

Wasting Light was released on 11 April 2011 in the UK and one day later in the US, emerging to the most enthusiastic reviews of the band's career. 'Most bands struggle to follow a Greatest Hits abum,' noted Johnny Dee in his 8 out of 10 review for *Classic Rock*. 'Foo Fighters have followed theirs with a record that sounds like another Greatest Hits album. They're unstoppable.' *Q* awarded the album 4 out of 5, and hailed the 'indecently thrilling' collection as a 'career-defining return'. *MOJO* too considered *Wasting Light* worthy of a 4/5 review, with Stevie Chick applauding 'high velocity thrills from the master of unreconstructed rock'. And *Rolling Stone*'s David Fricke wrote, 'If you ever thought Foo Fighters were Nirvana-lite because Grohl lacked Cobain's torment, get ready to apologise.'

The record-buying public responded with enthusiasm. In topping the *Billboard* chart, *Wasting Light* racked up first-week sales of 235,000 units in the US, their second-highest sales week ever. The album also hit the No. 1 spot on a further eleven national charts, including those of the United Kingdom, Ireland, Australia and Germany. In the months prior to the album's release, after analysing chart figures worldwide, media organisations had devoted countless column inches to the idea that rock music is 'dead', with veteran US DJ Paul Gambaccini, the self-appointed 'Professor of Pop', declaring, 'It is the end of the rock era. It's over, in the same way the jazz era is over. That doesn't mean there will be no more good rock musicians, but rock as a prevailing style is part of music history.' *Wasting Light* stands as a rather robust, defiant rebuttal of such a foolish notion.

The key to unlocking the album is contained within 'I Should Have Known', the most nakedly emotional song Grohl has ever penned. Grohl can be a maddeningly oblique lyricist, comfortable only when dealing with universal themes which give little of his own heart away, but 'I Should Have Known' is a raw, haunting tale of personal loss so laden with guilt and regret that listening in almost feels like an intrusion. Given added pathos by mournful accordion and fuzzed-out bass riffs supplied by Grohl's erstwhile Nirvana bandmate Krist Novoselic, the song will inevitably be interpreted as an elegy for Kurt Cobain, but while Grohl has acknowledged that it's a tribute to those he has loved and lost, the true inspiration behind the track is his lifelong companion Jimmy Swanson, who passed away on 18 July 2008 as a result of a drug overdose. In Swanson, Grohl always saw himself, or rather a version of himself that would exist had fate not dealt him a different hand; just as 'Word Forward' on Foo Fighters' *Greatest Hits* collection opens with the poignant lyric '*Goodbye Jimmy, farewell youth*', lines here such as '*I should have known, I was inside of you*' and '*I cannot forgive you yet, to leave my heart in debt*' carry an almost unbearable emotional charge.

But in undertaking this painful soul-mining, and revisiting the memories he shared with Swanson, Grohl uncovered the source materials for the most life-affirming album of his career. The songs on *Wasting Light*, delivered with the same breathless intensity and hunger Grohl brought to his earliest band practices in Springfield garages and basements, can be considered his 'thank you' notes to the artists that soundtracked the adolescence he shared with Swanson, and to the life experiences which blossomed as a consequence of that musical education. As such, there are nods to Grohl's past dotted throughout the album. 'I Should Have Known' features the lyric '*came without a warning*', a subtle allusion to the title of the opening track of Scream's début album *Still Screaming*. 'Bridge Burning' references Revolution Summer's definitive anthem 'Dance Of Days' and namechecks both Ian MacKaye's Embrace and Alec MacKaye's Faith. And in 'Arlandria', a song titled in tribute to the area of Virginia in which Grohl was raised, over bouncing, thrust-and-drag guitars the 42-year-old sings, '*My sweet Virginia, I'm the same as I was in your heart,*' a proud boast that the teenage punk within him will never be silenced.

At other points, links with Grohl's past are musical rather than lyrical. 'White Limo' melds the red-eyed bruiser-punk of Queens of the

Stone Age's 'Quick and to the Pointless' with the kinetic fury of Refused's 'New Noise' to deliver a rasping rave-up which Motörhead's Lemmy could have proudly fathered, while 'Rope', with its angular, colliding art-punk guitar riffs, could have been lifted from an unreleased Dain Bramage demo tape.

Wasting Light most explicitly acknowledges Grohl's formative musical influences, however, with the appearance of Bob Mould on the Hüsker Dü-esque 'Dear Rosemary'. Grohl met Hüsker Dü's frontman for the first time at the 9:30 Club's 30th Anniversary party in Washington DC on 31 May 2010, and was moved to tell his teenage hero that he'd been ripping him off musically for 15 years. The pair swapped phone numbers, and on 27 September Mould was invited to Grohl's home to trade vocal lines on 'Dear Rosemary'.

'I think he's known for a long time that I'm a huge Hüsker Dü fan, as is anybody from my musical generation,' Grohl told me. 'He's a legend, an American hero. So I texted him and said, "Hey, I have this song I think you should come down and sing with me on." And I've never done a duet, outside of the Norah Jones thing, and it turned into a duet and it works perfectly. He walked in and said, "Okay, well, where should I start?" and we said, "Well, why don't you start just by doing harmonies?" And he has such a signature sense of melody and composition, and the sound of his voice is the same – it hasn't changed whether it's *Copper Blue* or *Zen Arcade* or whatever, his voice is his voice – so when he started singing our jaws just dropped, like, "Oh my God, that's the voice!" And then I intentionally left the bridge unfinished so that the two of us could collaborate on a part, and it turned out so well that at one point he said, "Yeah, that's basically *Copper Blue* right there." It was so easy, he was a pleasure to work with and a pleasure to hang with.'

Inevitably, though, it was Krist Novoselic's guest appearance on the album which attracted most commentary. For snarky online commentators, the idea that Grohl would reunite three of the four men responsible for making *Nevermind* as the album's 20th anniversary approached was opportunistic and conceited. For Grohl himself, however, the motivation was pure and straightforward: Novoselic and Vig are family.

This is a Call

'I'd have to be pretty stupid to think it would go unnoticed!' he acknowledged in 2010. 'When we recorded with Butch last year I had so much fun just being in the studio with him again. We only recorded those two songs but it was the same feeling, it reminded me of making *Nevermind* in 1991 – not the music, just the experience of being with Butch. And we'd talked about making an album together again for years, we started talking about it in 2000 for the fourth record, his name always comes up whenever it's time to make a record. And after recording those two songs I thought, "Okay, it's time, it's time to work with Butch." And then I realised that it's also going to be the 20th anniversary of *Nevermind*. So I can either keep that from letting me make a record with Butch, or just not pay attention to it, because the idea of making this album with Butch in this way and having Krist come down and play on it is all for the sake of not being afraid of that. Does that make any sense?

'Ultimately what we're doing here isn't meant to recreate what happened 20 years ago, it's more of a reminder that we're here for the same reason, and we've all survived: we're fathers and we have families and we still love making music the same as we did 20 years ago. I know that when the album comes out there will be a ton of unneeded pressure and a lot of the focus will be on the fact that Butch and I are working together again after 20 years and that Krist Novoselic is playing bass on one song, and I'm okay with that, it's totally fine. I love our album, I think it's great, but it's a Foo Fighters record, it's not a Nirvana record, and it's important that people realise that I'm here to make a Foo Fighters record and not a Nirvana record. Krist and I are still great friends, we talk all the time and see each other a lot, and there's no question that this year will be a big year for Krist and I because of that anniversary, but what we're doing here isn't about that.'

Wasting Light is no *Nevermind*, nor was it ever intended to be, but it shares with that album an unselfconscious, unabashed love of volume, noise and melody, and a simplicity of purpose which echoes with memories of jam sessions in a spartan Tacoma rehearsal room before life got complicated. Grohl isn't looking to subvert rock 'n' roll, but rather to celebrate it – for Jimmy, for Kurt, for every kid whose life has been changed by a seven-inch slice of black vinyl delivering three chords and the truth – and nowhere is this more evident than on album-closer 'Walk', an anthem so open-hearted and optimistic it risks tipping into mawkish sentimentality. As waves of guitar build and roar behind him, Grohl screams, '*I never wanna die!*' over and over, a howl of exultation rooted in DC punk positivity and delivered with electrifying, undeniable conviction. Closing out an album which both consciously and unconsciously sets Dave Grohl's whole life into context, it's a sentiment that betrays the singer's fervent belief that his future starts here.

In the same week that *Wasting Light* débuted atop the *Billboard* 200, a new exhibition opened at the Experience Music Project in Seattle. Titled 'Nirvana: Taking Punk to the Masses', the interactive exhibition celebrates not only the music and history of Seattle's most iconic grunge collective, but also traces – via oral histories delivered on film by underground icons such as Greg Ginn, Ian MacKaye, Steve Albini, Mike Watt, Keith Morris, Mark Arm and the B-52s' Kate Pierson – the evolution and development of the American punk rock underground community. In display cases hewn from elm trees grown on Krist Novoselic's farmland in rural Washington, more than 140,000 cultural artefacts related to popular music are on show: among them the black Fender Stratocaster smashed by Kurt Cobain during the recording of 'Endless Nameless' at Sound City during the *Nevermind* sessions; the T-shirt Cobain wore in the 'Smells Like Teen Spirit' video; one of Dave Grohl's Tama drumkits; and Grohl's handwritten set-list for Foo Fighters' first Seattle club show at the Velvet Elvis, alongside thousands of flyers, photographs, ticket stubs and Krist Novoselic's teenage record collection. It's a fascinating, illuminating exhibition.

On the evening of 15 April 2011, the night before the exhibition opened to the public, Novoselic spoke in moving, emotional terms to an invited audience about the impact that this musical community had upon his own life, and the life of his closest friend, Kurt Cobain. He then paid tribute to old friends in Aberdeen, Olympia and Seattle, and thanked Dale Crover's mother for putting up with the presence of the

Cling-Ons at her home at 609 West Second Street. And he also gave a special shout-out to Dave Grohl.

'I love Dave,' said Novoselic. 'He released a new record this week … and it rocks. Dave's out there, and he works hard, and he's never lost focus. He's carrying the flame …'

There's a certain irony in Seattle's music scene luminaries getting misty-eyed over the music of their youth – didn't Dave Grohl, Krist Novoselic and Eddie Vedder join forces with Mike Watt to decry such nostalgia as '*someone else's sentimentality*' – but then in visiting the Emerald City in 2011 one might wonder if grunge ever really left its streets. Some of the scene's iconic venues may have disappeared – The Vogue is now a hair salon called Vain, the site of the OK Hotel is now home to chic waterfront apartments and art studios – but its key players continue to thrive: Soundgarden, Pearl Jam, Alice in Chains, Mudhoney and Melvins all have gigs and tours lined up for the latter half of 2011. As *Nevermind* turns 20, punk rock kids in dirty Black Flag and Dead Kennedys T-shirts still gather noisily outside Starbucks on the corner of 4th and Pine Street, and the Crocodile Café and Central Tavern still play host to gangs of dissolute teens with bad attitudes, shitty equipment and dreams of escape. Quite what these youngsters made of 20-year-old Casey Abrams's performance of 'Smells Like Teen Spirit' on manufactured pop talent show *American Idol* in March 2011 is anyone's guess, but Kurt Cobain would doubtless have enjoyed the delicious mind-warping irony of Aerosmith's Steven Tyler saluting Abrams as 'crazy' for his take on grunge's most iconoclastic anthem.

In December 2010 Dave Grohl indulged in a little grunge nostalgia of his own. On the day he was due to wrap the mixing of *Wasting Light* with Alan Moulder, Grohl booked Foo Fighters a surprise show at the tiny Paladino's club in Tarzana, California to première songs from the album. He decided to invite Krist Novoselic along to play 'Marigold', the *Pocketwatch* track which became the B-side of Nirvana's *Heart-Shaped Box* single, for a performance which would reunite the surviving members of Nirvana onstage for the first time since Foo Fighters' Bumbershoot festival appearance in 1997.

These days

The day before the show Grohl, Novoselic and Pat Smear got together in a Hollywood rehearsal room to run through the song. Once satisfied, Novoselic asked his two friends if they wanted to run through some 'mouldy oldies' for old time's sake: he suggested they might tackle 'Smells Like Teen Spirit'. And so, some sixteen years after he last played the song, Dave Grohl beat out the song's iconic opening tattoo once more.

Halfway through the performance, the studio manager opened the rehearsal room door and watched in silence for a few moments.

'That sounded pretty good,' he said finally. 'You guys should keep that.'

Grohl, Novoselic and Smear exchanged amused looks and burst out laughing. As the door of the room slammed shut again, Grohl picked up his drumsticks once more. As memories of days gone by rushed to his head, he composed himself and smiled. Then he looked at his friends, nodded and loudly counted in another song …

Sources

Quotations

All quotations are taken from the author's interviews, except as noted below:

Chapter 1

'It's kinda funny for a while ...' Neil Kulkarni, 'I Fucking Hated Hollywood',
Metal Hammer, December 1999.

'Porn stars become grocery clerks ...' Ben Mitchell, 'A Life Less Ordinary',
Q, December 2005.

'You and I are a lot alike ...' Andy Gray and Darcie Loreno, 'Rocker Talks to
Alley Painters', *Warren Tribune Chronicle*, 2 August 2009.

'Just because you're born here ...' Sarah Poulton, 'Music Is Art: Warren
Celebrates a Music Superstar', *www.valley24.com*, 25 July 2009.

'Pretty much at other ends ...' Michael Azerrad, *Come As You Are*, Main
Street Books, 1993.

'You're thinking "This can't be the United States of America ..."' Charles
Colson, 'Nixon: A Presidency Revealed', History Channel documentary,
February 2007.

'15 minutes from chicken farmers, and 15 minutes from the White House.'
Austin Scaggs, 'On a Honor Roll', *Rolling Stone*, 28 July 2005.

'Of course it caused a lot of pain and it caused a lot of struggle ...' Tom
Doyle, 'I Wanted to Take Acid and Smash Stuff', *Q*, July 2007.

'By the time I got a hold of the situation ...' Dave Everley, 'I Was a Teenage Punk Rocker', *Kerrang!*, 2 August 1997.

'To me that was just the best sound ...' Anon, 'I Saw the Light', *NME*, 1999.

'To this day [it's] still one of the most amazing songs ...' Anon, 'Songs in the Key of Life', *NME*, 1999.

'I had a chair that was next to my bed ...' Ken Micallef, 'Returning to His Roots', *Modern Drummer*, June 2004.

'They always said the same thing ...' Dave Everley, 'I was a teenage punk rocker", *Kerrang!*, 2 August 1997.

'Those guitars! Two strings! How cool! ...' Anon, 'Rebellious Jukebox', *Melody Maker*, 1997.

Chapter 2

'The term "punk" is bandied about an awful lot these days ...' Mick Houghton, 'White Punks on Coke', *Let It Rock*, December 1975

'This band hates you ...' Charles M. Young, 'Rock Is Sick and Living in London', *Rolling Stone*, 20 October 1977.

'Kids destroyed schools ...' Charles M. Young, 'Rock Is Sick and Living In London', *Rolling Stone*, 20 October 1977

'I'm working Monday through Friday ...' Paul Rachman and Steve Blush, *American Hardcore*, Sony Pictures, 2006.

'I stood there and thought "I could do this ..."' Paul Connolley, 'Rock Warriors', *The Times*, November 2002.

'I talked to the singer and I jumped on someone's head ...' Stevie Chick, 'Everyone Has Their Dark Side', *MOJO*, May 2005.

'It took me about a year before I finally found it ...' Stevie Chick, 'Everyone Has Their Dark Side', *MOJO*, May 2005.

'Ian's the only one who ever did the punk thing right ...' Brendan Mullen, 'This Band Could Be His Life', *L.A. Weekly*, 10 March 2005.

'They were detonating every song ...' Don Letts, *Punk: Attitude*, Freemantle Media, 2005.

'There was no music scene in Washington ...' Peter Hepburn, 'Ian MacKaye', www.cokemachineglow.com, 2 October 2004.

'Bad Brains influenced us incredibly ...' Mark Andersen and Mark Jenkins, *Dance of Days: Two Decades of Punk in the Nation's Capital*, Soft Skull Press, 2001.

'HR was the energizer ...' Nardwuar, 'Narwuar vs Ian of Fugazi', www.nardwuar.com, 7 July 2001.

'From the very beginning of the label we were told ...' Peter Hepburn, 'Ian MacKaye', www.cokemachineglow.com, 2 October 2004.

Sources

'We like to play out of town ...' Al Flipside, 'Black Flag', *Flipside*, December 1980.

'We think everybody should be subjected to us ...' John Kezdy, 'Black Flag', *The Coolest Retard*, 1981.

'There's more impact in playing for people ...' Steve Stiph, 'Black Flag', *Outcry*, 1980.

'In the middle of the show, I took a knife ...' Henry Rollins, *Get in the Van*, 2.13.61, 1994.

'Punk rock has more asshole ...' Vic Bondi, 'Vic, Ian and Dave', *maximumrocknroll*, September 1983.

'I have some really great practice tapes ...' Nardwuar, 'Narwuar vs Ian of Fugazi', www.nardwuar.com, 7 July 2001.

'It's sad, all those little kids that were on skateboards ...' Bill Bartell, 'Black Market Baby', *Flipside*, August 1984.

Chapter 3

'But nobody else blew me away as much as Bad Brains ...' Anon, 'The 100 Greatest Albums You've Never Heard', *NME*, 28 December 2010.

'It was a time when hardcore bands were these skinny white guys ...' Anon, 'The Greatest Gig I Ever Saw', *Melody Maker*, 1999.

'For me, punk rock was an escape ...' Anon, 'Page + Plant + Grohl', *Raygun*, 1998.

'There was some Nirvana book that glorified my parents' divorce ...' Ben Mitchell, 'A Life Less Ordinary' *Q*, November 2005.

'Imagine the lectures I'd get if I fucked up ...' Paul Connolly, 'Rock Warriors', *The Times*, November 2002.

'He thought that unless you practised for six hours a day ...' Paul Connolly, 'Rock Warriors', *The Times*, November 2002.

'We all decided that this is it, Revolution Summer ...' Al Quint, 'Fugazi', *Suburban Voice*, 1990 (Issue 29).

'Revolution Summer is a revival ...' Anon, *Flipside*, 1985 (Issue 74).

'The Do-It-Yourself element made everything more special ...' Ben Mitchell, unpublished extract from 'My Brilliant Career', *Q*, November 2007.

'I was smoking all day long ...' Chris Marlowe, 'I Haven't Smoked a Joint in Six Years', *Metal Hammer*, January 1996.

'The first time I took acid ...' Ben Mitchell, unpublished extract from 'A Life Less Ordinary', *Q*, December 2005.

'I'd never cracked a Bible in my life ...' Tom Doyle, 'I Wanted to Take Acid and Smash Stuff!', *Q*, July 2007.

357

'To me, Zeppelin were spiritually inspirational …' Dave Grohl, 'Led Zeppelin: The Immortals', *Rolling Stone*, 15 April 2004.

'Led Zeppelin, and John Bonham's drumming …' Anon, 'Sock It to 'Em JB!', *MOJO*, 2005.

'As a 17-year-old kid raised playing punk-rock drums …' Anon, 'Dave Grohl on Physical Graffiti', *Uncut*, 2005.

'Bonham played directly from the heart …' Anon, 'Sock It to 'Em JB!', *MOJO*, 2005.

Chapter 4

'Raised in a van by wolves …' Charles R. Cross, *Heavier Than Heaven*, Hodder & Stoughton, 2001.

'The first time I saw them …' Mitch Parker, 'Scream', *maximumrocknroll*, May 1983.

'When I first saw them …' Mitch Parker, 'Scream', *maximumrocknroll*, May 1983.

'This is the album where Scream went from being …' Anon, 'Rebellious Jukebox', *Melody Maker*, 1997.

'The best set of the year, so far …' Al Quint, 'Live Shows', *Suburban Voice*, Summer 1985.

'I don't think Hüsker Dü signing to a major label …' Bob Mould, 'What th' Fuck!!!!', *maximumrocknroll*, February 1986.

'The freaks, the fags, the fat girls …' Sean O'Hagan, 'Michael Stipe: I Often Find Myself at a Loss for Words', *Observer*, 6 March 2011.

'They started out with the ambition …' Michael Azerrad, *Our Band Could Be Your Life*, Little, Brown & Co., 2001.

'I said "Hallelujah. Go" …' Donna St George, 'For These Stars, Mom Rules', *Washington Post*, 11 May 2008.

'Even then, she knew me well enough …' Donna St George, 'For These Stars, Mom Rules', *Washington Post*, 11 May 2008.

'All parents want their kids to do brilliantly at school …' Dirk Siepe, 'Grohl Speaks', *Visions*, September 2000.

'The two of us were laughing so hysterically …' Dan Silver, 'Get in the Van', *Metal Hammer*, 1998.

'We were killing time between gigs …' Anon, 'Last Night a Record Changed My Life', *MOJO*, 2004.

'I always thought I knew the definition of heavy …' Anon, 'It Changed My Life', *Kerrang!*, 2001.

'He'd say, "That sounds too good …"' Pat Kearney, 'Let's Get Ready to Rumble', *The Stranger*, 25 April 2002.

Sources

'Though they don't want you to know it ...' Robert Christgau, 'Consumer Guide Reviews: Big Black', www.robertchristgau.com.

'It's still essentially wilderness country up here ...' Martin Aston, 'Freak Scene', *Nirvana and the Story of Grunge*, 2005

'I looked at those photos, and I immediately knew ...' Jason Crock, 'Bruce Pavitt and Jonathan Poneman', www.pitchfork.com, 7 July 2008.

'Not only did we put an emphasis on design ...' Steve Wells, 'Expresso Way to Your Skull', *NME*, 18 July 1992.

'Before Seattle I'd never been exposed to rock ...' Everett True, *Nirvana: The True Story*, Omnibus, 2006.

'Basically, this is the real thing ...' Everett True, 'Sub Pop, Seattle: Rock City', *Melody Maker*, 18 March 1989.

Chapter 5

'You have to understand, for me, Nirvana is more ...' Ed Power, 'Into the Light', *Irish Independent*, 8 April 2011.

'You could just say, "Hey Kurt, sing this!" ...' Gillian G. Gaar, 'Verse Chorus Verse: The Recording History of Nirvana', *Goldmine*, 14 February 1997.

'It just destroyed his life ...' Michael Azerrad, *Come As You Are: The Story of Nirvana*, Main Street Books, 1993.

'I remember hanging out at ...' Kurt Cobain, *Journals*, Viking, 2002.

'Most of what I remember about the songs ...' Gillian G. Gaar, 'Verse Chorus Verse: The Recording History of Nirvana', *Goldmine*, 14 February 1997.

'There are a lot of Croatian people here ...' Patrick MacDonald, 'In Search of Nirvana', *Seattle Times*, 8 March 1992.

'Kurt asked me if I wanted to be in a band ...' Anon, sleeve notes for *With the Lights Out*, Geffen Records, 2004.

'I think initially he was intrigued by it ...' Anon, *Nirvana: Taking Punk to the Masses* video interview, EPM/SFM, 2011.

'I thought they sucked ...' Greg Prato, *Grunge Is Dead: The Oral History of Seattle Rock Music*, ECW Press, 2009.

'We were uptight ...' Dawn Anderson, 'It May Be the Devil and It May Be the Lord ... But It Sure as Hell Ain't Human', *Backlash*, August 1988.

'In our press releases we would announce ...' Jason Crock, 'Bruce Pavitt and Jonathan Poneman', www.pitchfork.com, 7 July 2008.

'The Lamefest show was what really put Nirvana ...' Ian Winwood, 'Nirvana: The Day They Changed the World', *Kerrang!*, 26 October 2002.

'I feel like we've been tagged as illiterate, redneck, cousin-fucking kids ...' Nils Bernstein, 'Berlin Is Just a State of Mind', *The Rocket*, December 1989.

This is a Call

'I don't remember them saying, "You're in the band" ...' David Fricke, 'Nevermind 10 Years On', *Rolling Stone*, September 2001.

'The venue was down the street ...' Craig McLean, 'Dave Grohl: Grohl with It', *Independent*, 11 June 2005.

'I felt I had something to prove ...' Craig McLean, 'Dave Grohl: Grohl with It', *Independent*, 11 June 2005.

'His contribution transformed us ...' Krist Novoselic, *Of Grunge and Government*, RDV Books/Akashic Books, 2004.

Chapter 6

'We'd meet at her locker ...' Andrew Goldman, 'Drummer Boy', Elle.com, 28 July 2007.

'We're changing a little bit ...' Keith Cameron, 'Take the Money and Run', *Sounds*, 27 October 1990.

'I remember going "This is a really good song" ...' Carrie Borzillo, *Nirvana: The Day by Day Eyewitness Chronicle*, Thunder's Mouth Press, 2000.

'As we were mixing the album ...' David Fricke, 'Nevermind 10 Years on', *Rolling Stone*, September 2001.

Chapter 7

'Kurt had a mystical and powerful connection ...' Danny Goldberg, *Bumping into Geniuses*, Gotham Books, 2008.

'I saw this movie *Over the Edge* ...' The Stud Bothers, 'Dark Side of the Womb', *Melody Maker*, 21 August 1993.

'The director had a loud bullhorn thing ...' Anon, 'The Grunge Invasion', *Newsweek*, 28 June 1999.

'It was the first time I had seen ...' Ed Power, 'Into the Light', *Irish Independent*, 8 April 2011.

'When you tell a drummer "I think you should use ...' Ben Mitchell, unpublished excerpt from 'My Brilliant Career', *Q*, 2005.

'It was unbelievable. We went from selling ...' Anon, 'Nevermind – 10 Years On', *Rolling Stone*, 2001.

'One day we were this virtually unknown ...' Ian Winwood, 'Nirvana: The Day They Changed the World', *Kerrang!*, 26 October 2002.

'We were playing before Nirvana ...' Eric Weisbard with Jessica Letkemann, Ann Powers, Chris Norris, William Van Meter and Will Hermes, 'Ten Past Ten', *Spin Online*, August 2001.

'He was an oblivion seeker ...' Alexis Petridis, 'Courtney Love: "Sometimes I'm a little bit weird ... but never unpopular"', *Guardian*, 25 March 2010.

Sources

'He's had but an hour's sleep ...' Jerry McCulley, 'Spontaneous Combustion', *Bam*, 10 January 1992.

'I remember walking into their hotel room ...' Michael Azerrad, *Come As You Are*, Main Street Books, 1994.

'I remember thinking, "Wow, it's on now,' Eric Weisbard with Jessica Letkemann, Ann Powers, Chris Norris, William Van Meter and Will Hermes, 'Ten Past Ten', *Spin Online*, August 2001.

'We got to the point where we could ...' Anon, sleevenotes to *With the Lights Out*, Geffen, 2004.

'Everyone's been saying that ...' Anon, 'Kurt OD in Belfast: Nirvana Star Rushed to Hospital with "Mystery Stomach Bug"', *Melody Maker*, 4 July 1992.

'You had to say and do ...' Andrew Perry, 'Anarchy in the UK', *MOJO*, May 1998.

'Spend two days in tour fatigues ...' Keith Cameron, 'Love Will Tear Us Apart', *NME*, 29 August 1992.

'Any musician would be lying ...' Everett True, 'In My Head I'm so Ugly', *Melody Maker*, 18 July 1992.

'We rehearsed once, the night before ...' Alan Light, 'Interview: Dave Grohl, Foo Fighters Frontman', *Scotsman*, 24 November 2009.

'But we were wracked with nerves ...' Anon, 'Festival Questionnaire', *Q*, 2000.

'The hype about us cancelling was ...' Anon, 'Sky's Icon of 1992: Dave Grohl', *Sky*, 1997.

Chapter 8

'I'm like, "This is your fucking son,"' Craig Marks, 'Endless Love', *Spin*, February 1995.

'I think people who glamorise drugs ...' The Stud Brothers, 'Dark Side of the Womb', *Melody Maker*, 21 August 1993.

'Humping our own gear into CBGB's ...' Phil Sutcliffe, 'Something in the Way', *Nirvana and the Story of Grunge*, 2005.

'I felt this big ...' Phil Sutcliffe, 'Something in the Way', *Nirvana and The Story of Grunge*, 2005.

'I don't listen to records like that at home ...' Jon Savage, 'Kurt Cobain: The Lost Interview', *Guitar World*, 1997.

'Our A&R man at the time ...' Phil Sutcliffe, 'King of Pain', *Q*, October 1993.

'We'd never met Albini before ...' Ben Mitchell, previously unpublished excerpt from 'My Brilliant Career', *Q*, November 2007.

This is a Call

'When we talked to him before recording …' Phil Sutcliffe, 'Something in the Way', *Nirvana and the Story of Grunge*, 2005.

'We knew that Albini didn't wanna …' Keith Cameron, 'This Is Pop', *MOJO*, May 2001.

'We went out of our way to say things …' Brendan Mullen, with Don Bolles and Adam Parfrey, *Lexicon Devil*, Feral House, 2002.

'Krist, Dave and I have been working on this formula …' David Fricke, 'Kurt Cobain', *Rolling Stone*, 27 January 1994.

'I woke up at, like …' Craig Marks, 'Endless Love', *Spin*, February 1995.

Chapter 9

'After Kurt's death I was about as confused …' Anon, Foo Fighters' press release, 1995.

'My first reaction was, "What the fuck?" …' Clark Collis, 'Dave Grohl Q&A', *www.music-mix.ew.com*, 15 April 2011.

'Right when the thing with Stan Lynch …' Matt Snow, 'Learning to Fly', *MOJO*, December 2009.

'At one point Dave phoned me …' Jacob McMurray, *Taking Punk to the Masses: From Nowhere to Nevermind*, Fantagraphics Books, 2011.

'I wanted to fucking murder him …' Dorian Lynskey, 'The Man Who Fell to Earth', *Arena*, 2002.

'This was exactly the big …' David Daley, *Magnet*, November/December 1998.

'I approach every song trying …' Anon, 'Hey, What's that Buzz', *Guitar World*, May 2011.

'No one has ever said anything …' Tom Doyle, 'I'll Stick Around', *Nirvana and the Story of Grunge*, 2005.

Chapter 10

'I've made punk rock records …' Kim Hughes, 'Dave Grohl: From Punk Pounder to Foo Fighter', *NOW*, 1997.

'I love it for the way …' Anon, 'Rebellious Jukebox', *Melody Maker*, 1997.

'Dave had me do 96 takes …' Michael Roberts, 'Bring Back That Sunny Day', *Miami New Times*, 3 December 1998.

'I knew it was a cool song …' Morat, 'How to Write a Rock Anthem', *Kerrang!*, 17 June 2006.

'I had no idea what I was doing and I faked it and it worked …' Anon, 'Foo for Thought', *Raygun*, August 1997.

'It's important to break out from …' Mike Rubin, 'So Happy Together', *Spin*, July 1997.

Sources

'Had Franz not been in Wool at the time ...' Lisa Johnson, 'The New Model Army', *Kerrang!*, 18 October 1997.

'Of course he'll be writing with us ...' Lisa Johnson, 'The New Model Army', *Kerrang!*, 18 October 1997.

'We waited about a year for him ...' Michael Roberts, 'Bring Back That Sunny Day', *Miami New Times*, 3 December 1998.

'Nothing seems sacred here ...' Ben Myers, 'I'm Still Standing', *Kerrang!*, 18 September 1999.

Chapter 11

'This place is like our own little boot camp ...' Joshua Sindell, 'We Have Lift Off!', *Kerrang!*, 19 May 2001.

'There's freaky time signatures, it's fucking fast ...' Joshua Sindell, 'We Have Lift Off!', *Kerrang!*, 19 May 2001.

'It doesn't matter what they were ...' Ian Winwood, 'Courtney. Kurt. Drugs. Rehab', *Kerrang!*, 30 March 2002.

'So in 2000, as we were touring with Queens ...' Ben Mitchell, unpublished excerpt from 'My Brilliant Career', *Q*.

'Being in Queens was one of the greatest ...' Ben Mitchell, unpublished excerpt from 'My Brilliant Career', *Q*.

'Playing drums in Queens was like ESP ...' Austin Scaggs, 'On a Honor Roll', *Rolling Stone*, July 2005.

'I had a profound revelation ...' Austin Scaggs, 'On a Honor Roll', *Rolling Stone*, July 2005.

'We rushed into it and we rushed ...' Austin Scaggs, 'Foos Reclaim Their Honor', Rolling Stone.com, 25 April 2005.

'Those bands were something ...' Ian Winwood, 'Metal God', *Kerrang!*, 29 November 2003.

Chapter 12

'I really avoided talking to the press ...' Anon, 'James Hetfield: I Don't Like Talking Politics', WENN, 1 August 2002.

'All the hot air coming ...' Ian Winwood, 'I Put My Faith in the Cult of Elvis Costello', Guardian Online, 12 July 2007.

'I felt like I was being challenged by ...' Tom Doyle, 'Let Me Entertain You', *Q*, June 2008.

'I went back and forth to Los Angeles for years ...' Ian Gittins, 'Dave Grohl', *Man about Town*, April 2011.

'I was personally offended ...' Andrew Beaujon, 'Q&A: Dave Grohl', *Spin*, July 2005.

'Every day before Kerry got up to speak …' Andrew Beaujon, 'Q&A: Dave Grohl', *Spin*, July 2005.

'There was a moment when I thought …' Morat, 'Riders on the Storm', *Kerrang!*, January 2005.

'About what it meant for us …' Ian Winwood, 'I'm a Geek. I'm the Guy Next Door …', *NME*, May 2005.

'It didn't make a lot of sense not to try …' Ian Winwood, 'I'm a Geek. I'm the Guy Next Door …', *NME*, May 2005.

'I tried to be cool …' Dom Lawson, 'Into the Void', *Kerrang!*, May 2005.

'It didn't feel like the most important show …' Dan Gennoe, 'Monster of Rock', *Mail on Sunday*, 16 September 2007.

'We don't usually jump …' Anon, 'It's Like Being Knighted', *Uncut*, 2006.

Chapter 13

'The next project that I'm trying to initiate …' Stevie Chick, '"Everyone Has Their Dark Side": Dave Grohl – The MOJO Interview', *MOJO*, May 2005.

'How could it get any bigger or better?' Anon, 'Summer Rocks!', *Kerrang!*, 31 May 2008.

'I'm not at liberty to talk about it …' Johnny Firecloud, '24 Minutes with Brody Dalle of Spinnerette', *www.antiquiet.com*, 3 July 2009.

'The first song we recorded, we get a drum …' Ken Micallef, 'The Foo Fighters Take a Low-Tech Approach to High-Intensity Rock', *Electronic Musician*, May 2011.

Lyrics credits

'*Days change at night, change in an instant …*'
X, 'Los Angeles', written by John Doe and Exene Cervanka, published by Billy Zoom Music BMI, from the album *Los Angeles* (Slash, 1980).

'*last year I was 21 | I didn't have a lot of fun*'
The Stooges, '1969', written by Dave Alexander, Ron Asheton, Scott Asheton and Iggy Pop, published by Paradox Music BMI, from the album *The Stooges* (Elektra, 1969).

Sources

'I'm about to have a nervous breakdown | My head really hurts | If I don't find a way outta here | I'm gonna go berserk ...'
Black Flag, 'Nervous Breakdown', written by Greg Ginn, published by SST Music, from the EP *Nervous Breakdown* (SST, 1979).

'Never mind the Stars and Stripes, let's print the Watergate tapes'
The Clash, 'I'm So Bored with the USA', written by Joe Strummer and Mick Jones, published by Nineden Ltd./Riva Mus. Ltd., from the album *The Clash* (CBS, 1977).

'Chaotic Hardcore Underage Delinquents! Cannibalistic Humanoid Underground Dwellers!'
Mission Impossible, 'Chud', written by Mission Impossible, from the first Mission Impossible demo tape.

'Slow down!'
Mission Impossible, 'Life Already Drawn', written by Mission Impossible, from the first Mission Impossible demo tape.

'To err is human, so what the fuck are you? Working so hard to make me perfect too ...'
Mission Impossible, 'To Err Is Human', written by Dave Grohl, from the first Mission Impossible demo tape.

'I can't promise perfection, I can only try'
Mission Impossible, 'I Can Only Try', written by Mission Impossible, from the split EP *Thanks* (Sammich, 1985).

'If you're really upset and you don't know what to do, then shout it out or talk it out, don't crawl into your shell'
Mission Impossible, 'Into Your Shell', written by Mission Impossible, from the split EP *Thanks* (Sammich, 1985).

'Now I'm off to face a new horizon but I don't think I'll be alone.'
Mission Impossible, 'Now I'm Alone', written by Mission Impossible, from the split EP *Thanks* (Sammich, 1985).

This is a Call

'... *more from a three minute record than we ever learned in school*'
Bruce Springsteen, 'No Surrender', written by Bruce Springsteen, published by Bruce Springsteen (ASCAP), from the album *Born in the U.S.A.* (Columbia, 1984).

'*We're from the basement | We're from underground | We want to break all barriers with our sound | We're sick and tired of fucking rejection | But we're not down 'cause we got a direction.*'
Scream, 'We're Fed Up', written by Scream, from the album *Still Screaming* (Dischord, 1983).

'*Yesterday it rained so hard I thought the roof was gonna give | But now today's so bright, just wanna let it all in*'
Scream, 'This Side Up', written by Scream, from the album *This Side Up* (Dischord, 1985).

'*The sky's my limit*'
Dain Bramage, 'I Scream Not Coming Down', written by Dan Kozak and Reuben Radding, published by Dainger Island/Further Down Music, from the album *I Scream Not Coming Down* (Fartblossom, 1987).

'*smoke rising outta Dischord House*'
Pussy Galore, 'You Look Like a Jew', written by Jon Spencer, published by Vinyl Drip Int., from the EP *Groovy Hate Fuck* (Shove, 1986).

'*The spoken word is weak. Scream, motherfuckers, scream!*'
Steve Albini, 'Spoken Word Intro Thing', written by Steve Albini, from the album *Sub Pop 100* (Sub Pop, 1986).

'*Damaged by you | Damaged by me | I'm confused | Confused | Don't wanna be confused.*'
Black Flag, 'Damaged II', written by Greg Ginn, published by Cesstone Music (BMI), from the album *Damaged* (SST, 1981).

'*I'm a negative creep, I'm a negative creep, I'm a negative creep and I'm stoned*'
Nirvana, 'Negative Creep', written by Kurt Cobain, published by The End of Music/EMI-Virgin Songs, Inc. (BMI), from the album *Bleach* (Sub Pop, 1989).

Sources

'over-bored and self-assured'
Nirvana, 'Smells Like Teen Spirit', written by Kurt Cobain, Dave Grohl and Krist Novoselic, published by The End of Music, M.J.-Twelve Music and Murky Slough Music, all EMI-Virgin Songs, Inc., all BMI, from the album *Nevermind* (Geffen, 1991).

'With the lights out, it's less dangerous. Here we are now, entertain us …'
Nirvana, 'Smells Like Teen Spirit', written by Kurt Cobain, Dave Grohl and Krist Novoselic, published by The End of Music, M.J.-Twelve Music and Murky Slough Music, all EMI-Virgin Songs, Inc., all BMI, from the album *Nevermind* (Geffen, 1991).

'pretty songs'
Nirvana, 'In Bloom', written by Kurt Cobain, published by The End of Music/ EMI-Virgin Songs, Inc. (BMI), from the album *Nevermind* (Geffen, 1991).

'plays an old guitar, with a coin found by the phone'
Late!, 'Friend of a Friend', written by Dave Grohl, published by M.J.-Twelve Music, administered by EMI Music (BMI), from the album *Pocketwatch* (Simple Machines, 1993).

'or Flipside … one of those punk things'
Late!, 'Just Another Story About Skeeter Thompson', written by Dave Grohl, published by M.J.-Twelve Music, administered by EMI Music (BMI), from the album *Pocketwatch* (Simple Machines, 1993).

'Some say love it is a river …'
Better Midler, 'The Rose', written by Amanda McBroom, published by Chappell, from the album *The Rose: The Original Soundtrack Recording* (Atlantic, 1979).

'Teenage angst has paid off well | Now I'm bored and old'
Nirvana, 'Serve the Servants', written by Kurt Cobain, published by The End of Music/EMI-Virgin Songs, Inc. (BMI), from the album *In Utero* (Geffen, 1993).

'I wish I could eat your cancer when you turn black'
Nirvana, 'Heart-Shaped Box', written by Kurt Cobain, published by The End of Music/EMI-Virgin Songs, Inc. (BMI), from the album *In Utero* (Geffen, 1993).

This is a Call

'Cufk Tish Sips'
Nirvana, 'Tourette's', written by Kurt Cobain, published by The End of Music/EMI-Virgin Songs, Inc. (BMI), from the album *In Utero* (Geffen, 1993).

'Pain'
Nirvana, 'You Know You're Right', written by Kurt Cobain, published by The End of Music/EMI-Virgin Songs, Inc. (BMI), from the album *Nirvana* (Geffen, 2002).

'You can't fire me because I quit'
Nirvana, 'Scentless Apprentice', words by Kurt Cobain, music by Kurt Cobain, Krist Novoselic and Dave Grohl, published by The End of Music/EMI-Virgin Songs, Inc. (BMI), from the album *In Utero* (Geffen, 1993).

'Big train, big train, do you wanna ride my big train?'
Mike Watt, 'Big Train', written by Tony Kinman and Chip Kinman, published by Sony Music Entertainment Inc., from the album *Ball-Hog or Tugboat?* (Columbia, 1995).

'The kids of today should defend themselves against the 70's'
Mike Watt, 'Against the 70's', written by Mike Watt, published by Sony Music Entertainment Inc., from the album *Ball-Hog or Tugboat?* (Columbia, 1995).

'I don't owe you anything' and *'How could it be I'm the only one who sees your rehearsed insanity?'* and *'I've been around all the pawns you've gagged and bound'*
Foo Fighters, 'I'll Stick Around', written by Dave Grohl, published by M.J.-Twelve Music, administered by EMI Music (BMI), from the album *Foo Fighters* (Roswell/Capitol, 1995).

'This is a call to all my past resignations'
Foo Fighters, 'This Is a Call', written by Dave Grohl, published by M.J.-Twelve Music, administered by EMI Music (BMI), from the album *Foo Fighters* (Roswell/Capitol, 1995).

'Breathe out, so I can breathe you in ...'
Foo Fighters, 'Everlong', written by Dave Grohl, published by M.J.-Twelve Music, from the album *The Colour and the Shape* (Roswell/Capitol, 1997).

Sources

'*We're all gonna score. Fuck your drug war!*'
Harlingtox A. D., 'Treason Daddy Brother in Crime Real Patriots Type Stuff', written by Harlingtox A. D., lyrics by Bruce Merkle, published by Harlingtox A. D., from the album *Harlingtox Angel Divine* (Laundry Room, 1996).

'*I have always been a stupid fucker.*'
Harlingtox A. D., 'Obtaining a Bachelor's Degree', written by Harlingtox A. D., lyrics by Bruce Merkle, published by Harlingtox A. D., from the album *Harlingtox Angel Divine* (Laundry Room, 1996).

'*In all of the time that we've shared I've never been so scared*'
Foo Fighters, 'Doll', written by Dave Grohl and Foo Fighters, published by M.J.-Twelve Music, from the album *The Colour and the Shape* (Roswell/Capitol, 1997).

'*I'm not scared*'
Foo Fighters, 'New Way Home', written by Dave Grohl and Foo Fighters, published by M.J.-Twelve Music, from the album *The Colour and the Shape* (Roswell/Capitol, 1997).

'*the boats and the King Dome*'
Foo Fighters, 'New Way Home', written by Dave Grohl and Foo Fighters, published by M.J.-Twelve Music, from the album *The Colour and the Shape* (Roswell/Capitol, 1997).

'*Line up all the bastards, all we want is the truth*'
Foo Fighters, 'Stacked Actors', written by Foo Fighters, published by M.J.-Twelve Music, Flying Earform Music and Living Under a Rock Music, administered by EMI Virgin Songs, Inc. (BMI), from the album *There Is Nothing Left to Lose* (Roswell/Capitol, 1995).

'*Into the sun we climb. Climbing our wings will burn bright. Everyone strapped in tight, we'll ride it out. I'll be coming home next year.*'
Foo Fighters, 'Next Year', written by Foo Fighters, published by M.J.-Twelve Music, Flying Earform Music and Living Under a Rock Music, administered by EMI Virgin Songs, Inc. (BMI), from the album *There Is Nothing Left to Lose* (Roswell/Capitol, 1995).

This is a Call

'Mine is yours and yours is mine | There is no divide | In your honor I would die tonight.'
Foo Fighters, 'In Your Honor', written by Foo Fighters, published by M.J.-Twelve Music and I Love the Punk Rock Music, both administered by Songs of Universal, Inc. (BMI), Living Under a Rock Music, administered by Universal Music Corp. (ASCAP), and Flying Earform Music (BMI), from the album *In Your Honor* (Roswell/RCA, 2005).

'This is the last song that I will dedicate to you'
Foo Fighters, 'The Last Song', written by Foo Fighters, published by M.J.-Twelve Music and I Love the Punk Rock Music, both administered by Songs of Universal, Inc. (BMI), Living Under a Rock Music, administered by Universal Music Corp. (ASCAP), and Flying Earform Music (BMI), from the album *In Your Honor* (Roswell/RCA, 2005).

'The only thing I ever ask of you is you gotta promise not to stop when I say when'
Foo Fighters, 'Everlong', written by Dave Grohl, published by M.J.-Twelve Music, from the album *The Colour and the Shape* (Roswell/Capitol, 1997).

'Echoes, silence, patience and grace, all of these moments I'll never replace'
Foo Fighters, 'Home', written by Foo Fighters, published by M.J.-Twelve Music and I Love the Punk Rock Music, both administered by Songs of Universal, Inc. (BMI), Living Under a Rock Music, administered by Universal Music Corp. (ASCAP), and Flying Earform Music (BMI), from the album *Echoes, Silence, Patience & Grace* (Roswell/RCA, 2007).

'unwanted strangers, exploited and dangerous'
Them Crooked Vultures, 'Elephant', written by Them Crooked Vultures, published by Board Stiff Music (BMI), M.J.-Twelve Music, administered by songs of Universal Inc. (BMI), Cap Three, Ltd. (ASCAP), from the album *Them Crooked Vultures* (Columbia, 2009).

'Goodbye Jimmy, farewell youth'
Foo Fighters, 'Word Forward', written by Foo Fighters, published by M.J.-Twelve Music and I Love the Punk Rock Music, both administered by Songs of Universal, Inc. (BMI), Living Under a Rock Music, administered by Universal Music Corp. (ASCAP), and Flying Earform Music and Ruthensmear Music, both administered by Bug Music (BMI), from the album *Greatest Hits* (Roswell/Sony, 2009).

Sources

'I should have known, I was inside of you' and *'I cannot forgive you yet, to leave my heart in debt'*
Foo Fighters, 'I Should Have Known', written by Foo Fighters, published by M.J.-Twelve Music and I Love the Punk Rock Music, both administered by Songs of Universal, Inc. (BMI), Living Under a Rock Music, administered by Universal Music Corp. (ASCAP), and Flying Earform Music and Ruthensmear Music, both administered by Bug Music (BMI), from the album *Wasting Light* (Roswell/RCA, 2011).

'came without a warning'
Foo Fighters, 'I Should Have Known', written by Foo Fighters, published by M.J.-Twelve Music and I Love the Punk Rock Music, both administered by Songs of Universal, Inc. (BMI), Living Under a Rock Music, administered by Universal Music Corp. (ASCAP), and Flying Earform Music and Ruthensmear Music, both administered by Bug Music (BMI), from the album *Wasting Light* (Roswell/RCA, 2011).

'My sweet Virginia, I'm the same as I was in your heart'
Foo Fighters, 'Arlandria', written by Foo Fighters, published by M.J.-Twelve Music and I Love the Punk Rock Music, both administered by Songs of Universal, Inc. (BMI), Living Under a Rock Music, administered by Universal Music Corp. (ASCAP), and Flying Earform Music and Ruthensmear Music, both administered by Bug Music (BMI), from the album *Wasting Light* (Roswell/RCA, 2011).

'I never wanna die!'
Foo Fighters, 'Walk', written by Foo Fighters, published by M.J.-Twelve Music and I Love the Punk Rock Music, both administered by Songs of Universal, Inc. (BMI), Living Under a Rock Music, administered by Universal Music Corp. (ASCAP), and Flying Earform Music and Ruthensmear Music, both administered by Bug Music (BMI), from the album *Wasting Light* (Roswell/RCA, 2011).

Picture credits
Plate-section photographs have been supplied courtesy of: Donald Butcher/ Jon Fitzgerald: p1 (bottom); Amanda MacKaye: p2 (top); Mark Smith: p2 (bottom); Naomi Peterson: p3 (top); Ian Tilton/Retna: p3 (bottom); Martyn Goodacre/Retna: p4 (top left); Michael Lissen/Redferns: p4 (top right); Steve Eichner/Retna: p4 (bottom); Steve Pyke/Getty: p5; Lisa Johnson:

This is a Call

Bibliography

Anderson, Mark and Mark Jenkins (2001) *Dance of Days: Two Decades of Punk in the Nation's Capital*, Soft Skull Press.

Apter, Jeff (2008) *The Dave Grohl Story*, Omnibus Press.

Azerrad, Michael (1993) *Come As You Are: The Story of Nirvana*, Main Street.

Azerrad, Michael (2001) *Our Band Could Be Your Life: Scenes from the American Indie Underground 1981–1991*, Little Brown.

Berkenstadt, Jim and Charles Cross (1998) *Nevermind Nirvana: Classic Rock Albums*, Schirmer Trade Books.

Blush, Steve (2001) *American Hardcore: A Tribal History*, Feral House.

Borzillo, Carrie (2000) *Nirvana: The Day by Day Eyewitness Chronicle*, Carlton.

Chick, Stevie (2009) *Spray Paint the Walls: The Story of Black Flag*, Omnibus Press.

Cobain, Kurt (2002) *Journals*, Viking.

Cross, Charles R. (2001) *Heavier than Heaven: The Biography of Kurt Cobain*, Hodder & Stoughton.

Cogan, Brian (2006) *The Encyclopaedia of Punk*, Sterling Publishing.

Earles, Andrew (2010) *Hüsker Dü: The Story of the Noise-Pop Pioneers Who Launched Modern Rock*, Voyager Press.

Goldberg, Danny (2008) *Bumping into Geniuses: My Life Inside the Rock and Roll Business*, Gotham Books.

Foege, Alec (1994) *Confusion Is Next: The Sonic Youth Story*, St Martin's Press.

James, Mark (2008) *Dave Grohl: Foo Fighters, Nirvana and Other Misadventures*, Independent Music Press.

Love, Courtney (2006) *Dirty Blonde: The Diaries of Courtney Love*, Faber & Faber.

McMurray, Jacob (2011) *Taking Punk to the Masses: From Nowhere to Nevermind*, Fantagraphics Books.

Marcus, Griel (1993) *In the Fascist Bathroom: Writings on Punk 1977–1992*, Viking, 1993.

Mulholland, Garry (2006) *Fear of Music: The 261 Greatest Albums since Punk and Disco*, Orion Books.

Mullen, Brendan, with Don Bolles and Adam Pamfrey (2002) *Lexicon Devil: The Fast Times and Short Life of Darby Crash and The Germs*, Feral House.

Nedorostek, Nathan and Anthony Pappalardo (2008) *Radio Silence: A Selected Visual History of American Hardcore Music*, MTV Press.

Novoselic, Krist (2004) *Of Grunge and Government*, RDV Books/Akashic Books.

Parker, James (1998) *Turned On: A Biography of Henry Rollins*, Phoenix.

Peterson, Charles (1995) *Screaming Life: A Chronicle of the Seattle Music Scene*, HarperCollins West.

Prato, Greg (2009) *Grunge Is Dead: The Oral History of Seattle Rock Music*, ECW Press.

Robbins, Ira (ed.) (1997) *The Trouser Press Guide to '90s Rock*, Fireside.

Rocco, John (ed.) (1998) *The Nirvana Companion: Two Decades of Commentary*, Omnibus Press.

Rollins, Henry (1994) *Get in the Van: On the Road with Black Flag*, 2.13.61.

True, Everett (2006) *Nirvana: The True Story*, Omnibus.

The following magazines and fanzines have also been invaluable in researching *This is a Call*: *Alternative Press, Flipside, Kerrang!, maximumrocknroll, Melody Maker, Metal Hammer, MOJO, NME, Q, Rolling Stone, Select, Spin, Sounds, The Stranger, Suburban Voice, Uncut*.

Discography

Mission Impossible

Can It Be? (compilation) (Metrozine, 1985): 'New Ideas'
Alive and Kicking (compilation), (WGNS/Metrozine, 1985): 'I Can Only Try'
77KK (compilation) (77KK, 1985): 'Life Already Drawn'
Thanks * (split seven-inch EP with Lünchmeat) (Sammich/Dischord, 1985):
   'Helpless' / 'Into Your Shell' / 'Now I'm Alone'

Dain Bramage

I Scream Not Coming Down (Fartblossom, 1987): 'The Log' / 'I Scream Not
   Coming Down' / 'Eyes Open' / 'Swear' / 'Flannery' / 'Drag Queen' /
   'Stubble' / 'Flicker' / 'Give It Up' / 'Home Sweet Nowhere'

Scream

No More Censorship (RAS, 1988): 'Hit Me' / 'No More Censorship' / 'Fucked
   Without a Kiss' / 'No Escape' / 'Building Dreams'/ 'Take It from the Top' /
   'Something in My Head' / 'It's About Time' / 'Binge' / 'Run to the Sun' /
   'In the Beginning'

* Reissued as *Getting Shit for Growing Up Different*.

Live at Van Hall (Konkurrel, 1989): 'Who Knows, Who Cares?' / 'U. Suck A.'
– We're Fed Up' / 'Laissez Faire' / 'This Side Up' / 'Human Behavior' /
'Iron Curtain' / 'Total Mash' / 'Still Screaming' / 'Chokeword' / 'Feel Like
That' / 'Came Without Warning' / 'Walking by Myself'

Your Choice Live Series Vol. 10 (Your Choice, 1990): 'C.W.W. (Part II)' /
'I.C.Y.U.O.D.' / 'The Zoo Closes' / 'Hot Smoke and Sasafrass' / 'Fight' /
'American Justice' / 'Show and Tell' / 'Sunmaker' / 'No Escape' / 'Take It
from the Top' / 'Dancing Madly Backwards' / 'Hit Me'

Fumble (Dischord, 1993):'Caffeine Dream' / 'Sunmaker' / 'Mardi Gras' /
'Land Torn Down' / 'Gods Look Down' / 'Crackman' / 'Gas' / 'Dying
Days' / 'Poppa Says' / 'Rain'

Nirvana

Nevermind (Geffen, 1991): 'Smells Like Teen Spirit' / 'In Bloom' / 'Come as
You Are' / 'Breed' / 'Lithium'/ 'Polly' / 'Territorial Pissings' / 'Drain You' /
'Lounge Act' / 'Stay Away' / 'On a Plain' / 'Something in the Way' /
'Endless, Nameless' (hidden track)

Incesticide (Geffen, 1992): 'Dive' / 'Sliver' / 'Stain / 'Been a Son' /
'Turnaround' / 'Molly's Lips' / 'Son of a Gun' / '(New Wave) Polly' /
'Beeswax' / 'Downer' / 'Mexican Seafood' / 'Hairspray Queen' / 'Aero
Zeppelin' / 'Big Long Now' / 'Aneurysm'

In Utero (Geffen, 1993): 'Serve the Servants' / 'Scentless Apprentice' /
'Heart-Shaped Box' / 'Rape Me' / 'Frances Farmer Will Have Her
Revenge on Seattle' / 'Dumb' / 'Very Ape' / 'Milk It'/ 'Pennyroyal Tea' /
'Radio Friendly Unit Shifter' / 'Tourette's' / 'All Apologies' / 'Gallons of
Rubbing Alcohol Flow Through the Strip' (hidden track)

MTV Unplugged in New York (Geffen, 1994): 'About a Girl' / 'Come as You
Are' / 'Jesus Doesn't Want Me for a Sunbeam' / 'The Man Who Sold the
World' / 'Pennyroyal Tea' / 'Dumb' / 'Polly' / 'On a Plain' / 'Something in
the Way' / 'Plateau' / 'Oh, Me' / 'Lake of Fire' / 'All Apologies' / 'Where
Did You Sleep Last Night?'

From the Muddy Banks of the Wishkah (Geffen, 1996): 'Intro' / 'School' /
'Drain You' / 'Aneurysm' / 'Smells Like Teen Spirit' / 'Been a Son' /
'Lithium' / 'Sliver' / 'Spank Thru' / 'Scentless Apprentice' / 'Heart-
Shaped Box' / 'Milk It' / 'Negative Creep' / 'Polly' / 'Breed' / 'Tourette's' /
'Blew'

Nirvana (Geffen, 2002): 'You Know You're Right' / 'About a Girl' / 'Been a
Son' / 'Sliver' / 'Smells Like Teen Spirit' / 'Come as You Are' / 'Lithium' /
'In Bloom' / 'Heart-Shaped Box' / 'Pennyroyal Tea' / 'Rape Me' / 'Dumb /

'All Apologies' / 'The Man Who Sold the World' / 'Where Did You Sleep Last Night?'

With the Lights Out (Geffen, 2004): 'Heartbreaker' / 'Anorexorcist' / 'White Lace and Strange' / 'Help Me I'm Hungry' / 'Mrs Butterworth' / 'If You Must' / 'Pen Cap Chew' / 'Downer' / 'Floyd the Barber' / 'Raunchola/Moby Dick' / 'Beans' / 'Don't Want It All' / 'Clean Up Before She Comes' / 'Polly' / 'Blandest' / 'Dive' / 'They Hung Him on a Cross' / 'Grey Goose' / 'Ain't It a Shame' / 'Token Eastern Song' / 'Even in His Youth' / 'Polly' / 'Opinion' / 'Lithium' / 'Been a Son' / 'Sliver' / Where Did You Sleep Last Night/' / 'Pay to Play' / 'Here She Comes Now' / 'Drain You' / 'Aneurysm' / 'Smells Like Teen Spirit' / 'Breed' / 'Verse Chorus Verse' / 'Old Age' / 'Endless, Nameless' / 'Dumb' / 'D-7' / 'Oh, the Guilt' / 'Curmudgeon' / 'Return of the Rat' / 'Smells Like Teen Spirit' / 'Rape Me' / 'Rape Me' / 'Scentless Apprentice' / 'Heart-Shaped Box' / 'I Hate Myself and I Want to Die' / 'Milk It' / 'M.V.' / 'Gallons of Rubbing Alcohol Flow Through the Strip' / 'The Other Improv' / 'Serve the Servants' / 'Very Ape' / 'Pennyroyal Tea' / 'Marigold' / 'Sappy' / 'Jesus Doesn't Want Me for a Sunbeam' / 'Do Re Mi' / 'You Know You're Right' / 'All Apologies'

Sliver: The Best of the Box (Geffen, 2005): 'Spank Thru' / 'Heartbreaker' / 'Mrs Butterworth' / 'Floyd the Barber' / 'Clean Up Before She Comes' / 'About a Girl / 'Blandest' / 'Ain't It a Shame' / 'Sappy' / 'Opinion / 'Lithium' / 'Sliver' / 'Smells Like Teen Spirit' / 'Come as You Are' / 'Old Age' / 'Oh, the Guilt' / 'Rape Me' / 'Rape Me' / 'Heart-Shaped Box' / 'Do Re Me' / 'You Know You're Right' / 'All Apologies'

Live at Reading (Geffen, 2009): 'Breed' / 'Drain You' / 'Aneurysm' / 'School' / 'Sliver' / 'In Bloom' / 'Come as You Are' / 'Lithium' / 'About a Girl' / 'Tourette's' / 'Polly' / 'Lounge Act' / 'Smells Like Teen Spirit' / 'On a Plain' / 'All Apologies' / 'Blew' / 'Dumb' / 'Stay Away' / 'Spank Thru' / 'The Money Will Roll Right In' / 'D-7' / 'Territorial Pissings'

Late!

Pocketwatch (Simple Machines, 1993): 'Pokey the Little Puppy' / 'Petrol CB' / 'Friend of a Friend' / 'Throwing Needles' / 'Just Another Story About Skeeter Thompson' / 'Color Pictures of a Marigold' / 'Hell's Garden' / 'Winnebago' / 'Bruce' / 'Milk'

Foo Fighters

Foo Fighters (Roswell/Capitol, 1995): 'This Is a Call' / 'I'll Stick Around' / 'Big Me' / 'Alone + Easy Target' / 'Good Grief' / 'Floaty' / 'Weenie Beenie' / 'Oh, George' / 'For All the Cows' / 'X-Static' / 'Wattershed' / 'Exhausted'

The Colour and the Shape (Roswell/Capitol, 1997): 'Doll' / 'Monkey Wrench' / 'Hey, Johnny Park' / 'My Poor Brain' / 'Wind Up' / 'Up in Arms' / 'My Hero' / 'See You' / 'Enough Space' / 'February Stars' / 'Everlong' / 'Walking After You' / 'New Way Home'

There Is Nothing Left to Lose (Roswell/RCA, 1999): 'Stacked Actors' / 'Breakout' / 'Learn to Fly' / 'Gimme Stitches' / 'Generator' / 'Aurora' / 'Live-In Skin' / 'Next Year' / 'Headwires' / 'Ain't It the Life' / 'M.I.A.'

One by One (Roswell/RCA, 2002): 'All My Life' / 'Low' / 'Have It All' / 'Times Like These' / 'Disenchanted Lullaby' / 'Tired of You' / 'Halo' / 'Lonely as You' / 'Overdrive' / 'Burn Away' / 'Come Back'

In Your Honor (Roswell/RCA, 2005): 'In Your Honor' / 'No Way Back' / 'Best of You' / 'DOA' / 'Hell' / 'The Last Song' / 'Free Me' / 'Resolve' / 'The Deepest Blues Are Black' / 'End Over End' / 'The Sign' / 'Still' / 'What If I Do?' / 'Miracle' / 'Another Round' / 'Friend of a Friend' / 'Over and Out' / 'On the Mend' / 'Virginia Moon' / 'Cold Day in the Sun' / 'Razor'

Skin and Bones (Roswell/RCA, 2006): 'Razor' / 'Over and Out' / 'Walking After You' / 'Marigold' / 'My Hero' / 'Next Year' / 'Another Round' / 'Big Me' / 'Cold Day in the Sun' / 'Skin and Bones' / 'February Stars' / 'Times Like These' / 'Friend of a Friend' / 'Best of You' / 'Everlong' / 'Ain't It the Life'

Echoes, Silence, Patience & Grace (Roswell/RCA, 2007): 'The Pretender' / 'Let It Die' / 'Erase/Replace' / 'Long Road to Ruin' / 'Come Alive' / 'Stranger Things Have Happened' / 'Cheer Up, Boys (Your Make-Up Is Running)' / 'Summer's End' / 'Ballad of the Beaconsfield Miners' / 'Statues' / 'But, Honestly' / 'Home'

Greatest Hits (Roswell/RCA, 2009) 'All My Life' / 'Best of You' / 'Everlong' / 'The Pretender' / 'My Hero' / 'Learn to Fly' / 'Times Like These' / 'Money Wrench' / 'Big Me' / 'Breakout' / 'Long Road to Ruin' / 'This Is a Call' / 'Skin and Bones' / 'Wheels' / 'Word Forward' / 'Everlong' (acoustic)

Wasting Light (Roswell/RCA, 2011): 'Bridge Burning' / 'Rope' / 'Dear Rosemary' / 'White Limo' / 'Arlandria' / 'These Days' / 'Back and Forth' / 'A Matter of Time' / 'Miss the Misery' / 'I Should Have Known' / 'Walk'

Medium Rare (Roswell/RCA, 2011): 'Band on the Run' / 'I Feel Fine' / 'Life of Illusion' / 'Young Man Blues' / 'Bad Reputation' / 'Down in the Park'/

'Baker Street' / 'Danny Says' / 'Have a Cigar' / 'Never Talking to You Again' / 'Gas Chamber' / 'This Will Be Our Year'

Harlingtox A.D.
Harlingtox Angel Divine (Laundry Room, 1996): 'Treason Daddy Brother in Crime Real Patriots Type Stuff' / 'Orbiting Prisons in Space' / 'Recycled Children Never to Be Grown' / 'Obtaining a Bachelor's Degree' / 'Open Straightedge Arms'

David Grohl
Touch: Music from the Motion Picture (Roswell/Capitol, 1997): 'Bill Hill Theme' / 'August Murray Theme' / 'How Do You Do' / 'Richie Baker's Miracle' / 'Making Popcorn' / 'Outrage' / 'Saints in Love' / 'Spinning Newspapers' / 'Remission My Ass' / 'Scene 6' / 'This Loving Thing (Lynn's Song)' / 'Final Miracle' / 'Touch'

Probot
Probot (Southern Lord/Roswell, 2004): 'Centuries of Sin' / 'Red War' / 'Shake Your Blood' / 'Access Babylon' / 'Silent Spring' / 'Ice Cold Man' / 'The Emerald Law' / 'Big Sky' / 'Dictatosaurus' / 'My Tortured Soul' / 'Sweet Dreams' / 'I Am the Warlock' (hidden track)

Them Crooked Vultures
Them Crooked Vultures (Columbia, 2009): 'No One Loves Me & Neither Do You' / 'Mind Eraser, No Chaser' / 'New Fang' / 'Dead End Friends' / 'Elephants' / 'Scumbag Blues' / 'Bandoliers' / 'Reptiles' / 'Interludes with Ludes' / 'Warsaw or the First Breath You Take' / 'Caligulove' / 'Gunman' / 'Spinning in Daffodils'

Dave Grohl also appears on the following albums and EPs:
Buzz Osbourne, *King Buzzo* (Boner/Tupelo, 1992)
Backbeat Band, *Backbeat: Songs from the Original Motion Picture* (Virgin, 1994)
Mike Watt, *Ball-Hog or Tugboat?* (Columbia, 1995)
The Stinky Puffs, *A Little Tiny Smelly Bit Of ...* (Elemental, 1995)
Puff Daddy, *Been Around the World* (Arista, 1997)

This is a Call

Earthlings?, *Earthlings?* (Man's Ruin, 1998)

Reeves Gabrels, *Ulysses (Della Notte)* (E-Magine, 2000)

Earthlings, *Human Beans* (Man's Ruin, 2000)

Tenacious D, *Tenacious D* (Epic, 2001)

Tony Iommi, *Iommi* (Divine/Priority, 2001)

David Bowie, *Heathen* (ISO/Columbia, 2002)

Queens of the Stone Age, *Songs for the Deaf* (Interscope, 2002)

Cat Power, *You Are Free* (Matador, 2003)

Killing Joke, *Killing Joke* (Zuma, 2003)

The Bangles, *Doll Revolution* (E1 Music, 2003)

Garbage, *Bleed Like Me* (Geffen, 2005)

Nine Inch Nails, *With Teeth* (Nothing/Interscope, 2005)

Pete Yorn, *Nightcrawler* (Columbia, 2006)

Tenacious D, *The Pick of Destiny* (Epic, 2006)

Juliette and The Licks, *Four on the Floor* (The Militia Group, 2006)

Jackson United, *Harmony and Dissidence* (Deck Cheese, 2008)

Various Artists, *We Wish You a Metal Xmas and a Headbanging New Year* (Armoury, 2008)

The Prodigy, *Invaders Must Die* (Take Me to the Hospital/Cooking Vinyl, 2009)

Slash, *Slash* (Roadrunner, 2010)

Taylor Hawkins and the Coattail Riders, *Red Light Fever* (Shanabelle/RCA, 2010)

Mondo Generator, *Dog Food* (Impedance, 2010)

Index

Index

Index

Index